Genesis

Studies in German Literature, Linguistics, and Culture

Genesis

The Making of Literary Works from Homer to Christa Wolf

T. J. Reed

CAMDEN HOUSE
Rochester, New York

Copyright © 2020 T. J. Reed

All Rights Reserved. Except as permitted under current legislation, no part of this work may be photocopied, stored in a retrieval system, published, performed in public, adapted, broadcast, transmitted, recorded, or reproduced in any form or by any means, without the prior permission of the copyright owner.

First published 2020
by Camden House

Camden House is an imprint of Boydell & Brewer Inc.
668 Mt. Hope Avenue, Rochester, NY 14620, USA
www.camden-house.com
and of Boydell & Brewer Limited
PO Box 9, Woodbridge, Suffolk IP12 3DF, UK
www.boydellandbrewer.com

ISBN-13: 978-1-64014-082-0
ISBN-10: 1-64014-082-4

Library of Congress Cataloging-in-Publication Data

CIP data is available from the Library of Congress.

This publication is printed on acid-free paper.

Printed and bound in Great Britain by
TJ International Ltd, Padstow, Cornwall

For Richard Dorrington

Contents

Note on Quotations and Translations ix
Preface xi
Introduction: Processes 1

Part I. Antiquity

1: Homer's Audiences: Shaping the *Iliad* (and the *Odyssey*) . . . 19
2: Fourfold Genesis: The Bible between Literature and Authority . . . 37

Part II. Early Modern

3: An Alphabet of Experience: Montaigne 57
4: Beginner's Luck: Shakespeare's History Cycles 78

Transition—Tradition 100

Part III. Goethe

5: Cross-Purposes: Goethe's *Faust* 103
6: Occasions: Goethe's Lyric Poetry 125
7: Live and Learn: *Werther* and *Wilhelm Meister* 146

Part IV. Nineteenth- and Twentieth-Century German

8: Writing on the Run: Georg Büchner's Revolutions 163
9: "The Best-Laid Schemes. . .": Thomas Mann Unplanned . . . 174

10: Description of a Struggle: Kafka's Half-Escape	191
11: Atomic Beginnings: Brecht, Galileo, and After	209
12: Knowing and Partly Knowing: Paul Celan's Mission	220
13: Christa Wolf: A Fall from Grace	231
Afterword	239
Notes	241
Bibliography	281
Index	295

Note on Quotations and Translations

To meet the needs of comparatists as well as Germanists, German prose material is for the most part translated into English. The original is referenced in the endnotes, and in especially significant cases quoted in full there. Poetry is quoted in the original, with a translation following. Unless otherwise noted, all translations from German and French are mine.

Preface

THE PROCESS OF MAKING LITERATURE ranges from the creation of an individual work to the shaping of a corpus or the establishing of a major work as a classic part of written culture. A sense of the origins of meaning in this process is a firm foundation for understanding a work, not necessarily a final interpretation, but a way of staying close to the quick of creation and its direction.

This is too simple a theory to need much elaboration other than the practice of the case studies that follow. The proof of the pudding is in the eating. As Goethe said, "the phenomena *are* the theory."[1]

What follows does however rest on a reasoned position: that literary works are viable acts of communication between author and reader, generated in real historical contexts, shaped by the time, place, and circumstances in which they arose, and open to reconstruction with the help of the marks these forces have left on them. Literary biography has never lost its interest for a scholarly and a wider readership, and to look closely at the genesis of a work is to give that interest a sharper focus where it most matters, at the point where meaning is created from the materials of experience and the skills of the literary craft. Upon this common ground every genesis is then a different and absorbing human story.

The present book casts a wide net for a limited haul—the studies are small in number when set against the infinite corpus of literary works whose every genesis might be reconstructed. So this is only a representative selection, but it takes in a variety of types, from the writing of single poems and novels to the genesis of a genre, from a handful of plays to a complete writing career.

The first four case studies, of Homer, the Bible, Montaigne, and Shakespeare, treat classic early instances of complex genesis from outside my immediate professional field. They are designed to set the scene for the later German examples. I offer both kinds, in the teeth of Goethe's warning that "there are two things you cannot sufficiently beware of: obstinacy, if you limit yourself to your specialism; inadequacy if you go outside it."[2] So a degree of modesty is in order. But against that may be set Samuel Johnson's generous claim on behalf of the judgments of the Common Reader,[3] for whom literature is a field of free choice and opinion. It is perhaps not hubris for a Common Reader to survey a shared literary heritage and take on the role of a Common Critic. As central figures in that corpus, they selected themselves. Far from being the objects of a research project casting round afresh for examples, the works I discuss are those I have lived with and thought about over some decades. Their quality and prominence make them a self-evident canon. That they are nearly all male is historically determined. Socially and institutionally disadvantaged as women writers have always been, the fact remains that, in Simone de Beauvoir's words, "none ever reached the heights of a Dante or a Shakespeare."[4] So there is no matching female canon, no corpus of plays by Shakespeare's sister, for whom Virginia Woolf imagined an equal talent and a sad fate, no epic equivalent of the *Iliad*, unless we follow the intriguing notion that a woman wrote the *Odyssey*. Nor did women's writing find a place in the Old or New Testament, or in the canon of any other faith—doctrinal or prophetic texts by women were ignored or suppressed by the religious authorities. It will be seen, however, that the opinion of female critics, from Virginia Woolf to contemporaries, is appealed to at significant points in what follows: the chapter on Goethe's lyric poetry recalls the contribution of a woman who wrote some of "his" poems; and the final chapter treats a woman who was a leading East German writer, caught up in the pressures of historical change.

※ ※ ※

I am grateful to the friends who kindly (and encouragingly) read the chapters on their respective areas of scholarly specialism: Terence Cave for Montaigne, Katherine Duncan-Jones for Shakespeare, Christopher Rowland for the Bible, and Jürgen von Ungern-Sternberg for Homer; for the German chapters, to my colleagues Elizabeth Boa and Ray Ockenden; and to friends from yet other spheres who tested from other angles and for general readerly interest: Peter Hacker, Karen Hewitt, Dirk Meyer, Stephen Sedley, Claudia Zwiener, and the late Michael Gelder. My wife Ann, not for the first time, read every chapter as it was written.

As ever, valuable hints and other help came from many quarters. My thanks to Jeremy Adler, Rebecca Beasley, Helen Buchanan and Emma Huber (Taylorian Library), Chris Collard, Malgorzata Czepiel (Bodleian Library), Malcolm Davis, Carolin Duttlinger, Stephen Gill, Phillip Harries, Ann Jefferson, John Kelly, Tom Kuhn, Chris Llewellyn Smith, Charlie Louth, Martin McLaughlin, Christopher Metcalf, Andrea Meyer-Ludowisy (Senate House Library, University of London), Richard Parish, Georgina Paul, Roger Pearson, Elke Richter (Stiftung Weimarer Klassik), Janne Sørensen (Royal Danish Library), Karolina Watroba, and the late Colin Matthew.

I continue to be grateful for the use of a workroom and all the other facilities generously provided by the Queen's College, and for the support and stimulus of old friends at St John's.

The dedication marks a friendship dating from our National Service and student days, and remembers the many hills climbed together since.

Jim Reed
Oxford, October 2019

Introduction: Processes

To the sympathetic observer, there is pleasure in watching something of beauty or value being made or coming spontaneously into existence. A blossom is a highpoint in a plant's evolution and a single year's cycle. Parents watch a child grow in the womb into what from the moment of birth will be a distinctive person. Literary works are likewise the product of a human organism and come into being in an analogous way, containing "a potency of life as active as that soul was whose progeny they are."[1] The metaphor of procreation will recur. More than one writer thinks of his work as his child, himself even as its mother, not so much a male attempt to appropriate woman's unique role as a sense that literary creation too is an unstoppable process from deep within.

So works are not just there like objects in a landscape. They have to begin and gradually grow into what they are. Not that objects in a landscape are "just there," either. Eons of geological activity have created mountains and valleys, folds and faults. Everything has a history, and coming at it through its genesis is a way of understanding it in depth—understanding how a form has been shaped by traceable forces, so that even when it is the object of a discrete aesthetic perception, it is only one possible "still" within a continuous movement. Following that movement locates and illuminates the final form from many sides.

A work may take time and undergo all kinds of inner and external pressures and accidents on the way to its eventual form, assuming it ever finds one—for "ars longa, vita brevis." Pascal's *Pensées* are a mass of slips left at his death, halfway to thematic ordering. Short of mortality, anything is possible—vision, revision, addition, deletion, alternative drafts considered and discarded, even abandonment as a fragment or a frankly admitted failure;[2] everything is in flux. In an insight of Goethe's (who coined the term morphology for the science of evolving forms), "State is a foolish word, because nothing stands still, and everything is in motion."[3]

At the everyday level, readiness to understand another person's viewpoint is sometimes expressed as "I see where you're coming from"—not simply where you now stand, but more illuminatingly how you reached that position, from what assumptions and principles and through what experiences. A literary text is similarly an act of communication in which the receiver needs to grasp as fully as possible the direction of what is being communicated, where *it* came from as a clue to where it has arrived, and where it may yet lead.

So to approach literary works from the angle of their making involves finding out as much as possible about who and what the author was at the time of writing, what direction they were coming from, in what kind of career situation, what personal, social, cultural, political, historical forces were helping to shape the product of a primal creative impulse, maybe to further it, maybe to change or frustrate it. To ask these questions is the classic method of critical editions, here applied to a representative selection. If a work takes long enough to write, like Thomas Mann's *Magic Mountain*, which took twelve years, or Goethe's *Faust*, which took sixty, the direction of travel and the work's final shape and meaning may have changed radically, several times even. It isn't at all certain how far these two great artificers, or others reshaping their works over shorter timespans, were conscious of the ways the work was changing under their hands and exactly why.

Such shifts and drifts may have caused difficulties for the writer and may have left observable inconsistencies, awkward joins, and contradictions in the end product. Homer's *Iliad* and Goethe's *Faust* are rich in them, though an over-pious scholarly tradition has commonly tried to explain them away or sweep them under the carpet, on the squeamish assumption that consistency and seamlessness are the highest of artistic values—as if the originator of European epic and the author of the central work of a national literature had at all costs to be proved perfect. That is a misplaced ideal: imperfection is part of a work's history, its humanity, a measure of the complexity and difficulty of the creative task, and a foil to the work's piecemeal perfections. When Goethe chose not to excise from his *Faust* some motifs and passages that plainly cut across the logic of the plot, he was implicitly judging that their poetry was too valuable to be sacrificed in the name of consistency. The more ambitious the project, the more any faults have to be accepted as what the ancient critic Longinus called "the negligence of genius"; for "great geniuses are least 'pure,' and where there is grandeur, there must be something that has been overlooked."[4] Ruskin, too, argued eloquently for the positive value of imperfection, in architecture and in art more broadly: "No good work whatever can be perfect, and *the demand for perfection is always a sign of a misunderstanding of the ends of art*."[5] The assumption that what is great must be flawless—that some section of a Shakespeare play can't possibly be by Shakespeare, or that certain lines of the *Iliad* must be spurious—begs the question of critical judgment. The concise formula from Horace's *Art of Poetry* has become proverbial: "Homer sometimes nods."[6] To nod is human, to stay perfect and polished is not, and where there is an undeniable flaw or inconsistency, it is a feature to be sympathetically engaged with, just as a geological fault is part of the reality of the landscape to be crossed.

In the Beginning

... is not the word. A literary work begins as an impulse with direction but no certain outcome. Introspect for a moment: we rarely begin by knowing even how any single sentence we speak or write will end. Its final form isn't there from the start. The idea that we think in words in order to compose a sequence of words falls foul of infinite regress. Rather, meaning takes shape as we find words in our mental store that will match what is obscurely thought and felt. ("How do I know what I think till I hear what I say?" is more than just a joke.) That isn't the same as having only such thoughts as we already have words for. The expressive impulse is potentially inventive. We feel for words, move urgently towards words, whether it's from the sudden need to warn someone of danger or the emotional pressure to tell someone you love them. At most a word or two may be present to the mind as stepping-stones towards formulation, and it's always possible to compose an utterance with care; but that is more *a* speech than speech. A clear case is the difficulty of putting together something to be communicated in the language you barely know of the country you're visiting.

The literary process likewise begins tentative and inchoate, and writers know this well. A Philip Roth character, surely a projection of the author's experience, works in the night, "[his] head vibrant with the static of unelaborated thought."[7] Virginia Woolf was clear that something essential had to come before words: "Style is a very simple matter; it is all rhythm. Once you get that right, you can't use the wrong words. [...] A sight, an emotion, creates this wave in the mind, long before it makes words to fit it." So she finds herself "sitting after half the morning crammed with ideas and visions, and so on, and can't dislodge them, for lack of the right rhythm." And when she calls an American writer "too controlled, uses his brains not his body," she is on the same tack, and sounding unexpectedly close to D. H. Lawrence's notion of thinking with the blood.[8] Close also to Friedrich Schiller in the eighteenth century, for whom "the musicality of a poem is more often in my mind than the clear notion of content" and "a certain musical mood precedes the poetic idea."[9] The twentieth-century poet Günter Eich knew, physically, when he reached a convincing fulfillment toward which he had only been feeling his way unplanned: "In every line that is right, I hear the blind man's stick tapping that shows I've reached firm ground."[10] Or in Reiner Kunze's words, the poet is "looking for the word about which the only thing he knows is that it's not yet there."[11]

There is, incidentally, a prior uncertainty before the search for words seriously begins. Am I a writer? Is what I'm doing really "writing" in the full literary sense? Like the appetite that proverbially comes with eating, written words have to convince the writer that this is what he is. From an early poem of Goethe's, which he wrote in charmingly eccentric English, "A Song over the Unconfidence towards myself"—"I hum no supportable tune, / I can no poet be"[12]—down to the tortured self-doubts of Kafka's diaries, the problem recurs, and in some measure begins again with every new work. Each must prove its own existence, step by step.

But to return to the finding of words: the most striking account of the way pre-verbal impulse generates language, not specifically literary but the more persuasive for its anecdotal variety, is Heinrich von Kleist's essay "On the Gradual Shaping of Our Thoughts in Speaking." He tells how, after cudgeling his brain for hours over a legal case or a problem in algebra, he will turn and talk about it to his sister who sits sewing in the same room. Once he has started a sentence, his mind comes up with an ending that resolves the problem. Many a great orator will have opened his mouth not knowing what exactly he was going to say. When Louis XVI in 1789 sent a command for the Estates to disperse, Mirabeau stood his ground and at the climactic moment found the famous decisive phrase, "It will only be at bayonet point." This, for Kleist, is thinking aloud; language is "not a brake on the wheel of the mind, but another wheel running parallel on the same axle."[13]

In such situations, impulse and formulation are unique to the moment—they have to be firmly grasped *now*, as they won't come round again in just this form. It's as if a curtain has been briefly drawn back, then closed over the revelation. A philosopher (these processes are shared across the genres) describes the common experience of "phases of bright alertness in which thoughts are unexpectedly in motion or free flow"; and he warns against "leaving to your long-term memory what has suddenly opened up, in the hope that it will surely come back when wanted, as clear as ever. Anybody who has learned that the same clarity can hardly ever be recaptured will put the thoughts down on paper straight away."[14] Circumstances may not favor this. Goethe recalls leaping out of bed to capture an idea without having time to put the paper straight, caught short by poetry.[15] Montaigne says "My mind commonly gives birth to my most profound reveries [. . .] when I am least on the lookout for them, which vanish as suddenly, since I have nothing to hand to fix them, at table, in bed, above all on horse-back, where I have my broadest reflections."[16] This isn't to say that a related idea will not return in some other verbal guise, as witness the notes on obsessive themes in Pascal's never completed *Pensées* or in the aphoristic books of Nietzsche's middle period.

The appeal to common preverbal experience doesn't rest on Noam Chomsky's grammatical deep structures, much less on a distinct prior language such as Jerry Fodor's mentalese. It simply recognizes the time element in the expressing of thought and feeling, their necessarily wordless origin as they wait for a formulation that is not precisely foreseen. Perhaps all thinking is a series of preverbal inspirations, their open-endedness the ultimate origin of originality. Metaphorically we build a bridge out into meaning or, in a comic-cartoon image, we lay track in front of the train of thought as it careers along.

Once started, the bridge or track can be consciously worked on and extended. Impulse becomes intention, intention becomes plan, drafts once sketched can be reviewed and revised, all of them drawing strength from the originating impulse—the poet's insight or emotion, the dramatist's vision of conflict, the narrator's urge to tell a story. Giving these impulses coherent shape demands application. A work of literature is properly so called, because it's produced by the *work* of literature. "It isn't only sculptors who graft" said Balzac, himself a laborer on a heroic scale;[17] and Joseph Conrad recalled how he "had to work like a coal-miner in his pit quarrying all [his] English sentences out of a black night."[18] Yet the work may still be a delicate sensory matter, needing ritual objects and particular surroundings to stimulate thought—Virginia Woolf wrote with violet ink, Goethe and Thomas Mann needed extra smooth paper, Kafka the easy flow of a fountain-pen and the discipline of writing in stout notebooks rather than on loose sheets; Schiller kept rotten apples in his desk, the exiled Heine's verse came more easily when he once again breathed German air.

Tellingly, the conventional terms of criticism all have roots in manual work: "form" in the creating of a sculpted body; "style" in the impressing of signs on wax or clay with a stylus; "text" in the weaving of a fabric; "structure" in the building of an edifice—all needing to be glossed by these gerunds of purposeful activity. Once the form, style, fabric or structure is completed, time has done its work, process has become product, energy has been turned into object. The reality of those arts that are sequential in time, as literature and music are, may then be lost to sight, the metaphor of static form obscuring their temporal nature. "Form" is indeed a metaphor—the literal form of, for example, a novel is oblong, of variable thickness. The term's unthinking application to music was what Éric Satie was mocking when he was criticized for compositions that lacked form and responded by writing a set of pieces "in the shape of a pear."[19]

It is salutary to go back to the moments before completion, when a work didn't yet exist, even to the point when the writer was first putting pen to blank page, and to follow the process of creation through. Where we normally look at a work as a fixed piece of artistic culture, its creator was looking forward into an open space, at most fringed with an audience, was carried forward by the force of a conception and an impulse to complete it.

This perspective means that the single work, and beyond it the whole body of literature, is no longer taken for granted as something ready printed and bound, culture on tap for study or casual perusal. The product fixed in space can be felt as something still in motion.

So to follow a work's genesis is almost to go back and make it, watching it develop as its author watched, looking forward to a still uncertain outcome, solving difficulties, making adjustments, sometimes giving up and starting afresh. This is art in action, with no preset teleology to obey, yet with its own status: "Why should we not understand the production of a work of art as itself a work of art?" Paul Valéry wondered,[20] in short, as performance art.

Sometimes the work of genesis can be partly done for the writer. A line of verse or a stanza may seem blessedly given, may come into the mind ready-made. But the gift then makes distinct demands, setting a direction, a line of thought to follow, an argument to be continued, a stanza-form to be matched. The follow-up must be able to bear comparison with the initial gift, ideally to the point where they can't be told apart.[21] Such generous moments already touch on the phenomenon of inspiration, of which writers have left an account, often exciting in itself, though not necessarily proof of the quality of what they were inspired to write. Virginia Woolf again: "It has pressed and spurted out of me. If that's any proof of virtue, like a physical volcano."[22]

But is it? The most striking of such records, Nietzsche on the genesis of *Thus spake Zarathustra*,[23] raises expectations which that overwritten work itself may not fulfil. Yet the passage is so eloquent that it remained a marker German writers aspired to come up to, against the grain of a modern self-consciousness that was desperate to be carried beyond its own acutely felt limitations. The more so as Nietzsche was issuing an explicit challenge to modern times: Did anyone, at the end of the nineteenth century, have a clear idea of what poets of strong ages called inspiration? If not, he will describe it. He lists the physical symptoms that made it a revelation and gave him the sense of being the mouthpiece of overwhelming powers such that he never had any choice:

> Everything happens in the highest degree involuntarily, in a storm of felt freedom, of absoluteness, of divine power ... The involuntariness of the image, the simile, is the most remarkable thing; [...] everything offers itself as the nearest, the rightest, the simplest expression.[24]

Earlier notes of Nietzsche's had actually played down the notion of inspiration as a sudden ray of grace from heaven, something that writers had of course an interest in claiming, as he has just done himself, in contrast to the labor of slow gathering and selecting: "All great artists were great workers, tireless not just in inventing, but also in rejecting, sifting, reshaping, ordering," as Beethoven does in his notebooks. The subjective experience of inspiration is here plausibly understood as a sudden release after creative forces have been dammed up, producing the illusion of a miracle, "as if there had been no foregoing inner processes."[25] It may be a slow burn: Kant put a whole decade's intense thought into the five hundred pages of his *Critique of Pure Reason* in just ten months.

Not all creativity is so dramatic; it has calmer forms, as described by Joseph Haydn. Shut away in the Esterházy palace in Eisenstadt, he was clear that this situation well outside Vienna had proved an advantage:

> My prince was content with all my works. I could, at the head of an orchestra, make experiments, observing what created an impression and what weakened it, thus improving, adding, cutting away and running risks. I was set apart from the world, there was nobody in my vicinity to confuse and annoy me in my course, and so [his conclusion is a happy non sequitur!] and so I had to become original.[26]

Records of inspiration raise the question of consciousness in the creative act, which no doubt varies from case to case. Related is the further question of whether there are two distinct creative types, the spontaneous and the reflective, the one to whom writing comes easily, the other a burner of the midnight oil whose creative process has to be generated from cold—the one is the born poet, the other has to struggle against that old tag "poeta nascitur, non fit" in order to make himself one. Goethe and Schiller themselves embodied this distinction, at least in Schiller's view as he simultaneously introspected and observed, seeing in himself the conscious, reflective, and in Goethe the spontaneous, naïve poet. Out of it Schiller made the classic essay *Über naive und sentimentalische Dichtung* (On Primal and Reflective Poetry)[27] further locating the contrast in cultural history, ancients against moderns, with only the occasional latecomer a bearer of the old primal force of nature.

All this concerns the inner workings of the creative mind. The other factor in genesis is obviously the outside world, as object and obstacle. As object it is what provokes the original impulse to describe or express, celebrate, decry, lament. The writer is stimulated by the range of reality, challenged by its beauty or complexity, horrified by its violence—Montaigne by the ever richer experience of his own self interacting with the world and by the atrocities of the religious wars perpetrated around him, Shakespeare by the violent course of English history down to his own time, Goethe by the forms and forces in nature that he observes as a poet and a scientist, Tolstoy by the impact of the Napoleonic Wars on a Russian family and society at large.

As obstacle, the world actively intervenes to interrupt or prevent creation or to alter its course. "A person from Porlock" calls on Coleridge and stops him transcribing his dream-vision, "Kubla Khan"; typhus kills Georg Büchner partway through the writing of *Woyzeck*; the First World War and the turbulent politics of the Weimar Republic interrupt and reshape Thomas Mann's *Magic Mountain*; the dropping of the first atomic bomb undoes Bertolt Brecht's conception of Galileo as a hero of science and he tries to reverse the message of his play. Even while it is being processed into literature, the world changes and upsets the developing pattern of the work. For all sorts of reasons, the course of composition doesn't always run smoothly. In Virginia Woolf's words, "probably no book is born entire and uncrippled as it was conceived"[28]—the birth metaphor again.

In this view of authorial input, the author is far from being in full control, yet still remains the necessary center of concentric circles: personal, social, and political, subject to random or systematic pressures. It remains the author's creative act to assimilate the forces pressing in on person and work and to shape them into coherence. A writer's creativity is often at full stretch holding the many factors together, much as athletes at pressure moments have to surpass themselves and move into the "zone."

A successful result can be noteworthy in the broadest anthropological sense, a high-water mark for humanity, something to celebrate, in the single instance and all across culture. Celebration is not, of course, the whole story. We will see Goethe spoiling a fine poem with misguided revision, and Brecht failing to grasp just how far events have shifted the ground under his dramatic conception. Yet artistic genesis remains largely a positive story. So when Rilke measures mankind against his imagined overwhelming angel in the seventh Duino Elegy, he offers the arts as the height of human achievement:

> Aber ein Turm war groß, nicht wahr? O Engel, er war es,—
> groß, auch noch neben dir? Chartres war groß—und Musik
> reichte noch weiter hinan und überstieg uns.
>
> [But a tower was great, was it not? O Angel
> Great, even beside you? Chartres was great—and music
> reached still higher and outclimbed us.[29]]

To make an equal claim for literature may have seemed superfluous to Rilke, engaged as he was in its ostensive definition through his own grand poetic statement. In any case, the writer's art needs no angelic instance to appreciate and validate it, but simply the openness and sensitivity of other human beings.

In other words, a sympathetic, not necessarily uncritical public, beginning often with a circle of family or friends. The beginner Marian Evans was encouraged by her partner George Henry Lewes to become the major woman novelist George Eliot—a special kind of genesis! Publishers are sometimes themselves crucial and creative through their insight and support. Audience appetite and expectation in some form are one more element in the communicative nexus, setting norms for the writer to obey or rebel against, sometimes powerfully influencing a work's final form, with audience reception even codetermining genesis, as we shall see it doing with the *Iliad*. Occasionally audiences are directly appealed to for help, as when Schiller gets stuck in the writing of *Don Carlos* and publishes a cry for "the judgment of the world" on the three completed acts to help him go on in a new direction. He has been staring at the page for too long; a work ought to be "the blossom of a single summer"[30]—not the literal time-span, but a metaphor for the organic growth that ensures unity.

That is already a form of collaboration. A more intense form is the mutual audience of one, when two creative minds collaborate: Goethe and Schiller between Weimar and Jena, Wordsworth and Coleridge at Nether Stowey, Wilfred Own and Siegfried Sassoon at Craiglockhart hospital, Hugo von Hofmannsthal and Richard Strauss, writer and musician, corresponding between Rodaun and Garmisch—no other operatic composer ever had so fine a poet and dramatist as author of his libretto. Such relationships are a boost to the morale of both sides. They can offer constructive, or as Schiller once called it, "warning" criticism of each other's works, and they can coalesce in what are virtually joint projects: Wordsworth and Coleridge's *Lyrical Ballads*, Goethe's novel *Wilhelm Meister's Apprentice Years*, written in constant consultation with Schiller, the same two writers' satirical *Xenien*. There can be a dominant partner—Wordsworth over Coleridge; Goethe at the start over Schiller, but soon accepting Schiller's complementary otherness; Sassoon at a time when Owen was just beginning, and not yet the central voice among the poets of the Great War. "The work of two people can achieve a single entity," Hofmannsthal was able to say from experience. Indeed, he spoke of the opera *Ariadne* as his and Richard Strauss's shared child, a new version of the parental motif.[31] Doubles are a special kind of genesis.

"Theory"

This account of literary creativity, together with the case studies that follow, runs counter to the theories that disturbed and came to dominate literary criticism in the later twentieth century. The scare-quotes mark it out as a particular phase in the age-old reflection about literature. "Scare" is apt enough, for the theories emanating from France and widely taken up in the United States consciously destabilized traditional modes of reading, variously declaring the death of the author, the indeterminacy of meaning, the inadequacy of language to achieve expression, or contrarily its power to formulate independent of any human agent, or its inescapability as a prison-house.

The intention of this book was to be positive rather than polemical, allowing the case studies to speak for themselves, but this much needs to be said: the common thrust of all those listed notions was to dehumanize the human processes literature involves—indeed, "humanist" reading became a term of scorn. The human agent at the center was an early target, when the "death of the author" was proclaimed by Roland Barthes and Michel Foucault. It is really no more than a metaphor for a personal preference to leave the author out of account and concentrate on a wholly impersonal text. True, there had in the past been excesses of biographism, whereby fully formed literary work was turned back into facts of the author's biography. Yet the connection between the empirical person and the creative mind is too intricately causal and too evidently crucial to the productive process to be disregarded just because it has sometimes been oversimplified. Set beside the struggles, achievements, and cultural significance of writers, their obituary notice was implausible.

Ultimately "theory" started from a legitimate concern with literature's material medium of language, but it became overwhelmingly skeptical about the capacity of language to communicate, eventually dismissive of traditional critical approaches as mere chitchat about literature, and loud in proclaiming its own innovative rigor as part of a hard sell. But theory is not necessarily rigorous, any more than humanist reading is necessarily slack.

The concentration on language had its roots in the linguistics of the French-Swiss scholar Ferdinand de Saussure, who popularized the insight that a language is a system of arbitrary correspondences. The point is obvious to anyone who knows more than one language: a tree no more "is" a tree than it is an *arbre*, or a *Baum*—the spoken or written word is just a conventional sign. A community's collected signs then constitute its language, what Saussure termed *langue*. The notion of conventional signs goes back to eighteenth-century (especially German) aesthetics, and ultimately to Plato's Cratylus, but "signifier" and "signified" became terms much bandied about as if they were a revelation.

In ways not precisely traceable yet unmissable, the notion that language is in that one sense arbitrary spread like a stain to the use of a language by its speakers (what Saussure distinguished as *parole*) as if a set of correspondences, however arbitrary in origin, were not then a means to make significant statements—an obvious non sequitur. For there is no arbitrariness in what can be said about things once their labels have been agreed. "Tree" can be meaningfully linked to various agents—a climbing boy, a urinating dog, or Isaac Newton.

But in one of two flatly opposed developments, language became suspect, as if it were a wholly unreliable medium. First, it could allegedly never achieve final meaning, which must always remain indeterminate, in Jacques Derrida's term endlessly "deferred,"[32] for Roland Barthes "evaporated" in the act of writing.[33] In the second view, language was itself the self-sufficient creator of meaning. It was not the speaker who gave meaning to an utterance, but the linguistic system as a whole that produced it. This was itself only marginally less arbitrary than the notion that monkeys with typewriters would eventually recreate Shakespeare's texts. And with language itself in control of all utterance, we all, Jean Jacques Rousseau included, allegedly say "more, less, or something other than what we mean, or want to say."[34] The practical consequence was readings that could run counter to the immediate sense of a text, subject only to the limits of ingenuity. The language knew better than its user. The idea was to catch the writer out, to find inner contradictions, self-subversions, or discreditable attitudes, often sociopolitical—"subvert" was the buzz-word—the process known as "deconstructing."

Neither the indeterminacy of language nor its creative self-sufficiency was a plausible thesis. The notion that meaning is always indeterminate and deferred made nonsense of three-and-a-half millennia of written communication that had served the progressive sharing of human experience and the advances of civilization. In a pithy saying from Jürgen Habermas's 1965 Frankfurt inaugural lecture, "Mutual understanding is the purpose inherent in human language."[35] The idea of "deferred" meaning was another unrecognized metaphor for the range of fully determinate meanings arrived at by different individuals or by the same individual at different times. For in practice every reading is unavoidably determinate for a given reader at the moment of reading. We can read for richness of reference in a text, we can even read for ambiguity, but we cannot read for indeterminacy. Assigning a definite meaning to words is a necessary part of the cognitive act. That one person's determinate reading then diverges from that of other readers is the stuff and stimulus of critical debate, one of the pleasures literature offers.

It is unclear in any case how much effort habitually went into such resolutely negative reading before meaning was declared indeterminate. Like the literary labor it should serve, critical reading too is work, requiring one to begin with the careful application of knowledge—of a language, a period idiom within it, an author's idiolect within that. Difficult texts may need a considerable archaeology to bring meaning to the surface. Literary language works with intricate personal and cultural associations, finding new ways peculiar to the individual, even to the single work. In Goethe's aperçu, "It isn't much of an author who can be captured by a standard lexicon."[36] The fact remains that it isn't indeterminacy when the critic fails to make out meaning. Simply, nothing fails like a reading pre-programmed to fail.

As for the notion that it isn't the individual but only ever the linguistic system that does the creating, that hardly requires rational refutation. It stops short at the point where creation is about to begin.

Till then, what Saussure called *langue* is only the resource on which a speaker has yet to draw—a virtually limitless resource from which the skilled user selects and shapes. It was damaging for substantive human purposes when the real-world referents in works of science and philosophy were alleged to be no more than "an effect produced by language itself."[37] The equally misleading notion that language is a "prison-house" came from a title of Frederic Jameson's, derived in turn from a mistranslation of Nietzsche.[38]

As support for these notions of theory, a few authors were judged to be not dead after all, and were set up as beacons pointing the way to what was now presented as fact. Mallarmé was the first to see the alleged necessity of putting language in the place of the person previously considered its owner. A Samuel Beckett quotation—"What does it matter who is speaking?"—was invoked to support Foucault's notion that "writing creates a space into which the writing subject vanishes."[39] But to draw new dogma from a slight modern corpus was to ignore the voluminous record of centuries. Those named writers apart, all remaining unnamed authors had to be read skeptically, their overt meanings deconstructed.

For a certain cast of mind, negation allows a more flattering pose than acceptance. Given the theorists' various "aporias" (another favorite term, for unresolvable problems of understanding), seemingly reveled in rather than regretted, to trust yourself to a text or an author was not an option.

Yet no reading of literature can work without trust and empathy. The atmosphere of "theory" was consistently hostile, an environment in which understanding was unlikely. Above all, deconstructionists and other theorists showed little sign of the love that literature has traditionally inspired.

Love is a classic way into understanding, argued Nietzsche, a thinker not known for soft sentiment:

> *Love as a method.*—Anyone who wants really to *get to know* something new (whether it is a person, an event, or a book) does well to accept the new thing with all possible love [. . .] For example, you give the author of a book the greatest possible start and positively, with pounding heart as if at a race, desire him to reach his goal. For with this procedure you get right to the heart of the new thing, right to its animating center, and this is what getting to know it means. The understanding can come along afterwards with its restrictions.[40]

New theses are a legitimate challenge to an existing paradigm, though the means by which they acquire influence are not straightforwardly rational. By the time the pregnant key phrases—"death of the author," "endlessly deferred meaning"—have been even just mentioned a few dozen times, albeit in shocked tones, they are part of the intellectual scene, and it is already getting late to analyze and oppose them. From the start they thrived on sensation—fashion in intellectual matters operates in much the same way as the extremes of *haute couture*. As Hugo von Hofmannsthal noted in a different context, "Anything bizarre seizes the attention, exaggeration forces itself upon us."[41]

Novelty could appeal especially to the young, and persuading them was easier when the cart of abstract theory was put before the horse of substantive reading. Typical of what could trickle down to their practice is this vignette, from a seminar on Goethe's Persian-style collection, the *West-Östlicher Divan*:

> Ist's möglich, dass ich Liebchen dich kose,
> Vernehme der göttlichen Stimme Schall!
> Unmöglich scheint immer die Rose,
> Unbegreiflich die Nachtigall.
>
> [Am I really caressing you, dearest,
> Hearing your voice, its heavenly tone!
> Just as impossible seem always roses,
> And the nightingale singing alone.]

It seems a straightforward love-lyric. But wasn't "vernehmen" a compound of the verb "nehmen," to take? So wasn't the poem really about masculine take-over, male supremacy? The linguistic link is true but trivial—"vernehmen" is indeed a compound of "nehmen," but only a common, if slightly high-style verb for "hearing." Nothing in the poem is plausibly "taken" by or from anyone—only taken from the reader, since a lyrical expression of love and wonderment has become arbitrarily shot through with suspicion.

Students lacked the breadth of reading against which to test its notions that their elders had enjoyed in pre-"theory" days. They perhaps also lacked the confidence to confess to a dissenting enthusiasm for literature. True, the more perceptive began to find it less than exciting when their reading came out monotonously subversive week after week. Could it be that simple—or rather that complex?

Yet alongside theory's hard-sell of its allegedly superior rigor, it could also claim to be doing no more than what was traditional in literary studies—this in response to a perceived "resistance to theory." In a volume with that title, a prominent deconstructionist, Paul de Man, diagnosed it as a resistance "to the use of language about language"—but that is a use all criticism makes all the time; or a resistance to theory as a perceived "obstacle to scholarship and consequently to teaching"—but plausible theory has been vital since Aristotle as a stimulus to both. Finally, de Man attributed the resistance to theory to "a disturbed moral conscience," because it has been "the more or less secret aim of literary teaching to keep [structures of language] hidden from students."[42] Groundless professional defamation was hardly rigorous argument. Nor was the sleight of hand by which theory was presented as a simple "return to philology," that is, a close attention to texts, which is the basis of all teaching. Yet nowhere—and this was disingenuous to the point of dishonesty—did de Man acknowledge the distinctive character of recent theory, and the meaning the term "literary theory" had acquired. What was resisted was a decidedly anti-literary theory.

It must be recognized that traditional humanist reading had failed to make its underlying values explicit. It was all too easy for teachers to assume that the appeal of literature, touching as it does on elements of existence that the young already have experience of—thought, feeling, memory, personal and social relations—was direct enough not to need elaborate theorizing. As a result, literary study could appear to have no intellectual structure. So perhaps the sheep looked up and were not fed? A charitable view of "theory" is that it made this shortfall clear, that as George Steiner has noted, "the acrobatics of deconstruction have helped to reclaim for intelligence, have woken to excitement, much that lay inert and formulaic in the study of letters and the arts."[43] They certainly confirmed clarity about what it is we are doing.

Yet it remains ironic, and the ultimate illogic of the whole elaborate theoretical corpus, that its aporias involved denying determinate meaning while ignoring just the realities that help to determine it. This was to look a gift horse in the mouth.

For a time, literary theory enjoyed a heyday. Having disposed of or discredited authors as such, its exponents were left center-stage basking in the limelight, their secondary activity regarded as more significant (its own texts not admitting of any aporia) than the activity from which it formally derived.

To return to an acceptance of literature as a viable communicative system is not just to fall back on blinkered tradition. And if new theory is needed, it is to hand from a body of empirical investigation that starts out from everyday exchanges in real life, where communicative intention and unspoken implication are met by willing understanding and alert inference, in contexts knowable to both parties—exactly what happens in intelligent reading. This model, offered by Dan Sperber and Deirdre Wilson in their "relevance" concept,[44] transfers effortlessly to literature. It has in turn a sound basis in cognitive science, which has fruitfully investigated the processes that make possible intuition and empathy through an imitative response to the motions and emotions of an interlocutor, or to their representation in art. With this very positive alternative to skeptical theory, we are back in a world we can recognize.[45]

As we are with another school of practice close to the working-method of this book. Since the 1970s a very different French movement has been active at the Centre National de Recherche Scientifique under the banner "critique génétique."[46] It concerns itself with the detailed analysis of manuscripts, where I only draw on that aspect for broader critical purposes. Much account is taken of early drafts for their own sake, so that sometimes the prime aim seems to be to get back to the author's creative consciousness itself, making the work seem secondary. So there is a risk of losing sight of the wood for the trees.

Nevertheless, the "critique génétique" school is devoted to texts in human contexts, to the processes by which writers match words to realities as precisely and faithfully as possible.

And behind communication and literature as a means lies a sympathy with human beings, who are the substance creative writing engages with. "Humanism" in literary practice means a positive openness to all those who have shared the common human experience and added something to the written record. It speaks eloquently in a letter the young Goethe wrote when Christian friends invoked the spiritual testimonies on which their faith was founded:

> Do I need testimonies that I exist? Testimonies that I feel?—As it is, I value, love, worship the testimonies that show me how thousands or just one before me have felt what gives me firmness and strength. And so it's the word of human beings that is for me the word of God, whether priests or whores have collected it and rolled it up into a canon or strewn it about as fragments. And with all the depth of my soul I fall upon my brother's neck Moses! Prophet! Evangelist! Apostle, Spinoza or Machiavelli. I can say to every one of them, dear Friend, it's the same for you as for me.[47]

Goethe remained consistent in his practice, drawing with exemplary gratitude on his predecessors in literature and thought—Linnaeus, Spinoza, Pindar, Shakespeare, the Roman lyricists, the Persian poet Hafiz. Near the end of his life he sums up in less exuberant but deeply felt terms his allegiance to the "sterling people" from the past who have left a written record of thoughts and feelings that they believed might survive them. These people are his secular "communion of saints," following whose example he owes a communication of his own to the future.[48]

Goethe's literary partner Schiller had earlier teased out what such interaction among human beings could achieve. He sees them as together constituting a great organism in which every individual is a single sense, each perceiving the world in a manner as distinctive as the different human sense organs do. They only need to communicate with each other to compose a full picture. The theoretical mind may have difficulty grasping how this can work, yet "real life shows at every moment that it is possible, right down to the most minute level of particularity, through the general medium of language."[49] What, if not such community—with the dead, the living, and future generations—gives human life a broader substance and coherence?

Such deeply humane insights were once the assumptions on which literary studies drew. In recent scholarship, realization has been dawning of what has been lost through the systematically unsympathetic reading that goes along with "theory." Voices are now being raised against the "unbearable knowingness of scepticism"[50] and arguing for a return to a sympathetic "immersive reading" that "can bridge the separation between humans."[51] It looks as if humanism is making a comeback, and not before time. The need goes beyond literature. Now more than ever, civilized society depends on reliable communication, for as Montaigne declared, "We are only human beings and hold true to one another through the word."[52]

Part I
Antiquity

1: Homer's Audiences: Shaping the *Iliad* (and the *Odyssey*)

Starting

THE STUDY OF LITERARY GENESIS begins in ancient times with the founding cases of scholarship and controversy, Homer and the Bible. This chapter touches on motifs that will recur later. It also suggests a modest alternative answer to some long-standing Homeric questions.

The *Iliad* and the *Odyssey* mark the genesis of a genre. Homer is the first great epic author in Western literature, the first whom people identified, or perhaps they simply created him, a legendary and symbolic poet-figure, old, blind, but richer for that in grand and compelling visions. At all events, nothing is reliably known about a real person. Homer—I stick nevertheless to the traditional name—was also the first to suffer the death of the author (a rather different kind from the once alleged death of modern authors) when his role as the sole creator of the *Iliad* and *Odyssey* was questioned. Doubts arose from inconsistencies, irregularities, contradictions that stuck out like the proverbial sore thumb. It has never quite healed, but has at best been awkwardly plastered over.

The epics attributed to Homer certainly had a complex and confusing genesis; it has been called "a long process about which we know nothing."[1] That is too sweeping, since it overlooks a lot that we do know about an enormous cast of people involved in the creation and afterlife of the *Iliad* and the *Odyssey*: an unknown number of unknown authors of earlier oral poems; an unknown number of unknown live performers from before and after the epics were given written shape; a large number of scholars and commentators, ancient and modern, known (Aristarchus, Eustathius, and Zenodotus; d'Aubignac, Perrault, and Wolf . . .) or unknown, who purified, criticized, cut, censored, and bowdlerized the texts. In sum, enough knowns and unknowns to make a fair body of knowledge. Roles are clear, though names and dates are largely lost. Their relation, to the texts and to each other, still leaves wide areas of uncertainty that have nourished controversy for centuries, keeping generations of scholars busy down to our own day trying to see through the complexities to the true substance. So the genesis of Homer's epics is also the genesis of genetic criticism.

Anger and After

"Iliad" is a slightly misleading title. The poem isn't an epic history of Ilium (Troy), or even of the entire siege by the Greek armies. Beyond the ebb and flow of battle in the killing fields outside the city, which in itself hardly constitutes a plot, it is the story of one man's anger and the consequences. The first determinant of the poem's genesis is thus a focus on psychology, on the wounded pride of Achilles, humiliated by his chief Agamemnon, who has arrogantly snatched his leading warrior's prize of honor, the captive girl Briseis. The whole epic is an inverted pyramid resting on a petty point, the squabble between two spoiled and self-willed men.

The poem could as well have begun from the opposite angle, the flaw in the generalissimo: "Greed—goddess, sing the greed of Atreus's son Agamemnon." The actual opening runs: "Rage—goddess, sing the rage of Peleus's son Achilles, murderous, doomed, that cost the Achaeans countless losses, hurling down to the house of death many sturdy souls . . ."[2] Robert Graves duly called his version, aptly enough, *The Anger of Achilles*.[3]

The poem's action takes place within less than two months and it begins in the ninth and last full year of the siege. We are projected not *in medias* but *in ultimas res*—or nearly *ultimas*, since the famous ruse of the wooden horse and the final fall of Troy are omitted. That leaves us wondering why, if there was to be no victorious end to the siege, Homer chose to begin the poem so late. For this leaves some episodes puzzlingly placed.

Homer's original hearers—and "hearers" will be crucial to the poem's genesis—may have cast their minds back still further than Paris and the goddesses, to the very existence of Helen as a prize and a provocation. It was one of Zeus's many escapades with mortal women that begat her and with her a whole grim history:

> A shudder in the loins engenders there
> The broken wall, the burning roof and tower
> And Agamemnon dead.[4]

As in Christopher Marlowe's lines, which make it ultimately Helen's face that "burnt the topless towers of Ilium,"[5] the god's orgasm is an original cause brought together with its distant effects as subject and object of a single verb. Leaving out the stages in between is a special kind of ellipsis for which I know of no term in rhetoric, but it brings home starkly the necessity of fated outcomes, from the fall of Troy down to the murder of the returning Agamemnon by his vengeful wife Clytemnestra.

Where poetic evocation can be brief, epic has to spell out the stages of the story in full. But of that substance the *Iliad* was only heard a small part at a time. What the very earliest hearers heard wasn't yet the *Iliad* at all, but separate ballads that would one day go into its making, each complete enough in itself to make a rounded evening's performance by a professional bard.

The *Odyssey* portrays a typical occasion. When Odysseus is feasted at Alcinous's court, entertainment is provided by the blind bard Demodocus, perhaps the original for the legend of a blind Homer. He sings, of all things, tales of the siege of Troy that Odysseus has not long ago left behind—the latest events in the outside world were perhaps the most in demand by an audience. For the court, it is entertainment, but for Odysseus it's a cause to weep. (Od. 8:74 and 300.) Phemius too, the bard pressed into service by Penelope's unwanted suitors back on Ithaca, sings of the other returners from Troy, again in Odysseus' lurking presence. (Od. 1:178 and 22:348) A bard is thus both a recorder of the recent past—almost a news channel—and a herald of the grander epic treatment to come. Homer himself may well have performed his own work, perhaps, in the words of the eighteenth-century scholar Richard Bentley, "for small earnings and good cheer"—just some pickings from the evening's feast.

In Plato's dialogue *Ion*, Socrates interviews a real-life bard on his way back from winning a competition at Epidaurus. Such festivals were the most prestigious feature of a bard's working life, culminating in the Grand Panathenaia held annually, and on a grander scale every four years, in honor of Athene, the patron goddess of Athens.

These performance specialists were the rhapsodes. The word has nothing to do with an ecstatic state, though that commonly arose in performance and gave rise to the modern sense of "rhapsodic"—Socrates says they are divinely possessed and pass their excitement on like magnetism down the links of a chain.[6] But rhapsode originally meant no more than a maker, literally a stitcher, of poems. The slightly odd metaphor becomes very apt when the performance materials are later joined together by a poet or poets to make the larger tapestries of the *Iliad* and the *Odyssey*. Over the centuries scholars have differed over whether the performances and their legendary content were just the *inspiration* for the large-scale epics, or whether they provided textual *material* that was stitched together to constitute them. This itself would have been a demanding enough creative task, matching and smoothing to make whole cloth. Either way, the work of composition was made easier, perhaps made possible at all, by the invention of writing, which meant that checking and changing in the light of an overview became practicable in a way it would scarcely have been for unsupported memory.

Even written material, as far as writing had then evolved, can't have made composition exactly easy. Single written sheets were combined into rolls, effectively scrolls, of up to thirty-five feet. That made long texts hard to manage: "When one had to hold the roll in the right hand and re-roll it with the left, reading column after column of text, the inconvenience of very long rolls is very apparent."[7] (The word processor now has us "scrolling" back and forth again, but at least it moves fast and has the short cut of a Find function.) Add to this the arrangement of text on a sheet with no break between words ("scriptio continua"), all capitals, with hexameter-length lines possibly running alternately from left to right and back—known as "boustrophedon," that is, in the manner of an ox turning to plough the return furrow:

RAGEGODESSSINGTHERAGEOFPELEUSSONACHILLES
LOSSESCOUNTLESSACHAEANSTHECOSTTHATDOOMEDMURDEROUS
HURLINGDOWNTOTHEHOUSEOFDEATHMANYSTURDYSOULS

And those are just the opening lines of the *Iliad* (see above). The further you went into a scroll, the harder it must have been to work at the detail of comparing, conflating, compiling, while still keeping an overview of the whole. The day of the codex, the early form of the book, lay far in the future.[8]

The Sore Thumb

So even on the assumption that a single poet composed the *Iliad*, it is no surprise to find things that stick out, awkward or inadequate joins, overlaps, or uncorrected slips. Even the most exhaustive and closely argued reconstruction of how the *Iliad* was put together by a supposed poet "P," working over many years of revision and expansion, adding "tectonic" and "episodic insertions" to a "primary layer," to arrive finally at a complex weave, not to say patchwork—even this ultimate positive account still admits there are numerous instances of not quite matching up, of failing to correct a detail, of places where the initial program appears to be completely forgotten," where there is "a breach of continuity in the execution," where "lost contiguities between portions of the text have been forced apart by insertions," or where "tell-tale signs are left of a double account."[9] It has been compared to the growth of a medieval cathedral over centuries, later elements disturbing earlier, always continuing, long unfinished.[10] Given the immense scope of the project, these flaws are what an ancient critic argued should be accepted as "the negligence of genius," for "great geniuses are least 'pure,' and with grandeur there must be something that was overlooked."[11]

Even once a written text had been firmly established, probably in sixth-century BCE Athens under the tyrant Pisistratus, it was still subject to changes, interpolations, and corruptions as it was handed down and as sections of it went on being performed and adapted by rhapsodes—Plato's Ion is a declared Homer specialist.

These complexities left ample room for conjecture on the authorship of individual sections, especially in the *Iliad*. Since no working drafts by poets or texts used by rhapsodes were preserved, and since an immense number of non-identical manuscripts of the finished epics (188 of the *Iliad*, about half that of the *Odyssey*) had come into being by the heyday of scholarship in ancient Alexandria around the third century BCE, conjecture rested on stylistic, formal, grammatical, metrical, and other aesthetic and even social and eventually archaeological grounds: Did a passage feel like authentic Homer (whatever that was taken to mean) or was it the work of some other hand? Could he really have meant this word, or was it perhaps an alien insertion, or a copyist's mistake? Was it even correct Greek, or consistently the right dialect of Greek? Could Homer have written something so socially improper (Princess Nausikaa with her women doing the laundry herself in a stream outside town)? Could a particular item of armor have existed in Homer's time (whenever that was)? Was a given character consistent? Was there an overall unity? Was there even a single Homer? Worse still, could a great poet at times have written sub-standard lines—a field day for impressionistic judgments.[12]

The fundamental question was first systematically asked by Friedrich August Wolf in his *Prolegomena ad Homerum* of 1795. In its boldest formulation, he proposed "that this entire connected series of the two continuous poems is owed less to the genius of him to whom we have normally attributed it, than to the zeal of a more polite age and the collective efforts of many, and that therefore [. . .] they do not all have one common author."[13] The scholarly sect created by this breaking of a taboo became known as Analysts, their opponents, who hold that the epics are wholly the work of Homer, or some unknown single poet, as Unitarians. Separatists are those who claim that the *Iliad* and the *Odyssey* had different authors, of whom one may even have been a woman.[14]

On the questionable details, no two scholars' conjectures matched, "since the criteria they were using—inconsistency of character, imbalance of structure, irrelevance of theme or incident, clumsiness of transition—are notoriously subjective."[15] Bernard Knox's impatience is understandable, but it is simply not true that every critical assertion is subjective. Some rest on concrete observation. It may not much matter if the odd Greek or Trojan warrior is killed only to turn up alive a bit further on. With all the deaths in the *Iliad*, that is a mistake any single author might make; it isn't evidence for multiple authorship or conflation of earlier texts.

But the most obtrusive difficulties relate to the story's overall timing. For strange things happen in this ninth year of the siege. In book 2, the armies and the places and clans they come from are reviewed, the Greeks at great length (2:543–894), the Trojans more briefly (2:927–89: this latter breaks off as if fragmentary); part of the review is a catalogue of the ships that brought the Greeks to Troy in the first place. Why does it happen so late? None of this is a flash-back, or a recollection, or a reminder of the start of the war, which is where it would have obviously belonged. On the contrary, it is unambiguously part of the narrative present. It also leads in to an obvious tactic that would have been something to attempt, and record, at the very start of the siege. For Zeus has urged Agamemnon to "attack at once, full force" (2.33). It all reads as if the two sides had never yet met in battle.

Likewise, when King Priam soon afterwards looks down from the walls of Troy at the advancing Greeks (the "teichoscopy"), he needs Helen to tell him who the figures he's spotted are. One of them is so regal in appearance that he must surely be a king? And fancy that, it is indeed Agamemnon in person. Odysseus similarly gets identified, then the greater Ajax and Idomeneus (3.203 et seq.) So nine years in, the leaders of the besieging force are still not yet known to the besieged. So much for what must always have been a first principle of military intelligence: know your enemy.

Similarly in book 3, a duel is agreed on between Paris and Menelaus, the adulterer and the husband he cuckolded, as a means of settling the conflict over Helen without everyone else having to go on fighting. This too would surely have been an earlier suggestion to prevent the years of bloodshed that have ensued. The duel anyway proves indecisive, indeed it is a blind motif: grotesquely, Paris on the point of defeat is whisked away by Aphrodite to, of all places, Helen's bed, where he declares he is more desperate to make love than ever before—this too after nine years. Well, maybe. (3:439 and 516) At all events, no more is heard of the duel as a tiebreaker, even though Menelaus was clearly winning.

Evasions

How do commentators present these things? Of the way those sights and events of the ninth year are narrated as if the war were just beginning, it is "perhaps enough to say that for the reader this *is* the beginning of the war."[16] But it's obviously not enough. It is an elementary confusion of the time in which we're reading and the time-frame of the events we're reading about, an invitation to give up asking the question the critic can't or won't answer. Knox, in his introduction to the Fagles translation, calls those episodes "scenes that recall earlier stages of the war."[17] Not at all—they are in the narrative present, they are happening right now. The Prolegomena volume to the authoritative Basel *Iliad* Commentary lists the catalogue of ships, the Paris-Menelaus duel, and the teichoscopy (it makes no mention at all of the review of the armies) but similarly explains them all as "a reversion that delves into the past." The catalogue of ships is wrongly labelled "the gathering of the fleet in Aulis nine years in the past," while the teichoscopy "cannot of course have happened as late as the ninth year of the war.[18] But it can and it has. All these arguments are simple bluff, flying in the face of what the text says. The episodes are neither memories nor repeats designed to call to mind identical past events. It's all happening now.

Scholars may agree to let sleeping dogs lie, but in publications aimed at a popular readership such sleight of hand will not do. Cheating the Common Reader, who may not indeed be so easily fooled, is not the best way to promote a classic. E. V. Rieu, in his first-generation Penguin Classics translation—the most important modern English interface with the general public—took evasiveness to the point of positively browbeating the reader into acquiescence:

> It will astonish people who know nothing of the "Homeric question" to learn that these splendidly constructed poems, and especially the *Iliad*, have in the past been picked to pieces by the men who studied them most carefully and should presumably have admired them most. They alleged certain incongruities in the narrative and argued that the *Iliad* is the composite product of a number of poets of varying merit, who [. . .] lived at different times and each patched up his predecessor's work, dropping many stitches in the course of this sartorial process.[19]

Rieu then makes what at first sight seems an open-minded offer:

> I cordially invite new readers to try to find some [inconsistencies] for themselves.

But then cordiality turns into schoolmasterliness:

> No marks will be given for the discovery of passages where Homer, after killing a man in battle, brings him back to life—this might happen to any author. One mark (out of ten) is allotted for minor incongruities in timing, as when Odysseus does more things [in twenty-four hours] than the most energetic hero of a modern adventure story could have done in three days. [. . .] I might allot as much as two marks to the enquiring spirit who asks how it came about that Priam, who has had the Achaean chieftains knocking at his gates for nine years, has to ask Helen who is who. But full marks will be given only for the detection of a real flaw which cannot be explained away.

Yet Rieu makes no attempt to explain away the visible real flaws.

Such apologias not only pooh-pooh the question instead of answering it; they prejudge the issue ("these splendidly constructed poems"), they beg the question ("enough to say"), they play fast and loose with concepts ("a real flaw"). Similarly, a volume in the Oxford Past Masters series—another essay at the popular interface—claims that there are "few significant inconsistencies"[20] but doesn't say what would count as significant, or why the few that actually are significant still don't matter, or how many there would have to be for us to take them seriously.

It is a common assumption that there was, if not a single poet, then one editing hand that brought the sections together, and that this was not only dependent on prior rhapsodes but may have been partially undone by later careless or creative colleagues, before or after a written redaction came about. Scholars, as illustrated above, nevertheless feel impelled to assert an ultimate cohesion. Their judgment is readily swayed by the authority of cultural and scholarly tradition, and it is all too easy to claim universal agreement—that "the impression felt by every hearer and every reader, whether in ancient or modern times" (how can we possibly know?) is that "each poem is somehow" (how exactly?) "a unity."[21]

Sometimes good sense prevails and the textual puzzles are not swept under the carpet. "It is hard to believe that a poet as good as Homer is unaware of matters to which we attach importance."[22] That must mean, promisingly, that things which seem irregular to us were consciously left so, perhaps for good reason. But the writer immediately goes out on a limb of his own: "It is not enough to argue that Homer was a primitive poet, for he is outside any scheme of ancient and modern, primitive or advanced." Yet no writer can conceivably stand outside that scheme; and if there is to be anything like a solid understanding of what Homer is about and why his texts are as they are, it must take into account precisely the particular conditions of his primitive age.

One aspect of those conditions was given a lot of scholarly attention in the twentieth century, namely the practice of oral epic narrative as (re)-discovered by Milman Parry among Yugoslav *guslari*, who depended heavily on repeat formulas to support the performer's memory.[23] Parry's observations and arguments are commonly said to have revolutionized Homeric scholarship. They certainly had widespread influence, but they had their own not quite secure logic. For what Parry's team observed in modern Yugoslavia at most proves that memory and improvisation on something like the scale of the Homeric poems are humanly possible. It doesn't prove that this obtained in Homer's case, any more than do the similar (Italian) cases already known to Friedrich August Wolf in the eighteenth century, or others (Estonian, Latvian) known to nineteenth-century scholars, or the many cases documented in modern studies of oral performance all over the world.[24] Albert Lord's extension of Parry's arguments labelled more and more structures formulaic until virtually nothing escaped the term, leaving little room for the free play of language and imagination. But if Homer's longer formulaic repetitions were no more than a basic aid in performance, it isn't clear why they would all have been included in the eventual written redaction. The Yugoslav findings also pay little attention to quality—and none to one other simple, and significant, factor.

"Play it again, Sam": A Taste for Repeats

It isn't only Rick and Ilsa for whom hearing the old tune and words stirs memories and emotions.[25] Children want familiar stories told in the familiar way, and cry out against variation. Repetition is a major factor in art and in human responses to art: poetry lives by recurrent rhythms, rimes, meters, stanza patterns; songs have refrains; classical symphony and sonata have a recapitulation; dance has repeat rhythmic patterns; word games rerun a sequence and add something more to it.

It seems the Greek audiences were no different. Parry's spotlight fell exclusively on performers, leaving the hearers in the shadows. Yet it is their reactions that provide the one thing we do know about the whole Homeric genesis, though not much is usually made of it. *We know the original audiences must have liked what they heard, because it survived to become the final text.* Beside this certainty, invocations of prior poets, early tales, later rhapsodes, vanished versions, redactional dates, and even modern memory-virtuosos all pale into lesser significance. The much talked-of centuries-old ballad tradition needs to be understood as a series of dialogues with audiences. The rhapsodes couldn't have rescued Homer's epics for posterity without the decisive input of their hearers. If these people hadn't liked the content and mode of a particular performance, it would never have been kept in the repertoire, let alone turned eventually into lasting written form. Imagine the after-supper scene: the warm stir of audience assent, even applause interrupting delivery (think the responses of a jazz audience to individual riffs) and this piece of narrative survives; the cold hush of disapproval and it's dead.

In modern print cultures an unrecognized writer can defy contemporary taste for a lifetime and hope for literary immortality at some later date, when fashions have changed and the work will be read more sympathetically. Things that are written go on existing—"scripta manent"—to be later rediscovered, either as a long-neglected published work or as a never-published manuscript. But performance doesn't last. Oral poetry vanishes with the singer's breath. Unless hearers continue to want his offering, it won't reach the future.

The usually complex aesthetics of reception allows this simple application, to an ancient audience that knew what it liked. So instead of concentrating, as scholarship largely has, on the way textual repeats and formulaic composition may have helped the poet to compose or the rhapsode to deliver, we should try reading Homer's texts as the product of their piecemeal popularity. And where anything seems out of line, unnecessary, intrusive, inconsistent, we should ask why it was nevertheless favored by its early hearers, with the result that it got included in the work's later redaction. It may be true that there is "little evidence in Homer of the criteria by which his audiences would have judged his poems."[26] But the one massive piece of evidence that must imply their criteria is the text itself.

There is a written record of which the favorite pieces were in performances by rhapsodes working from the now written-out *Iliad*.[27] There will have been favorites long before the stage of redaction was reached. Without knowing in detail which all of these pieces were, we know we must have them, they must be embodied in the text that has come down to us. In a paradoxical cart-before-the-horse process, the pattern of audience reception helped to determine the epic's genesis.

There is further evidence everywhere in Homer of things that people liked and must have wanted to hear about again and again: things familiar to them from daily experience—the preparation and enjoyment of meals (meat was only ever roasted, not boiled, with never a vegetable in sight!); ceremonies and sacrifices (the succulent thighs reserved for the gods); well-made objects, finely crafted armor, soundly constructed buildings. At such points, it is as if the poet pauses in carrying us with him along the narrative line of action and turns full-face on a scene, inviting us to join in his own absorption as he contemplates some deeply satisfying piece of the world. He also loves to follow the processes through which the things he's evoking were created. As the shrewdest of eighteenth-century German critics saw, Homer keeps description vivid by transforming the static into the dynamic, as when Hephaestus is shown forging a shield for Achilles that is richly covered with human activities, all of them described. (18.540–709). Objects existing in space become actions consecutive in time, as is right for the live movement of literature as against the immobile juxtapositions of painting.[28] In the same way, Odysseus is described in the process of building the raft on which to leave Calypso's island (Od. 5:529–87).

There is also ample evidence regarding which features of formal presentation the hearers preferred. Most strikingly it was repeats, of all shapes and sizes: the famous adjectival tags—swift-footed Achilles, the wine-dark sea, the earth that feeds us all, the rosy-fingered dawn, and its less remarked but finer counterpart, "the sun went down and the roads of the world grew dark"; the formulas of fatality—"and darkness came down over his eyes" or "his armor clanged about him"; the recurrent passages of narrative when battle is joined, or as gods and goddesses flit hither and yon between Olympus and earth, arguing and fighting among themselves and intervening in human struggles; the long messages spoken by a sender and delivered verbatim to the receiver, never reduced to mere indirect speech, always word-perfect (no Chinese whispers here:

Homer's characters speak with clarity and remember with ease). Passages of a few or even many lines recur both within a page of each other and many books apart. In neither case would the repeats be of any obvious use in helping a performer to take a breather and gather his wits. Rather, he is rehearsing over and over again things that are delightful to savor, or thoughts that are worth pondering. There is a clear parallel in the chorus repetitions of Aeschylean tragedy, where there is no question of a need for help in memorizing or improvising, but where the content of utterances is required to be taken with full existential seriousness.[29]

Knox, here getting warm, speaks of the audience "relishing a repeat of such a virtuoso passage—this is one of the pleasures of oral poetry in performance." Against that, Bowra, at one point excusing the absence of a description, says that its repetition would have been tedious—but tedious for whom? No amount of repetition seems to have tired Homer's hearers. Bowra's response assumes that Homer and his Greeks shared our taste and criteria and that we must excuse as a fault something that positively documents *their* taste and *their* criteria. That, precisely, is part of the primitive context that Bowra claimed Homer stood outside of.

So, to return to the classic cruxes quoted earlier: how do they read if we think ourselves back into the attitudes of their audience and ask what made sense to them, and above all what gave them pleasure? Instead of pretending that the review of the armies in book 2 "is" the beginning for the reader, or that it "recalls" earlier stages of the war, we assume the audience simply *liked* such grand display and that any chance to build it into the performance was welcome, however late in the course of the siege. There was distinct pleasure in the description of an army. We know how stirring the recital of fighting men's names and the places they come from can be. Think of Henry the Fifth's Crispin Day speech or Michael Drayton's Agincourt poem, their brief intensity drawn out to several times the length in this grand Homeric review, allowing hearers from all over Greece to indulge their local patriotisms: so many regions and races are listed, far more numerous in the Greek than in the list of the Trojans and their allies—the audiences after all were Greeks! The same applies to the catalogue of ships.

The fascination of both these martial spectacles is confirmed from an unlikely source, the love-poetess Sappho:

An army of horsemen, say some, of foot-soldiers, say others,
again others of ships, is the most beautiful thing
on the black earth—but I say, whatever
anyone holds dearest.

Which for her, in contrast to the panoply of war, is a girl called Anaktoria:

> Her charming step I would rather
> see and the radiant light on her countenance
> than the Lydians' chariots and fully accoutred infantry.[30]

Why the Lydians, who were not even Greeks, is not clear. What is clear is that Sappho is dissenting from a widespread, if limited (though perhaps not exclusively masculine) taste. The popular choice is between cavalry, infantry, chariots, and ships. Sappho may even have had those passages of the *Iliad* in mind, since Helen and Troy are named in the poem's next lines. And why the equally belated duel between Paris and Menelaus will have been a crowd-pleaser isn't far to seek. It's a dream of the ordinary soldier that the high-ups should have to fight out the conflict for themselves—it recurs in *All Quiet on the Western Front*.[31] As for the comic-titillating switch to Helen's boudoir. . .

As against the imperative to please, neither the audience nor the poet himself will have been much bothered about these evocative episodes coming so implausibly late in the story of the siege. The pleasure taken in quality, in quiddity, trumps logical consistency—if, indeed, either the performer or the hearers even had that concept then.[32]

Different timing of the *Iliad*'s starting point would of course have avoided any such problem of plausibility from the start. It would also have avoided the ultimate unresolved problem already touched on above: why doesn't Homer narrate the scene of the fall of Troy—colorful, violent, conclusive, and surely a powerful crowd-pleaser?[33] More importantly, it was the story's logical climax and the obvious reason for starting the poem in Year Nine. All we get is a harbinger of the city's downfall, in the defeat of Troy's irreplaceable defender Hector by Achilles. And that outcome adds one more question to the complex puzzle of the timing: why, if Achilles was so overwhelmingly superior to all other fighters, did he never give the Greeks a decisive advantage in the eight years when he *was* active?

Trying to imagine the audience and its tastes as determinants of the text poses further transcultural questions that are not easy to answer. How did they react to violent death in battle, which is the overwhelming content of the *Iliad*? And how happily did they accept the hierarchical pattern whereby "heroes,"—scholars commonly use the term without scare quotes[34]—the named Big Guys, efficiently slaughter hoi polloi? At best these unfortunate minor figures get a mention of their names (where did all the names come from?) and sometimes of their origin in a more peaceful time and place. But nowhere does a David defeat a Goliath, and only once does a minor actor even wound a major figure. Sometimes it only takes three lines to dispose of nine nonentities together in what is chillingly called a "blur" of killing; sometimes a single death gets *con amore* treatment with three whole lines to itself. Repetition of the one grim act is endlessly varied as bronze drives through flesh and organs at every possible angle and point of the anatomy. Rated most hideous wound of all is a spear-thrust "between the genitals and the navel" (13:570). But at least in these hand-to-hand combats men always die at once, unlike the drawn-out sufferings of the mortally wounded in later wars. Still, this was a grim enough entertainment. Was violence felt as a normal part of life, always in the offing in some form for the audience too? Or was it something safely distant in time and circumstance, part of the past "heroic" age, to be enjoyed in safety like the phenomena of the Sublime that eighteenth-century aesthetics could appreciate with what Edmund Burke called delightful horror?

One other repetition has a strange mixed resonance all its own. Before launching his "cunning" attack, Agamemnon resolves "according to time-honored custom" to test the men by telling them the war is all over. Zeus, he declares, is a cruel god. He promised they would take Troy, but it was all treachery, nine years have gone fruitlessly by (you wonder how they ever let themselves in for a siege that was divinely prophesied to last a whole decade). They will clearly now never succeed. So the new order of the day is to cut and run and sail home (2:130–39 and 157–65). La guerre de Troie n'aura plus lieu! It's another soldier's dream—imagine the generals on the Western Front saying something similar in 1914–18. The men need no second telling, and in no time are graphically described "knocking the blocks out underneath the hulls." Odysseus has a job getting them all back, he gives them a dressing-down as deserters and cowards, ignoring the fact that it was not their idea, they were obeying a command. They, plainly, had no inkling of any such time-honored custom. All in all, a pretty piece of generalship by Agamemnon.

But Agamemnon makes word for word the same speech seven books later, when the Greeks are faring badly and his morale is genuinely suffering a low. The wording is now apt, he means what he says about Zeus's treachery and the impossibility of taking Troy. It's "Cut and run!" in all earnest. This time Diomedes, the one Greek fighter with recognizably officer-like qualities, restores the situation, accusing his superior of a total lack of courage. (9:20–57). Agamemnon's morale will sag once more later, albeit with different wording, at the point where Odysseus calls him to his face a disaster (14:102).

Robert Graves gives a lively account of Homer as a satirist, with Agamemnon his main target,[35] as you might expect from an infantry officer who led the proverbial lions with asses for generals in 1914, and survived to tell his story in *Goodbye to All That*. A final nasty touch to the portrait of Agamemnon is when Menelaus intends to spare a vanquished Trojan and his brother makes him go through with the killing. Mercy is rare in the *Iliad*, but nowhere else and by nobody else is a small spark of humanity, otherwise only glimpsed in Hector, so ruthlessly extinguished.

And Agamemnon, remember (though it goes unmentioned in the *Iliad*) is the man who was prepared to sacrifice his daughter Iphigeneia to get the Greek ships a fair wind for Troy.

Yet satire has to be tempered with realism. Even Graves recognizes that Homer the satirist is "walking on a razor's edge and must constantly affirm his adherence to the ruling aristocracy, however stupid or cruel."[36] In book 2, it didn't take long for Odysseus to pull rank, bring the troops back after Agamemnon's foolish test, restore the hierarchical order,[37] and beat up the barrack-room lawyer Thersites, even though what Thersites accuses Agamemnon of—ruthless self-seeking and keeping the best prizes for himself when others have borne the heat of the day—is exactly what Achilles had thrown in his face in their confrontation. The troops, strangely, go along with Thersites's humiliation, even though he is, as it were, their union representative. Hierarchy, if not something the audience enjoyed having their noses rubbed in, will have been something they were familiar with and accepted. It was all very well for those upper-crust figures proving their prowess and getting saved in need by a god or a goddess, leaving the rank and file unsaved and unsung. Indeed, the only man-to-man fight among the Big Guys in which no immortal intervenes is that between Hector and Ajax in book 7, and even this is broken off and the intention to resume never fulfilled. For the rest, Paris is rescued by Aphrodite, Aeneas is likewise favored by her, and Achilles in the final duel with Hector is decisively helped by Athene. As Hector had been by Apollo when he fought Patroclus, whom the god first catches from behind and strips of his armor (916–24) so he can be stabbed—a unique exception—by a minor Trojan, leaving Hector to finish him off. None of this is particularly heroic.

Against all the privilege and pretension, the common men's rush for the ships is a brief safety valve for the anti-heroic view of things. This is not yet Falstaff's fight-dodging and critique of honor in *1 Henry IV*, or Blüntschli's chocolate-filled holster in Shaw's *Arms and the Man*, or Brecht's sermon against a land that needs heroes in *Life of Galileo*. But for an audience that knew and loved its *Iliad*, and especially if it was not always an upper-class but sometimes, perhaps often, a popular, even a plebeian audience (illiteracy being no barrier to the enjoyment of a live recital), there could be nice point in borrowing Agamemnon's despairing speech from book 9 and bringing it forward from the serious context to show the down-to-earth truth of what the troops really felt and wanted. (It can't of course be known at which of these points the episode was first located in the text.) And since epic poetry was not yet clearly distinguished from fact and history, since historiography had yet to be born and the Muses Homer invokes were thought of as a source not just of inspiration but of memory and reliable knowledge—since epic, in short, was the nearest thing there was to a true account of events and their causes—the whole episode can be seen as a kind of counterfactual wishful thinking: if only the rank and file had been given a free choice, if they had not all been tribal underlings and pressed men...

So it may have been no great shock for hearers to find, in another much discussed crux, that when an embassy is sent to conciliate Achilles, Greek dual-number verbs are used of Odysseus and Ajax, but for this form three's a crowd, so the other named member of the party, the minor figure Phoenix, is syntactically excluded, not just because he "goes on in advance," as in Rieu's embarrassed misrepresentation of the narrative (p. 165). It is true Phoenix does later have a substantial role to play in trying to make Achilles see reason, but only when he stays behind after his superiors have left. He is then at ease in the singular verb of his lesser social status, accepted by Achilles only because he is his old tutor. People in general must know their place, and language may help to make it plain; though I have yet to come across a scholar entertaining the notion that a mere academic couldn't expect to share a verb with the ruling classes.

Once we start seeing things from the audience point of view, other—admittedly speculative—possibilities open up. Book 10 is widely regarded as an interpolation by another hand. Its matter does indeed diverge markedly from the dominant pattern of battle and the changing fortunes of war. Odysseus and Diomedes go out on night patrol to see what the Trojans may be planning. They encounter the Trojan Dolon, who is outside the city walls on a matching mission. They capture and kill him. The scenario may have offered audiences a welcome change from the traditional set pieces of Big Guy exploits plus divine interventions, or fairy-tale passages as when Achilles fights against a river, or the higher-plane scenes among the gods. The patrol episode has an altogether less archaic feel; it is closer to the realities of war as hearers may have experienced it and as readers in our own time will readily recognize it. Whoever wrote it, book 10 will have been an audience-pleaser, as it continues to be.

Last "Twists and Tricks"

Circumstantial evidence of audience taste is a prominent feature late in the *Odyssey*. When book 21 opens with the words "The time had come," the modern reader assents with relief. Odysseus has been back on Ithaca since book 13, with half the poem still to run. The suitors' expected comeuppance is getting to feel overdue. Has Homer been building up the tension by making us wait—a whole eleven books long? Goethe and Schiller theorized about the "retarding elements" (retardierende Momente) that help make both drama and epic work.[38] But now one such element, which presumably was popular with ancient audiences, starts—for us—to tip suspense over into impatience.

For no sooner has Odysseus set foot back on Ithaca than he begins his incorrigible fantasizing. First he lies to a shepherd-boy (actually his faithful patron goddess Athene in disguise) with the fantasy tale of another identity in which he committed murder and had to flee the country. But Athene knows her man all too well,

> foxy, ingenious, never tired of twists and tricks—
> so, not even here, on native soil, would you give up
> those wily tales that warm the cockles of your heart!
> (Od. 13:332–34)

Odysseus' faithful old shepherd Eumaeus is next to be lied to, with an alleged "whole truth" (itself a meta-lie) that is in fact a fabrication of inordinate length. Admittedly Odysseus makes out he is a Cretan, and they were notorious liars. (Od. 14:220–407) Almost the last to be imposed upon is Odysseus' wife Penelope, this time with a tantalizing tale that this impostor, perversely pretending not to be the Odysseus he really is, once met Odysseus—"falsehoods all, / but he gave his falsehoods all the ring of truth," as he does, with yet another meta-lie: "I will tell you the whole truth" (Od. 19:187–283 and 300–353), which duly sets Penelope's tears flowing. When Odysseus finally does tell her the real truth, she takes some convincing, which serves him right. Aptly, it is only his knowledge of the privacy of the marital bed, massively structured round a live olive tree, that authenticates him.

Odysseus has earlier narrated his own true adventures (at least, we assume they're true—we only ever have his word for it, since none of his men have survived with him, and the sole firm fact is that he's been away for ten years) to the Phaeacians; so the narrative pump has been recently primed. But now on Ithaca and safely among his own people, there is no need for deception. Yet only to Telemachus does he reveal who he is, and even that only after first remaining silent while Eumaeus rehearses the lies the "stranger" told him the day before; and even then it takes Athena's injunction to stop Odysseus prevaricating further: "Now is the time, now tell your son the truth. / Hold nothing back so the two of you can plot / the suitors' doom." It has indeed become a tactical necessity. So at last the truth can out: "That man and I are one" (Od. 16:100–124; 188–94; 233).

But for as long as he can, Odysseus leaves all the others in the dark, with his several false identities and the imagined misadventures of an invented person. The repeated lying must be an inner compulsion—it "warms the cockles of his heart." Maybe it's even genetic—his grandfather Autolycus was a noted thief and liar, blessed by Hermes, the god of trickery. (Od. 19:448–49.) At all events, the consequence is that lying for its own sake has become part of Odysseus' image and will have created audience expectations, to be savored in the fulfillment by each assembly. You can imagine the whispers going round the audience: There he goes again, what will it be next? Nor is he in the least reviled as a liar. Rather he is recognized as "the master improviser" (Od. 19:186). His improvisations are feats of narrative in themselves, truth is seemingly not a moral issue, fabricating is a work of the imagination, and Odysseus' lies are part of Homer's art.

They are also part of a pattern. Though they "retard" the action, they do not create suspense, but rather linger and diffuse it. The modern reader may feel they are getting in the way of the story line, but for the original hearer they will have enriched it. They are further hints at the popular taste, like the much-loved repeats and digressions discussed above, and like Homer's one substantial flashback, the story of how the young Odysseus got a scar from a boar's tusk which identifies him when the old servant Eurycleia washes his legs (Od. 19:443–47).[39] But that is a delightful piece of the unfolding plot, a small homecoming in itself, with nothing deceitful about it.

Odysseus goes on lying to the very end. When the action is all over and the suitors have been slaughtered, for the first time he seeks out his father Laertes on a remote farm, who is still ignorant of events. Should the son straightaway declare himself and let the rejoicing begin? No, "I will put my father to the test, / see if the old man knows me now, on sight, / or fails to after twenty years apart" (Od. 24, 238–41) .Though Odysseus weeps to see his father in his working rags, "a man worn down with years, his heart racked with sorrow" (Od. 24:258), he can still muster the cool calculatingness to spin yet another yarn, twisting the knife by once again pretending to be someone who has met Odysseus (Od. 24:270–309 and 338–52). Only the "black cloud of grief" that visibly comes over Laertes makes his son put an end to the pretense. For us the scene leaves an unpleasant taste in the mouth, but it is all the more surely a sign of the once very different power and popularity of this virtual sub-genre.

What have those twenty years apart brought Odysseus—or robbed him of? The *Odyssey*'s positive balance is meagre. Experience, yes—he may have returned to Ithaca "plein d'usage et raison." But in Joachim Du Bellay's supreme sonnet of homesickness, "Heureux qui, comme Ulysse, a fait un beau voyage . . .," the world of salt sea and adventure yields pride of place to the gentle air of Anjou in the poet's native village. In its quiet way, that opposition is true to Homer's many stark contrasts between violent death and the happy scenes that dying warriors left behind forever. Odysseus has at least survived and reached home, but the twelve ships' crews of young Ithacans he took with him to Troy have not—it isn't much noted what a disastrous leader he, as much as Agamemnon, has been on the erratic return voyage, driven by curiosity to take needless risks. He himself has lost his best years as husband, father, and benevolent ruler of his island. All the loot plundered from Troy and other places has gone missing, leaving him with just the gifts the Phaeacians made at his final port of call. Penelope can still be described, despite the twenty years they have been separated, as a "golden Aphrodite" (Od. 19, 57) whom the suitors lust after (or is it really just her rank and property they want to lay hands on?) It seems more likely Odysseus will now live on, as Tennyson's poem "Ulysses" has it, "matched with an agèd wife." As for the rest, Menelaus has his Helen back and they are leading the implausibly placid domestic life Telemachus finds when he calls on them in Sparta: no suggestion in Homer of the long connubial years evoked in Rupert Brooke's poem "Helen and Menelaus," where she has become a scold and Menelaus "sacks a hundred Troys twixt noon and supper." Meanwhile, Agamemnon has returned in triumph to be murdered in his bath by his wife and her lover, an act of vengeance for the assumed sacrificial killing of their daughter Iphigeneia. Paris has been killed after killing Achilles. Achilles has besmirched his high renown by dragging dead Hector three times round the city walls and sacrificing twelve young Trojans at Patroclus's funeral ceremony. Troy is no more. The wholesale slaughter and sacrilege, the rape and enslavement of Trojan women, things the text foresees but doesn't narrate—it is sometimes suggested that they would have too much discredited the victorious "heroes"[40]—have duly happened.

Things happen. For the first time they are fixed in words on a large scale. Reality is looked squarely in the eyes. Homer, says Plato, is the first tragic poet. Archaic these poems may sound, the instruments of death may be primitive, but little else changes. Homer's epics are foundation stories for events that will recur throughout history, often in even more hideous, dehumanizing, dishonoring, forms.[41] When we speak of their "universal appeal," that means the conviction they carry, not some easy delight.

Faced with their monumental achievement, it is trivial to try to argue away, on some misplaced timeless notion of perfection, the irregularities rooted in their very historicity. Homer's sore thumb was always the live contact with an ancient reality.

2: Fourfold Genesis: The Bible between Literature and Authority

Odd One Out

Does the Bible belong here? Is it a literary work? It isn't even a "work" at all, but a collection, an anthology, a positive library—Carolingian catalogues listed it as "bibliotheca," and its modern name derives from an ancient Greek plural.[1] Each of the sixty-six constituent books—Old Testament thirty-nine, New Testament twenty-seven—has its own genesis. So far from being the single voice of God, as people once believed, the Bible is now taken, not just by secular minds, to be the work of many human hands, authors, part-authors, redactors, working from multiple sources, leaving problems of coherence and consistency that make the Homeric situation look positively simple. For example, the Pentateuch is made up of four constituents; the story of Jacob and Esau is said to be "stitched together" (that metaphor from accounts of Homer's epics) from three documents; there are late additions to 2 Samuel; Isaiah has at least three distinct strands; the last speaker in Job is thought to be an insertion; the book of Numbers is made up of sources with long and complex histories of their own; the Psalms are an anthology spanning seven centuries; there were once three versions of Mark's gospel; a further source lies behind Matthew and Luke, with possible links to the discovered gospel of Thomas.

Duplications are evident. There are two Creations in Genesis; the making of Man and Woman happens twice; light is created and only later the light-giving heavenly bodies; money that Joseph puts back in his brothers' sacks as they leave Egypt is discovered twice; David is twice presented to Saul; there are two reports in close sequence of the miracle of the loaves and fishes (Matthew 14 and 15). None of these texts show authorial awareness of their own reduplications. Uncertainty in the dating of the Hebrew Bible texts is measured not just in centuries but in whole civilizations. Not surprisingly, there is "widespread disagreement about practically every biblical book's unity, authorship and historicity."[2]

The arguments surrounding them are based on scholarly conjecture, stylistic intuition, hypothetical reconstruction—necessarily, for want of documents. Even the earliest manuscript survivals are vastly later than their textual content: the Dead Sea (Qumran) scrolls, discovered in 1947, which include fragments of almost all the Old Testament books, still only date back to the first century B.C.E., remote from their presumed textual origins somewhere between the ninth and second centuries B.C.E. Other treasured documents are later still and irrelevant for purposes of genetic precision; the Aleppo and St Petersburg manuscripts, for example, are merely medieval. To encompass such a multiplicity of geneses over such spans of time, all in a brief chapter, must seem impossible.

Yet the Bible can hardly be passed over in silence, for it was in at the very start of modern textual scholarship, the genesis of genesis. The so-called higher criticism of the Bible began alongside, was virtually intertwined with, the first systematic modern work on Homer. Wolf, he of the Homeric *Prolegomena*, and the leading theologian of the day, Johann Gottfried Eichhorn, were students together in the Göttingen seminar of the eminent classicist Christian Gottlob Heyne. They went on cross-referring to each other's work for support, the priority in method not clear, but not a bone of contention between them.[3]

Status

To apply the notion of genesis to the whole case can only mean asking what kind of work came newly into being at the different stages in the Bible's long history—a matter of the changes it underwent in human attitudes to it; and that involves precisely the question of its literary nature.

Some parts of the biblical corpus—poems, stories, aphorisms—are inherently literary, and will certainly have been accepted as literature in their ancient origins; and in recent decades they have become a fresh focus of specifically literary criticism. But the immense span in between had a radically different status, as both more and less than literature. More, because bringing them together and charging them with transcendent meaning as the foundation of two religious faiths made them authoritative in a way no purely literary production can ever be. At the same time, less—less free than literature by its nature is, because they were now doctrinally constrained and constraining. They set significance above beauty, were paradoxically both "literature and anti-literature."[4] Their new authority was implicit in that other label—scripture, "the writing," as if there were no other writing and it alone counted. As, for many people over those centuries, it did.

All this gives the Bible's genesis, overarching its constituent books, four distinct phases: first, the writing and preserving of the ancient texts; next, their drawing together into what became a doctrinal canon; then their rebirth as literature in the eyes of modern critics. The fourth, in-between, genesis, on the border both chronologically and essentially between canon and rebirth, is the appearance of translations into the vernacular, culturally most dramatic in English and German. Translation made the Bible effectively a new creation, belatedly opening it up to ordinary people, who, in an extreme paradox, had till then been barred from reading the book on which their faith was founded. The new accessibility played a major role in the genesis of Protestantism.

Origins

Deep in their past, the ancient texts, Babylonian, Assyrian, Ugaritic, Sumerian, even Canaanite, belong to a common root of Middle Eastern culture, which offers parallels and putative sources for such major themes as the Creation or, in the Babylonian Gilgamesh epic, the Flood, complete with Ark, rescued animals, mountain mooring, and exploratory dove. The Old Testament actually names three of its own ancient sources for Israelite history, though they have not survived.[5] For at least some of that material there may well have been a tradition of oral performance, but far less is known about it than can be inferred about Homeric occasions. *Gilgamesh* will surely have been recited, and there are heroes enough in the biblical material to have stirred a live audience—Moses, Jacob, Joshua, David, figures part history, part legend (was it really David who killed Goliath or some otherwise unknown warrior?).[6] The Psalms were plainly composed for the speaking voice, not the reading eye. Likewise the Song of Songs. The prophets too will have been heard before they were ever read, probably with an uneasy attentiveness, especially in times of national disaster, when past prophetic warnings had proved justified and might do so again, a situation quite unlike the Homeric audience's innocent delight in fine tales.

If the original texts were literary in form, some were already religious in substance—a creation myth, a flood and a new start for mankind and the animals, folkloric stories about the commands and acts of a primitive deity who didn't just control events from outside but was constantly there as a real presence, impressive and oppressive. There was no doubting this god's existence. Generous in his promises and his help in invading foreign lands and massacring their inhabitants, severe in his punishment of disobedience through the agency of Israel's enemies, he was as human as any Greek god in his group favoritism and—the other side of the coin—in his anger and jealousy, as he competed with the gods of other tribes, these often conceived as fully real, and sometimes able to steal the allegiance of his serially unfaithful Chosen People.

Pick and Mix

What begins in Genesis as a mythic origin of all humanity soon narrows down to the more or less continuous history of that single people, and eventually becomes the textual foundation of their religion. Exactly when and how that happened is again a matter of conjecture, though there was pressing need for a cohesive communal text after the Babylonian conquest and the destruction of the Temple at Jerusalem in 70 C.E. when the majority of Jews were scattered in exile, with obvious consequences of potential disunity and schism. The grounds for accepting texts in a canon[7] are equally unclear. Writing itself in its beginnings from the sixth century B.C.E. had a charismatic, almost sacred status. To say of something "It is written" already carries weight, not least, as Kant ironically remarked, with those who haven't read it.[8] Editorial decisions on inclusion in the canon or exclusion from it may have been determined less by doctrinal niceties than by intrinsic interest—the Old Testament has proportionally more narrative than religious teaching. The more ancient a text, the more it was respected and the better its chances of acceptance. Tradition played its part in ensuring that familiar material was kept in. The reluctance to omit anything time-honored, and conceivably even divine, such as the words Moses was said to have received on Sinai, is sometimes invoked by scholars to explain the above-mentioned duplications. Conversely, anything too modern, such as later prophecy, was not a serious candidate—prophecy generally was held to belong to an earlier age. (In things preternatural, the past is always easier to believe than the present.) There could be problems of content too: the sensual Song of Songs was a potential embarrassment that eventually had to be safely enclosed in religious allegory.

A Jewish canon was developing as early as the fifth century B.C.E. but was not fixed until the end of the first century C.E. It was apparently not a concern in Jesus' day, and the early Christians—the Evangelists and Paul—were certainly not writing consciously to contribute to it. Anything but, since a canon is a conservative institution, and the Christians were an innovative, not to say revolutionary movement. So for the New Testament in the first two centuries C.E. there was little relevant discussion among them and no consensus on what counted as scripture. But gradually the new movement too needed its book as it wrestled with internal dissensions and sought a way of accommodating the Jewish scriptures in its own often contradictory collection of writings and reminiscences. In 367 C.E. the twenty-seven constituents of the New Testament were declared canonical by Athanasius. What from this point on can properly be called the Old Testament became the plinth and prophetic harbinger of the New. Until then it was simply the Hebrew Bible, the foundation, along with rabbinical commentaries, of the Jewish faith, drawn on as such (though critically and creatively) by Jesus. But its status was felt to be downgraded by the term Old Testament, which from the Jewish standpoint is unacceptably "supersessionist." Still, only the rare deviationist like Marcion in the second century wanted to cast off the Old altogether.

For Christians, a practice of back-formation developed, seeing Jesus' life and actions prefigured in persons, dicta and events of the Hebrew scriptures, each confirming the other,[9] true to the saying that the Old Testament contains the New, the New Testament reveals the Old.

Declaring a canon changed the spiritual and intellectual world radically. It changed the nature of the texts themselves by including them in a corpus not to be fundamentally questioned. In a different way from the *Iliad*, reception helped determine genesis—only now was the Bible an entity. The whole then validated the parts. Rejected texts were relegated to the Apocrypha. These were human decisions, but they claimed suprapersonal authority, establishing an orthodoxy that commanded obedience and by the same token defined heresy. True, independence of mind was too deeply rooted in human nature to be prohibited by decree, so dissent continued, and not just among wild-eyed sectarian outsiders. In the fifth century C.E. such major figures as Jerome and Augustine were at loggerheads over whether to include apocryphal writings in the canon (still a disagreement to the present day between Catholics and Protestants). Earlier, as prominent a theologian as Origen was anathematized and declared heretical. Canonical certainty spawns intolerance. Christians had no monopoly on this. Spinoza would be excommunicated by the Amsterdam Jewish congregation, "expelled, cursed and damned with the consent of God," for not believing in Moses' authorship of the Pentateuch.[10] Human authority likes to dress itself up as divine. Even more drastic action could follow against individuals or groups, the most extreme being the thirteenth-century Albigensian crusade to exterminate the southern French Cathar sect, the only crusade the Church ever waged against Europeans.

Inspiration

The canon's status was strengthened, indeed made absolute, by claiming that its contents were divinely inspired. This was almost a necessary corollary for a religion that needed a means to establish its authority, especially when Protestantism did away with the Church's power to impose its decrees. The apocryphal writings, originally works of much the same stamp as those in the canon, were arbitrarily not allowed to have been inspired. But just what did "inspired" mean?

Inspiration is a familiar enough phenomenon from secular literature. The Muses had been inspiring the poets of antiquity (mousopneustia) long before New Testament Greek coined the parallel notion of divine inspiration (theopneustia). Writers down to modern times (Coleridge, Goethe, Nietzsche, Rilke, Kafka. . .) have left accounts of the experience for which an "incoming breath" from some higher source is a metaphor for the heightened mood, the unhindered flow of composition, the sense of being more than their normal selves. What more, or what that is distinctive, was claimed for the way the Bible was written?

"All scripture is given by inspiration of God," wrote Paul (2 Timothy 3:16). That this was a backward look at the Hebrew Bible is confirmed by Peter: ". . . prophecy came not in old time by the will of man: but holy men of God spake as they were moved by the Holy Ghost" (2 Peter 1:21). When prophets arraigned the Children of Israel, they ritually began with "Thus saith the Lord." They could hardly say less—a hot line from Yahweh was the guarantee of their authority. Yet beyond the two apostles' assertions and the prophets' claim to be passing on a message from on high, the Bible gives no details of how exactly inspiration operates, what it feels like, how it shapes what is written. Shouldn't the way in which the Bible's authors worked have been revealed so as to harden the concept and distinguish it from normal human creativity? Or was it after all no more than that? In what ways does an inspired text look different from other texts? And does the term apply piecemeal to every Bible passage, every line, every word, regardless of content—narrative, poetic, historical, legal, genealogical; violent, banal, boring, immoral; the rivalries, the treacheries, the rapes, the massacres? As so often with grand statements about the Bible and its style, the claim to be inspired is nowhere backed up with chapter and verse or precise critical argument.

The potential power of the concept, which would later be invoked not just for the biblical originals but for their translators and translations from the Septuagint on,[11] is weakened when no one is able to say exactly what it connotes or what its precise results are. That leaves it an unexplained mystery, as arbitrary as its natural consequence, the further claim to infallibility.[12] This latter is applied without any recognition of the limitations inherent in a given genre. For example, all historiography is by its nature open to debate and controversy,[13] so the Bible's "historical" books, those massed records of the Israelite past, are either not infallible or not history.

True, there are moments of inspiration in the sense of high creative and psychological intensity—the visions of Job, Ezekiel, Daniel, Zechariah, to say nothing of Revelation—and the dramatic Pentecostal gift of tongues to the apostles in Acts 2. The prophets can be imagined working themselves into a heightened state in their onslaughts on the wayward Israelites. But none of this throws light directly on the way composition occurs.

Inspiration thus caused more problems than it solved. Theologians tried variously to cope. The simplest way was to assume that God dictated a message and his human secretaries took it down. That would make the Bible text, in Heine's mock-reverent phrase, "God's memoirs."[14] It assumed a face-to-face confrontation and spoken exchange such as are indeed common enough in the Israelites' reported early experience of their Lord. The prophets all claimed to have had that experience. Jeremiah 36 comes as near to the dictating and writing process as can well be imagined, down to the detail of Yahweh prescribing scrolls for his message, which Jeremiah then dictates on to a scribe, after which Yahweh has to prescribe more scrolls repeating the same content because king Jehoiakim has burnt the first set. Most significantly of all, the ten commandments are delivered direct to Moses, who has throughout been meeting on easy terms with the Lord. Other prophets are instructed to convey a specific message, usually the ever-topical one of the Chosen People's backsliding and imminent punishment. As a last word, the Bible's final book, Revelation, was "sent and signified by [God's] angel unto his servant John" (Rev. 1:1).

Nevertheless, the dictation theory seems no longer to have much support. The notion is harder to maintain in books that have no prophecy scenario, where sorting out agent from origin is more difficult. There have been attempts of varying complexity to reconcile the divine and the human. For Luther there had been no dictation by the Holy Spirit, but an illumination that made the knowledge of God personal to the individual, after which the actual writing was a human, not a supernatural act. Perhaps the authors were somehow moved to produce the words God wanted. Or their individuality and even their literary style were fully their own, but had themselves been prepared all along by God for his own purposes. Such solutions merely shift the problem one stage back. As the next best thing to the voice of the Lord, Rembrandt paints an angel at Matthew's shoulder, no doubt prompting the composition of his gospel. At least one recognized writer could imagine the writing process very concretely, though without leaving any role for human agency. John Donne envisages the Holy Ghost in person "penning the Scriptures of the New Testament" and "delighting himself not only with a propriety but with a delicacy and harmony and melody of language, with height of metaphors and other figures which may work greater impressions upon the readers, and not with barbarous or trivial or market and homely language."[15] Donne's fulsome eulogy takes no account of the rough Greek of the New Testament, and he forgets that Jesus' parables work upon readers precisely through their homely language.[16]

But this is to anticipate, for Donne's is already a literary judgment, albeit still determined by the Bible's authority. Donne was judging from the originals and didn't favor the new translations. These, though, were now giving the Bible its culturally and historically decisive new genesis.

Words on the Page

The Bible had taken a long time to reach its ultimate readership. Humbler Christians, those who could read at all, lacked the languages—the Hebrew and some Aramaic of the Old Testament originals, or the Latin into which Jerome translated them (the Vulgate), or the version made for Greek-speaking Jews of second-century Egypt (the Septuagint), or the Greek of the New Testament, also done into Latin by Jerome.[17] All the time these versions remained a sealed book to ordinary people, the Church was free to keep Christianity a mystery religion and to determine all questions of belief in accordance with its own tradition of interpretation—direct access to the Bible text might cause an upset through outsiders, as it eventually did through a rebellious insider. Luther's main challenge to the Church was his insistence on the primacy of a Bible now made readable to all: "sola scriptura." That was surely a simple matter against the centuries of intricate doctrine.[18] It did however leave the problem that scripture alone could no more guarantee a single *understanding* than any other written text, as Luther's earliest critics pointed out. Divergent readings led from the start to further schisms within the Protestant movement.[19]

Yet translation was crucial, because support for Luther's movement beyond the narrow world of theologians and the clergy depended on a broad popular following. This potential force was the reason translation had always been subversive. In England, from the fourteenth-century Lollards and Wycliffe's version on, translators were pursued as heretics. In the 1520s, even possessing the Bible in English was punishable by death. Reading it had to be a secret, heretical practice. Even family members denounced and persecuted each other. Young William Maldon tries to hide his copy in his bed-straw and escapes hanging at his father's hands only through his mother's intervention.[20] Sir (later Saint) Thomas More has heretics tortured and burned. Almost as shocking was the public burning of William Tyndale's New Testament—the word of the Lord, burnt! Tyndale himself followed it, going to the stake at Vilvoorde near Antwerp in 1536.

Luther was always in danger of the same fate. His translations into German were sensational and decisive: first of the New Testament (done in eleven weeks, published in 1522) then of the whole Bible (twelve years work, published in 1534 and thereafter tirelessly revised till 1545, a year before his death).[21] His was not the first German translation, but like Tyndale in England, who met him and drew on him as a model, he worked from the original Hebrew and Greek, so could claim greater authenticity than the eighteen earlier German versions that had been based on the Church's Latin Vulgate.

Luther struck a direct, down-to-earth tone close to the everyday language of the people, asking what a German would have said in a given situation. That incidentally made his Bible, despite his specifically Saxon-Thuringian background, a factor in creating a common German language and ultimately the language of its literature—it was an avowed shaping influence on writers down to modern times. Luther recognized that the lowly register was potentially a problem—could God and the texts of the faith be properly represented in such lowly terms, what rhetoricians looked down on as *sermo humilis*? Yet Christianity, despite Augustine's stylistic class-consciousness, had come to see the paradoxical value of presenting transcendent matter in earthly, even earthy language. Luther followed his instincts and was richly vindicated. The sales of his Bible were phenomenal. Curiosity and the desire to read it were like a dam bursting. His fame as an adversary of Rome and author of an unbroken flow of polemical pamphlets in the often crude vernacular played its part. There was no need to put his name on the Bible's title-page, "Wittenberg" was enough. They knew where he lived. Though some Protestants preferred Zwingli's Zurich version, by the time Luther's local printer Hans Luft retired in 1572, he had produced some 100,000 copies, unique for the period. To these must be added an unknown number brought out by the pirate printers whom Luther and his patron Hanfried (Duke Johann Friedrich of Sachsen-Weimar) vainly tried to warn off in their prefaces.[22]

The English Authorized Version, or King James Bible, of 1611 was less radical and less controversial, the work not of one man but of forty-seven, with no writerly ambitions of their own. On the contrary, they avowedly compared and revised previous translations so as to make, as their preface said, "out of many good ones, one principal good one."[23] Rather than focusing on matters of style, they were concerned with finding exact equivalents for the wording of the original, as if the Hebrew and Greek words had each their own sacred content, which a too idiomatic translation risked spilling like some precious liquid. Indeed, there were sometimes doubts whether a translation could ever still *be* the sacred text at all. That led King James's men to stick as closely as possible to the Hebrew, but mixing it with other styles—sometimes Latinate (pejoratively dubbed "the ink-horn mode"), sometimes colloquial, sometimes frankly obscure.[24]

Still, at least the practice of translation was now accepted as a practical liturgical (and political) need. It was as if the old cries of heresy, the persecutions and the burnings of translators, had never been. They were so far overcompensated that the AV's place in the national culture came to be exalted out of all proportion to its modest beginnings, to the point where its historian can speak of AVolatry.[25] It became a commonplace to praise its language to the skies, while never substantiating the claim with chapter and verse, let alone serious analysis—at the wild extreme it has been called "the best translation *ever made in any language*."[26] The AV translators' modesty has been overlooked at the personal expense of Tyndale, whose stylistic genius created many of the most memorable and best-loved phrases of the New Testament[27] and half the Old. So when in the nineteenth century the notion of inspiration was extended from the Hebrew and Greek originals to the English text of the Authorized

Version, the original inspiration must have been Tyndale's, for which his only reward was martyrdom.[28]

Despite the AV's growing acceptance, a man of learning like John Donne reserved his regard for the Hebrew and Greek originals, claiming to appreciate qualities in them that "could not appear in translations"—a shaky argument, since the features he praises (elevated metaphors and other figures) are objectively there in the text, whatever the language. He raises the stakes further by setting these features against the best that classical antiquity has to show: "If we would take all those figures and tropes which are collected out of secular poets and orators, we may give higher and livelier examples of every one of those figures out of the scriptures than out of all the Greek and Latin poets and orators."[29] Only he doesn't do that. Elsewhere he does name names—"St Paul is a more powerful orator than Cicero," "David is a better poet than Virgil," "the harmony of poetry and the sweetness of composition never met in any man so fully as in the prophet Isaiah"[30]—yet still with no quotation as evidence. The first to make real and unbiased comparisons, of the book of Job with Sophocles's *Oedipus Tyrannus* and *Oedipus Coloneus*, was Robert Lowth in the next century, concluding that the products of the two cultures were fundamentally different, neither of them superior.[31] Lowth was unique in analyzing the Hebrew texts at all.

Overall the uneasy coexistence of Christianity and the Classics had been a fact of European culture since the Renaissance, not least within individual minds that had been shaped by both streams, as we shall see in Montaigne. Faith then normally had to have absolute priority, pagan literature had to be denied before ever a cock crowed. Donne's put-downs of the Classics are common currency. The doubly learned Milton is an even more striking case, harsher still on the Classics. He scorns their "swelling epithets thick laid / As varnish on a harlot's cheek," not worthy to be compared with "Sion's songs," which were written by men "from God inspired."[32] This is part of Christ's answer when Satan tries, with notable eloquence, to interest him in Greek culture—an unlikely non-biblical invention with which Milton goes out of his way to do down classical antiquity. Meanwhile his own poetic practice is heavily marked by the Classics as he expands a few pages of Genesis into an epic of wholly un-biblical dimensions and stylistic sophistication.

Dismissals of classical antiquity may not always have come from a conscious position of strength. In a reversal of normal usage, a writer of the next generation applies the term "bigoted" to the cultivated elite who favored Homer and Virgil and rejected all non-classical authors as heretical![33] The phrasing implicitly recognizes the Classics as a rival orthodoxy.

Rejecting the Classics was only a special case of a long-standing rejection of all secular literature as evil and corrupting. When Abraham Cowley extols biblical texts as "either already most admirable and exalted pieces of poetry, or the best materials in the world for it," and declares the wars of Joshua superior to the *Iliad* and the *Aeneid*,[34] he also attacks contemporary writing for its flattery of the great, its erotic obsession, and its senseless fables. It has been stolen by the Devil for his own purposes.[35]

Rather than adjudicate on the rival claims of two ancient cultures, the prior question is why Christian apologists felt they had to assert the Bible's literary superiority as well as its promise of salvation. The answer is simply that, if the Bible was inspired and its truth was infallible, it must surely be superior in every respect to all other writing. As an awkward converse, if it were found to be in any way less than perfect, that might discredit the divine inspirer. So it would have been safer not to mount those grand claims in the first place, as was argued half-defensively by John Wilmot, Earl of Rochester, notorious as a rake and free-thinker, yet still a man with a writer's eye. He "did not understand that business of inspiration." He stuck, aesthetically, at the incoherences of style in the Scriptures, the odd transitions, the seeming contradictions and, ethically, at "the cruelties enjoined on the Israelites in destroying the Canaanites, circumcision and many other rites of the Jewish worship, [which] seemed to him unsuitable to the Divine nature."[36]

But pious commentators were never going to give up their eulogistic prejudgment and attachment to authority. Grand posturing by grandees continued through the nineteenth century.[37] This would surely have to yield place to serious analysis, once the Bible was to be truly read as literature. But how far could that go?

Born-Again Literature

Restoring sacred texts to the condition of literature is as radical as was their first shift to transcendent status. If carried through consistently, it must set itself no limits, and no judgment can be taboo. There was resistance to that. When an early contributor wrote that no literary criticism of the Bible could hope for success which was not reverent in tone,[38] he still had one foot in the world of religious belief, with its obligation to accept and affirm. But literature does not deal in unquestioned reverence. It has its own canon (this book is working in its higher reaches) but there are no foregone conclusions. The literary canon is in principle only ever provisional, and is routinely challenged. It would be foolish not to try reading Homer or Shakespeare on the rumor of their greatness. But even Shakespeare's reputation is vulnerable—Tolstoy rated him below Harriet Beecher Stowe and *Uncle Tom's Cabin*.

So if the Bible is to be truly read as literature, divested of its transcendent claims, it must be as open to discussion as any other literary work. Judgment has to move from the certainty that to the question whether. There are winners and losers. Over against the idyll of Eden, the archetypal drama of the Fall, the first fratricide, the tale of Noah's ark, the tribulations of Israel in Egypt, the achievements of Moses, the moving story of Ruth, the twists and turns of Joseph's career, the vicious conflicts of David's, the limpid beauty of the twenty-third psalm, the stable-warmth of the Christmas story, the eloquence of Jesus' parables, his miracle cures, the horrors of his trial and crucifixion, and the mystery of the resurrection, must be set a great deal of "intractably nonliterary, even anti-literary, material," mainly in the Old Testament: in Leviticus, the prescriptions for ritual burnt offerings, aptly labeled an "unappetising vein of gristle";[39] in Numbers, the regulations for military call-up; in Kings 1, the political struggles between names otherwise unknown to history; and, ever present to the point of tedium, the Israelites' relation to the "god of their convenience,"[40] their faith constantly erratic despite the tangible evidence that he exists, that he keeps his promises and will carry out his threats.

If we actually compare literary effects and check, say, biblical against Homeric, as Cowley failed to do, then rather than lesser and greater there is simply, as Lowth said, profound difference. Joshua's battles lack the graphic grimness of the *Iliad*, but they record Yahweh's strategic commitment to his Chosen People as something stronger than the shifting allegiances and piecemeal interventions of the Greek gods. No wooden horse is needed when simple trumpets can bring Jericho's walls down. The Old Testament's genealogies—all those begettings—are not narratives but mere records of continuity, not concerned with the poignancy of individual mortality as the *Iliad* is when Homer evokes a warrior's family origins at the moment of his death. Nor do they have the political point of Shakespeare's genealogies, which spell out the dynastic claims of rivals for the English throne. The book of Numbers rehearses again and again the military call-up formulas—"by their generations, after their families, by the house of their fathers," "Of the children of . . .," "Those that were numbered of them . . ."—as if filling in so many War Office forms. The effect is very different from the *Iliad*'s review of the Greek contingents, which is picturesque and digressive, with epic similes thrown in for pleasure. As for prophets, the Old Testament figures are in a different class from Teiresias or Laocoon, more consistent in opposing royal power with their own, and commonly proved right by events (those who got their predictions wrong were reviled—this seems a little hard—as "lying prophets"!).[41] They were often critical, even radical, regularly invoking the interests of widows and orphans, an appeal to social justice that had tradition in the Torah. Their prophecies became part of a theological system, subjected to reworkings once they already "had the catastrophe behind them." The prophet had transmitted Yahweh's word, which embodied the course of history, so the prophet was already a historian. (The historian, after all, in Friedrich Schlegel's aphorism, is merely "a backwards-looking prophet.")

The classic analysis of what differentiates biblical from secular writing remains the opening chapter of Erich Auerbach's *Mimesis*, where the scene of Odysseus' old nurse Eurycleia recognizing him by an old wound is contrasted with the Bible's narrative mode in Abraham's near-sacrifice of Isaac.[42] This concentrates so intensely on the thread of grim purpose that it isn't concerned to describe the characters' appearance, or the country they pass through on the way, or even—amazingly—Abraham's feelings or Isaac's puzzlement as they approach the killing place. It is all very far from Homer's relaxed digressions on the look and feel of everyday things, the rich context of action, the remembered antecedents of events, in this case the hunt in which a boar's tusk gashed the young Odysseus' thigh. But Homer's hundred-line flashback to that incident doesn't create suspense about what will happen next. Rather, we temporarily forget the stage the main story has reached. The hunt is treated as something to be retold in its own right, part of a rich social world firmly rooted in the past but easily evoked in the present.

In contrast, the Abraham-Isaac story creates inescapable suspense, though not through uncertainty. It is the suspense of horrified expectation of the coming sacrifice, right up to the deity's last-minute change of mind. And to all this the religious text demands assent. It is, in Auerbach's word, "tyrannical"; it claims to be not just *a* true picture, but *the only* truth. "Scripture stories do not, like Homer, court our favour ... they seek to subject us, and if we resist, we are rebels."[43]

This much on narrative perspective. As to stylistic texture, for lack of filled-in detail the effect of the biblical narrative is minimalist, almost skeletal. That remains typical,[44] on the larger scale, too, of whole life-stories. Goethe called Joseph's career "a most charming natural narrative, except that it seems too short, und one feels tempted to fill out the detail."[45] Goethe never did, leaving it to Thomas Mann to write the two thousand pages of *Joseph and His Brethren*.

Is the Bible's minimalism a conscious method, or just a feature of undeveloped, primitive writing? Is it technique or unplanned effect? Writers on the Bible as literature are usually, by the nature of their project, sympathetic readers. That can go a little far in giving the benefit of the doubt, preferring to see subtlety and sophistication rather than primitive simplicity. The old inconsistencies are explained away, the duplicate creation stories as "a deliberate juxtaposition intended to convey the breadth and complexity of what it means to be human,"[46] the two creations specifically of Man and Woman as dual aspects like a Picasso portrait. Absence is read as implied presence, "a brilliantly laconic style" as having an "uncanny ability to intimate psychological and thematic complexity."[47] Praise inclines to superlatives. The phenomena of light and darkness, necessary enough things after all, are termed "virtuoso effects of the master of polarities," and "everything converges and fits perfectly at the highest level."[48] When Ezekiel is called "a philosopher of history of the first magnitude," what standard of comparison is being applied—Thucydides, Tacitus, Sima Qian, Voltaire, Herder, Gibbon, Burckhardt?

Specialist analysis can certainly convey the real strengths of the Bible's narrative and lyrical traditions, the former more easily because structural—the use of parallelism, for example[49]—the latter less easily because it involves sound patterns and verbal echoes that are rooted deep in the Hebrew language. We can only, but do then willingly, take on trust the effects that specialists describe, for example that the book of Job is a highpoint of Hebrew poetry.[50] But prose narrative has syntactical features that remain constant enough between original and translation to allow a non-specialist judgment, above all of the Bible's persistent parataxis, with the ubiquitous "And" that begins so many sentences. "And" is the most primitive way to connect sense-units, coordinating them without determining any relation other than temporal sequence or spatial location. Scarcely ever is there a conjunction indicating any form of cause or angle of vision (since, although, so that, and so on). Sometimes plain "and" may seem to be suggesting a fated sequence, but that cannot apply to every case. The AV's "and" renders the Hebrew "waw," but this can apparently imply a wide range of relations between clauses.[51] Not so the English word. It seems over-subtle, again, to see the AV's unvaried usage as a conscious strategy designed to "leave narrative structures open to the widest possible range of meanings," and thus avoid interpretative partiality and potential sectarian strife.[52] If that really is so, it comes at the price of monotony. It is a relief to read translations that vary it—German syntax at least offered Luther alternatives, for example, "Da kam er . . ." instead of "Und er kam . . ."—or just omit the conjunction, as a recent German version regularly does.

The familiar Bible stories are in any case memorable more for substance than for style, as archetypes rather than as performances. But beyond stylistics, when biblical texts are seriously read as literature and the submissiveness fundamental to all religious belief is removed, central episodes are open to ethical questioning. Why does Yahweh accept Abel's offering, but for no stated reason reject Cain's, with the consequence that the understandably "wrothful" Cain murders his brother? Why does Yahweh draw Satan's attention to Job, virtually boasting of Job's virtue and inviting the adversary to do his worst?[53] The book of Job is sometimes called "the Old Testament's King Lear."[54] But Lear brings his fate on himself, where Job's sufferings are a harsh test gratuitously initiated by the deity. As for the near-sacrifice of Isaac with which Yahweh "tempts" [*sic!*] Abraham, it is grotesque to suppose it leads to "a much deepened togetherness, both between father and son and between the Lord and his obedient follower."[55] We need only imagine Abraham's torment over the three days travelling to the appointed place, and Isaac's terror as he lies bound on the altar under his father's knife, to feel that the more likely result for them both would be acute post-traumatic stress taking years, if ever, to overcome. That is awful enough if a savage deity first intended the sacrifice but then just as arbitrarily thought better of it. It is the more profoundly and subtly cruel if it was the intention all along to stay Abraham's hand at the last minute. The standard explanation, that it was a test of Abraham's obedience, demands that we accept what all humane feeling resists, that the demand to sacrifice a child was a proper probing of a father's faith by his god.

Read as literature and with an anthropologist's eye, this and other stories embody the way early cultures represented human tragedies as the acts of an inscrutable deity beyond or before any concept of divine justice.[56] Even then, the Abraham-Isaac scenario scarcely fits any normal human situation. No other myth of sacrifice or near-sacrifice by a father rests on a deliberate test by the deity. Jephthah and Idomeneus are bound by their own foolish vows; Agamemnon ruthlessly bargains for a fair wind to take his armies to Troy, without the consoling knowledge that his daughter will at the last minute be saved by Artemis. The Isaac story becomes usable only as a grim allegory, in Wilfred Owen's charge against an irresponsible older generation, that in 1914–18 it "slew half the seed of Europe, one by one."[57] If the primitive original can still today be read with positive acceptance by a literary critic, then the critic is suffering the phantom limb of religious subservience.

Such pulling of punches, on substance as on style, naturally raises the question of motivation. Why did critics shift the Bible to the ground of literature in the first place? After all, such authorities as Jerome and Augustine back in the fifth century had found it "deficient from a literary point of view."[58] Yet it was there, a massive presence in Western literature, a preeminent source of stories and motifs throughout literary history, albeit essentially for religious, not literary reasons; for without the inner pressure of Christian belief and the social pressure of orthodoxy, the history and religions of the Jewish people and the stories woven into Christianity had no more necessary claim to close literary attention than the products of any other ancient culture. True, when it came to it, the Bible had as many good stories as classical antiquity, but what was decisive was the way these dominated the imaginative world of Christians from an impressionable age and were, in the fullest sense, taken as read by the surrounding culture.

Perhaps deep down in the Bible-as-literature movement is a nostalgia for belief, or at least an apology for a society no longer believing the Bible's religious content. Some form of recognition is felt necessary. A Christian literary scholar may simply not accept this suspension of belief. "Those who talk of reading the Bible 'as literature' may sometimes mean reading it without attending to the main thing it is about, like reading Burke with no interest in politics."[59] That is tantamount to claiming it can only be read with its own "special hermeneutic"[60]—which is not a literary reading at all. T. S. Eliot put it more acerbically still: "Those who talk of the Bible as a 'monument of English prose' are merely admiring it as a monument over the grave of Christianity."[61] But this is altogether to deny the independent interest of the Bible's literary qualities, which the Bible-as-literature movement presupposes.

Little, incidentally, has been said here about the New Testament as literature, for the obvious reason that it was never literature to begin with. Unlike the old Testament, it had no original status to depart from and return to. Like any prose text, it can of course be analyzed for structure, style, and rhetoric, or admired for the beauty of some of its phrasing. Jesus' parables are miniature allegories, but they have the limited purpose of teaching. The Gospels are a campaign to convince readers of a divine incarnation. Acts records the vicissitudes of a growing movement and is the first example of Christian apologetics. The Epistles were written to exhort, encourage, or criticize early Christian communities, not to explore inner complexities in the way the epistolary novel does. These were all serious purposes that borrowed quasi-literary means; they were never created for enjoyment. If insight and phrasing sometimes rise to eloquence, even to poetry, still the intention was always practical.[62] Strictly speaking, the New Testament can only be read *as if* literature.

There is a need for more clarity about the Bible as literature. From the conservative side, making it an object of study in itself is only legitimate on condition of an "enduring social and intellectual respect for, with the implication of at least some significant public adherence to, Christianity and/or Judaism."[63] That is a demand for orthodox conformity, and a misunderstanding of what literary study claims to be. Less conservative is the acknowledgement that the Bible is always "a looming, uneasy, sometimes authoritative presence."[64] It is visibly difficult for critics to escape its aura altogether, even for Alter and Kermode, whose volume is still the most substantial scholarly treatment, aiming to bring "a new rigour and seriousness to the Bible-as-literature movement."[65] Yet the editors too were avowedly "not careless of the religious character of the material." Does that mean they were wanting to not-have their cake and still eat it? And when they call the Bible "a work of great literary force *and authority*," it's hard not to see that as an acceptance of the Bible's special compelling status. Indeed, they say its claims on us are so strong that "we somehow must understand [it] if we are to understand ourselves."[66] That belongs, if anywhere, to our individual position in life. It does not belong to literary criticism.

The Unauthorized Version

The concept of authority has only limited use in literature, and where invoked has to rest on hard realities. To take instances at random, Conrad writes with authority on ships and the lands of the Far East where his professional life had been lived, Tolstoy with authority on Russia's Caucasian tribes because he had lived among and skirmished with them, Saint Exupéry with authority on the experiences and emotions of a pioneer aviator, and Jane Austen on Georgian manners and the limits imposed on women's lives by the marriage market. Authors in post-dogmatic times are each an authority on their own experience, of the world they know and of their distinctive inner life within it. "Author" has its full sense, as an initiator of fresh meaning. As such, they are answerable to nobody and nobody to them.[67] What they write is an offer, never a demand, certainly not (in Auerbach's word) a "tyrannical" one like that of the Bible. Literature's great offer embraces infinite possibilities and fulfillments, uncertainties and intense partial truths. It is the Unauthorized Version.

Part II
Early Modern

3: An Alphabet of Experience: Montaigne

Withdrawal

IN 1571 THE BORDEAUX JURIST, Michel Eyquem, Sieur de Montaigne, retired for good (or so he thought) from public life to spend his remaining days—he was thirty-eight, it could be considered oldish then—in the "liberty and tranquility" of his family estate and "the bosom of the Muses." He established a retreat in one of his château's two towers, with a library of some thousand books, the perfect environment and resource for a life of reflection. On the beams he had painted the resolve to leave his mind "in complete idleness to amuse itself." But as weeds spring up in a fallow field, idleness produced all manner of "chimeras and fantastic monsters." The horse (he switches metaphors—riding was a valued part of his life) had bolted. These things needed getting a grip on and "shaming into order." So he started writing. (1, viii; 70)[1]

Just what the monsters were is unclear. Nothing monstrous appears in Montaigne's earliest "essays." In their original form, they are not much more than entries in a commonplace book, short conventional pieces about popular sayings—"that we arrive at the same end by different means"; or about narrowly practical problems—"should a besieged commander venture out to parley?" a typical real-life (and -death) dilemma in a France torn by religious wars. These pieces were not going to set the Garonne on fire.

A personal note may slip in, as when Montaigne admits to having a terrible memory—this as a prelude to a piece "On Liars" (liars need to remember what they've said to whom [1, ix; 71]). But by the time he comes to publish the first edition of his *Essais* in 1580, the personal element has become their declared whole and sole point. Not however with any wide literary ambition. A prefatory note To the Reader states that he is leaving an account of his "conditions and humors" for family and friends to remember him by when he is no more. For this "domestic and private" purpose he is "himself the substance of his book," so it's not worth anyone else's while to spend their leisure on "a subject so frivolous and so vain." Don't bother!

Disclaimers and self-depreciation will remain a leitmotif of the whole work, a façade of modesty fronting an increasingly bold and confident practice. He has after all by this time chosen to make the domestic and private account public, and weightily so, in two volumes, of fifty-seven and thirty-seven chapters respectively. True, these do not claim to be polished pieces in the modern understanding of "essay" (the term is to that extent a mistranslation).[2] Montaigne was still only initiating, all unknowingly, a genre; for him the word meant no more than a try-out, a tentative shot at treating a subject, an "effort" in the sense of the modest colloquial phrase "Here's my latest effort." Still, there were now ninety-four pieces, some substantial, in the extreme case a book-length piece of over a hundred and fifty pages, which, set among other, shorter pieces, gives the whole collection a bizarre profile.

Even this substantial item, though, stays within the framework of convention, being a philosophical-theological disquisition on the competing roles of faith and reason, a far from new topic, which ends by undermining all claims to knowledge on either side with a systematic skepticism.[3]

The Catholic faith, which Montaigne subscribed to passively rather than passionately, was one half of the culture in which he grew up, although the members of his wider family were fairly evenly divided between Catholic and Protestant.[4] His own Catholic conservatism was purely practical. He deplores Protestant innovation primarily because of the atrocities religious schism has led to, though he admits that the stimulus of novelty might have attracted him in younger years. (1, lvi; 380) There was even a phase when the Bordeaux Parlement itself was sentencing and killing Protestants—conceivably a reason, alongside frustrated political ambitions, for Montaigne's decision to retire at just this moment.

The other half of Montaigne's culture was Antiquity, with its schools of philosophy, heroic histories and canonical poetry. He quotes extensively from ancient doctrine, historical anecdote, and classical verses, and in early essays arms himself with orthodox Stoicism against the threat of death, which it is needful to have constantly in mind.

Openings

That dual culture was his and not his, in each case knowledge and attitude congealed in dogma and tradition: inheritance, not experience. Three landmark episodes in Montaigne's life begin to open up this latter, deeper, individual source: a retrospect on his early education; memories of an ideal friendship; and reflection on the violence of a near-death episode.

Invited to advise a noble lady on how to educate the son she is gallantly (and as it turns out rightly) presumed to be carrying, Montaigne in all modesty—the bluff this time is a disclaimer of any special competence, since no gentleman wants to be seen as an expert on anything—offers "the one fantasy I have that goes against common usage" (1, xxvi; 197). Against, that is, the pedantic practice of packing young heads with parrot-knowledge while leaving their judgment unformed and their practical abilities undeveloped. Montaigne is inspired by memories of the enlightened approach that "the best father ever" brought back from his soldiering days in humanist Italy for his son's early education. Having first been put out to be nursed in the village and held at the font by lowly people, already a pointer to the social sympathies befitting a lord of the manor (3, xiii; 311), he was then privately taught to speak fluent Latin by a German tutor who spoke no more French than the child yet did. Family and servants had to "Latinize" too, with a basic smattering, to support the learning environment. At six the boy was sent to a conventional school, the Collège de Guyenne in Bordeaux, founded in the year he was born but already a prestigious institution among ambitious families.[5] It somewhat corrupted his Latin, but he was allowed to read what he liked, and he built up a rich stock, of poetry especially, which the essays were later to draw on. He left at thirteen, and may have gone on to university in Toulouse or Paris—we don't know.

In his advice to the Comtesse Diane de Foix, Montaigne argues for an education in things, not words; truth, not rhetoric; doubt and self-criticism, not fixity; inquisitive openness to the world; and practical skills. Learning must be deeply digested, not superficially stuck on. Lessons are for life—surely Aristotle didn't teach the young Alexander abstractions? And the pupil must be encouraged not chastised, and sometimes listened to by the teacher, so that learning is loved, not feared and hated—all now, for us, the long since unquestioned principles of liberal education. Less universally practiced is his father's notion of always waking the tender young mind with music (1, xxvi; 198).

Experience of a different order was Montaigne's lost friendship, made more poignant by its brevity. Etienne de la Boétie, his lawyer colleague at the Parlement (law courts) of Bordeaux, died a Stoic-Christian death, with Montaigne at his bedside, aged only thirty-two.[6] They had known each other for just four years. But in that time they had become "one soul in two bodies" in an "entire and perfect friendship" such as may happen "once in three hundred years," and surpassing (this for Montaigne was saying a lot) the classic friendships of antiquity. (1, xxviii; 232) How could such a rich and intense relationship have come about? Montaigne tries to explain it in abstract terms as "beyond my rational understanding, by a force inexplicable and fated that brought about this union." This is the 1580 text. A sentence added in the posthumous edition of 1595[7] restates the mystery in irreducibly concrete terms: "Because it was him, because it was me" (236). The earlier formulation is left standing in the text, but it has been rendered superfluous by that moving epigram. Life without such a friend is a dreary fag-end; his loss becomes a cult. Montaigne's library, where half the books were La Boétie's dying gift, becomes a monument to their friendship.[8]

Then at some point just before retirement, experience had burst in violently. On a routine ride near home, one of Montaigne's people, a powerful man on a powerful mount, for no clear reason rides full tilt into the little man on the little horse—Montaigne!—and throws him to the ground. They carry him home for dead, but he gives signs of life, vomits quantities of blood, and begins to be aware. He observes his own movements, sensations and emotions, all strangely pleasant and peaceful, and for a time painless (2, vi; 47), though he believes he is dying. It would indeed have been an agreeable death, and he draws a moral without which the tale would have been "slight and vain" (modesty again—it is nothing of the sort, the narrative is graphic and gripping). Crucially, it all felt so different from the death Stoicism required you to constantly reflect on and inwardly prepare for, a doctrine formally rehearsed in the essay "That Philosophizing Is Learning to Die." Practice—the new essay is called "On Practice"—has turned out to be agreeably unlike theory. "To make yourself easy with death you only have to come close to it." That, at all events, is his new personal position; it doesn't claim to be a lesson for others.

The original text ends with this restriction, once more to his private realm. But the 1595 edition adds three further pages which begin by flatly reversing that last view: "Still, please don't mind if I nevertheless communicate it. What works for me may conceivably work for somebody else." Montaigne then mounts a lively defense of his practice of self-study and self-revelation. It is admittedly "a thorny enterprise" to trace the "opaque depths of the mind's inner twists and turns." Few of the ancients ever did, so it is "a new and extraordinary amusement." He has been engaged in it for some years now, neglecting all other matters unless they bear on himself. No other science is so useful. Such self-concern may, he admits, be thought a vice, mere boastfulness; but that is to judge it by its excesses. Is drinking wine wrong because some people get drunk? He draws support from the example of saints and philosophers, though himself expressly neither, from Socrates in particular, (always an absolute touchstone) and elsewhere from the Huguenot practice of confessing in public, as against the enclosed confessional of Catholics. (3, v; 62) Self-study is only self-indulgent if you stay on the surface and don't probe deeper; while to avoid complacency and stay humble you need only compare yourself with the great spirits and heroes of the past (2, vi; 48).

Elsewhere again, he says that if there are things you don't want to confess to, you shouldn't have done them! For his own part, he reckons to display himself honestly and in full: "it is my essence" (2, vi; 50). From being a personal quirk, self-revelation is becoming a moral duty and a criticism of others' hypocrisy. The apologia for self-study leads on to asserting the value of the thing studied, his particular existence: "My business and my art is living." He has come some way from the anxious Stoic looking over his shoulder at death, and is beginning to celebrate life. In the three added pages this is an older Montaigne, looking back at his near-death experience from some fifteen years later. He was no doubt impressed and convinced by the remarkable insights he found in his earlier account.

He is also even further away now from the pretended privacy of his preface "To the Reader." But that statement is left still standing at the threshold of the *Essays*. Along with Montaigne's repeated derogatory terms for his practice, which often plumb the depths of self-abasement— "grotesque and monstrous bodies" (1, xxvii; 231), "gallimaufry" (1, xlvi; 331), "foolish undertaking" (2, viii; 56), plus the reflection that his works may at some future date serve to wrap a slab of butter at market (2, xviii; 326)—it leaves a discrepancy unresolved. But then it was Montaigne's ethic as a writer, and it is a further aspect of his honesty, not to change anything he had once made public. Since this is an emphatic answer to a central question of literary genesis (and also as a way to give the flavor of an extended passage of Montaigne's prose) his principles are worth stating in full—incidentally, as his account evolved through the second and third editions of 1588 and 1595, marked by the prefixed letters.[9]

> (b) I add, but I do not correct. First, because someone who has mortgaged his work to the world, it seems to me, doesn't have the right. Let him put it better elsewhere if he can, and not corrupt the job that he's already sold. From such people we shouldn't buy anything till after they're dead. Let them think carefully before they publish. What's the hurry?
> (c) My book is always one and the same. Except to the extent that I try to renew it so the purchaser [i.e. who has the earlier edition] doesn't go away empty-handed. I make it my law to attach to it (as it's no more than a piece of rough and ready marquetry) some supernumerary gesture. They're only make-weights which don't discredit the original form, but give some special value to each of the following ones by some small attempted subtlety. [...]
> (b) Secondly because for myself I fear to lose by any change; my understanding doesn't always progress, sometimes it goes backwards. I hardly mistrust the second or third form of my fantasies any less than I do the first, the present any less than the past. We sometimes correct ourselves as foolishly as we correct other people.
> (c) My first publications were in 1580. Over the long span since then I've aged, but I certainly haven't become an inch the wiser. Myself now and myself then are indeed two people; but when better? I really can't say. Growing old would be fine if we only marched in the direction of improvement. But it's more like the shapeless movement of a staggering, dizzy drunkard, jack-straws blown by the wind as it will. (3, ix; 177)

That Montaigne never corrects is not strictly true. He was a perfectionist in matters of fine detail. There are innumerable corrections—as many as ten on a single page of printed text—but only of spellings and misprints, along with minor clarifications, rephrasings, and adjustments to syntax. Corrections of this trivial kind are minutely registered in the latest critical edition, the ten on that randomly chosen page.[10] An earlier essay had made the same point about adding, not correcting, which was itself later modified to make the further fine distinction: "well, perhaps some word or other, but to vary, not to remove" (2, xxxvii; 421). Montaigne also elsewhere concedes that he does make changes in response to comments by friends, "for reasons of civility," to encourage them to speak freely about his work (3, viii;139). He did not, however, change his Gasconisms—he was after all a Gascon at heart. Only when in Paris did he feel French (3, ix: 185).

Clearly, "not correcting" means he doesn't make substantive changes, doesn't take out parts of an earlier text in order to substitute something different. (The shifts of emphasis that do arise from the dialogue between the two selves, which he is quite aware of, remain to be discussed.) So the *Essays* grow by enrichment, not alteration. Their genesis is to that extent a simple story, with no extruded paralipomena, no radically divergent versions, apart from his oscillations over the value of the whole enterprise; and even there it is increasingly clear that his self-depreciation is more mannerism than earnest. A different kind of complexity arises through the sheer volume of afterthoughts, newly remembered quotations and anecdotes, and individual touches that Montaigne felt moved to add to his ever-fuller self-portrait. The added quotations rarely if ever determine the line of an argument; they merely illustrate or confirm it.

Layers

This constant enrichment is embodied in the successive editions of the *Essays* published in Montaigne's lifetime and just after his death. Books 1 and 2 of 1580 were followed by the 1588 edition, which added a book 3. Also added in this edition were some six hundred insertions, large and small, scattered over the text of the two earlier books. (Some minor ones had already been made when the two-book edition was reissued in 1582.) And after the major enlargement of the corpus with book 3, Montaigne still couldn't leave well alone. He went on making manuscript additions to be inserted in a further edition that had not yet been put in hand when he died in 1592. These, as substantial as the 1588 set and still more numerous (about a thousand), were gathered by an ambitious young writer, Marie de Gournay, whose devotion to him and his work were a surprise late experience for the aging Montaigne, such that she acquired the status of an adopted daughter, a *fille d'alliance*. It was she who, breaking consciously, indeed assertively, into the male world of publishing, put together from complex and chaotic materials a new text that was published in 1595. It was a signal achievement and still provides the basis for modern editions.

To what effect? The contemporary purchaser and reader of this posthumous edition, that is to say someone who had bought and read one or more of the earlier editions (they had indeed sold fairly well and made Montaigne a considerable name)—such imagined persons must have been aware, as the author intended, of the greater mass now in their hands, and perhaps also of some subtle drift in the content. But it was scarcely possible to grasp the whole complex development with any precision. That would have been a gargantuan task even for a scholar.

A sufficient scholar appeared in the twentieth century. Pierre Villey sifted the textual layers of the *Essays* and designated them, (a) for 1580, (b) for 1588, and (c) for 1595.[11] Since Villey's 1923 edition, and up until very recently, it has been accepted publishing practice to intersperse the text with these identifying letters, or some analogous symbol.[12] Thus at any moment you know when the phrase, the paragraph, the page(s) you're reading were published or added. The additions can be any of those things, and they may be integrated at any point within the original text, not simply tacked on at the end like the defense of self-study that Montaigne added to the riding episode, but inserted anywhere, fore, aft or midships. Typically, the early essay 1, iii ("That our affections carry us away") in its final 1595 form opens with two whole pages of (b) text, with more (b) insertions to follow, ending with over a page of (c). Together these passages make up more text than the original had, and the content is correspondingly less conventional. This means that the writer in 1588 and 1592 (for 1595) was reaching back to scatter his afterthoughts across the whole corpus from its earliest state.

Montaigne would have approved of Villey's helping the reader to follow the evolution of his work: it was his declared wish (c) "to represent the progress of my humors, and to make visible each piece in its birth" (2, xxxvii: 421).[13] But he could hardly do it with the extreme precision Villey was to achieve.

The sequence of genetic layers can be grasped intellectually through Villey's letter code, but to make truly "visible each piece in its birth," a useful idea is to highlight in different colors some sample pages of a not-too-precious paperback edition. That also serves to bring home what a terrifying task faced the compositors, who had to insert into an existing text Montaigne's six hundred afterthoughts in 1588 and his thousand more in 1595.[14] There is surely no other edition of a literary work where such step-by-step information about the constitution of the text is built into the text itself, hardly even interrupting its flow. Such intricacies are normally captured and commented on in appendixes. Villey's notation makes any such separate commentary superfluous: his system is elegantly simple, the letters are once for all self-explanatory. (Later editors may add an occasional footnote when one of Montaigne's minor verbal changes grows into a more substantial variant.)

The system does however in one way cut across Montaigne's other, ultimate, intention. Though he was aware of the way his essays were taking shape, and wanted their evolution to be clear, his aim was also to compose a straightforward linear text that could be read as such. In other words, alongside the wish to show the genetic process, there was, consciously or not, the drive inherent in the very process of writing itself, to abolish the development across time in favor of a timeless object, to achieve coherent and consistent utterance—even though in Montaigne's case much of the message he communicates is precisely the inconstancy and fluidity of the phenomenon under scrutiny. The most recent Pléiade edition referred to above takes that deepest wish to heart and for once leaves out the traditional Villey lettering, even restoring the original unparagraphed text. That puts us back in the situation of an innocent reader in 1595, at the price of some strain on our attention span!

On the basis of his meticulous differentiation of the three compositional phases, Villey further posited a clear line in Montaigne's evolution, from an early Stoicism via a skeptical crisis to a life-affirming conclusion that came closer to Epicureanism. This is still a more than plausible thesis, though sometimes said to be an oversimplification. It is certainly speculative, but the foundational identification of the three layers is factually watertight.[15] These were in any case only the largest shifts in a production and an author whose very nature was change. Montaigne was attempting to put salt on the tail of reality down to its minutest units. As he puts it in one of his most celebrated statements,

> (b) The world is nothing but a perennial motion [branloire]. All things move without ceasing. [. . .] Constancy is only a more languishing motion. I cannot guarantee my subject. [. . .] What I am portraying is the flux of things [French: le passage]—not from one age to the next, or, as the people say, from seven years to seven years, but from day to day, from moment to moment. (3, ii; 20)

In/constancy

So it seems there was nothing for Montaigne to do but resign himself to recording the shifts, mutations, and contradictions he saw in the world around him. The very first essay calls Man (a) "a subject diverse and unstable"; (1, i: 41). The writer is himself avowedly a mass of contraries, (b) "shy and insolent, chaste and lustful, garrulous and taciturn, labored and delicate, clever and stupid, gloomy and cheerful, lying and truthful, knowledgeable, ignorant, and liberal, and miserly, and prodigal [. . .] I can't say anything entire, simple, and solid about myself without confusion and without mixture, nor in a single word" (2, I; 9). At a simpler level, of two different ways in which people might observe him looking at his wife, (b) "now coldly, now amorously, neither is pretense" (1, xxxviii; 286). Oddly, he doesn't seem to have or make use of a clear-cut concept of mood in anything like the modern sense. Sometimes inconstancy in phenomena might be better called complexity. On occasion Montaigne misjudges as inconstant a perfectly appropriate discrimination, approving Empedocles's criticism of the Agrigentines, who (c) "abandoned themselves to pleasures as if they had to die tomorrow, but built as if they were never to die at all" (2, I; 7). What's inconstant about that? It's a sanely considered priority.

Yet Montaigne is tolerant of variety. There are (a) "a thousand contrary ways of living; and, unlike most people, I am easier with differences than with similarities between us." He can empathize with other people's ways. (1, xxxvii; 281) Indeed, in grave matters such as religious conviction, it is arrogant and dangerous to try to impose one's own fixed belief on others. That way mortal conflict lies. Yet all the time, within and despite the vast human variety, constancy does remain possible as an ideal. Although even antiquity can show no more than a dozen men who (a) "organized their lives into a certain and assured course," this remains "the principal aim of wisdom." Virtue (he quotes Demosthenes) begins with reflection, and "its end and perfection is constancy" (2, i; 6).

Was Montaigne himself really so inconstant? Alongside the plethora of often trivial details of his personal habits, tastes, foibles, and quirks—a selection fills four pages of Donald Frame's biography—there are already from early on firm statements of value, most fundamentally of the value of life and of what makes human beings what they are: (a) "To disdain our life is ridiculous. For in the end it is our being, it is our all. Things that have a nobler and richer being may look down on us; but it is against nature that we despise ourselves [. . .] It is similar vanity to wish to be something other than what we are"; worst of all, to be angels (2, iii: 24–25). There is no sign of skeptical doubt when he speaks of (a) "the true face of things," of "truth and reason," of "knowing the truth of things by the force of reason" (1, li; 362–63) .There can be truth in language, the honest use of which is what holds society together. That makes lying (a) "a vile vice" because words are "the means by which we communicate our thoughts and our wishes," they are "the interpreter of our soul," and if words deceive us, "it breaks off all our dealings and dissolves all the links of our civilization" (2, xviii; 328). This message was important enough to be repeated more concisely later: (b) "Lying is an accursèd vice. We are only human and hold true to one another through the word" (1, ix; 73).

He is himself (b) trusting by nature (1, v; 61), even in the most pressing matters. He has somehow, miraculously, come through these terrible times of civil war and the ever-presence of marauding soldiery by a kind of sublime trustingness. He has paradoxically never put his house in a state of defense, on the principle that this would only provoke attack, since difficulty stimulates desire. Would marauders bother with a place that has open doors and a welcoming old janitor? It was a brave bluff, and he carried it through by putting on a confident face on the one occasion when soldiers did get into the house. They left without doing violence, and their leader later told him why. Montaigne's house, even though (b) potentially endangered by its strategic location (3, ix; 184), was perhaps, he claimed, (c) the only one in France that could look back on thirty years of peace amid recurrent war (2, xv; 280). Something similar seems to have worked on an occasion when he was waylaid en route in the forest. He was robbed, a ransom was discussed (typically, he says they overestimated what he would be worth), but the gang thought better of it and returned his things and his liberty. (b) His calm face and the firmness of his speech had again apparently done the trick (3, xii; 272–73). True, on another occasion he was less fortunate, losing (b) men and horses, and seeing a promising Italian page killed (2, v; 37). He doesn't expatiate further on this episode. Confidence is in any case at all times a gamble—it may impress or it may provoke. Many of Montaigne's anecdotes concern the uncertain psychology of such critical confrontations, no mere theoretical issue in an age when acts of unsurpassable savagery were being stoked by religious fanaticism. One earlier case must have stuck in his mind. In the Bordeaux salt riots of 1548, the mayor went out to face down a mob, lost his composure halfway, and was torn apart. There could be no reliable answer; it was always touch and go.

Montaigne's lucky escapes were instances of practical constancy, the outward face of the settled mental state he aspired to in an unstable world. Deep beneath it was the general idea of being in his "assiette." The word derives from *s'asseoir*, to sit: he probably has in mind the experienced rider securely in the saddle. That was where Montaigne most loved to be—for as much as eight or ten hours at a time, into advanced years and despite the affliction of gallstones (3, ix; 187). For one thing, ideas came when he was out riding (3, v; 91). Like other writers (Goethe, Nietzsche) he needed movement as a stimulus (3, iii; 44), the only drawback being that it was hard to keep hold of an idea while on horseback.[16] He even said he could wish to die in the saddle rather than in bed (3, ix; 191)—as indeed he already almost had. There were other homely metaphors for the desired settled state, centrally that of home itself, of being "chez soy." In the literal sense, that evokes Montaigne at leisure in his tower among his books, with much of his property visible from the windows, but for the moment not needing to do anything about it. He was never a keen estate manager, claiming with his usual overdone modesty not to know the simplest things about the country tasks he had been born and brought up among; he alleges that (a) he couldn't even tell a cabbage from a lettuce (2, xvii; 315). This literal "chez soy" was also (b) the best place to write (3, v; 90). But deeper down, the metaphorical "chez soy" was his real self, the substance beneath all appearances and away from people and pressures: (a) "the greatest thing in the world is knowing how to be in oneself." [French: à soy]." It was "a back room behind the shop" (1, xxxix; 292).

That inner core of a man observing, reflecting, and judging, can be sensed from the very start of the essay project, among and despite the swirl of change that constitutes the world and embraces the observer of the world. There is always the sense of a balanced *jugement* in action, an *entendement* that is not disoriented, a mind *au dessus de la mêlée*. His readiness to speak confidently for himself and about himself grows steadily stronger. This against a background of authority, the canonical texts from antiquity that he never ceases to quote, and the Catholic orthodoxy that he never ceases formally to profess. By the time he comes, after a break of several years,[17] to write a third book of essays, he has amassed experience, and he knows it. He has always recognized the possibility (a) "that for those who use their time well, knowledge and experience grow in step with life" (1, lvii; 389). But he was not, in that early passage, applying the insight to himself. Now he can.

A third book was never part of a plan, as the title of book 2 ("second," not "deuxième") makes clear. The largely favorable reception of the first two books from 1580 on (3, ix; 178) may have given him the confidence to start writing again. But most probably it was the head of experience that had built up and was demanding to be released. It had now become a positive (c) "hunger" for self-revelation (3, v; 62), strengthened by the sober sense, (c) which he states along with more of his habitual self-depreciation, of his own value (2, xvii; 298).[18]

Involvement

What was that further experience? Over the eight years since books 1 and 2 were published, Montaigne had been drawn back again, unwillingly at first and never without reservations, into the public realm from which on his retirement in 1571 he thought he had escaped.[19] To begin with, in 1581 he was voted Mayor of Bordeaux, while away on an Italian journey and without even knowing he was a candidate. The news came in the form of a somewhat peremptory order, which he tried to decline, but it was reinforced by royal command and he was hauled back home, travelling in slow stages, plainly dragging his feet.

That journey, incidentally, was another major experience, seven months of mind-enlarging travel as he followed his fancy, feeling at ease among foreign peoples, Italians, Germans, and Swiss, their customs and cuisines.[20] When courteously offered service in the French manner, he declined—(c) "I always threw myself on the tables that were thickest with foreigners" (3, ix; 199). In Rome he was honored to have citizenship conferred on him, though it wasn't for his writings. Papal censors did read and approve these, to the extent of making only mild objections and not insisting that he act on them. Montaigne duly didn't.

A more important purpose of the journey was to visit various spas in search of relief from the painful condition of gallstones, which he had been suffering from since 1578. The illness, too, was a central part of daily experience, narrated fully in the travel journal—but so too was the discovery that he could tolerate the pain as part of life, "umanamente," and enjoy no less, in some ways more, life's positive gifts. He had long known Pliny's judgment (a) that the stone was the worst of all illnesses (2, iii; 26), and he had seen his father suffer and die from it.[21] But as with his own near-death experience, the reality turned out to be more bearable than expected. And there was no pleasure quite like the relief when a stone was extruded.

On receipt of the command from the Bordeaux *jurats* (councillors), he spelled out with his usual, now tactical modesty the qualities he lacked for the post. He was "without memory, without vigilance, without experience, and without vigor." So they knew what they were not getting. He did in all honesty admit to an equal number of balancing qualities: he was "without hatred, without ambition, without avarice and without violence" (3, x; 217). His father had been mayor before him, and that was both a warning (he had been completely taken over by the stress of business) and a further pressure to accept the office and make the best job of it he could. This he did to such good effect, largely through not being proactive—in his phrase, "by abstinence from doing" (3, x; 235)—that he was reelected, albeit against some opposition, for a second term, something that had only ever happened in Bordeaux twice before.

In an age when violence and treachery were more common than integrity, Montaigne earned a reputation as "a man of a spirit free and foreign to factions."[22] In the years following his reelection as mayor, Montaigne acted as intermediary for Henri of Navarre, later Henri IV of France. Henri asked him to become still more closely attached, but it was too late; Montaigne died soon after. Not before spelling out what this role would have required—telling his master, unlike the flatterers, home truths about his actions and the way they were being seen. (3; iii; 288). As a humane man in a fanatical age, he advised "a young prince" (no doubt Henri) to practice benevolence rather than take revenge. (3, iv; 50) It was nobler and perhaps (*pace* Machiavelli) more effective. This much practical involvement was already a case of an intellectual—if that is what we may properly call Montaigne—playing a small but effective part in political affairs.

Montaigne declined to write directly about the events of his time, as he was invited to do by contemporaries who thought his view would be less distorted by passion than some, while yet being close to the action. But he does discuss the principles involved in a public rôle. It is the first topic in the new book 3: "Of the Useful and the Honorable"—useful, that is, to a political cause, as against the honorable limits that conscience sets to engagement. In other words, expediency versus morality.

In hard reality, public purposes—at the extreme, *raison d'état* (Montaigne doesn't use the term)—may require treachery, lies, and even (c) massacres. Montaigne had a visceral hatred of cruelty, to which he compulsively and eloquently reverts. He was horrified at what the formerly civilized French were doing to each other in the name of religion, with large-scale massacre fresh in living memory (the slaughter of Protestants on the night of Saint Bartholomew occurred in August 1572) but for the moment he merely says that this takes a different kind of people.[23] His own activity as a negotiator has been frank and open, something still possible in these terrible times and apparently even bringing out a similar response from the other side. He was happy not to feel the passionate commitment to a cause that is often motivated more by people's personal interests than by the cause itself. Not for any cause would he allow himself to lie, and he made clear to the high personages he had to deal with that there were limits to how far he would go in their service. "The public interest must not require everything against the private interest," that is, against one's conscience (3, I; 18). It was his rule of thumb that you can deal "loyally" with mutually hostile parties, "if not with an equal, then at least with a moderate affection which does not engage you so deeply for the one side that they can require absolutely anything from you. [. . .] You can go with the flow of troubled waters, but not fish in them" (3, i; 9).

Non, je ne regrette rien

Montaigne is not shy of declaring what he has practiced, and "Of the Useful and the Honorable" is less a confession than a proud claim to have stuck to his principles. The second essay of the new book confirms it: "On Repenting" is more about *not* repenting of what he has done. It is also about his certainties of what, despite "the flux of things," he essentially is: "[I have] a pattern ["patron"] inside me as touchstone for my actions, I have my laws and my court to judge me" (3, ii; 23). Anyone who listens to his inner voice will discover "a form of his own, a master-form" [*forme maistresse*] that struggles against outside influences and "the tempest of contrary passions." It allows him to hold firm: "I am more or less always in my place, in the way ponderous heavy bodies are. If I am not at home, I am never far off" (3, ii; 26)—that home metaphor again, now more than ever vital when he is under pressure. Still, Montaigne is at ease with not expecting too much of himself: (c) "My conscience is content, not as the conscience of an angel, but as the conscience of a man"—once again, a firm earthly delimitation is set against vain and impracticable transcendence.

With his clear conscience, he now dares "not only to talk about myself, but to talk only about myself" (3, viii; 157). In fact it isn't the only thing he dares to talk about. He has the confidence to hold forth on anything and everything that has gone into his life's experience—this is a last survey before departing, and in the end all subjects are connected (3, v; 91). "I speak true, not my fill of what I might say, but as much as I dare; and I dare a bit more in aging," something that custom allows to older people (3, ii; 21). Most strikingly, he devotes the longest essay ("On some Verses of Vergil") to sex—to human sexuality in general and to his own career in particular as, apparently, something of a ladies' man in his day. He is here at his frankest, coming near the knuckle of the conventional decencies with forthright statements and confessions and a vocabulary only partly hidden away in the Latin of his quotations ("mentula," "rimula" for the male and female sexual organs). But why should he not talk openly about this action, "so natural, so necessary and so just?" We talk readily enough about killing men, so why not about making them? (3, v; 63) His private remembrance is full of sap and succulence—the kisses whose scent lingered long on his moustaches, the nights when he managed it six times (quoting, though adapting, verses of Ovid, who claimed nine) but there is a realistic balance. He knows the highs and lows of male experience, from the disaster of failed performance to the pleasure of giving pleasure. "Anyone who the morning after can await without shame the disdain of those lovely eyes that have witnessed his slackness and inadequacy has never known the happiness and pride of turning them misty from the vigorous exercise of a devoted and active night" (3, v; 102). If I fail, she is not to blame, it is nature that has done me "this most enormous damage." As for marriage—Montaigne was married, fathering several children of whom only his daughter Léonor survived—it was seen in his day largely as a quite separate, more sober matter than sex. Somewhat to his surprise, he turned out to be more faithful than he had expected (3, v; 68). He confesses (c) to two mild infections (3, iii; 42).

Now however his vital forces are fading, though not altogether his inclination. Love might still restore lost power to his declining person (3, v; 108).[24] Meantime, he hopes that the sexual content of this essay will help his book progress from an item put on display in the living room to something for milady's chamber (3, v; 62). It seriously deserved to, since it is not just salacious in the manner of his neighbor Brantôme's *Lives of Galant Ladies*, but socially analytical, evenhanded in its treatment of the sexes, tender towards women, critical of men's indiscretions and lack of consideration, critical more radically of their dominance through custom and prejudice, which has created (c) unequal social forms (3, v; 76). At base, both sexes are cast in the same mold, they are alike in their desires and their capacities. He agrees with Plato (c) that women are as fit for all offices as men (3, v; 112). Measured against the norms of his time, Montaigne is a feminist.

But beyond even the matter of the sexes, he is arguing for a balance of spiritual and corporeal. Against ancient and widespread religious and philosophical traditions that do the body down, he sets a human constitution that is "marvelously corporeal" (3, viii; 145). He hates "that inhuman wisdom that would make us disdainful and enemies of bodily culture" (3, xiii; 318). Those people who would have us renounce bodily functions as something base—why don't they give up breathing?—and (c) are they preoccupied with abstractions like squaring the circle when they lie on their wives? (3, xiii; 319)

He accepts and positively celebrates physical existence in general, even its downside: his gallstones are "the rent owed to old age" (3, xiii; 301). Compared with other diseases it even has advantages, and he writes a virtual apologia for it: it needs no tiresome course of medicines, it has supplanted all his other ailments, it is self-curing when a stone is passed— "there is nothing in the pain suffered that can outweigh the pleasure of so prompt an improvement" (3, xii; 304) .It has intensified his enjoyment of the good things of life. In any case, the affliction has only come on at a late stage. For the rest, he has been lucky with the course of his life and his health: "I have seen the herb and the flowers and the fruit; and am now seeing the dry season. Happily, because naturally." He is grateful for "the long felicity of my past life" (3, ii; 32). These late pages are touched by poetry.

The early stirrings of life-affirmation have become immensely stronger. The Stoic obligation to keep death always in mind is now rejected as causing more torment than the thing itself. To fear suffering is already to suffer what you fear. Rather than having a liberating effect, the anticipation of evil casts a shadow over all present living. Humorously put, (c) "why get your fur coat out on Midsummer's Day just because you might need it at Christmas?" (3, xii; 261–62)

Montaigne does still reflect on death, but concretely now, on its possible locations and circumstances: preferably not at home surrounded by mourning family and friends, but somewhere far away. Death in Venice perhaps? Or it might find you journeying through the wintry Grisons. And better to die on horseback than in bed anywhere (3, ix; 191). Or death might find him on his estate planting his cabbages (1, xx; 134–35)—except they might of course be lettuces. And where the now distant essay on learning to die said you must (a) "be always booted and ready to depart," the late insertion on the same page now gives a relaxed answer:

(c) "I am at the moment in such a state, thank God, that I can move out ["desloger," aptly the word for leaving home] whenever I please, without regretting any single thing, unless it be life itself" (1, xx; 134). What was once sternly prescribed has now been calmly achieved. He deserved a kinder death than the drawn-out one he in the event had.

He now reflects far more on life than on death. The one attitude is after all the reciprocal of the other. It only needed the maturing processes of time and experience to shift the emphasis, to flip from Wittgenstein's duck to Wittgenstein's rabbit,[25] from anticipating death to embracing life. The old essay on learning to die now has a further, happier conclusion added: (c) "If you taught men to die, you would be teaching them how to live" (1, xx; 135). Montaigne is more than just an escaped Stoic; he is a patent if undeclared Epicurean. He consciously makes the most of such pleasures as old age still allows, starting with his memories of good times. He "passes" present time only when things are unpleasant; when they are good, he holds on to time and savors it. It will all be lost eventually, but without regret—we are "losable by our natural condition" (3, xiii; 323). This is not heroic humanism, though the classic quotation from Terence was of course up there on a beam in the tower.[26] In the end we are only playing rôles, mostly farcical ones at that, in what medieval and Baroque writers were to label the *Theatrum mundi* (3, x; 223). Indeed, we are (c) all ultimately just wind (3, xiii; 318)—another very Baroque thought.[27] Still, Nature must meanwhile be our essential guide (3, xii; 325). As Montaigne had written years before when dedicating his translation of Raimond Sebond to his father, Nature is a book the study of which makes nobody a heretic.[28] That is to say, what she prescribes cannot be wrong. To the last, Montaigne is observing and revealing himself. His final essay includes a virtual self-interview full of personal minutiae—he doesn't wear glasses, still walks with a firm step, wears only thin hose in all seasons, doesn't eat salads or fruit, except melons—as if there was a public out there avid for yet more personal details (perhaps by now there was). Incidentally, an "unexpected profit" from publishing this much about himself is that it gives him "a sort of rule" to live by, in that he doesn't want to betray the history of his life by doing anything to change it (3, ix; 193).

Que sais-je? Tout un tas de choses!

It is not however all self-indulgence. Montaigne draws serious conclusions from a lifetime's insights. That final essay, aptly, is called "On Experience," and it establishes a modest but firm practical solution to our natural desire for knowledge: "When reason fails us, we use experience, which is a weaker and less worthy means, but truth is so great a thing that we must not disdain any medium that will lead us to it" (3, xiii; 275). Appeals to experience are scattered back as (c) insertions into the earliest essays: "I find by experience . . ." "I will state my experience about this subject . . ." (1, xiv; 97 and 103). It all echoes that other great Renaissance empiricist Leonardo da Vinci's self-description as a pupil of experience ("discepolo della sperientia").

Montaigne's self-knowledge has gradually extended to other selves, to become a broader wisdom still: "From the experience I have of myself, I find enough to make me wise, if I were a good pupil" (3, xiii; 284). "This long attention that I employ in considering myself sets me up to judge passably of other people" (286). He has found that no event or form is quite the same, but then nor is any entirely different (280). Study them, put them together, and they make a coherent whole: "Wisdom is a building solid and complete, of which each piece has its place and bears its mark" (287), the mark, that is, which a master-mason uses to indicate where a stone is to fit into a structure.

Yet there is no grand philosophizing manner, no Cartesian-style "I think, therefore I am" (which was, incidentally, to prove less than adequate for getting a grip on the external world). Rather it is a plain empirical approach: I experience, therefore I am, am a real and distinctive part of a recognizably real world. It remains tentative, any certainty offset by phrases that regularly soften and moderate the arguments.[29] Indeed, Montaigne's modesty makes express allowance for a possible reader's need to aim off in a direction altogether contrary to his own: "This fricassee I'm daubing is only a register of my lifetime try-outs which, for the sake of inner health, is exemplary enough, if you take the lesson against the grain" (289).

So Montaigne ended up feeling he knew quite a lot, and for working purposes quite enough. It is unfortunate that the saying most associated with him, and commonly misunderstood as summing him up, is the motto "Que sais-je?" for which according to legend he at some point had a medal struck. If he did ever subscribe to that phrase, it must date, like the skeptical quotations painted on the beams in his tower, from early in his career of observation and reflection. It is squarely invalidated by the whole enterprise of the *Essays*, and it is misleading to quote the tag as if it were Montaigne's—or indeed any—serious highpoint of philosophical insight. It was never more than a starting point, a necessary maxim of humility and caution. To have settled for it as a conclusion would have been defeatist. Instead, Montaigne now had a sound knowledge of human beings and their affairs, drawn from history and his own times, and he had firm moral values drawn from that knowledge. The question "Que sais-je?" had been taken much deeper by the question "Que suis-je?" and both had been amply answered. Skepticism was like the balance in physics between equal and opposite forces, which results in a point of inertia. For the world of ideas, that would have meant orthodoxy must remain undisturbed, leaving conformism to rule by default. Accumulated experience had by now proved powerful enough to tip the balance.

Modern terms can only be approximate, but roughly speaking, Montaigne was a liberal. He was *against* prejudice, blind partisanship, ruthless ambition, fanaticism, cruelty, imposed authority, undeserved social status, ceremony, pretention, jargon, and empty abstraction. He was *for* honest self-knowledge, free communication, undisturbed private life, spontaneity, tolerance, sociability, and cosmopolitanism. From the *Essays* you would have known what kind of man you were meeting. It might even be called constancy.

With all that, and despite the political troubles all around him, was Montaigne a happy man? His friend Pierre de Brach certainly thought so.[30] Those late expressions of gratitude for the life he had led and the health he had enjoyed clearly suggest as much. If so, it was, as André Gide argued, "not for his own selfish satisfaction, but just as much for the happiness and profit of other people, considering what instruction, what counsel for the whole of humanity the mere example of a happy man can be."[31] At its simplest, it comes down to the declaration "We must spread joy and cut back sadness as much as we can" (3, ix; 192). It hardly needs saying how rare the celebration of that ideal has become in modern writing. But perhaps it is what has made Montaigne such a congenial and supportive mind for so many Common Readers across the ages. Friedrich Nietzsche put it most eloquently: that such a man has written truly increases the enjoyment of living: "He would be the man for me if the task were set us of making ourselves at home on the earth."[32] As of course it is.

In fundamentals, Montaigne had his classical sources (Seneca, Plutarch especially) and models (Cato, Scipio, Epaminondas) but above all one historic figure: "It is fortunate that the man most worthy to be known and to be presented to the world as an example should be the one of whom we have the most certain knowledge. He has been illumined by the most clear-sighted men who ever were: the witnesses we have of him are admirable for their fidelity and competence" (3, xii; 249). The following pages have a reconstruction of his trial, fairly full in (b) and further elaborated in (c). Surely this Christian, this orthodox Catholic, must be talking about Jesus Christ and the gospel authors? No, it is Socrates, and the clear-sighted witnesses of Socrates' life and death are Plato and Xenophon. Without apology or a sideways glance at orthodoxy, Montaigne's unquestioned ideal is provided by a Greek philosopher. "It is he who brought human wisdom down from heaven, where it was wasting its time, to give it back to mankind, where it has its most just and most demanding task, and its most useful one." Against some hundred references to Socrates scattered across the Essays, many of them substantial and eloquent, there are just six passing references to Christ, none of them suggesting any particular piety. There are numerous references to God, but those would make Montaigne no more than a deist. Religion in the

Essays otherwise figures most prominently in its corrupt form, abhorred as the misguided motive for internecine violence. Orthodox Montaigne certainly was, to the point of closing his eyes to what his own argument against miracles implied for belief, David Hume *avant la lettre*. But he notes sardonically that you need to rate your religious "conjectures"—itself a clearly negative term—pretty high if they are to justify burning another human being. Yet expressly for the sake of social harmony he doesn't confront blind belief with rational arguments (3, xi; 244–45). In any case, the declared subject of this essay, "Of Cripples," to which he gets round right at the end, is a lightweight popular belief, that cripples are especially good in bed.

Montaigne's explicit religious conformity, as well as being a necessary personal precaution, had social and political grounds. "Innovation" in theology had shaken the state and led to civil war, the ultimate evil. His response was pragmatic, not dogmatic. "He may well have seemed a good Catholic," wrote Sainte-Beuve, "except that he was scarcely a Christian."[33] He bent his knee, but resolutely not his mind (3, viii; 150). Fideism, the watertight separation of faith and reason, is too sophisticated—too intellectual—a term for Montaigne's position, which was simply not concerned with theological reflection.

That celebration of Socrates suggests which of the two components of Montaigne's cultural heritage, Christianity or the Classical world, had marked his mind most profoundly. The stamp of classical antiquity is clear again in the closing lines of the last essay, the envoi of the whole corpus. They are, literally, an apotheosis of the human condition and its acceptance: "It is an absolute perfection, and as it were divine, to know how to loyally enjoy our being. We look for other conditions because we do not understand the use of our own, and go beyond ourselves through not knowing what it is right to do (c). It's all very well getting up on stilts, but on stilts we still have to walk on our own legs. And on the highest throne in the world we are only sitting on our own backside (b). The finest lives are, in my view, the ones that fit into the common pattern (c) the human pattern, with order, but (b) without miracles and without extravagance. Well, old age has some need to be treated more tenderly. Let us commend it to that god, the protector of health and wisdom, but of a joyful and sociable kind." That god is the Roman god Apollo, and Montaigne closes with a stanza addressed to him by the aging Horace:

> What I have gathered, let me enjoy it now,
> Son of Latona, and with a mind intact
>   Spend an old age in no way shameful,
>   And may the poets' lyre not be wanting.[34]

"C" Change

No sooner had Montaigne brought out his 1588 edition than he began scribbling more afterthoughts in the new copy.[35] The habit was hard to break. But he never saw them in print, some key phrases of that wonderful peroration included. They went into Marie de Gournay's posthumous edition, to form what is known since Villey as the (c) layer.

There is no sign Montaigne was planning any new essays, though it is conceivable there could eventually have been a fourth book. For among his hopes for a rejuvenation by love, one—significantly added to that passage after 1588—is clearly that it would strengthen his writing powers, "would take me back to wise and healthy studies by which I could make myself more esteemed and more loved, lifting from my spirit the despair of itself and of its practice, and acquainting it with itself again," restoring "the vigor and joyfulness of the soul" (3, v; 108). Even without such rejuvenation, he had already declared his resolve to go on writing: "Who cannot see that I have taken a route which I will pursue, without cease and without labor, as long as there is ink and paper in the world" (3, ix; 159).

Writing had plainly become a major preoccupation, perhaps *the* dominant experience of Montaigne's last fifteen years, and must always have been a felt background to every other practical involvement: working with words to get thoughts into shape, however irregular, never finally satisfied with the result; watching the way each essay groweth as it listeth; leaving the shifts of emphasis in and between essays to sort out their mutual relation in the dialogue of the years.

"Without cease," yes, but surely not "without labor"? Imagine the hours Montaigne must have put into reading and rereading what he had written, feeling his way back into past lines of argument, thinking out his present position on them, drafting a response, deciding where to insert the new section; all the time making those innumerable small perfectionist adjustments; and whenever yet another classical parallel occurred to him, checking and adding quotations from among the thousand books on the shelves in his tower. All this surely made the man who at first affected to be a mere dilettante into a writer in the fullest sense. Can he really have been one of those people "who don't have much to do with books," someone who "for the last twenty years has not read a book for an hour together"? (3, viii; 155) Believe that who will.

As it turned out, the four-year span from 1588 to 1592 was Montaigne's last chance to rethink and add. Since he didn't live to see the 1595 edition and be provoked to yet more afterthoughts on that latest text, there was never a (d) layer. But the project of self-exploration, which he had invented and pursued so fruitfully, remained potentially endless. At the very least, he left the whole remaining alphabet of experience for later writers to explore.

Appendix:
Essays quoted or referred to in this chapter

(NB: The numbering can differ very slightly between editions. This is the numbering of the Micha edition.)

1, i	That we arrive at the same end by different means
1, v	Should a besieged commander venture out to parley?
1, viii	Of Idleness
1, ix	Of Liars
1, xiv	That the taste of good and evil depends in large part on the way we think about them
1, xx	Of the power of the imagination
1, xxvi	Of the education of children
1, xxvii	It is madness to judge "true" and "false" by our own lights
1, xxviii	Of Friendship
1, xxxi	Of Cannibals
1, xxxviii	How we laugh and cry at the same thing
1, xxxix	Of Solitude
1, xlvi	Of Names
1, li	Of the vanity of words
1, lvi	Of Prayers
1, lvii	Of Age
2, i	Of the inconstancy of our actions
2, iii	Custom of the island of Cea
2, v	Of Conscience
2, vi	Of Practice
2, viii	Of the affection of fathers for their children
2, xi	Of Cruelty
2, xii	Apology for Raimond Sebond
2, xvii	Of Presumption
2, xviii	Of Denials
2, xxxvii	Of the resemblance of children to their fathers
3, i	Of the useful and on the honorable
3, ii	Of repenting
3, iii	Of three kinds of human interaction
3, iv	Of Diversion
3, v	Of some verses of Virgil
3, vi	Of Coaches
3, viii	Of the art of conversing
3, ix	Of Vanity
3, x	Of managing one's will
3, xi	Of Cripples
3, xii	Of Physiognomy
3, xiii	Of Experience

4: Beginner's Luck: Shakespeare's History Cycles

Near-Oblivion

THE GENESIS OF SHAKESPEARE'S dramatic oeuvre is rooted in the materials of history and—as with the *Iliad*—in the tastes of his first audiences; but the material circumstances of its production meant that much of it might never have survived to become history itself. For a long time, Shakespeare's amazing nonchalance about the fate of his plays left the final phase of fixing the texts in print to chance, with the consequence that some were never printed in his lifetime at all. There is no sign that he did anything to further publication. Since he left no record of his actions or omissions, his motives can only be guessed at.

Direct traces of Shakespeare's writing career are few. Signatures apart, only one small piece of text thought to be in his hand is preserved, a section of the drama *Sir Thomas More* on which he is known to have collaborated: three pages, only a part, albeit a vital part: More's speech to xenophobe rioters appealing for a humane response to political refugees.[1]

There exists, though, a striking account of *how* Shakespeare wrote, from men who knew whereof they spoke. The actors Henry Condell and John Heminge,[2] who in 1623 put together the First Folio after Shakespeare's death, had been for years his fellow-shareholders and collaborators in the troupe for which he both acted and did virtually all his writing, the Chamberlain's (later the King's) Men. The two editors were concerned "to procure [for] his Orphans, Guardians,"[3] a variation on the metaphor of paternity common in writers, in this case remedying a neglectful kind. Condell and Heminge laid the foundations of Shakespeare's later fame by rescuing the half of his dramatic production that had never yet been printed—eighteen plays, including several of his finest, which would otherwise certainly have been lost—and by republishing the others, which had earlier appeared in haphazard sequence, some of them in a form not designed to last.[4] The already published titles did at least include all but one of the histories (discounting the minor *King John* and *Henry VIII*). They were his significant early successes, although not yet labelled as "histories" to distinguish them from any other genre.

The two former colleagues' theatrical roots gave them access to textual material that was somehow still just recoverable from the past disorder. But they also, unnecessarily for the purpose of promoting their volume—this was not yet the Romantic age—celebrated Shakespeare's spontaneous way of writing: "His mind and hand went together, and what he thought, he uttered with that easiness that we have scarce received from him a blot in his papers."

This is as authentically close as we can get to Shakespeare with quill in hand. It has the ring of real experience—memories of the writer in action observed over many years, perhaps even in the process of redrafting a text under pressure at a late juncture in a stage production. There is no reason to think his colleagues' account is an "idealised description [...] adulatory rather than accurate."[5] Indeed, an earlier comment by a fellow dramatist confirms this view of Shakespeare's gift in the grandest anthropological terms. The poet's best lines

> show
> How far sometimes a mortal man may go
> By the dim light of Nature.[6]

For what it's worth, it was also a commonplace of Stratford local lore in later years that Shakespeare had been "a natural wit, without any art at all."[7]

Beaumont's comment was a riposte *avant la lettre* to the reservations of Shakespeare's otherwise admiring contemporary, Ben Jonson. For all Ben's devotion, he deplored the way Shakespeare's writing "flowed with that facility that sometime it was necessary he should be stopped." The two editors, Jonson said, had wrongly chosen "that circumstance to commend their friend by, wherein he most faulted."[8] Blunt language indeed, springing from Jonson's own poetics, on which he expands in a prefatory poem to the First Folio, where he argues for the necessity of Art as a conscious craft: "Who casts to write a living line, must sweat," must "strike the second heat / Upon the Muses' anvil." The anvil metaphor ill fits the mythical Muses, and the image of hard graft doesn't allow for a poet who in the Prologue to *Henry V* could appeal for a heaven-storming "muse of fire" and invoke the power of imagination, his to create and ours to follow his flights. Jonson didn't conceive that there might be two fundamentally different types of creator, the intuitive sure touch and the conscious deviser—the one as if sleep-walking (Goethe will use that image for his inspirations), the other sometimes brought to a standstill by too much self-awareness (extreme case Flaubert's "torments of composition" in pursuit of the "mot juste"). Just such a typology of poets would later be brilliantly worked out in Friedrich Schiller's 1795 essay "On Primal and Reflective Poetry." By that time Shakespeare had become the pivoting point to a new aesthetics: he was in both senses the original genius.[9]

Critics who follow Jonson's line often mistake the point that Heminge, Condell, and Beaumont were making, as if they were failing to remember Shakespeare's revisions of his own texts—amply documented in variants across and between the Quartos of the 1590s and the First Folio—and as if the fact of revision in any way disproved his easy spontaneity. Revision is no objection. "Flow" is a matter of the relation at any instant of hand and pen to paper, the organic product of a contact that was second nature to writers throughout the ages between orality and the coming of the word-processor. A new draft may have flowed just as easily as the original passage, which it not only replaces but may often enlarge and deepen. The revising eye spots not just flaws to be corrected but growth-points that will carry first imaginings further, the flow resumes with renewed energy. (It is in any case questionable whether Shakespeare's language at its most intense, in the full flow of metaphor, hyperbole, and rhythm, could ever have been pieced together by a deliberate Art such as Jonson was preaching.)

Lines inserted near the end of *A Midsummer Night's Dream* show exactly how flow takes off from points in an existing text in the process of revision. Duke Theseus's speech about two kinds of madness:

> Lovers and mad men have such teeming brains.
> One sees more devils than vast hell can hold.
> That is the madman. The lover, all as frantic,
> Sees Helen's beauty in a brow of Egypt—

is developed further by a third case of madness that takes off syntactically by first repeating the word "such . . ." from that first line:

> Lovers and mad men have such teeming brains,
> *Such shaping fantasies, that apprehend*
> *More than cool reason ever comprehends.*
> *The lunatic, the lover and the poet*
> *Are of imagination all compact.*
> One sees more devils than vast hell can hold.
> That is the madman. The lover, all as frantic,
> Sees Helen's beauty in a brow of Egypt.
> *The poet's eye, in a fine frenzy rolling,*
> *Doth glance from heaven to earth, from earth to heaven,*
> *And as imagination bodies forth*
> *The forms of things unknown, the poet's pen*
> *Turns them to shapes, and gives to airy nothing*
> *A local habitation and a name.*
> 					Act V, sc. 1, lines 2–22[10]

The Duke's intended put-down of all kinds of over-heated minds becomes a celebration of the poet, especially of the imagination's power to explore beyond the already known. These added lines show Shakespeare's imagining taken further, to generate some of his best-remembered phrases. Such local expansion can be multiplied over and over. Additions to *Hamlet* enlarged the original text to twice its length.

Play-Writer

Beyond that brilliant expansion of Duke Theseus's speech, how did Shakespeare see his own talent and its role? He left no self-analytical diary or letters, so we can only draw inferences from his practice. They come close to Bertolt Brecht's self-description as a "play-writer" (*Stückeschreiber*), an aggressively modest word designed to keep the solemn label "Dichter" at arm's length—the German word means not just poet but a writer with achievements (or at least pretensions) in any of the genres. Brecht's term sticks to the down-to-earth reality of the boards. In much the same way, Shakespeare worked directly for the stage, often shaping a role to a particular actor, above all Richard Burbage. Shakespeare could sometimes only fully conceive a role if the company had a suitable player, a competent boy actor, say, to take on a major female role such as Rosalind or Cleopatra. The poet's eye and fine frenzy were then his necessary means.

That publishing was not for Shakespeare a consummation particularly to be wished is plain from his not bothering to have half his plays printed even during the long leisure of his retirement from London to Stratford-upon-Avon. The power and subtlety of his dramas were apparently not matched by an awareness of their quality, or by any ambition for immortality as a dramatist, unlike the claims he made for the Sonnets. The contrast with those formal poems indeed brings out the more sharply his astounding insouciance about the plays.

Part of the explanation may be that plays as a form were ephemera produced in their hundreds in the England of the day and mostly since lost. They had a very low status in the entertainment market, not far above the bear-baiting and cock-fighting arenas, the brothels, taverns, and gambling-houses which the theaters stood among in the "liberties" outside London's walls. The stage was duly denounced as immoral by the religious authorities, the Puritans especially. Even Heminge and Condell refer to the plays they were in the act of publishing as trifles,[11] though perhaps more in deference to the volume's two noble dedicatees, as if to say, why would people of your elevated status bother? All this may have kept Shakespeare's self-esteem within limits. True, from early on he was also a highly regarded narrative poet, his *Rape of Lucrece* and *Venus and Adonis* are impressive in both substance and outward dress, the second of them by far his most enduringly popular printed work. In contrast, the sixteen plays that he did see published in his lifetime were nearly all cheap pamphlets in quarto format, essentially occasional productions—opportunistic follow-ups to stage successes, or defensive measures to stop rival companies stealing his own company's property and production rights, or ways to make a bit of money when the theaters were closed in times of plague, or means to raise more capital for the Globe when the company was building it for their own use.

The First Folio was an initial step towards a specifically literary reputation, with Ben Jonson's prophetic praise of Shakespeare as a voice "not for an age but for all time" on a par with the ancient Greeks, and this in a volume whose grand format had been reserved till now for Bibles (oh yes, and for Jonson's own grandly titled *Works* of five years earlier, themselves a major advance in establishing literary authorship as a profession). But it looks as if Shakespeare, like Brecht, was never in his own estimation more than a provider of actable material, in the contemporary term a play-maker, a play-*writer*—something different from the similar-sounding play*wright*, which despite echoes of hands-on practicality (shipwright, wheelwright, wainwright) belongs to the vocabulary of High Literature.

Correspondingly little fuss was made over Shakespeare's death, whereas Richard Burbage's was publicly lamented as the passing of the great figures he had acted—Richard III, Hamlet, Lear, Othello, Brutus, Coriolanus, Antony, Prospero. Never a side-glance at the man who created them.

Getting It Together

This much sense of how Shakespeare worked, and to what conscious end, still doesn't throw light on any particular genesis. There is no manuscript material to help, since none has survived from the copy used to set the First Folio, much less the quartos. Nor is it known for certain what copy-text—what *kind* of copy-text, even—any of these were printed from. Condell and Heminge dismiss the texts with which readers had had to make do before their new edition as "stolne and surreptitious copies, maimed and deformed by the frauds and stealths of injurious impostors, that expos'd them" ("expos'd" in a damaged condition, like unloved, unwanted babies, continues the metaphor of neglectful paternity) but they do not specify how they themselves have managed to achieve texts that are now "cur'd and perfect of their limbs."[12] Did they or their compositors work from an old fair copy of Shakespeare's? For something had, in their phrase, been directly "receiv'd from him." Or was it from his rough drafts, conventionally known by the bibliographers' term "foul papers," an unlovely name for things that scholars would dearly love to get their hands on? Or from a prompt-book fresh from recent performances, or not so fresh from seasons of hard use and running alterations? Or did they have to rely on actors' memories of productions, especially of each one's individual role? Actors, like the Homeric rhapsodes, were professional memorizers; they will have played a given part many times, and they may have teamed up with colleagues who remembered *their* parts, and between them put together a complete text. Actors did apparently often make copies for their friends. How did they manage that? Perhaps, as Samuel Johnson speculated, someone "wrote down, during the representation, what time would permit, then perhaps filled up some of the omissions at a second or third hearing, and when he had by this method formed something like a play, sent it to the printer."[13] Stenography, both the thing and the term, already existed. According to Thomas Dekker in 1607, prostitutes too, trawling for clients in the theaters, got to know play-texts by heart.[14] (Whether they were ever consulted is another matter.)

Dr. Johnson's wording "formed *something like* a play" is suitably cautious. The various possible routes into print, with conceivably more than one of them operating at a given time, some carrying the writer's afterthoughts, some just other people's approximations, some the cuts and additions the company made in Shakespeare's lifetime or after his death—this hit-and-miss process resulted in texts that vary both in detailed phrasing and in larger units between quartos and First Folio, and between quartos among themselves. There are also infinitely many small verbal divergences, much like Montaigne's minute adjustments, which may go back to the writer himself, or to the mishearings of memorizers, or to misreadings by a copyist or typesetter. Some of these people are shadow-beings identified by their work patterns (Compositor A, B, C. . .), some are named individuals, like the high-quality scribe Ralph Crane, or the error-prone apprentice John Leason, who was allowed to work on the First Folio, with predictable results.[15]

These multiple uncertainties have given rise to endless arguments over which is the best complete text, or, if conflation is the chosen approach, which bits of which texts might best be pieced together. (Conflation is no longer thought respectable by editors, though still not uncommon in performances). There were "good" and "bad" quartos, of more or less reliable provenance. One of them has this variant of Hamlet's most celebrated soliloquy: "To be or not to be, I [=Ay], there's the point. /To die, to sleepe, is that all? I all: / No, to sleepe, to dream, I mar[r]y there it goes . . ."; after which several familiar lines are missing entirely.[16] Even if we allow for the phenomenon of potential growth-points, that sounds more like somebody else's half-remembered gist of Hamlet's speech than a first formulation from Shakespeare's own hand.

This is not even to mention debates about the actual authorship of individual passages, scenes, and sections. Because it was a common practice of the day for dramatists to collaborate, it was easy to claim that a less than perfect passage could surely not be by Shakespeare but must have been written or revised by someone else. Imperfection could not be his. But precisely that is what the offending examples would call in question—realistically enough, since Shakespeare, like Homer in Horace's phrase, may sometimes have nodded. So the subjective cherry-picking of individual passages was a circular argument, based on the same misplaced perfectionism/apologism as happened with Homer. Co-authorship remains, though, a documented widespread practice of the time. Recent scholarship has aimed at a more objective distinction between authors through minute stylometric comparisons and attributions to specific known collaborators of Shakespeare's.[17]

An embarrassment of riches remains to be pondered over. Even the variant punctuation in two printings of Hamlet's reflections on "What a piece of work is man," in one the phrases divided by exclamation marks (F 1), in the other by commas (Q), conjures up two different Hamlets, one declamatory, the other brooding.[18] The armchair reader of the variants can experience, as it were, two different actors' interpretations; a synoptic effect.

All that, again, is not even to mention the yet more radical claims that the whole corpus of the plays was the work of someone else altogether, any one of variously preferred candidates who had wider and higher worldly experience than the mere country-boy and actor Shakespeare; for works must—so the argument common to all of them runs—be rooted in biographical reality.[19] But had Sophocles before creating *Oedipus* murdered his father and married his mother? The empathetic power of a unique imagination to "body forth the form of things unknown" is not dreamt of in the anti-Stratfordians' philosophy.

Ready-Mades from History

Among all these genetic imponderables, there is little chance of catching Shakespeare in the act of devising a dramatic action. The less so since it is something he scarcely ever did for himself, famously preferring to borrow the material and title of someone else's earlier effort—an anonymously published *King Leir* drama,[20] or Bandello's *Romeo and Juliet* novella[21] (plus three other works of Bandello's from which Shakespeare made comedies). Perhaps the dependence on ready-made material was a case of needs must when a new stage piece was urgently called for. Or perhaps other writers' work sparked a deeper affinity and inspiration, offering growth-points on a scale that could transform a whole dramatic entity; for Shakespeare's creative act lay in giving alien matter a new soul—a new depth to the characters' psychology, a new pith and poetry to their speech.

This outward dependence on old models is true of Shakespeare's whole oeuvre, but the need for material that would appeal to the theater-going public must have been most pressing in his beginnings. That was one reason to turn to history, a ready-made story if ever there was one, ready-made too in that the existing chronicles—of Holinshed, Hall, More—already had occasional elements of dramatic shaping.

But where would the appeal of history lie? To begin with, it was "a common entertainment."[22] In its most primitive form it offered plain information, tinged perhaps with national narcissism, but aimed obviously at an audience that was happy to take its facts raw—what the poet Samuel Daniel called "the bare *Was*" of the past,[23] far from being refined into history-as-interpretation. An extreme case is quoted by Tillyard from another writer's *Richard III*, published in 1594. It ends with a survey of later reigns, starting with Henry VIII and coming down to the Elizabethan present, though leaving out the sectarian conflicts and persecutions that successive reigns over that time-span had witnessed: "When he had reign'd full thirty-eight years, / Nine months and some odd days and was buried in Windsor, / He died and left three famous sprigs behind him. / Edwd the Sixt: / He did restore the gospel to his light / And finish'd that his father left undone; / A wise young prince giv'n greatly to his book. / He brought the English service first in use / And died when he had reign'd six years, five months / And some odd days and lieth buried in Westminster. / Next after him a Mary did succeed, / Which married Philip King of Spain. / She reign'd five years four months and some / Odd days and is buried in Westminster. / When she was dead, her sister did succeed." "Minutely informative" indeed![24]

Shakespeare can sound little better than this when dry information has to be communicated, as when a claimant to the throne spells out (his version of) the genealogical facts. Richard Duke of York, challenged to make the case why the barons should support his claim, answers

> Then thus:
> Edward the Third, my lords, had seven sons:
> The first, Edward the Black Prince, Prince of Wales,
> The second, William of Hatfield and the third,
> Lionel, Duke of Clarence; next to whom
> Was John of Gaunt, the Duke of Lancaster;
> The fifth was Edmund Langley, Duke of York;
> The sixth was Thomas of Woodstock, Duke of Gloucester;
> William of Windsor was the seventh and last.
> Edward the Black Prince died before his father,
> And left behind him Richard, his only son,
> Who after Edward the Third's death reigned as king,
> Till Henry Bolingbroke, Duke of Lancaster,

> The eldest son and heir of John of Gaunt,
> Crowned by the name of Henry the Fourth,
> Seized on the realm, deposed the rightful king,
> Sent his poor queen to France, from whence she came,
> And him to Pomfret; where, as all you know,
> Harmless Richard was murdered traitorously.[25]

With interjections from Salisbury and Warwick, York runs on for another eighteen lines of dynastic detail. After all of which, Warwick's response is unintentionally comic: "What plain proceeding is more plain than this?" As the Arden editor says, "almost a music-hall riposte."[26]

It isn't just that the dialogue in this passage is as wooden as that of the chronicle play. Even as an intended help in untangling the rights and wrongs of contested legitimacy, which is the ultimate issue throughout the Histories, it's a lot for readers to get their head round, and harder still for an audience to take in live in the theater. That is a measure of the resistance that has to be overcome if the stuff of history is to be turned into drama.

Did verse help? Did it have enough audience appeal to make it worth marshalling dry matter into meter? Or was it by now simply taken for granted as a convention established by Shakespeare's predecessors, by the old verse-drama *Gorboduc* and more powerfully by his short-lived contemporary rival, Christopher Marlowe? Marlowe's handful of dramas showed the convention of verse not just working but possessed of a potential to generate mouth- and mind-filling magnificence of language. It took an especial stylistic flair if the subject matter of history, inherently wooden and factual and acted out by personages more prosaic than poetic, was to raise the verbal temperature. There would always be an ironic gap between high style and brute fact—brutal in the most literal sense; figures who address each other, as was the upper-crust custom, as "gentle So-and-so" mostly have blood on their hands or in their minds. Even the murdered York, who has given as good, or as bad, as he got, is celebrated by one of his sons as "the flower of Europe for his chivalry."[27] Perhaps they saw no contradiction, "gentle" had become a cliché attribute of rank.

It is a further irony that a middle-class writer was here doing these noblemen proud, clothing their power-lust and hatreds in pentameter and metaphor; the grandeur was not inherent in their characters or actions. Fine language is not common in power politicians, who live by cliché. The point is made by an exception, Elizabeth I, who "always spoke well and, as her most famous speeches prove, could on occasion use the language of Shakespeare with an eloquence that her predecessors emulate only in his pages."[28] Her speeches in the face of the threatened Spanish invasion in 1588, like Winston Churchill's in 1940, still have the power to move.

Takes All Sorts...

Even the euphemisms of a set poetic form could not disguise the underlying grim realities of historical events. It left untouched the violence of conflicts fought out on stage, unlike the practice of classical drama from the Ancient Greeks to Racine, where dreadful acts are only reported, by watchmen on the walls (teichoscopy) or by messengers. Was the taste for violence a psychological release after the restrictions of the medieval miracle and morality plays, from which the Elizabethan stage was ultimately descended? Shakespeare's early *Titus Andronicus*, with fourteen deaths, a woman's hands chopped off and her tongue torn out, another woman's sons beheaded and served up to her in a pie—atrocities only in part taken over from Philomela's story in Ovid's *Metamorphoses*—tops the league. As one of Shakespeare's great successes, it was extreme, but not unique. In the later parts of *Henry VI*, the Wars of the Roses characters constantly slang and slaughter each other. It is a hard-nosed message about politics and civil strife, less remote from people's recent memories than the *Iliad*'s slaughter probably was from its hearers; but it is also a violence deliberately foregrounded to be savored by spectators whose other entertainments were bull- and bear-baitings, cockfights, and public executions. Courting their custom meant creation was also collusion.[29] It made history a "common entertainment" in the fullest sense. Is the taste for blood perhaps being sent up in Peter Quince's gross alliterations as Prologue to "Pyramus and Thisbe": "With bloody, blameful blade / He bravely broached his boiling bloody breast."[30]

Marlowe's *Tamburlaine* already catered for that taste. The play's content, history shading over into myth, is the notorious tyrant's boasts and threats, ruthlessly carried out. He enslaves conquered rulers, conducts mass slaughter, burns one town because his consort died there, drowns the population of another town, man, woman, and child: all violence for its own sake. The perverse appetite is brought out by way of a gruesome vignette—

> That I may view these milk-white steeds of mine,
> All loden with the heads of killed men,
> And from their knees, even to their hoofes below,
> Besmer'd with blood

—that ends with a light aesthetic relish: "that makes a dainty show."[31]

At that, a first installment was so popular that the public called for a second, which continues in much the same vein, albeit ending with Tamburlaine's death, when disease proves he isn't superhuman and fortune's wheel is not ultimately in his hands. Until then his self-glorification as "my mightinesse," as "the scourge of God and terror of the world" (1,

86, and 196), generates its own rhetoric, adding verbal excitation to gore and destruction. Though just for a change, when he is courting the captured princess Zenocrate, the grandeur of his promises has something of Enobarbus's description of Cleopatra in her regal barge:

> A hundred Tartars shall attend on thee,
> Mounted on Steeds, swifter than Pegasus.
> Thy garments shall be made of Medea silke,
> Enchast with precious juelles of mine own:
> More rich and valorous than *Zenocrates*.
> With milke-white Hartes upon an Ivorie sled,
> Thou shalt be drawn amidst the frosen Pooles,
> And scale the ysie mountains lofty tops:
> Which with thy beautie will be soone resolv'd.

But the play's subject didn't offer room for very much in that vein.

Could some part of the public have enjoyed such peaks of style separate from the substance? Were there in fact two publics, looking for different things, the "wiser" from their place in the Globe's gallery seats, the groundlings jostling down below? For these customers there was incidentally some foolery, another obligatory crowd-pleaser. Marlowe's printer cut such stuff as "unmeet" for "so stately a historie," and Marlowe in his prologue turned his back on "clownage" in order to "leade you to the stately tent of War."[32]

From Pope and Johnson down to our day it has been argued that Shakespeare was indeed aiming at two distinct audiences, trying to both make money from the mob and create something subtler for the discerning, who included lawyers at the Inns of Court and, increasingly through his career as his company became the King's Men, the Court itself. For his more basic subsistence, he needed "to hit the taste and humour that prevailed";[33] hence his plots "are crowded with incidents by which the attention of a rude people was more easily caught than by sentiment or argumentation."[34] It is readily conceivable that Shakespeare was "frustrated by the limits this imposed on what he could write" and on his "desire to experiment [. . .] with increasingly complicated social, historical and political issues."[35] For this carried the risk that he might, in both senses of the word, lose his audience. The higher elements would have to somehow be entwined with the violent action, for those with ears to hear.

Beyond the problems of communicating plot details, what kind of poetry could the makers of history be made to speak? That Shakespeare could already write fine dramatic verse is proved by another early work, *Romeo and Juliet*. That too, incidentally, is about historic conflict, a small-scale civil war:

> Two households [. . .]
> From ancient grudge break to new mutiny,
> Where civil blood makes civil hands unclean.[36]

But this fundamental tragic cause is overlaid by its consequences for the "star-cross'd lovers." The knot of poignant if-onlys, of fatal misunderstandings and mistimings, is home territory for a poetry that needs to rise to the lyrical. The familiar text hardly needs quoting.

It was a different matter to devise speech for the starkly unlyrical agents of real history. In the *Henry VI* trilogy, oaths are taken and broken, allegiances pledged and switched, enmities reconciled and renewed; there are disputes and taunts, betrayals and murder, atrocities and revenge; today's victor becomes tomorrow's victim, internecine dissent on every hand ruins the realm, with "virtue chok'd by foul ambition"[37]—all making a plain linear action as monotonous as the monomania with which rivals struggle for the crown. Paradoxically, the flow of history scarcely inspired poetic flow; hard fact and hard characters were stubbornly inert material. Here if anywhere the necessary fallback was, for once, the kind of conscious Art Ben Jonson preached.

For this there were means to hand. A major element in the curriculum at Shakespeare's grammar school, not for nothing so called, was rhetoric. The tropes and techniques taught at the time are traceable down to the detail of the grammar-books and readers that beginners will have used.[38] And where is rhetoric in place if not in the mouths of politicians? It can spin out little to make much, by way of anaphora and other forms of repetition. It does this most obviously when Henry, perched on a molehill well away from battle (from which he has been banned lest his feebleness harm his cause) longs for the simple life of a shepherd and imagines watching

> the minutes how they run:
> How many makes the hour full complete,
> How many hours brings about the day,
> How many days will finish up the year,
> How many years a mortal man may live.
> When this is known, then to divide the times:
> So many hours must I tend my flock,
> So many hours must I take my rest,
> So many hours must I contemplate,
> So many hours must I sport myself,
> So many days my ewes have been with young,
> So many weeks ere the poor fools will ean,
> So many years ere I shall sheer the fleece.

All of which would finally "bring white hairs unto a quiet grave."[39] Besides that multiple anaphora, surely the longest on textual record, there is a good deal of dramatically superfluous speech. The elder and younger Talbot debate at great length whether the son should abandon the stricken field or stay and die along with his father.[40] Murders and acts of revenge are given elaborate preludes, of intention, defiance, or appeal for mercy, before the deed is done. Richard Duke of York, perched on another molehill to be mocked before being killed, a pleasure that Henry's Queen Margaret can vocally take her time over, is still allowed his own lengthy speech.[41] Exchanges in subsidiary scenes sometimes feel like padding: wordy resolves to join battle at once, or to ride urgently to London.[42] And on occasion there is time, even in the press of action, to construct poetic effect by means of an epic simile, as when Queen Margaret translates a moment of crisis into thirty-five lines of nautical imagery—mast overboard, anchor, sailors, and tackle lost, but pilot still at the helm. . .[43] or when she takes time to poeticize the foes who are even now hot on her heels, in the image of hounds chasing a hare.[44] When simple situations or motivations have to be dramatized, irrelevance and "the obviousness of elaboration"[45] threaten.

But without any decoration at all, the central conflict can leave plain sequences of verbal violence, name-calling, claim and counter-claim: "I am thy sovereign." / "I am thine."[46] Once again the humbler music hall or pantomime is not far away: "Oh yes I am." / "Oh no you're not."

Some characters remain striking, as actors in past events that have shaped the audience's present. The public of the day reportedly acclaimed the portrayal in Part One of the soldier-hero Talbot, who died fighting for England's French possessions when left in the lurch by quarreling nobles; in Part Two, Humphrey of Gloucester stands almost alone as a man devoted to the common weal, and is murdered for it; in Part Three, Jack Cade leads a people's uprising, complete with his own cod genealogy parodying those of the great; Henry's fierce, unloving Queen Margaret is present in all three parts of *Henry VI*, binding them together, as does the presence of Henry himself, rendered helpless in the political snake pit by his piety and unregal weakness; and at the close of Part Three, Richard of Gloucester already stands out, offering a preview of the murders that his bid for the throne will require in the play that concludes the first history cycle, *Richard III*.

"Once more unto the breach. . ."

Violence was not yet tragedy, and what Shakespeare had so far shown was history as, in Gibbon's famous definition, "little more than the register of the crimes, follies, and misfortunes of mankind,"[47] this time as committed or undergone by the one nation. In a crude way it was more epic than dramatic, and has sometimes been glorified with the title of a national epic. In these four early dramas, Shakespeare met the challenge of staging history and peopling it, though hardly yet giving it shape or asking whether it had any meaning. The occasional suggestion of coherence is merely conventional. When Queen Margaret warns the French king, "Yet heavens are just, and Time suppresseth wrongs,"[48] it is wishful thinking, nowhere borne out by what follows. There is never any trace of a deus ex machina.

It is true there is an overall moral judgment, as simple as the brutal action itself, namely that the high-ups almost to a man (and woman) are in it for themselves, their last thought the well-being of the realm, the upshot of their ambitions prolonged civil war. Rank, wealth, and power merely create the appetite for more. Only Henry stands in a sense outside events, though too weak to rise above them. His Christian principles (notably not shared by any of Shakespeare's churchmen) can't compete with the Realpolitik of the rest.

Further down in society there are other contrast figures of moderation, people contented with their lot. The Kentish sheriff Alexander Iden (who, allegorically enough, kills the rebel Jack Cade) rejects the "turmoil'd court": "This small inheritance my father left me / Contenteth me, and worth a monarchy."[49] And long before the conflict has broken out into civil war, a skeptical Mayor of London exclaims, "Good God, these nobles should such stomachs bear! / I myself fight not once in forty year."[50] Even the arch-intriguer Warwick asks at the end if it was worth the loss of everything he once enjoyed, so that now "Is nothing left me but my body's length."[51]

The message is ultimately subversive, discrediting the ruling classes as unfit to govern (a common perception down to our day). That is why history plays—and plain histories too—were always suspect to the authorities, often censored and on the verge of being banned. Players and authors were interrogated when their productions seemed to hint at a similar story playing out in the present, most acutely the Essex rebellion against Elizabeth. She herself, never secure on the throne in the political and religious turmoil of the times, famously saw the deposition acted out in *Richard II* as an ominous parallel—"I am Richard, know ye not that?" The play was not allowed to be put on again in her lifetime. Sir Thomas More hit off the relation of fact to fiction with a neat reversal: "King's games [were] as it were stage plays in which poor men were but lookers-on."[52] They will have looked on with the shrewd and skeptical eye of the common people.

What Shakespeare's first history cycle almost wholly lacks is the inner world of thought and feeling. Queen Margaret's love affair with Suffolk is a very minor strand. Any kind of extended reflection is rare. Only when we get to the future Richard III, late in *Henry VI* Part Three and on into the play that bears his name, does a kind of inwardness unfold. In Richard it is still the same single-minded lust for power, but newly and intensely self-aware and self-expressive. His frequent asides probe and reveal his mind, and since an aside is a small soliloquy, they open up the route to an admittedly still distant Hamlet. As yet the content is only a villain's conscious villainy, with no complications of doubt or self-questioning, at least not until the eve of the battle of Bosworth, when the ghosts of his victims appear. There in any case this first cycle ends, cutting off further development. Victorious Richmond is poised to reconcile the warring Roses, reign as Henry VII, and start the Tudor dynasty that will lead down to Shakespeare's Elizabethan present.

But could things be that simple? Get rid of the "bloody dog" Richard and all will be well? Henry VII gets a fairly good press from historians, though not without reservations.[53] Despite the apparent happy ending, something drew Shakespeare on, or rather chronologically back. Having come as close to his own time as he perhaps dared—not till the end of his career will there be a (somewhat pussy-footing) *Henry VIII*, with no reference to religious conflict—there was nowhere to go but the deeper past. Where did Henry VI's travails originate? Was there more complexity to history?

There was certainly more complexity to politics. Paradoxically, politics in any substantive sense is something else the first cycle lacks. True, there was the ruthless pursuit of power, but no goal beyond attaining and enjoying it; there was ambition to be king, but no conception of kingship, no aura to the crown; there was desire to rule, but no sense of what that might involve—leadership, direction, policy, a philosophy of government. What was different about the earlier decades?

The first play of the new cycle, *Richard II*, was already at least in gestation with *Richard III* barely dry on the page.[54] (Was it perhaps the identical name that helped direct Shakespeare's interest?) The new drama begins with more of the same: a conflict over succession. This Richard is not a villain like his later namesake, but still no "good" king: he is wasteful, self-indulgent, exploitative, surrounded by sycophants, immune to moderate advice. He is deposed, forced to abdicate, a process less immediately violent than those in the first cycle, although he is later murdered to fully secure Bolingbroke's succession as Henry IV. So, not yet much change. Subtlety begins in the portrayal of a fallen ruler and a broken man. What is left when Richard has lost his hallowed rank? Brooding soliloquys now burgeon, Richard's readiness to abdicate in recognition of his past failings is mixed with his stubborn attachment to auratic status. The absolutist idea of Divine Right and the mystical notion of the King's Two Bodies[55] die hard in him. Is being the Lord's Anointed an indefeasible state? Political theory has always jibbed at justifying rebellion, on the grounds that even tyranny is preferable to the instability that is likely to follow its overthrow. But is a king's claim to reverence unaffected by his misrule? Richard goes on asserting his regal essence almost to his nadir. Much has been made of Richard as a tragic figure, yet his past record means the effect is no more than pathos. He is a character hard to empathize with. That isn't to gainsay the peculiar poetry generated by humiliation. But losing kingdom and kingship only becomes fully tragic in Lear.

Do Richard's victors take seriously the idea that supplanting a king was sacrilege? It comes back to haunt Henry IV, spawning rebellion in others and a lingering guilt in himself, although the reason why "uneasy lies the head that wears the crown" is more obviously the straightforward fear of being unseated. Whether or not Shakespeare believed in the sin of usurpation, and in the connection between this crime and its punishment (known since Tillyard as the Tudor myth), his characters sometimes do. Even Henry V, the innocent next generation, still on the eve of Agincourt implores divine pardon for his father's act. His final pious thanks for the seemingly miraculous victory and the Te Deum he orders, suitably long-drawn-out in Kenneth Branagh's film version, are a sigh of relief that no penalty has been divinely exacted in the form of defeat in a crucial battle.[56] History, it appears, was perhaps after all more a matter of hard political and military fact than of nemesis and eschatology. In the unsurprisingly grim term of a Polish critic it was all just a Grand Mechanism.[57] As cynical realism says, nothing succeeds like success—in the contemporary epigram of Sir John Harington "Treason doth never prosper: what's the reason? / For if it prosper, none dare call it treason."[58] Still, elements of remorse, doubt, and uncertainty give the characters a new depth.

As do the clash of temperaments and the conflicting strategies among rebels in a common cause, impulsive Hotspur, misty-mystical Glendower, cold, calculating Worcester. Their shift from one-time supporters who helped put Bolingbroke on the throne to disillusioned nobles who now resent his ingratitude and fear becoming his victims, who now idealize "that sweet lovely rose" Richard II and justify their present rebellion as moral restitution for their past acts[59]—these swings are plausible politics beyond anything in the first cycle. So is Worcester's dishonesty in withholding the king's conciliatory offer because it might undo his side's motivation to fight. So too is Northumberland's failure, after much high rhetoric, to put his sword where his mouth is. But there is also now room for a little generosity, for touches of humanity such as were wholly missing from the first cycle: Vernon's two descriptions of Hal to Hotspur, Hal's epitaph on the Hotspur he has just killed, and his releasing of the captured Douglas unransomed.[60]

A different kind of humanity is added in the East Cheap scenes, which are commonly said to show the broader social picture. So very broad it is not. There has been excessive enthusiasm for this half (it is fully half) of *Henry IV* Part One. It isn't clear that what we are seeing is what Edward

Thomas called "the vital commoners,"[61] since the dominant figures are a knight, of sorts,[62] and a wayward Prince of Wales. Nor is it clear that the lengthy passage at 2, iv is "the finest tavern scene ever written,"[63] as if tavern scenes were a rich genre, and as if this one's period repartee were even halfway comprehensible to a modern audience or a reader without footnotes. Its popularity hangs on fat Falstaff. The two parts of *Henry IV* are sometimes even referred to as the Falstaff comedies.[64] From early in the play's stage history, Falstaff has been a cult figure, with suggestions that he may even have been one reason Shakespeare wrote a Part Two at all, though the greater likelihood is that the political material outgrew the bounds of a single play, a natural occurrence in large-scale genesis.[65] Falstaff's yet further appearance in *The Merry Wives of Windsor* is rumored to have been at Queen Elizabeth's command—if true, an ironic meeting of extremes, since Falstaff's appeal must originally have been to the groundlings' crude taste. (This last adventure of his, attempts at seduction by a man plainly past it, does nothing for his human standing or interest.) His inflated status ever since surely has to do with the wish of the refined to show they can be as broad-minded and earthy as anyone.

Falstaff isn't just earthy, and certainly not just a jolly fat man, Father Christmas in period costume. He is neither noticeably "witty in [him]self," as he claims, nor "the cause that wit is in other men."[66] His plan to make comic capital out of decent Justice Shallow's Gloucestershire country household—which really does provide a heart-warming broader social picture—so as to "keep Prince Harry in continual laughter the wearing out of six fashions," suggests he is a first-class bore. Worse is his callousness. The poor men he recruits to fight at Shrewsbury are for him just "food for powder. They'll fill a pit as well as better. Tush, man, mortal men, mortal men"; and after the battle when "there's not three of my hundred and fifty left alive," he writes off these remnants in full knowledge of their miserable future—they "are for the town's end to beg during life." This from a man who certainly will not have risked his own life leading them, before he took the chance to stab dead Hotspur and ludicrously claim to have vanquished him, and who thinks he can secure an easy future for himself by "leering" up at old-pal-Hal as he rides by to his coronation.[67] The one word, leering, expresses all that is wrong with Falstaff's expectations and the dis-order Hal now rejects.

This much lest we idealize Falstaff, deplore his due rejection by Henry V, or sentimentalize his death. That he is somehow the salt of the earth needs to be taken with a pinch of same. But liking him or not isn't the point. Take him for what he is, a convincing bit of social reality, and he is then part of the whole human picture, what the young Goethe, overwhelmed by his first reading of Shakespeare, experienced as Nature absolute and immediate: "And I cry: Nature! Nature! Nothing so Nature as Shakespeare's characters."[68] Goethe's enthusiasm for Shakespeare helped inspire one of his early break-through works, the historical drama *Götz von Berlichingen*, which started an Anglo-German chain-reaction: a translation of *Götz* was Walter Scott's first published work and set the seed for his historical novels. And since *Götz* also began a native German tradition of open form, free of the (long misunderstood) unities to move through time and space, Shakespeare became, in another large-scale genesis via Goethe, Lenz, and Büchner, the ultimate ancestor of Bertolt Brecht's epic theater.

Goethe names no names in his rhapsodic Shakespeare speech, but it is clear the histories are very much in his mind, and much later he singles out *Henry IV*: "If everything of this kind that was ever written were lost, one could completely reconstitute poetry and rhetoric from it."[69] Quite how isn't clear, and for a moment it seems possible Goethe could have meant *Henry V*, for its Prologue is indeed a concentrated poetics, encompassing both the poet's inspired invention and the appeal to the audience to respond with our "imaginary forces." Still, the two parts of *Henry IV* do perhaps between them have substance enough to serve Goethe's purpose, not least through the eloquent and highly flexible verse of which Shakespeare was by this second cycle a master.[70]

Versatility

Shakespeare's verse form is the iambic pentameter— x / | x / | x / | x / | x / | (x). Well, yes. But the line is a loose container for real speech, which must already have made it palatable even to cruder audiences. The irregularities that abound have unnecessarily worried editors down to today. Alexander Pope's own meticulous metrical practice led him to add a syllable here and there to mend Shakespeare's. Recent scholars have gone on agonizing over "deficient" lines, sometimes bizarrely suggesting that a gap be filled by forcing two syllables to sound as three— "portly" by heavily rolling the "r," "Douglas" by heaven knows what means, and at the extreme "Henry" as "Henery," which takes us back again to music hall.[71] In reality, good verse moves within its set matrix with flexible stress in obedience to rhythmic impulse and semantic sense. True, absolute regularity can be impressive, even awesome. Racine's relentless majestic alexandrines have an almost hypnotic effect, drawing us ever deeper into the narrow obsessions of a tight circle of agents and a tense action. But that was designed for a refined Parisian taste. Shakespeare's verse, like his plots, moves freely and opens out into wider-ranging action and expansive metaphor.

Above all, his verse allows shifts that match the speaker's thought and feeling to the particular situation. Often it must have been left to the actor to shape the line, once again a case of theater before literature. Some irregularities dictate a specific spoken stress to mark a highpoint of feeling, as when the king ruefully contemplates Hotspur's bright fame, while "riot and dishonour stain the brow / Of my young Harry. O, that it could be proved / That some night-tripping fairy had exchanged / In cradle clothes our children where they lay."[72] The inserted "O" creates a dactyl (/ x x) to make the wishful point. Later, when Hal is praising his brother John's fighting prowess—

    / / / x   /   x x x /
"O this boy lends mettle to us all!"[73]—

the same exclamatory "O" stands in for a whole two-syllable foot before the iambs start—or alternatively it starts a sequence of four trochees, or even two spondees (/ /, a real rarity in English verse). Similarly, a seeming four-foot line of John of Gaunt's puts double weight on each of the first two words, creating a single spondee in place of two iambic feet, to make up full measure and convey Gaunt's intended emphasis:

    / / x / x / x /
"Think not the king did banish thee"[74]

Technically, it is often the dactyl that lets in one of the common sound-patterns of spoken English (it is a mistake to think iambic is our dominant natural rhythm) and enlivens a line, including the most famous line of all,

    x / x / x x / x x   / x
"To be or not to be, that is the question."

It would of course be possible to place the stress on "is," by main force restoring the iambic pattern—once again, the reading is in some measure up to the actor.[75] Not so with another superb dactylic intrusion in *Macbeth*. Not, as might have been, "the all too massive seas incarnadine" but "the *multitudinous* seas incarnadine"—x / x x x x / x / x x[76]— where the rhythmic rise and fall wonderfully renders the swelling weight and breaking of a wave. The pattern of the next line is impressive in a quieter way: a dactyl followed by three stressed syllables "making the green one red"—/ x x / / /[77]

When Shakespeare matches words and world like this he has gone beyond metrics to what one of the rhythmically most sensitive English poets called "the roll, the rise, the carol, the creation."[78] Less grandly, there are instances of informal free stress-distribution, such as Lady Percy's delightful teasing of her husband after his comments on the Welsh lady's singing:

```
  /     /    / x  / x   x   / x x
```
"Then should you be nothing but musical"[79]

—plainly the stress of the sense falls on "you," and arguably on both syllables before it. So, a spondee and a trochee, with two dactyls to follow. Not an iamb in sight! Here as in countless other instances across his whole oeuvre, Shakespeare is not confined to a procrustean meter. And in a darkened theater and the thrill of live performance, who's counting anyway?

Unhappily Ever After?

Are the Histories history? Many readers and spectators confess to getting their knowledge of the Tudor period from Shakespeare's plays. Run through in chronological sequence (of the events, not of the plays' genesis) they can look like a national epic of sorts. That they were not so meant seems clear precisely from the reverse order of their composition. Nor were they ever staged as a sequence in Shakespeare's lifetime, or indeed for long after, until Franz von Dingelstedt put them on in Weimar in 1864.

The author of the Histories was certainly not a historian. No doubt he knew the chronicles—Holinshed, Hall, More—but even here dependence is rarely demonstrable in detail and is sometimes left far behind.[80] The closest verbal dependence on a source, this from Roman history, is in *Antony and Cleopatra*, 2, ii, 198, the account of Cleopatra's barge in its progress down the Nile. Even here dependence is only a starting-point. Colorful touches transform Plutarch's already evocative prose into the magical poetry of Enobarbus's erotically suggestive soldier's tale. The queen's golden barge "burned on the water," the sails were "so perfumèd that / The winds were lovesick with them," the silver oars "made / The water which they beat to follow faster, / As amorous of their strokes"; and more besides.[81]

As a technique, facts found in the putative sources get compressed (distant events are brought close together), combined (two rebellions become one, as do two popular uprisings), persons are radically altered (Hal's rival and coeval Hotspur was in reality the same age as Hal's father) or enriched (Hal's deeds are all fiction—at the battle of Shrewsbury he neither rescued the king his father nor killed Hotspur). The dramatist is not a scholar aiming at objective accuracy. If he reads, it is not thoroughly but intensely, he is not the judicious owl but the opportunistic magpie, picking up materials and motifs for their imaginative potential.

Hotspur is by some margin the fullest such enrichment. His way with words is a breath of fresh air (too modestly he disclaims "the gift of tongues"). His headlong arguing when he will not stop to listen to his elders, comical but convincing, is of a piece with his urge for immediate attack, which, given the uncertainties of all military action and the vital role of morale and surprise, might well have had better success than the circumspect tactics which then fail. ("De l'audace, encore de l'audace, toujours de l'audace," as Georges Danton said.) Hotspur is all spontaneity and integrity, engagingly rounded out in the intimate playful dialogue with his wife, which has the poignancy of imminent loss. He is a supreme piece of dramatic imagining.

If the first history cycle was "a lumbering wagon looking for a good road,"[82] the second has found one and is briskly under way, with believable characters on board. Yet for all their difference in quality, the two cycles together make a consistent point. After Henry V's Agincourt triumph, the second cycle ends with a gloomy prospect of things to come, events that "lost France and made his England bleed," "which oft our stage hath shown,"[83] that is, in Shakespeare's own first cycle. That admittedly ended with the promise of a new day under Henry VII, but the afterword to *Henry V* suggests all too persuasively that any happy ending is precarious and almost certainly temporary. History *has* no ending. Elizabeth's reign too, despite the later cliché of its glories, was precarious, a highpoint of religious struggles and persecutions, with the throne and the nation constantly under threat from Catholic conspiracy within and Spanish invasion without. Instability seemed imminent as the childless queen aged and the problem of her succession became more pressing. All this was dramatic material indeed! But to have treated it openly would have been too near the knuckle, or indeed the neck.[84] Censorship, in Shakespeare's day by the Master of the Revels, or the threat of repercussions for author and actors, is another factor in genesis: what might otherwise have been written but never was is a defining shadowland. Shakespeare stayed notably clear of the central issue of his time, religious conflict, even in *Henry VIII*, a late work co-authored with John Fletcher, which focuses not on the obvious theme of the king versus Rome but on a truly tragic Catherine of Aragon versus Wolsey. *King John* likewise avoids making anything of the Magna Carta. For the rest, there could at most be veiled parallels with the present in dramas that were set safely in the past.

But avoiding any political message still left the meta-political point sharply clear: the truism that the Grand Mechanism is always at work, Fortune's Wheel always turning, happiness and unhappiness at best alternating. Since that is a constant of human affairs, it may induce no more than a shrug of resignation. At all events, the histories that dominated the first phase of Shakespeare's writing career, grim as their content was, were not yet tragedies of the depth and bleakness he would go on to create. But in these early works he had flexed the muscles of his dramatic imagination and poetic invention, and their success on stage and in print had made him the leading dramatist of his day. He was poised for the greatest literary genesis of them all.

℘ ℘ ℘

Appendix: Dates of Works Published in Shakespeare's Lifetime

1593	*Venus and Adonis*
1594	*The Rape of Lucrece*
	Titus Andronicus
	2 Henry VI[85]
1595	*3 Henry VI*[86]
1597	*Richard III*
	Richard II
	Romeo and Juliet
1598	*Love's Labours Lost*
	1 Henry IV
1600	*2 Henry IV*
	Henry V
	The Merchant of Venice
	A Midsummer Night's Dream
	Much Ado about Nothing
1602	*The Merry Wives of Windsor*
1603	*Hamlet* (flawed edition, replaced 1604/5)
1608	*King Lear*
1609	*Pericles*
	Troilus and Cressida

Transition—Tradition

There is less of a gap than might appear between the two main sections of this book, the wider European and the specifically German. The introductory chapters, besides being large-scale examples of genetic process, are linked in substance with what follows, indeed are in large measure its precondition. Homer, the Bible, and Shakespeare were live forces in the minds of modern European writers, in German no less than in the other vernacular languages. Montaigne too, with his innovative, rich picture of a single private world, surely emboldened later explorers of human character and experience.

From the rediscovery of Antiquity in the Renaissance and onward, Homer was its central literary symbol. Homeric epic was a source of mythical figures and actions and of the very conception of narrative, recognizable even as it mutated in the eighteenth century into the new phenomenon of the novel, which for Hegel was "the modern bourgeois epic" capturing a new prosaic reality[1]*—increased psychological and social complexity in place of violent action and tribal custom. The Bible, for its part, was a treasury of story and myth alternative to the classical heritage and, in its Protestant translations into English and German, a shaping influence on the literary language of those cultures. Bertolt Brecht of all people, the enfant terrible of the 1920s, when asked about the sources of his style, said "You'll laugh: the Bible." Serious-to-solemn German literary occasions fell instinctively into Luther's syntax and rhythms, as English ones did into the structures and rhythms of the Authorized Version; their presences are subliminally felt, and no less powerful for that. Shakespeare reigned over literature at large as an object of reverence and a challenge to creative emulation. Goethe's revolutionary first drama Götz von Berlichingen took over Shakespeare's formal freedoms and an immunity to the constricting classical "unities." Büchner's and Brecht's plays moved in the same broad stream. Poets down to Paul Celan tempered their style on translations of Shakespeare's sonnets. "Shakespeare without end," the motto Goethe set over his working life, helped to shape the German national literature of the later eighteenth and the nineteenth century. Shakespeare's plays became virtually part of it, in repeated waves of translation, especially the masterly interpretative versions of August Wilhelm Schlegel and Ludwig Tieck. The Shakespearean pentameter line was the accepted stage language from the mid-eighteenth to the late nineteenth century. German literature was not shut in on itself. A rich tradition was alive within which the writers now to be treated were working.*

Part III
Goethe

5: Cross-Purposes: Goethe's *Faust*

No work by a single author ever had so long a genesis as Goethe's *Faust*: over thirty years from the young poet's first drafts at some point in the early 1770s down to the publication of the completed Part One in 1808, then a further quarter-century until the last of twelve thousand lines were written in 1832, just in time before the poet died.[1] Over that sixty-year time-span, organic change and external chance were enough by themselves to undermine any consistent conception and final unity. But from the very start the writer was at cross-purposes with his chosen subject; and when a second story-line forced its way into the plot, the two strands were at cross-purposes with each other. This never-resolved dual disharmony complicated the genesis and shaped the text right to the end.

A Problem Subject

Why should the rising star of German literature in the 1770s have chosen to revive the old Faust story at all? Goethe's early successes were firmly contemporary and he was firmly secular. The Shakespeare-style history play *Götz von Berlichingen* fed a growing present interest in the German past and had a message for the political present. The novel of unhappy love and suicide, *The Sorrows of Young Werther*, captured the younger generation's emotional and social unease and became a European sensation. Goethe was also writing poems, as yet unknown to a wider public,[2] celebrating earthly existence with an intensity never before achieved in the German language and never surpassed since. In contrast, Faust belongs to an already fading scene of fears and fables, where the destiny of a sinning soul is played out between heaven and hell, with damnation his inevitable end. This deeply Christian moral tale was narrated in Spiess's chapbook of 1587 and dramatized in the same spirit in 1590 by Christopher Marlowe as *The Tragical History of Doctor Faustus*.

But by the late eighteenth century, Germany as one center of the European Enlightenment was slipping the bonds of Christianity and the constricting view of the world it imposed, Goethe as much as anyone. Brought up in a household no more than conventionally Christian, he was a born free spirit with an impulse to see and think for himself, central principles of the Enlightenment in whose atmosphere he grew up. His thinking was very much of this world. As a boy he already had the heretical idea of "directly approaching the great god of nature whose wrathful utterances were long forgotten in the face of the beauty of the world and the manifold good things that we enjoy in it." It was impossible to give god a shape, rightly so, for there could be "no finer worship than the kind that needs no image but arises out of our inner dialogue with nature."[3] He responded with relish to what he called "the free world," "the open world"[4]—plainly epithets transferred from his own feeling of liberation. The exhilaration of his individual existence made it "the highest bliss to dwell in oneself." He set that happy condition against the pathological lack of independent feeling of his Christian friend Johann Caspar Lavater,[5] and met Lavater's desperate assertion of Christian truths with his own conviction of "the truth of the five senses."[6] This and other letters to Christian friends are striking sketches of a spiritual and intellectual independence.

Goethe did pass through a brief Pietist phase in 1768, when he returned in a state of near collapse from university in Leipzig. But it was clear, to members of his sect and to himself, that despite honest efforts he was not cut out to be passively pious. In their view he was too "flighty through attachment to the world" for any earnest commitment. He had a different faith, in his own personal future as a writer, and he knew this ambition was the main obstacle to seeking grace.[7] The oxymoron: flighty—attachment, states a necessary conflict. For a poet, attachment to the world goes with the job, allowing no competing interest in the constructs of transcendent belief.

The young poet tries on myths to fit this identity. His Prometheus reproaches Zeus for not providing help or consolation (never things that the Greeks expected of the father of the gods, more like what Christians expected of theirs) and is defiantly self-sufficient: "Musst mir meine Erde / noch lassen stehn, / Und meine Hütte, / Die du nicht gebaut, / Und meinen Herd, / Um dessen Glut / Du mich beneidest." (You must leave my earth / Still standing / And my hut / That you did not build / And my hearth / For whose glowing heat / You envy me.)

Another mood, another myth: Goethe's Ganymede is all ecstatic response to the world and the power behind it: "Wie im Morgenrot / Du rings mich anglühst, / Frühling, Geliebter!" (How in the red of dawn / All around you glow at me, / Springtime, beloved.) The boy's ecstasy points onwards and upwards to union with a quite differently conceived Zeus, an all-loving father, again more a borrowed Christian than a Greek motif. The two poems look less like a balance or contradiction than successive stages: "Prometheus" clears the ground of a false dependence, "Ganymed" expresses a new spontaneous devotion.

How could Faust, of all figures, fit into this revolutionary vision of the world? It is not as if the Faust story positively enthused Goethe, in the way that discovering the autobiography of the medieval knight Götz von Berlichingen had done, generating his first dramatic success. He had come across Faust as a puppet play and knew the Spiess chapbook. (He didn't get to know Marlowe's drama till almost fifty years later, in 1818.) True, at university once more, this time in Strasbourg, he had the Faustian experience of glimpsing the range of possible knowledge and the impotence of academic method to embrace it, especially the inadequacy of learnèd language to match reality: all natural enough responses in an impatient student at any time. Natural responses too in a career-weary academic such as Faust as Goethe portrays him, fobbed off with empty titles—"Heisse Doktor und Professor gar" (Doctor they call me, and Professor even)[8]—and frustrated by a monotonous and materially unrewarding life. How to break out of a claustrophobic workroom and word-bound learning and penetrate Nature's inmost secrets? This is not the original Faust's crude pursuit of pleasure and power, and there is no suggestion in his opening monologue that he is venturing on ground that religion forbids. In Goethe's semi-enlightened age, the pursuit of understanding—"Dass ich erkenne, was die Welt / Im Innersten zusammenhält" (HA 3:367; That I may know what holds the inmost world together)—could no longer be the sin it had been in days when religion and scripture were the only permissible sources of knowledge and God's grace the necessary precondition for understanding: "dominus illuminatio mea." What Goethe's Faust first manages to call up as he experiments randomly with magic spells—"Ihr schwebt, ihr Geister, neben mir; / Antwortet mir, wenn ihr mich hört!" (428–29; Spirits, I feel you hovering close, / Answer me if you can hear!) is likewise not the devil of the legend, but a mighty Earth Spirit. This is a pure invention of Goethe's that has no place in the Faust legend or its Christian context, and, as it will turn out, a highly problematic place in the further action of the play; but its substance is deeply true to the poet's earth-bound imagination. The Earth Spirit embodies the ebb and flow of nature's fundamental forces. Only when it spurns Faust as a creature too puny to be bothered with—"Du gleichst dem Geist, den du begreifst, / Nicht mir!" (512–13; You match the spirit you can grasp, / Not me!)—is he open to offers from a lesser source. Cue Mephistopheles.

So far this is hardly dependent on the original story, which in a later conversation with Eckermann Goethe would dismiss as "not up to much."[9] At least with the entrance of Faust's traditional antagonist, he seems to be moving into line with the legend. Yet still far from completely. This Mephisto, in any case only a second-best after the wholly unorthodox Earth Spirit, isn't even the expected figure of evil, but a stylish cavalier, a sardonic wit, more worldly-wise than hellishly wicked.[10] Only on occasion does he strike a chilling note, and then apropos the fate not of Faust but of their innocent joint victim Gretchen. Much of the time Mephisto is a comic act, and just as the devil is said to have the best tunes, throughout both parts of the drama he has some of the best lines, starting with the "Prologue in Heaven" where he is an impudent visitor: "Von Zeit zu Zeit seh ich den Alten gern, Und hüte mich, mit ihm zu brechen." (350; I like to see the Old Man now and then, And take good care not to fall out with him.) The Lord tolerates him as a jester who will all unwilling and unwitting contribute to the grand plan, a plan so positive that the Lord himself already predicts that it will end, at the most extreme remove from the legend, with Faust saved.

How can that happy ending be brought about in what still calls itself a Faust drama? The outcome had to hang on some kind of pact—the Faust of legend signs away his soul in return for twenty-four years of power and knowledge. When, at a very late stage in the genesis of *Faust Part One*, Goethe at last sets out the stipulations of a pact, he shies away from anything so straightforward as the old bargain. Mephisto still offers crude services (1656), not realizing that Faust has become a more complex customer. What Faust does now want is a set of bizarre *un*satisfactions that will draw him ever further into the fullness of human experience, to the point of self-destruction. (1676) He wagers that no moment will ever be so beautiful that he could wish it to last, and if ever he did admit that, specifically in the formula "Verweile doch, du bist so schön" (1700; Linger a while, you are so lovely) that would be his end. He would have to serve Mephisto over there in return for services rendered here. He brushes that aside as irrelevant—earthly life is the source of all his pains and pleasures, and he neither knows nor cares what lies beyond (1656). This amputates one limb of the legend's plot, and there is accordingly no mention of Faust's soul. Even Mephisto doesn't use the word until the very end of Part Two. Lines fully drafted for him to speak in the pact scene—"Dein Fleisch und Blut ist wohl schon etwas wert / Allein die Seel ist unsre rechte Speise" (Your flesh and blood are maybe worth a bit, / But it's the soul that we are hungry for)—were not finally included in the text at all.[11]

Child Murder

Complicated enough, and perhaps too complicated for Mephisto, who sometimes even seems to be working against the aim he is meant to be pursuing, as he feeds Faust with banal insignificance—"flache Unbedeutenheit" (1861)—when he should be tempting him with experiences that would provoke the agreed words. But before this intricate pact-cum-wager was ever devised, when the only Faust materials yet written were an opening monologue, the Earth Spirit apparition, and a scene where Mephisto is already there teasing a freshman student, Goethe had already created a complete second strand, barely relevant to the fate of Faust and powerfully diverting attention from him. It can scarcely be called a subplot, since it comes to positively dominate Part One. It is the tragedy of a young woman made pregnant and abandoned by Faust, in which her moving simplicity as a poetic creation upstages both the sophisticated intellectual and the cynical devil. Sex was traditionally on Mephisto's menu, debauchery features in the Spiess chapbook, and Faust's brutal demand when he first sights Gretchen—"Hör, du musst mir die Dirne schaffen!" (2619) and "Ist über vierzehn Jahr doch alt" (2627; Listen, you must get me the girl; She's over fourteen, isn't she?)—briefly descends to that level. But the tone soon changes, and Goethe's most striking departure from the legend turns the side issue of sexual trifling into a harrowing story of seduction and infanticide.

External events were almost certainly the source. As a young lawyer practicing in Frankfurt in the 1770s, Goethe must have known about the case of Susanne Margarete Brandt, who in 1772 was abandoned by her lover, killed their child, and was executed in a dreadful public ritual.[12] It was a local sensation, her prison and the scaffold where she was decapitated were a stone's throw from the Goethe family house, a précis of her trial was in his father's document collection, and he will very likely have heard the current cynical phrase that he puts in the mouth of Mephisto, "Sie ist die erste nicht" (HA 3:137 and 415; She's not the first). Goethe could have made a separate drama of it—the two plots remain essentially distinct and infanticide was a common enough social subject of the day that generated other plays and poems.[13] But an existing work-in-progress offered a ready-made framework for an expressive need. The sequence must surely have been this way round: a Faust drama could just about accommodate a love affair, whereas a newly conceived love affair had no need of a Faust as its romantic lead.

It was a further problem to have an elderly professor in that role, later solved by rejuvenating him in the scene "Hexenküche" (Witch's Kitchen). But he was still a figure of legendary status that went far beyond the bounds of a lowly social drama, while conversely this small-scale yet deeply moving tragic involvement got in the way of the legend's grand themes. The emotional power of both the Brandt case and the Gretchen action it inspired is clear from the fact that Goethe completed this strand of the action straight away—its power made it almost an independent work—leaving the rest of the play hanging unfinished. Such prompt completion was untypical of Goethe's rich but disorderly desk, which was always full of half-finished projects.[14] The lifelong stop-start work on Faust is the greatest example of that disorder; but in the long sedimentary growth of this enormous work, the Gretchen tragedy is a volcanic eruption.

A fast-moving set of brief scenes, contrasting with the extended scenes of the opening Faust sequence, shows: the couple's meeting in a realistic burgher and domestic setting; Faust's courtship, helped by Mephisto's magic; the comedy of the go-between Frau Marthe, who learns her husband has died in foreign parts and promptly tries to catch Mephisto as his successor; Gretchen at the spinning wheel longing for Faust (the text for the most moving of Schubert's songs); Gretchen, pregnant, appealing for help to the Virgin; Gretchen mocked by an evil spirit; her brother Valentin vilifying his fallen sister; Faust's regrets at bringing destruction on Gretchen's orderly world; his tirade against Mephisto for ruining her and concealing her fate from him; his appeals to the infinite spirit he believes sent Mephisto, to turn him back into the dog he first appeared as; Gretchen imprisoned for killing their baby; Faust and Mephisto seen galloping headlong on black horses to rescue her. Demented but clear-sighted, Gretchen refuses to be rescued, throwing herself on the divine mercy; Mephisto cries "Sie ist gerichtet" (She is judged). End.

Even before Faust's rejuvenation, the affair is lyrically persuasive once Faust's lust turns into love. It is certainly love that Gretchen gives back, from an uncorrupted heart and with a physical passion that overrides her conventional upbringing and beliefs. Her spinning-wheel monologue is powerfully physical,[15] and the scene where she questions Faust's lack of Christian faith ends with her accepting a drug to keep her mother from disturbing their night together (a drug that will kill her).[16] With Gretchen there is at last a Christian figure in this profoundly un-Christian version of a Christian story. She instinctively sees through Mephisto's smooth manner to his cold core, she is lovingly worried about Faust's soul, and finally as horrified by her lover as by his dark accomplice. Mephisto's judgment at the end of this 1770s sequence, "She is judged" (ist gerichtet) will be overridden in 1808 by a Voice from Above, "Is saved" (Ist gerettet). Goethe needed this much mitigation of his own poetic power, for he now found the harrowing final scenes he had written in stark prose unbearable, and tried to "veil them in verse."[17] In whatever form, the Gretchen action remains a problem for a Faust play.

Three Stages[18]

Goethe's problems and attempted solutions across three decades to the completion of Part One are embodied in three preserved texts. Assigning every scene a number to trace its shifting locations in successive versions will give some sense—even at a glance, without going into the detail—of Goethe's struggles, and of the way the work took shape.

Some things that are only dramatically realized at a later stage must have already been part of Goethe's conception. Only in the final text (16c) do we see Faust murder Gretchen's brother Valentin (they fight, and Mephisto paralyzes Valentin's sword-arm). But we know from *Urfaust* (17) that Faust has a blood-guilt back in town, and (19) that Valentin is buried beside Gretchen's dead mother and murdered child (see table 5.1).

Table 5.1: Scene-by-scene comparison of Goethe's three versions of *Faust*. Numberings indicate the order in which the scenes were composed.

I. *Urfaust* (1770s)		II. *Faust, a Fragment* (1790)		III. *Faust* Part One (1808)	
1	"Night." *Faust's opening monologue; appearance of the Earth Spirit; Faust's conversation with his assistant Wagner.*	1	Night	23	[NEW] Dedication.
---	[The GREAT GAP ("große Lücke"). *No entrance of Mephisto; no pact.*]	20	[Faust, Mephisto] *lines 249 to 346 become end of pact scene in Part One, lines 1770–1867.*	24	[NEW] Prelude on the stage.
2	Mephisto already there, in dressing-gown: student.	2	Mephisto and Student.	25	[NEW] Prologue in heaven.
3	Auerbach's beer-cellar.	3	Auerbach's beer-cellar.	1	Night. *Much extended, ending with Faust's near-suicide.*
4	Open road. *Mephisto is discomfited by a roadside cross.* [*This scene was never used later.*]	21	[NEW] Witch's kitchen	26	[NEW] Outside the town. *The townspeople emerge, converse gratefully with Faust.*
5	Street. *Faust's meeting with Gretchen.*	4	Open road.	27	[NEW] Faust's study. (i) *Mephisto enters, but escapes again*
6	Evening. A small well-kept room. *Faust contemplates Gretchen's bedroom.*	6	Evening. A small well-kept room.	28	[NEW] Faust's study. (ii) THE PACT (*ending with the lines from 20*)
7	Avenue. *Faust and Mephisto plot the seduction.*	7	Avenue	2	Mephisto with student.

(*continued*)

I. *Urfaust* (1770s)	II. *Faust, a Fragment* (1790)	III. *Faust Part One* (1808)
		3 Auerbach's beer-cellar. (*versified*)
		21 Witch's kitchen.
8 Neighbor's house. ⎫	8 Neighbor's house. ⎫	5 Street.
9 Garden. ⎪	9 Garden. ⎪	6 Evening. A small well-kept room.
10 Summerhouse. ⎬	10 Summerhouse. ⎬	7 Avenue.
The courtship ⎪	*The courtship* ⎪	8 Neighbor's house. ⎫
11 Gretchen's room. ⎪	11 Gretchen's room. ⎪	9 Garden. ⎬
12 Martha's garden. ⎭	12 Martha's garden. ⎭	10 Summerhouse. ⎭
13 At the well. *Gretchen is now pregnant.*	13 At the well.	22 [*Relocated*] "Woodland cave."
14 At a shrine. *She appeals to the Virgin.*	22 [NEW] Woodland cave.	*The now interrupted . . .*
	Composed of Faust's serene monologue	11 Gretchen's room. ⎫
	[NEW] *and the self-reproaches from*	12 Martha's garden. ⎬
	16b [OLD]	*. . . courtship*
15 Cathedral. *An evil spirit mocks her.*	14 At a shrine ⎫	
16 Night, outside Gretchen's house.	15 Cathedral. ⎭	
16a *Valentin's monologue reviling Gretchen.*	*The action ends without the concluding*	
16b *Faust's self-reproaches.*	*scenes from the Urfaust.*	
17 Faust, Mephisto (*untitled*). *Faust vilifies*		
Mephisto.		
18 Night. Open country. *Faust and*		
Mephisto on their way to rescue Gretchen.		

13 At the well.

14 At a shrine.

16 Night. Street in front of Gretchen's house.

16a [OLD] *Valentin's monologue.* [NEW] *Faust kills him.*

15 Cathedral.

29 [NEW] Walpurgis Night

30 [NEW] Walpurgis Night dream.

17 Dull day. In the country

18 Night. Open country.

19 Dungeon. [*versified*]

19 Dungeon. *Mad but clear-sighted, Gretchen refuses rescue.*

The *first stage* is based on a manuscript of work-in-progress that Goethe brought with him to Weimar in the autumn of 1775. In December he read scenes to the court,[19] and Louise von Göchhausen, a cultivated little hunch-backed lady and favorite of Dowager Duchess Anna Amalia, made a copy. It is easy to imagine this live wire of the court circle badgering Goethe for his text. Her transcript was discovered in 1887 by the scholar Erich Schmidt in the Göchhausen family papers and published as "Faust in ursprünglicher Gestalt" (Faust in its original form), known for short as "Urfaust." Both titles are misleading, since the text was never a distinct original version. Still, with minor reservations—the scenes Louise copied may not have been all Goethe read to the court, or all he had—the manuscript does show roughly the form the work had reached by 1775. It embraces early inspirations (Faust's opening monologue and the appearance of the Earth Spirit) and above all it proves the priority Goethe gave to completing the Gretchen tragedy. We can't blame him for the fragmentariness and discontinuities of the *Urfaust*, since it was never for him a discrete text. It is only a distinct stage at all because of Erich Schmidt's discovery, and because for almost fifteen years from 1775 Goethe seems not to have touched the project again.

The *second stage* is a text he did round off, or more precisely break off, and publish in 1790. It adds some new scenes, the "Witch's Kitchen" and the interlude in a "Woodland Cave," but it leaves out the final scenes of the tragedy. This makes the fragment truly fragmentary—apparently, if Faust's story was not to be completed, then nor was Gretchen's. So contemporary readers were left not knowing what happened next. (We have to avoid reading into the Fragment what only later readers of Part One and of the earlier *Urfaust* could know.) Meantime, by cutting the final scenes the Fragment kept the focus marginally more on Faust than on Gretchen. This text went into volume 7 of Goethe's first collected edition, of 1787–90, a project aimed at refreshing his somewhat faded early reputation. (By now, *Götz von Berlichingen* and *The Sufferings of the Young Werther* already lay fifteen years back.) Publication of the Fragment might have drawn a line under the whole project; indeed it was probably meant to do just that. Goethe may have been not just resigned to leaving the work unfinished,[20] but at this stage positively wanting to get a no longer live project off his desk—not least because he was now embracing a new classical aesthetic.

The *third stage* is the final *Faust Part One*. It comes after a significant shift in Goethe's creative career. At 3 a.m. on September 3, 1786, he slipped out of Carlsbad, where the Weimar court was staying ("They wouldn't have let me go otherwise")[21] and set out for Italy, to fulfil a yearning that went back to his childhood and his father's stories of his own Italian journey. He stayed in Italy for nearly two years. Goethe took *Faust* along as part of a larger plan to clear his literary backlog, built up largely through administrative work for the Duchy, and to get enough copy together for that collected edition. But what he wrote in Italy suggests there is now a yet further disharmony between the poet and the subject to add to the original cross-purposes. He felt a closer affinity to two other dramas that went with him. *Iphigenie auf Tauris* was an Ancient Greek subject reworked from Euripides, completed in prose in 1781, but needing to be revised and versified; *Torquato Tasso* was a refined psychological drama set in an Italian Renaissance court. They were to become central pillars of the new classical poetics towards which Goethe had been moving and which his long sojourn in Italy emphatically confirmed: dignified figures, measured action, iambic pentameter blank verse. Nothing could have been further removed from the Gothic gloom and Christian devilry of *Faust*.

So of the two scenes written in Italy, "Witch's Kitchen," composed incongruously enough in the gardens of the Villa Borghese, adds irony to the hocus-pocus that Faust reluctantly has to undergo in order to be rejuvenated. The other, "Woodland Cave," begins in more expressly classical mode, with a serene blank-verse monologue of thanks for the insights into nature that the Earth Spirit has granted him, and a complaint that Mephisto's company was part of the package. Awkwardly for the plot, Faust's gratitude flatly contradicts what the Earth Spirit actually did and said, while the complaint can only be a conjecture of Faust's, perhaps going back to an earlier conception of Goethe's, about what agency sent Mephisto.[22] These inconsistencies will be carried over into Part One.

Why, having published the Fragment in 1790, did Goethe not simply leave it at that? Declaring it a fragment would have made that easy. But it seems the work had a will of its own, for in 1794 Goethe wrote to his new friend Schiller, "I don't dare open the packet that holds Faust imprisoned." Schiller was already pressing him for any further scenes that might exist beyond the published Fragment. Goethe temporized. He couldn't copy out the existing material for Schiller without doing more work on it (this was his creative conscience stirring) and he hadn't the courage for that. Still, "if anything can in future make me feel able to, it is certainly your sympathetic interest."[23]

Three years passed before it did, in which time Goethe was preoccupied with revising and completing the novel *Wilhelm Meister's Apprenticeship*, also with Schiller's help. Paradoxically, Italy, or rather the hindrance to a planned further Italian journey, was co-responsible for his taking up *Faust* again. Napoleon's campaign in the north of the country made travel there unsafe, at least for some while. Goethe needed something he could work on while waiting, "so I've decided to go at my Faust." It would mean "dissolving" what was already written, "disposing the great masses" (that sounds as if a good deal more was indeed in stock) and "preparing the idea." Would Schiller kindly think the thing through in one of his sleepless nights—the friend's insomniac work-routine was well known—and set out the demands he would make of the whole? Schiller was to be Joseph to Goethe-Pharaoh's dream.[24] The die was cast. The central work of German literary culture would eventually come into being, though it took some further prodding from Goethe's publisher Cotta (with whom Schiller intrigued to put on the pressure) and much later from Goethe's amanuensis Eckermann.

In the event Goethe did a great deal more than just tinker with the material in 1797. He became resigned in a new sense, resigned now to completing the work. He added new scenes, some of them vital: Mephisto's arrival on the scene, where his presence in older sections had simply been taken for granted and never explained; and above all a pact. Also a superb scene "Vor dem Tor" (Outside the Town) where the people emerge from the darkness of walls and winter into the springtime countryside and Faust is drawn close to them—"Hier bin ich Mensch, hier darf ich's sein" (940; Here I am human, for once can be).[25] Further, a Walpurgis Night fantasy that gives free rein to yet more Nordic hocus-pocus.

Most significantly, Goethe tries to get a systematic grip on the whole project by standing back and placing it in a framework. Or rather three frameworks. The first is autobiographical. Two days after the last-quoted letter to Schiller, Goethe wrote a dedicatory poem ("Zueignung") that looks back to the unclear visions of his youth. The magical power these have now regained over him is partly nostalgia for past times, old loves and friendships, and partly the long outgrown but now revived longing for their "quiet, solemn spirit realm." His "severe heart" is softened, and what he possesses—his new classical principles—feels for a moment remote, as the realities of a vanished time surge back. It is a moving palinode by the mature poet to his Storm and Stress youth, and a commitment to reliving it. The dedication is not to any other person, not even to those long-lost friends, but of the poet to the work itself.[26]

The second frame is a "Prelude on the Stage" in which Poet, Director, and Jester stand on the boards debating what kind of a show they will put on. It is the old conflict in cultural policy between what the public wants and what the cultivated believe it needs. The figures are representative rather than autobiographical, though their views certainly draw on Goethe's experience of the first two of those roles. The piece doesn't relate very specifically to this play, and was used, and probably first conceived, for other Weimar theatrical occasions.

But with the third frame, the "Prologue in Heaven," we are squarely on to the essentials of a Faust action. What is to be its metaphysical scope and significance? Who can tell us if not the Lord in person, here seen at home on high? After fulsome praise of the creation from the three archangels, and some jaundiced criticism of the whole set-up by Mephisto, who is up here on one of his periodic visits, with its saucy reference to the Old Man, the Lord takes the initiative: "Kennst du den Faust?—Den Doktor?—Meinen Knecht!" (299–300; Do you know that Faust?—The doctor?—Yes, my servant!) So the authorities are aware of Faust, though it isn't clear why the Lord should respond to Mephisto's lament about the hard lot of human beings by singling out this one man. But it does confirm Faust's representative status, as in the legend. To that extent, Goethe has moved back into the penumbra of the original. Heaven or hell is where we expect to be in a Faust play.[27] Thematically, the Prologue is part of the refocusing process, meant to rescue Faust structurally from his victim Gretchen. But Goethe's rapprochement with the original has limits. This is no wrathful Lord and, on the surface at least, no malignant Mephistopheles. Though Mephisto bets he can lead Faust astray, the Lord not only promises to lead Faust from confusion into light, but to prove that "Ein guter Mensch in seinem dunklen Drange / Ist sich des rechten Weges wohl bewusst." (328–29; A good man in his dark instinctive drive / Is conscious of the right way in the end)—"good man" meaning not so much a virtuous man as your average decent person. Mephisto is granted only a limited freedom of action, just enough to stir the slothful human being into activity (340–42). And error is an inevitable result of activity, hence pardonable—that will be decisive at the end of the play. On this showing, there will not be much suspense. But then, this is the higher view of an infallible deity, who knows everything in advance. Goethe has revived the layout of the Christian tale for the sake of giving his work its old local habitation and name.

Decision Time

Not that the old scenes now tucked neatly into the new framework. Originating at widely different times, they left loose ends and contradictions. What, for example, is the Earth Spirit's own habitation within this orthodox cosmogony? By his own account, he indwells in all the forces of nature and fashions the living garment of the deity. (508) Yet no such services are acknowledged by the Lord, nor by the Archangels—as they might well have been in their praise of the Lord's own "incomprehensibly high works" (249–50). And if Heaven's permanent residents know nothing of this Earth Spirit, nor does their visitor from below. Mephisto gives no hint to confirm Faust's belief that he himself was sent by the Earth Spirit. On the contrary, he is explicitly set going by the Lord, as a rascal ("Schalk") useful to spur the slothful into activity; while his actual Earthly associates are paraded in the "Witch's Kitchen" and the orgies of the "Walpurgis Night" on the Brocken mountain, with no trace there of the Earth Spirit. He remains excluded from the newly created framework, as he is from the further working out of the plot. He is an early inspiration lying athwart the Christian worldview, from which Goethe had early departed and to which he was now gravitating back. There is no explaining away this contradiction between cosmogonies. Goethe has simply "become confused in his own mythology."[28]

The problems of structure and consistency come together in "Wald und Höhle" (Woodland Cave). What Faust celebrates in his opening monologue—"Erhabner Geist, du gabst mir, gabst mir alles / Warum ich bat. [. . .] Gabst mir die herrliche Natur zum Königreich" (Sublime Spirit, you gave me, gave me everything / I asked for. [. . .]. Gave me the glory of nature as my realm . . .)[29]—is the opposite of what happened. The Earth Spirit humbled him, as Faust has just ruefully recalled in the pact scene a short textual span ago: "Der große Geist hat mich verschmäht, / Vor mir verschließt sich die Natur." (1746–47; The great spirit spurned me, / Nature is closed to me.) There could not be a clearer contradiction. Then there is the further puzzle of how Faust can be so deeply contented out here in a natural setting when he has wrought destruction on Gretchen, as his self-reproaches immediately afterwards eloquently recognize—this in the final section of the scene, taken over from the late *Urfaust* 16b, Night. Outside Gretchen's house. By this time, at that point in the *Urfaust* and equally in this new scene for the *Fragment*, Faust has already seduced her, she is pregnant and ruined and he reviles himself as an inhuman outsider who burst into her orderly life like a raging torrent that sweeps away an alpine cottage. Yet for all his awareness of guilt, he accepts the consequences as unalterable. "Mag's schnell geschehn, was muss geschehn. / Mag ihr Geschick auf mich zusammenstürzen, / Und sie mit mir zu Grunde gehn!" (HA 3:415–16, italics added; Let what must happen happen quickly, let her fate come down on me too and she be destroyed *along with me*.)[30] Where the scene now stands in *Fragment*, he has abandoned her to her fate, and he seems to be callously accepting the outcome. That was already so in its *Urfaust* location at 16b, but at least there it was not preceded by Faust's revelling in the enjoyment of a serene nature-vision.

In Part One, however, "Woodland Cave" is relocated early in the courtship as just an interlude in the developing romance. It is puzzling that Faust has there left Gretchen at a point where his passion is plainly keen and their love has not so far been consummated. Or has it? Some lines plainly say it has. "*Faust:* So tauml' ich von Begierde zu Genuss / Und im Genuss verschmacht' ich nach Begierde." (3249–50; *Faust*: And so I stagger from desire to enjoyment, / And in enjoyment thirst for new desire.) Or again: "Was ist die Himmelsfreud in ihren Armen? / Lass mich an ihrer Brust erwarmen! / Fühl ich nicht immer ihre Not?" (3345–47; What is the heavenly joy I feel in her arms? Let me warm myself [i.e., even when I warm myself] at her breast! Do I not always feel her plight?)[31] And *Mephisto*, apropos her breasts: "Ich hab' Euch oft beneidet / Ums Zwillingspaar, das unter Rosen weidet." (3336–37; I've often envied you the twin pair that nestles under roses.) Faust's "always" and Mephisto's "often" were both natural in their original place after the seduction. They are impossible to overlook in their new position before it. Even if we brush them aside and accept the scene where it now stands, an even more fundamental problem arises. In *Urfaust* and *Fragment*, Faust was lamenting his responsibility for what had already happened. In Part One, with the scene located so early, he is lamenting a fate he has not even begun to bring about, embracing a guilt for things he has not yet done and could still hold back from doing. Banal though it may seem to say so, that makes this most moving of tragedies strictly unnecessary. Such fatalistic foresight, if we took it at face value, would bespeak a quite different order of callousness. These considerations cannot have crossed the poet's mind.

It seems unavoidable to see the relocating of "Woodland Cave" in Part One as a mistake. The point is not to rap Goethe over the knuckles for inconsistency, but to enter sympathetically into the confusion that such a long and complex genesis was bound to create, with scenes of various dates pulling this way and that between plot strands that had been at odds from the outset. A striking metaphor of Goethe's own suggests how he could seem to have a grip on the problem when talking it through with Schiller, and then lose it again: "It's like when a powder has settled out of a solution. As long as you [Schiller] are shaking it, it seems to come together, as soon as I'm by myself it settles on the bottom again."[32] Any piece of text that Goethe inserted unchanged in a new position risked creating confusion. Every verbal revision needed to be checked for what it implied for what went before; the consequences of every adjustment or failure to adjust had to be thought through. Scenes in a drama are rarely interchangeable with impunity. It helps if we imagine Goethe at various points from the late 1780s onwards playing Patience with pieces of text spread out on his desk, or juggling them in his mind, each with its own original force and implications. He had to cope with an "old existing highly confused manuscript,"[33] out of which for purposes of the *Fragment* it was already a challenge to arrange some scenes into a roughly coherent text. Later, for purposes of Part One, it was an even greater challenge to shape all the scenes he had into a fully consistent completed form.

So what, concretely, was the player of Patience to do when, in the late 1790s and early 1800s, he set about definitively enlarging, revising, tidying up, and ordering his genetically and thematically scattered material? A first simple step would have been to cut the Earth Spirit altogether, leaving the Christian framework undisturbed. (There will be not even an echo of the Earth Spirit in *Faust Part Two*.) But was Goethe to sacrifice, in the cause of consistency, one of his most inspired pieces of writing? Moreover, the Earth Spirit's apparition was already published, out in the world, and early readers of the *Fragment* felt it was the most powerful scene of all.

Again, cutting the entire "Woodland Cave" would have solved its knot of problems at a single stroke. But was he to sacrifice Faust's (and his own post-Italian) expression of harmony with nature, just because it both contradicted the Erdgeist's observed effect and was blithely out of tune with the tragic love action? Was he to sacrifice the grand outburst of Faust's guilty conscience which was now also inserted early, in "Woodland Cave," almost as if in compensation for Faust's nonchalant escape into nature? Or should he let them all stand where they were for their own poetic quality, and unity be damned? This can be put more basically as the instinct of poetic economy: I wrote it, I have it in stock, I must use it or lose it.[34] It was effect versus tidiness, substance versus structure, poetry versus plot.

All of which presupposes that Goethe even had a clear view of the problems and the choices with which they faced him. The writer's long familiarity with his own diverse approaches, thirty years of shifting conceptions and their successive part-realizations, may have weakened the capacity, even for so powerful a poetic mind, to spot a mismatch. We must simply take the real man in his creative dilemmas seriously, not contrive excuses to smoothe away obvious unevenness, as unitarian scholars have so often done on the presumption that Goethe of all people cannot have been unaware of them and did somehow actually succeed in resolving them in a final unity that must at all costs be demonstrated.[35]

If it was indeed Goethe's conscious priority to keep valuable poetic substance, he was obeying a pressure we can go along with, because it surely finds its reciprocal in the reception of literature by lovers of language and poetic formulation. We would not want to be without visions of this power—in Goethes *Faust* or in poetic creation overall. They generate the vivid impressions by which literature lives in our imagination, and they arguably have a stronger effect than the arrangement we call form. Even the most perfectly balanced structures are not necessarily sources of the greatest aesthetic pleasure. The symmetry of Schiller's *Maria Stuart* for example, where alternate acts focus on the rival queens, followed by a neat moral coda, is intellectually satisfying but cool beside the immediate effects of their (fictive) central meeting and the play's grim display of Elizabethan Realpolitik. And there are many structurally less than elegant masterpieces that we savor with all their sins upon them, not least some of Shakespeare's, above all for the sheer force of poetic language. Supreme substance leaves its imprint on the memory. Quiddity rules. "Have for once the courage to give yourself up to your impressions," Goethe once said to Eckermann (May 6, 1827). It is a collusion of reader with author rooted deep in the literary culture we inhabit. Perhaps there is an analogy in music, where listeners may consciously delight more in texture than structure, in the timbre of instruments, the delicacy of a voice, the melodic richness and rhythmic impulse of a movement, rather than the formal complexities that are elucidated in program notes. Which is not to say that these do not have their effects too. And not for nothing are there synoptic gospels.

Unitarians, who deny there even are any inconsistencies, have on their side a lengthy and emphatic statement of Goethe's own, as reported from a conversation about *Faust* on August 19, 1806, which Schöne quotes as the authority for "trusting Goethe to have surely noticed" such things.[36]

> In poetry there are no contradictions. These exist only in the real world, not in the world of poetry. What the poet creates must be taken as he creates it. The way he has made his world, that is how it is. What the poetic mind generates must be received by a poetic sensibility [*Gemüt*]. Cold analyzing destroys poetry and produces no reality. Only fragments are left, which serve no purpose and only get in the way [*inkommodieren*].[37]

Are we to say "touché," and let Goethe carry the point? Surely not. At this moment in the conversation he clearly had his back up at being criticized, and it is hard to take his sweeping statement seriously. The poetic world he appeals to isn't in fact arbitrary; it has its own standards of coherence and consistency which are not so remote from the realities it represents. A poetic world that lacked even the possibility of contradictions could make no great claims to achieving coherence. Goethe arrives at a more balanced view when not overreacting to criticism of his own work:

> No damage is done to sacred writings, any more than to anything else that has come down to us [*jeder anderen Überlieferung*], when we treat it with critical sense, when we uncover places where it contradicts itself, and how often something original, better, has been covered up, indeed distorted, by later additions, insertions and adjustments.[38]

That fits *Faust* like a glove. Goethe's many other comments on his *Faust* range from assertion to concession, a favorite term being "incommensurable"—a work not to be measured or compared with any other. That may well be true, for better or worse, of *Faust*. Nevertheless, if its contradictions and inconsistencies cannot be explained away without implausible hypotheses that recall the epicycles early astronomers used to account for irregularities in the movements of the heavens, we might better take a realistic view that frankly recognizes the writer's fallible humanity.

So the point of a genetic look at Faust is not to talk down a universally acknowledged masterpiece. We need to distinguish. Goethe is a great poet, in the precise sense of a master of language, phrasing, rhythm, of colloquial and personal idiom. These qualities make him a supreme creator of memorable characters and their spoken interplay: Faust and

Mephisto (arguably rather more Mephisto, truly one of the great roles of the European stage), both of them rich in pithy phrases that have long since become current as popular wisdom or humor;[39] Faust and Gretchen (decidedly more Gretchen, in all the power of her unsophistication); and elsewhere Egmont and Alba, Iphigenie and Thoas, Tasso and Antonio. Even more significantly, through a lifetime's lyrical writing Goethe is the supreme creator of his own poetic character in a ceaseless dialogue with the world that achieves unequalled insights into nature and humanity—just the things for which Faust, and through him surely Goethe himself, gives thanks to the Earth Spirit.

Character rather than action was accordingly Goethe's way into drama, which is why prominent figures in his early writing are on the borderline between poetic monologue and dramatic situation: those identity models Prometheus, Ganymed, Mahomet, and several "Wanderer" protagonists. *Faust* might equally have stopped short at lyrical empathy with one more legendary figure in a concise poem. It might not have turned dramatic at all, had there not been the figure personifying earth's forces to confront Faust, or the pedantry of his earth-bound assistant to frustrate him. Compared with Schiller's primal theatrical talent, dramatic structure was never Goethe's starting point or his forte. Where a play is elegantly crafted—*Iphigenie auf Tauris*—it is by following the line of Euripides' original, albeit with enhanced psychological insight and moral substance; but then these, precisely, are Goethe's strengths. Not surprisingly, when he goes back to Faust in 1797, he asks Schiller, the man of structuring intellect, for guidance through the labyrinth of material that the decades of separate inspirations have created. But after Schiller's death in 1805, with the whole of *Faust Part Two* still to write, Goethe was on his own.

New Purposes

After a long initial delay from 1806, with only sporadic work on a Helen of Troy action, intensive work on *Faust* gets going again in 1825. The individual acts are clearly dated and the genesis is relatively straightforward, once we accept the vastly expanded scale and changed poetic mode of an action that now takes in the wider world of history, politics, myth, and science. Underlying this enormous range of new material, the same cross-purposes persist between the Faust and Gretchen plot-strands and between the poet and his traditional theme. Indeed they bracket it, for the action of Part Two starts with Faust forgetting Gretchen, a more radical detachment than his absences in "Woodland Cave" and "Walpurgis Night," and it ends with his salvation, a radical departure from the old morality tale. Gretchen's final intercession for him weaves the two long-standing disharmonies together.

On those earlier occasions in Part One, Faust did eventually remember her, and their last meeting in her cell, followed by the execution she so graphically foresees and from which he is unable to rescue her, must have left a lasting trauma. Yet if he is to be free for new high-level adventures untrammelled by a mere human connection, Gretchen has to be definitively abandoned, both by the man who ruined her and by the writer who had rescued her for human sympathy. Character and author both now have new purposes.

When Part Two opens, Faust is safe in an idyllic setting, "reclining on a flowery lawn." True, he is "uneasily seeking sleep," but spirit voices, led by Shakespeare's Ariel no less, soothe away memories of his shattering experience and profound guilt. He can now time-travel to a Holy Roman Emperor's court, observe political corruption and social chaos at work, be present at a classical Walpurgis Night, go thence to the aftermath of the siege of Troy where as a Nordic knight he rescues Greek Helen from a vengeful Menelaus, to be then involved in medieval battles, and finally engage in land reclamation, piracy, and manslaughter at the coastal fief which his dubious deeds have earned him, before dying and rising to a grandiose heaven.

All this realizes the promise of the pact to range over human experience. It does it so amply and distractingly that the issue on which the pact centered—will Faust ever rest content with a supreme experienced moment?—gets largely lost to sight in the sheer mass and variety of material and the symbolic or allegorical weight Goethe gives to its elements. This is even true of the one motif that does come from the Faust legend and is central to Part Two, the conjuring up of Helen of Troy. First glimpsed as an image in a peep-show for courtiers, Helen is then retrieved by Faust from the mysterious realm of "the Mothers" as a flesh-and-blood woman on whom he fathers a son. The immense elaboration of this episode—the virtuoso recreation of Greek verse-forms, the play with mythological creatures in a "crowded theme-park of classical antiquity,"[40] the marriage of Ancient and Modern—makes it the culmination of Goethe's love-affair with antiquity and a symbol of his achieved classicism. By its theme and its sheer extent it is more a work-within-a-work (as indeed the Gretchen action in Part One had been) than a link in the drama. So much so that there is a failure to make the decisive connection with the terms of the pact, for at the highpoint of Faust's and Helen's relationship its key provision is in substance met. The couple are savoring their fulfilled moment:

Faust: Nun schaut der Geist nicht vorwärts, nicht zurück,
Die Gegenwart allein—
Helen: ist unser Glück. (9381–82)

[*Faust*: Now we look neither back nor forward, we
Find in the present—
Helen: our felicity.]

Yet nothing results. Their serene contentment is seemingly not noticed by Mephisto, though he is present in the classical guise of one of the hideous Graiae. Is he so literal-minded that only the agreed form of words ("Linger a while, you are so lovely") will trigger his triumph? Is he, or is Goethe, as forgetful of what the pact stipulated as Faust now is of his past guilt? Schöne sees the contradiction but makes nothing of it, merely noting that Faust is "freed from the stipulations of the pact."[41] That ignores the dramatic question: should he be?

The couple's union admittedly does not last; the death of their son Euphorion through over-reaching[42] breaks it up, and Helen must follow him back to the underworld. Happiness and beauty, according to a saying that she quotes, cannot be permanently joined. (9940) But permanence was not the issue in the pact, only a single highpoint of experience. That has come and gone unnoticed, and Faust is soon off on his next adventure, borne on a cloud formed by Helen's robes. Nearer by, a wisp of mist clings round him and takes the shape of a delightful image, a "jugendstes, langstentbehrtes, höchstes Gut" (10055–56; a long-lost highest good of early youth). Though unnamed, it can only be Gretchen—so, not forgotten by Faust as completely as she was meant to be at the outset of Part Two. Nor by Goethe, to whom alone, and not to Faust, the quoted words properly apply: Gretchen was not the love of Faust's early youth, but the creation of Goethe's. As with the dedicatory poem, this is literary nostalgia. So is it Faust's conscience or Goethe's that has retrieved Gretchen?

The same question applies more pressingly at the work's close, where "a penitent, once called Gretchen" makes a comeback to intercede for Faust and lead him onwards and upwards—this within a heaven of dynamic movement, where choirs of angels, learnèd and mystical Fathers, and the Virgin in Glory are scattered across the depths and heights of "Bergschluchten" (Mountain Gorges), a poetically more appealing Realm of the Beyond than the conventional picture of the afterlife as an endless contemplative stasis. Vanished without trace is the heaven of the Prologue along with the Lord and his deferentially lyrical archangels. (Of Christ there has throughout the work never been more than passing mention.)

Does this final vision represent Goethe's serious belief? Perhaps at most through the motif of movement in which Faust's immortal part, his "Unsterbliches,"[43] is to join. For the rest, Goethe was consciously resorting "to sharply defined Christian figures and conceptions" in order to present something "so suprasensuous and hardly imaginable" as the final ascent of Faust's soul, which would otherwise have risked getting "lost in vagueness."[44] The final show of transcendence does not have the substance of belief that the Mater dolorosa once had for a despairing Gretchen. But at least Gretchen has now been richly remembered—by Goethe at least. From Faust himself, there is not a spoken word or a flicker of response in the whole elaborate scene.[45]

Gretchen's intercession resolves one instance of cross-purposes, that between the Faustian theme and the young woman's tragedy, but at the price of massively reinforcing the other, that between the secular poet and the original legend. For paradoxically, the Christian figure of Gretchen furthers a happy ending that departs absolutely from the Christian story. And it is not just that no Faust rightly so named should properly be saved.[46] This particular Faust has gone on piling offence on offence, right down to Act Five, where he is complicit in the murder of two old people, Philemon and Baucis, whose small property had made Faust's landholdings annoyingly incomplete. This is hardly the "ever higher and purer activity, right to the end," that Goethe claimed for his Faust.[47] There is no sign that the Lord has, as promised in the prologue, led a confused Faust into clarity (308–9), nor that Faust has on his own account been obscurely conscious of the right way (329). He might have, surely should have, gone down in a pit of guilt, not out in a blaze of glory. A tragic Faust drama—and Goethe's subtitle is, after all, "tragedy"—ought to end in damnation and remorse and at best a last-minute hoping against hope, as when Marlowe's damned Faustus presumes at the last in vain on salvation:

> O, I'll leap up to my God! Who pulls me down?
> See, see, where Christ's blood streams in the firmament!
> One drop would save my soul, half a drop.

Goethe presumes far more than this on behalf of his Faust, namely that he actually *is* saved, on the ground that anyone can be saved who constantly strives, and actually will be saved if met by love descending: "Wer immer strebend sich bemüht, / Den können wir erlösen. / Und hat an ihm die Liebe gar / Von oben teilgenommen . . ." (11936–39).[48] True, the Lord has said in the Prologue that all human striving entails error (317), a dual leitmotif that is the only link between the heaven of the opening and the heaven of the close; and Faust has certainly erred with a vengeance. He is guilty of the deaths of Gretchen, her mother, her brother, and her child, of the old couple violently relocated and their guest, and perhaps of other human sacrifices darkly hinted to have been involved in the land-reclamation work. Against the alleged "ever higher and purer activity right to the end," there is this massive negative balance, all allegedly to be offset by the virtue—if it can be called a substantive virtue—of striving. It goes far beyond the mere secularization of the legend. It is no wonder Faust says nothing as he rises through the heights of heaven. What could he possibly say for himself? Not surprisingly, after more than a century of exploitation for purposes of national identity—as the quintessential German character in the nineteenth-century Empire, as a model for Nazi activism, as the visionary of a socialist society in the

East German Republic—the play and its protagonist are rightly now more often read as a warning.[49]

And has Faust not, incidentally, already lost his wager with Mephisto by uttering, in the moment before he dies, the exact form of words agreed in the pact? (11581) This time Mephisto does react, but is then cheated of his prey, perhaps because of the conditional tense in which Faust wraps the formula "I would be able / entitled to say . . ." ("dürft' ich sagen"), a quibble critics have made much of. A more substantial justification lies in the sense Faust gives the words. He has not succumbed to any earthly indulgence, so that to the short-sighted Mephisto's puzzlement he has spoken the words to "den letzten schlechten, leeren Augenblick" (11589; the last, poor, empty moment) The words do however evoke a community's defense of reclaimed land against the sea, a need stretching too far into the future to be narrated but symbolically contained in a present moment of vision. Without such compression, there was logically no way Faust could ever have won the wager. Endless activity could not be encompassed in a finite work. Hence it was possible for Mephisto to win if Faust's activity at any moment ceased, but impossible for Faust, who could have only ever endlessly put off closure. Still, human activity is declared a fundamental value, regardless of its moral content. That comes perilously close to the position of Goethe's contemporary Hegel, who declared history rational, and scornfully dismissed the "litany" of moral objections raised by those who had fallen foul of its not obviously rational processes and their ruthless agents.[50]

If Goethe wanted to celebrate and justify human activity, he could not have chosen a less appropriate vehicle than the Faust story, even in his own radical adaptation. This is a final case of cross-purposes. Choice, of course, was not how this genesis happened. Rather, the young poet was obscurely drawn to the legend, only to find himself diverging from its inherent line and always desperately working against its grain. The result was a highly problematic lifelong striving of his own.

6: Occasions: Goethe's Lyric Poetry

Fulfillments

GOETHE IS AT CROSS-PURPOSES with the conception of *Faust* in yet another way and even more fundamentally. Faust will lose the wager with Mephistopheles if he ever admits to contentment with an individual moment. His certainty that this will never happen is a dismissive judgment on all possible experience. Yet Goethe the poet declares, and his lyrical poetry embodies, the flat opposite. Over a long lifetime he repeatedly captures experiences of fulfillment with an intensity matched by no other German poet—moments of love, of beauty, of insight and pleasure in the natural world, of sheer exuberance in his own felt existence, often closely traceable to their originating moment. In the late poem "Vermächtnis" (Legacy) there is a paradoxical suggestion of permanence, that "der Augenblick ist Ewigkeit" (the moment is eternity.)

Not that Goethe's captured moments are grandiose. They arise from everyday occasions too familiar to be exciting (though he did once in young years have to throw himself from a bolting horse)[1] and too obvious to be poetic—until, that is, they are transformed through the poet's fresh and vigorous vision. When Goethe in old age comes to survey what he has all along been doing, "occasion" (Gelegenheit) becomes the central concept of an uncomplicated poetics.

Historic change pivots on the term. Where once it meant moments of public significance—births, marriages, victories, deaths—for which the worldly great, and later also citizens of substance, commissioned poems (*Casualcarmina*), it could now mean anybody's moments, experiences from the common life made memorable by feeling or insight—hence the other standard term "Erlebnisdichtung" (poetry of experience).[2] It was a democratic appropriation.

That did not mean its range was narrowly private. On the contrary, it opened up the wider world to a lyrical realism:

> The world is so large and rich, and life so multifarious, that there will never be a shortage of occasions for poems. But they must all be occasional poems; that is to say, reality must provide the motive and the material. A special case becomes general precisely because the *poet* treats it. All my poems are occasional poems, they are stimulated by reality and have their ground and roots in it.[3]

The genesis of such poems was also distinctively new. Occasions rooted in everyday life generated free spontaneous utterance; it was no longer a question of calculation in accordance with the rules of classical rhetoric. The words came with the case. Acts of creation in "the flashpoint of the moment"[4] and in identifiable places (the most celebrated is the wooden hut on whose wall Goethe wrote the best known of all German lyrics)[5] are well enough documented for his geneses not to be mere Romantic legend or a deliberately cultivated image. Indeed, when Goethe reports individual cases, he is more like an anthropologist observing his own talent, almost with surprise, wholly as nature. Poetic impulse could propel him out of bed to get a poem down without stopping to put the paper straight, caught short by poetry.[6] He describes the process in the early fragment "The Eternal Jew," a version of the Ahasuerus legend: "Um Mitternacht wohl fang ich an, / Spring aus dem Bette wie ein Toller; / Nie war mein Busen seelevoller . . ." (MA 1.1:238; It's midnight when I start to write, / Jump out of bed as if I'm mad, / Never so full of inspiration . . .). The manuscript text embodies it, spread diagonally across the first four pages.

Goethe regarded such natural products with reverence, but he keeps solemnity at bay with a touch of humor. He felt towards his poems like a hen who sees her chicks chirping around her. This is the autobiographer's late retrospect, but equally down-to-earth and un-vatic are his notes sometimes made on the spot and at the moment, as in a letter enclosing one small improvised poem: "This is something I sang recently deep in a magnificent moonlight night climbing out of the river that flows through the meadows in front of my house."[7] That is the river Ilm and its park, with the Gartenhaus where Goethe lived in his first Weimar years.

Singing to himself what just came into his mind was a habit. A letter to Carl August from an inspection tour of the ducal forests ends with a goodnight greeting, followed by an afterthought: "One more word before I go to bed. As I was riding through the night towards the Fichtel mountains the feeling of the past, my destiny, and my love came over me, and I sang to myself: 'Holde Lili, warst so lang All mein Lust und all mein Sang. / Bist, ach, all mein Schmerz—und doch / All mein Sang bist du noch.'" (Sweetest Lili who so long / Were all my pleasure all my song. / Now alas are all my pain— / Yet all my song you remain.)

The poem is simple and unpunctuated, but putting it on paper has creative consequences. Goethe repeats the goodnight greeting, adds further good wishes, and these become the start of another poem: "Gehab dich wohl bei den hundert Lichtern / Die dich umglänzen / Und all den Gesichtern / Die dich umschwänzen / Und umkredenzen. / Findst doch nur wahre Freud und Ruh / Bei Seelen grad und treu wie du."[8]

(Fare you well in the bright-lit places / Mid all those faces / Where flatterers sidle / And tipplers idle. / Real joy and peace you'll only find / With other true souls of your kind.)

This is no great poem either, though it does already link fresh experience to traditional literary motifs in a coherent sentiment. Taking shelter in a forester's house with "natural good people" points up the old ethical contrast between court and countryside, and leads to the hope that Goethe's employer and friend might leave the artificial court world behind in favor of the natural values that deep down are his too. But the two poems and their sequence illustrate Goethe's creative workings. A past love gives the substance, riding gives the rhythm, a poem results and is memorized. Writing it down renews the creative mood and verbal impetus, and gives rise to something more complex. After that, he draws a line without another word—otherwise where might it stop? For poem generates poem, as rhythm and reflection keep the mind working on a level above the prosaic world. As far as any cultural product can be, this is the work of a natural process. Poetry came, in Keats's phrase, "as naturally as leaves to a tree."[9]

Nor was it just a phenomenon of youth. In 1814 Goethe writes eight poems in a day towards his Persian-style collection, the *West-Eastern Divan*. It is like the conjurer's colored handkerchiefs, each pulling the next out of the hat. Such connectedness is a factor in the making of cycles. At its latest and most sublime, it is what sustains the creation of the massive "Marienbad Elegy," a tragic outburst over the old man's last impossible love, twenty-three massive stanzas written over the three days of the journey back from Bohemia to Weimar. Scribbling on an old calendar und not too much disturbed by the jolting of the coach, he could tidy the day's yield at successive post-stations. All that gave the poem, in Goethe's understated comment, "a certain immediacy."[10]

But already half a year before the forest inspection trip and its poem-sequence, an occasion had already produced one of Goethe's finest lyrics. In the autumn of 1775 he travelled to Switzerland, accompanied by three aristocrats (his publications, especially the successful novel *The Sufferings of Young Werther*, had given him social status). They all got themselves up in Werther uniform, blue coat, yellow waistcoat and trousers, and a round grey hat. More seriously, Goethe was escaping from an engagement to Lili which mixed delight with discomfort, leaving the young couple uncertain if they had a future together. The Goethe and Schönemann families had differences of religion and social origin, Goethe's sister Cornelia emphatically warned him off Lili, his father felt an aversion to this young *grande dame* who seemed unlikely to fit into his household, and for the poet himself the prospect of having to settle down to marriage and a tedious legal career in his home town was hard to accept. But above all there was a clash between character and convention, between his own natural way of being and Lili's glittering circle. Why did she draw him irresistibly into that splendor when he was happiest by himself in a quiet evening room? Was it even still his real self that she kept at her side among all the lights, at the gaming table, opposite such intolerable other visages?[11] Lights and faces again, the outward show of society. "Warum ziehst du mich unwiderstehlich, / Ach, in jene Pracht? / War ich guter Junge nicht so selig / In der öden Nacht?" And later: "Bin ich's noch, den du bei so viel Lichtern / An dem Spieltisch hältst? / Oft so unerträglichen Gesichtern / Gegenüberstellst?" Yet against that there was her powerful attraction. Lili was not just a pretty face, but at seventeen already a woman of culture and intelligence. "I was never so near to my true happiness as when I loved Lili," Goethe said long after.[12] All this, and the evidence of her later life,[13] gives persuasive substance to the poems written to her and about her[14] and helps explain the fascination that made a break so difficult for him. So at the end of the poem "To Belinda," Goethe attempts a desperate reconciliation. Are nature and this charming socialite really such different worlds? The spring blossoms out in the fields are not more charming than she is. "Reizender ist mir des Frühlings Blüte / Nun nicht auf der Flur, / Wo du, Engel bist, ist Lieb' und Güte, / Wo du bist, Natur."

That forced compromise could hardly hold for long. Hence the escape to Switzerland. There, on the fifteenth of June, Goethe joined a party of nine on a boat trip down Lake Zurich. He was on his way, after abandoning his three no longer so congenial aristocrats, to at least see the fabled Swiss mountains before Lili drew him back to Frankfurt, "homewards and love-wards." The boat took them past grandiose scenery, but even eighteenth-century nature-lovers needed a change. So they played a word-game, *bouts rimés*, in which someone sets two pairs of rhymes for the next person to make a humorous quatrain out of; this person then sets the next player two new pairs. Goethe had a notebook and pencil, probably a gift from his host Johann Caspar Lavater, since the date at the top of the first page is in Lavater's hand: "Den 15 Junius 1775. Donnerstags morgen auf dem Zürchersee" (June 15, 1775. Thursday morning on Lake Zürich). Goethe took the first turn, the notebook and pencil went the rounds and were then back in his hands. The nine pieces of doggerel are followed by this:[15]

Ich saug an meiner Nabelschnur	I suck at my umbilical cord
Nun Nahrung aus der Welt.	Nourishment from the world.
Und herrlich rings ist die Natur	Splendid is nature all around
Die mich am Busen hält.	At whose bosom I am held.
Die Welle wieget unsern Kahn	The wavelets cradle-rock our boat
Im Rudertakt hinauf	To the pulling of the oars

Und Berge Wolken angethan	And mountain-tops all capped with cloud
Entgegnen unserm Lauf.	Dip to meet our course.
Aug mein Aug was sinkst du nieder	Eye, my eye, why droop What golden
Goldne Träume kommt ihr wieder	Dreams return to past beholden
Weg du Traum so gold du bist	Dreams though gold you be away
Hier auch Lieb und Leben ist.	Here too life and love hold sway.
Auf der Welle blinken	On the wave are sparkling
Tausend schwebenden Sterne	Thousand hovering stars
Liebe Nebel trincken	Darling mists are drinking
Rings die thürmende Ferne	Towering heights afar
Morgenwind umflügelt	Round the shadowed inlet
Die beschattetete Bucht	Morning breezes blow
Und im See bespiegelt	Mirrored in the water
Sich die reifende Frucht	Ripening fruit hangs low[16]

Simple verse, in a party game, has again warmed the medium and helped to generate a poem, this time the real thing. Goethe perhaps had at the back of his mind the fact that, twenty-five years ago almost to the day, the revered Klopstock had conceived one of his greatest odes on, and on, this same lake: "Der Zürchersee." So the setting had an Apolline aura, to which Hölderlin too would later respond. Did Lavater perhaps even make his gift of the notebook in expectation poetry would come of it? This time, moreover, Apollo had been invoked by name, for the second quatrain of *bouts rimés* reads "Wozu sind wohl Apollos Affen / Als wie zu *bouts rimés* geschaffen?" (What are they for, Apollo's apes, / But to make end-rhymes into shapes?) The party were indeed aping Apollo, not suspecting the serious effect it would have.

Goethe's poem expresses three phases of feeling in a symmetrical pattern—eight lines, then four, then eight again, though as yet laid out as eight-twelve. It opens with the speaker deeply at home in the natural setting; his happy mood is then threatened by memories of a different world, but he dismisses them and the lake scene returns, now self-sufficient. An observer is only implied, his own maturing process subtly suggested at the close.[17] The varied metrical movement of the original matches the formal balance, from relaxed iambics at the opening, via the trochees of the intermezzo that harks back and the spondee that dismisses doubts, to the lilting dactyls scattered through the last section. This is exquisite "Erlebnisdichtung," a poem that captures two opposed experiences and a feeling of the conflict between them. The story is totally lucid without biographical background, though the crucial name, Lili, is supplied in a further small poem, entitled "Vom Berge in die See" (The Lake Seen from the Mountain) that stands at the top of the next page in the notebook: "Wenn ich, liebe Lili, dich nicht liebte / Welche Wonne gäb mir dieser Blick / Und doch, wenn ich, Lili, dich nicht liebt, / Wär, was wär mein Glück." (If I, dearest Lili, did not love you / What would be my pleasure in this scene / And yet, Lili, if I did not love you, / What can my happiness have been?) The heading carries the humorous reference "Vid. Das Privat Archiv des Dichters. Lit. L."—"See the poet's private archive under L."—parody of Goethe's law-office practice.

The Lake poem is an elegant construct, it might seem. Yet the manuscript suggests it was once again composed spontaneously in the moment, in the boat, with pencil on knee, visibly in a free-flowing hand, with no afterthoughts, crossings-out or substitutions. Apart from three minor errors[18] and the absence of punctuation, it looks like a fair copy. Surely there must have been a prior rough draft. But where? What could have been rougher for Goethe's purpose than this flimsiest of notebooks, just eight pages which were later used mainly for brief travel jottings.[19] And the poem-text follows on without a break after the rhyming game. Even if, improbably, a rough draft had been written on other pages, there seems no reason, rough notebook that it was, why they should have been torn out. There wouldn't have been much notebook left. The only alternative would be that, as with the first of the two forest poems, Goethe memorized this longer and more complex text during the boat trip and wrote it down later, still using pencil, as was his normal practice (the scratching of a quill pen disturbed what he called his "sleep-walking" creative process).[20] Such a feat of memory seems unlikely—he later told Sulpiz Boisserée that it was a positive worry if poems came into his mind complete when he was out walking or riding, and he had to take care not to think them through for fear of losing them altogether. The trouble was, movement was crucial, generating good ideas and formulations; as he put it: "Sitting down I'm not up to much."[21] The causal connection between bodily and mental activity is a truism of poetic and intellectual genesis.[22]

The manuscript has more to reveal yet. In the left-hand margin, two parallel oblique strokes mark the end of the *bouts rimés* before the poem begins. They are familiar from Goethe's long early letters, where they separate the successive days, or parts of a day, on which he is writing. And there is another pair of them after the first eight lines of the poem. Or should we rather say: after the first poem? For it seems clear that Goethe saw these lines as a completed unit immediately after writing them and before starting again and writing twelve more. The strokes, not always reproduced in critical editions, are a crucial clue: Goethe wrote two poems, first an intense impressionistic account of invigoration by nature, then later—how much later?—two further phases of feeling, each distinct in content, though themselves as yet making one block. Joining the two poems made a single story, but it was only even later that their author saw the coherence, and the formal symmetry of the three phases. Joining the two units and splitting the second gave the poem the form published in 1789: eight-four-eight.[23] Here structure really does matter, because it is intimately part of the substance. Perhaps this was one of the earliest occasions when Goethe recognized how natural his poetic processes were. For an isolated phrase stands on a later page of the notebook, "Unmittelbaarer [sic] Ausdruck von der Natur" (immediate expression of nature).[24]

The new layout does allow one nuance of this absorbing history to get lost. There was clearly a gap in time—a moment? an hour? the even look of the handwriting suggests it was not long—before the serene mood of the opening was disturbed by the afterthoughts that set Goethe writing four more lines. But there was then no such gap before the past was dismissed and present happiness reasserted in a further eight lines. The line "Here too life and love hold sway" rejects the golden dreams with an unhesitating declaration, and introduces new images from the natural surroundings without a break in the writing. Indeed they follow intimately *from* that declaration, as if after a colon: each detail embodies the general statement, as in a baroque *exemplificatio*. Not however as a product of rhetorical calculation, but as a reality that imposed itself on an open eye and mind. All which is at least a modest answer to Max Kommerell's doubt whether we fully know a single minute of Goethe's life.[25] Here we surely do.

The events on Lake Zurich in 1775 are the outstanding instance of Goethe's spontaneous creativity, and they put down a more general anthropological marker for what the human mind is capable of.[26] Scholars subservient to a modernist poetics sometimes discount all such cases, dogmatically treating the records of genetic circumstance as legend and asserting that these poems too are unavoidably the conscious contrivance of rhetoric. But rhetoric would be at best a metaphor for the intuitive skills Goethe had developed over five years writing a new kind of poetry, and since the poetic quality is itself the only evidence for rhetorical calculation, the judgment simply begs the question. Decisive in the present case, even if all else were to be thought cool calculation, is the fact that Goethe himself only realized after the event how formally perfect his poem had turned out to be. When a full picture of compositional circumstances is joined by a demonstrable poetic perfection, inspiration is the unavoidable judgment.

Mistrusting the miraculous is a routine part of the modern skeptical outlook. But Goethe's acts of spontaneous creation are not miraculous, merely extreme cases of something taken for granted in other human activities, namely the coming together of impulses under outside pressure to produce outstanding results. There is nothing irrational about this, it is simply the mind working at a higher pitch. The psychology of such situations was analyzed in Heinrich von Kleist's essay "On the Gradual Formation of Our Thoughts in Speaking" quoted in the introduction. One obvious parallel activity would be sport, where players fully in the zone or flow surpass themselves to achieve something nearly impossible. That one of the greatest of poets should have been able effortlessly to achieve sovereign form ought not to be surprising. It sets a criterion for less spontaneous poetry to come up to—indeed, if there were no such *live* norm, what is it that the constructing poet would be striving to construct? Surely not a mere illusion of a harmony such as nobody could ever really attain? Beyond that, spontaneity validates poetry as, in a phrase of the Romantic poet Novalis, "the peculiar mode of action of the human mind," even if, in a sublime paradox, he calls it "nothing very special"![27]

Revisions

Besides bringing out the poem's inherent form through the new layout, Goethe made other changes to what he now called "Auf dem See" (On the Lake). Typically of his revisions, he removed the diary-like heading (several other early poems had dates removed, and/or a title added or adjusted)[28] making the occasion more general without sacrificing its vivid particularity. More importantly, Goethe took out the umbilical-cord image, leaving it only vestigially present in the new second line; but in its place he managed an equally powerful opening by subtler means. They could indeed not be simpler. He starts with the most basic conjunction "Und"—"And":

> Und frische Nahrung, neues Blut   And fresh nourishment, new blood
> Saug ich aus freier Welt;   I suck from the free world;

The beginning concisely captures continuity—the delighted realization that nature is always there to sustain you when you arrive, as the poet had, from some other place and experience, to pick up an unbroken thread. It integrates the speaker in the natural world as profoundly as did the original image of the child in the womb. Conjunction indeed!

Soberingly, one of Goethe's editors suggests that "Und" merely marks a more banal continuation from a preceding poem. In the layout of the 1789 edition, "Auf dem See" does indeed follow immediately after "Lilis Park," a comic narrative in which the poet is a bear kept by his mistress in her menagerie. That would be a very tenuous link to the powerful renewal by the outside world in "Auf dem See"; and it is odd, banal even, to think of a lyrical poet—and this of all lyrical poets—reshaping a serious poem merely so as to connect it with the preceding comic one in a printed sequence.

There are surely effects of a different order in the changed opening of what is self-evidently a major lyrical utterance. Both poems, it is true, arose from the uneasy engagement with Lili, but they are so different in mood and mode that they can hardly be seen as a pair; while to claim that Goethe "only ever" starts a poem with "und" when he wants to link it with a predecessor[29] plainly begs the question: every case needs to be considered on its merits before you generalize, and this one's poetic merits are clear. At most, once the new opening was there it may have helped determine the placing of the two poems in 1789. But the new opening was created, it can be shown, best part of a decade earlier, before any edition of the poems can have been even thought of.

For in 1999 a further version was discovered in the Türckheim family papers. Its title, "Zurchseefahrt [*sic*] im Juni 1775," still explicitly connects it to the occasion, but no longer by the umbilical cord—the "Und" opening has already replaced it, with slightly different wording from the final published version: "Und frische Kraft und frisches Blut / Trinck ich aus freier Welt" (And fresh strength and fresh blood / I drink from the free world). The altered layout of the lines, eight-four-eight, is also already present. The direction of further minor changes makes it obvious that this must be an intermediate version, not a further revision to the 1789 text.[30]

We previously knew only that Goethe revised the poem at some time between 1775 and 1789, the evidence suggesting that he did it late in that span, shortly before publication. He told Schiller in September 1788 that he was "polishing his poems."[31] Ten years earlier in that span, certainly, he had not yet done any large-scale revising, because a manuscript collection he put together for himself in 1778 still has important original features which were later changed. "An Schwager Kronos" (To Coachman Kronos) still tosses "sticks, roots and stones" athwart the syntax and the coach's progress, while the poet's final arrival in the underworld as an honored prince has the triumphant chutzpah of the original; "Eis-Lebens-Lied" (Ice-Life-Song) still has that title; and "Seefahrt" (Voyage) still carries its date.[32]

The newly discovered version of the Lake poem, however, persuasively dates its revision to 1779. In that year Goethe again travelled to Switzerland, this time accompanying Duke Carl August on what became an adventurous, even foolhardy mountain excursion. (They ventured into the high snows, and the Duke had not yet fathered an heir.) On the way, Goethe called in on the two women he had loved and left, Friederike Brion of eight years back and Lili of four. It was a journey of friendly reconciliation with them both. At this distance from the broken engagement, with Lili now happily married and possessed of a "fine house, respected family, prominent social rank," in short, with "everything she needed"—note the tense of the verb[33]—it was not tactless, was perhaps even a typically unconventional compliment, to present her with two poems that their relationship had inspired, both written on the earlier Swiss journey, the greater of them (Goethe may well have already realized) particularly fine.[34] But perhaps it would not do to turn up on Lili's doorstep with that crude obstetric image? It has always seemed likely that Goethe deleted the umbilical cord as too strong meat for the poetry-reading public, composed probably in large part of women—there were especial anthologies published for ladies, and spontaneous aversion to that metaphor is confirmed by at least one present-day lady friend. It now seems that a female public was not just presumed but real, composed of the one woman Goethe was on his way to visit. Which means the poem was inspired both in its first conception in 1775 and in its final form in 1779 by Lili Schönemann-von Türckheim—Lili in her successive social incarnations. It was a kind of happy ending.

Throughout the drawn-out genesis of "Auf dem See," Goethe plainly did not lose touch with the poem's original emotion. What Wordsworth said about the "mood in which successful composition generally begins" applies at least as much to successful revision. Initial composition, in Goethe's case, often shows little gap between the originating occasion and the poetic response, and what Wordsworth called the "spontaneous overflow of powerful feelings" already fits those cases precisely.[35] But revision is even more a case of "emotion recollected in tranquillity," meaning not, as the phrase is often misunderstood, cool detachment from an originating emotion, but, as Wordsworth's full context makes clear, the process of getting back into it, "till by a species of reaction the tranquillity disappears and an emotion kindred to that which was before the object of contemplation is gradually produced and does actually exist in the mind." The visiting Goethe's aesthetic-cum-social problem with a text he had written four years earlier transported him back to that time sufficiently to stimulate the fine alternative opening. Whereas in any mood short of such full recollection, the result will be the work of a critical mind responding to what an earlier self wrote. As W. B. Yeats frankly said, the poet is remaking himself.[36] Moreover, he is now in a world of words, no longer directly of emotions. He has to somehow have the courage of his old (that is, his young) emotions. For if a man isn't young at twenty-two, how can he be when he's forty?

The greater the time-gap, the less likely he is to achieve poetic constancy. Körner put it with admirable clarity on the news that Schiller was about to revise his early poetry:

> I'm unhappy about too severe a revision of your poems. You've changed your manner. A lot of things must displease you that have traces of a youthful wildness but are perhaps suited precisely to the spirit of works that are in their own way estimable. You needn't

tolerate offenses against language and meter But I would already plead for leniency towards images of a certain luxuriant kind. I know they don't satisfy the more mature taste. But the *date* printed above each poem is enough for your justification.[37]

On that principle, the revision of "Auf dem See" could not be better. It not only sustains the harmony with the originating occasion across the interval of several years, but for the first time sees not faults but innate perfections.

≈   ≈   ≈

A less happy ending, poetically and personally, is another major poem that Goethe reworked for the 1789 edition and then called "Willkomm [later "Willkommen"] und Abschied" (Welcome and Parting). Again there is biographical background—it is one of the group the young Goethe wrote in 1771 to the Alsace pastor's daughter Friederike Brion, the other old flame he was to visit on the reconciliation tour of 1779. Once more the original is lucid and self-sufficient without that specific knowledge:[38]

Mir schlug das Herz; geschwind zu Pferde,	An impulse—mount! And off, careering
Und fort, wild wie ein Held zur Schlacht!	Wild like a hero to the fight.
Der Abend wiegte schon die Erde,	Earth was already lulled by evening
Und an den Bergen hieng die Nacht.	And on the mountains hung the night.
Schon stund im Nebelkleid die Eiche	Already clad in mist, the oak-tree
Ein aufgethürmter Riese da,	Rose like a giant of towering size,
Wo Finsterniss aus dem Gesträuche	And from the thicket's depth the blackness
Mit tausend schwartzen Augen sah.	Peered out with hundreds of dark eyes.
Der Mond von seinem Wolkenhügel,	The moon through haze looked out all gloomy,
Schien kläglich aus dem Duft hervor;	Perched high upon its cloudy hill;
Die Winde schwangen leise Flügel,	The winds so softly winging round me
Umsausten schauerlich mein Ohr.	Breathed in my ear a horrid thrill.
Die Nacht schuf tausend Ungeheuer—	Night spawned a thousand monsters, but

Doch tausendfacher war mein Muth;	My courage was thousandfolder yet,
Mein Geist war ein verzehrend Feuer,	My mind was a consuming fire,
Mein ganzes Herz zerfloss in Glut.	My heart entire melted in heat.
Ich sah dich, und die milde Freude	I saw you, and delight so tranquil
Floss aus dem süßen Blick auf mich.	Flowed over me from the sweet look.
Ganz war mein Herz an deiner Seite,	My heart was wholly at your bidding,
Und ieder Atemzug für dich	For you alone each breath I took.
Ein rosenfarbes Frühlings Wetter	All of spring's freshness rich with roses
Lag auf dem lieblichen Gesicht,	Was gathered in your lovely face.
Und Zärtlichkeit für mich, ihr Götter!	And tenderness, ye gods! I hoped for
Ich hoft' es, ich verdient' es nicht.	But never could deserve such grace.
Der Abschied, wie bedrängt, wie trübe!	The time to part pressed hard upon us.
Aus deinen Blicken sprach dein Herz.	Your looks said all there was to say.
In deinen Küssen, welche Liebe,	How much love was in your kisses,
O welche Wonne, welcher Schmerz	O how much bliss and how much pain!
Du giengst, ich stund, und sah zur Erden,	You went, I stood with downcast gaze,
Und sah dir nach mit nassem Blick;	And watched you go with tear-filled eyes.
Und doch, welch Glück! geliebt zu werden,	And yet, what fortune to be loved
Und lieben, Götter, welch ein Glück!	And heavens! To love, life's highest prize!

Goethe made deep changes for 1789. What they show happening is very much what Körner feared Schiller would do in his revisions. You can almost hear the no longer youthful Goethe thinking: surely a hero wildly galloping off to battle isn't the right image for a lover off to a romantic tryst (the battle of the sexes was not yet a cliché). Hence a prosaic substitute was found—"no sooner said than done."[39] Likewise, the courage to meet a thousand monsters, itself already for the same reason inappropriate, cannot as in the original be linguistically or logically "thousandfold*er*," so it becomes "fresh and cheerful";[40] the mind that was "a consuming fire" and the heart that "melted in heat" yield to vacuous exclamations—"In my veins what fire! In my heart what heat!"[41] The substitute phrases hardly belong in a poem at all—they certainly don't touch the reality of youthful feeling. Goethe has censored out of existence his early exuberance, and with it his former self.[42]

These changes are points of manner and taste, the risk-averse older view displacing the authentic younger vision. But Goethe also made decisive structural changes, to the times of day in the narrative and to the lovers' roles at the end. The original is played out in late evening, and at some point, for reasons not stated, the lover has to leave. In the revised story, his departure is emphatically at dawn, hence after the traditional night of love, as in the medieval *taclied*, or in Romeo and Juliet ("It was the nightingale and not the lark").[43] It has become a very different relation, pressed into a conventional category. "But alas with the morning sun Departure presses my heart"; and "I went, you stood with downcast eyes, and looked after me with tears in them."

Presumably it was the same pressure away from a distinctive occasion towards poetic convention that dictated the change in the closing choreography. If the lover has arrived, surely he should be the one seen in the act of departing?[44] That creates symmetry, but an artificially imposed one, quite unlike the symmetry that came about spontaneously as the deep shape of the Lake Zurich occasion and its expression. If we follow the intricacies of the changed ending, it no longer rings true. As things first stood, before the lover leaves *he* stands watching *her* go (perhaps back into the house) and the pain of parting brings tears to *his* eyes. "Und doch" (And yet). He answers *his* tears with *his* affirmation: what happiness it is to be loved and to love!! In the revised version, *he* goes while *she* stays, *she* is now the one looking down at the ground, yet *he* somehow knows that *she* has tears in her eyes as *she* watches *him* go. The adversative "And yet" has lost its referent—his reaction to his own emotion. The tears outdone by happiness are no longer his tears, the happiness, once affirmed with good right on his own behalf, is no longer his. Hers then? But that is something he can at best patronizingly presume; at this distance he can no more know her conclusions than he can actually see her eyes. That leaves the last two lines as a free-floating sentencia. Goethe has kept for convenience the outward structure and rhyme scheme of the poem's last four lines so that at first glance all seems well; but the poem's vital thread has been lost.

Confusions

"Welcome and Parting" as revised above was published in 1789 and became the canonical text, held in high esteem by poetry lovers and scholars, the poetic flaws unnoticed. True, unless they went back to the *Iris* printing "Mir schlug das Herz," they had nothing to compare it with, until the Hamburg Edition in 1948 printed the original and revised texts in parallel, providing the basis for genetic insight and aesthetic discrimination. Otherwise the original version was only to be found listed piecemeal as variants in the apparatus at the back of critical editions, which is no place to appreciate and compare poetic effect. Genetically speaking, it was the changes that were the variants, so this order of presentation got things the wrong way round anyway.

Worse, the revised texts of this and other early poems have been regularly printed and discussed, deep into the twentieth century, as if they *were themselves* the early poems, and this even in publications expressly committed to a chronological and evolutionary view: an edition of the complete works in chronological sequence; the complete poems in chronological order; a study by a prominent scholar of *Goethe in the Changing Imagery of His Poetry*.[45] In every case, the later versions are printed as early poems, to the point where the last-named book enthuses over formulations of a youthful genius and "miraculous" combinations which are actually the cautious re-phrasing of a writer now aged forty. Even the most authoritative Goethe scholar of the mid-twentieth century, though aware of these discrepancies, chose to disregard them.[46] A mistake in textual editing becomes a falsification of literary—and personal—history.

Obligations

The revised text of "Welcome and Parting" is inauthentic because it fails to hang together as a poem. That doesn't yet have anything to do with the biographical facts of whether and when the poet and his beloved met and what passed between them. So the criticism isn't a case of the much-mocked phrase of nineteenth-century biographistic scholarship, "Hier irrt Goethe!" (Here Goethe is mistaken). A poem has a life of its own, yet the life flows from the occasion, and in this instance the occasion has been distorted, and the altered details don't cohere. But that does after all have a biographical consequence. The dawn scene Goethe imposed on the story would have compromised Friederike and made the poem an impossible gift on the 1779 visit. He would have had to arrive on her doorstep poetically empty-handed, as he no doubt did. (Quite what we are to make of the fact that Friederike had in her possession a copy of just the poem's first ten lines is a puzzle—did Goethe at some stage make her such a half-hearted gift, avoiding the embarrassment of the full revised story?)

The visits to both women in the event passed off cordially, so that Goethe recorded feeling "able to live in peace with these reconciled spirits."[47] The two poems as revised, one for the better, one for the worse, went into the 1789 volume. Poetry and truth were kept apart. But only just. If occasions were rooted in human reality, they must surely be someone else's reality too. To that extent faithfulness to occasions can entail a personal obligation, in some cases even to historical truth. We have seen the problem—though for him it was not a problem since he had a firm ethical solution—in Montaigne. It was a continual issue for Wordsworth, who "encouraged historical, even biographical, interpretations of the poems, while actually presenting revised, even transformed texts."[48] Famously, *The Prelude*, subtitled *The Growth of a Poet's Mind* and purporting to capture authentically the early stages of that process, went on being revised throughout Wordsworth's life—a very different sort of growth.

So did Friederike eventually see the revised poem when it was published? Did she, later still, read the lengthy section of Goethe's autobiography that recounts his love for her and his rides out from Strasbourg to her Sesenheim home?[49] Though for obvious reasons he doesn't quote the poem there, the link would have been clear enough. What the revised text says about their relationship might well have caused her distress.

In a more extreme case still, Goethe exploited his relations with a young engaged couple and his own allegedly near-suicidal passion for the fiancée, plus the actual suicide of a colleague likewise unhappy in love and career, to make a sensational romantic amalgam, *The Sufferings of Young Werther*. The friends, Christian and Charlotte, proved remarkably tolerant, secure enough in their private feelings for each other and their public reputation not to worry too much about their (mis)representation in a novel everyone in 1774 was reading; but it was a close-run thing.[50]

That early tragic passion in Goethe's life is balanced by a late one, a moving instance of poetry struggling to contain experience. At the age of seventy-four, he fell wildly in love with a young woman of seventeen, Ulrike von Levetzow, whom he met in the early eighteen-twenties in the spa society of fashionable Marienbad. She responded with an innocent affection, but his marriage proposal was too grotesque to be considered seriously. Shattered by the rejection, in the coach back to Weimar Goethe wrote a massive Elegy, scribbling intensively from stage to stage in last year's calendar-diary and working on it in the evenings.[51] The original document plainly registers the jolts of a journey on rough roads, what the young Goethe had evoked fifty years before in "An Schwager Kronos" as an allegorical ride into immortality. More significantly, it shows the mix of emotional inspiration and concentrated craftsmanship. Once back home, an ultimate fair copy bound in red morocco became for Goethe a cult object, read aloud to him repeatedly as consolation by his old friend Zelter. The poem's mass (138 lines in six-line stanzas), its taut argument and unrelenting intensity make it difficult to paraphrase or excerpt. It recalls the whole course of the affair from moments of supreme happiness down to the depths of despair, voicing the trauma of a man whose stable and fulfilled life has suddenly been made meaningless. The poet is left abandoned by his companions, a King Lear figure in a bleak landscape of rock and moor.

Worse, emotionally speaking, was to come. In probably the blackest mood Goethe ever knew, certainly the blackest ever documented, he composed a further fifty-line outburst, in even more rugged chunks, addressed "An Werther" (the early novel had recently been reissued). What he says to his long-dead fictional friend could not be darker. By going on ahead Werther has not lost much. Is there any consolation in poetry? Goethe had long ago suggested so. At the close of his drama *Torquato Tasso*, the poet consoles himself for a disastrous life with the thought that when humankind falls silent in its pain, a god gave him the power to utter what he was suffering: "Gab mir ein Gott zu sagen, was ich leide."[52] The address to Werther ironizes this claim, yet Goethe had already placed those words as the epigraph over his great elegy. So had poetry got him over the love-crisis or hadn't it?

Goethe was manipulating a culture of his own creating, drawing both deep doubt and tentative strength from earlier and earliest work. There was also a new poem to be found a place in the nexus. Dating from just before the Levetzow affair, "Aussöhnung" (Reconciliation) was a hymn to the soothing power of music. At Marienbad Goethe had heard Anna Milder-Hauptmann sing and the Polish pianist Maria Szymanowska play. The chronology of events was thus i) serene experience and praise of music; ii) traumatic love-experience and its harrowing record; iii) reflections on Werther and suicide that devalue life. That makes a steep downward slope ending in an abyss. Goethe finally resisted its pull. We can imagine the three poems lying on his desk, as variously disposable as the scenes for *Faust Part One* had been. Their genetic sequence told an unambiguous story of a movement deep into existential darkness. Goethe chose not to make that story public, real as it had been, but to reverse the order: first the suicidal thoughts, then the love-experience, finally the praise of music, and reconciliation. The three linked poems became the "Trilogie der Leidenschaft" (Trilogy of Passion).

Was this deliberate arrangement another betrayal of the truth of occasions? Perhaps this time it was more a declaration of the truth of a larger occasion, a moment of standing back and resolving to recover (Goethe had also been physically ill). And this time it was all about himself, so no living person was traduced and no experience was misrepresented. All three poems are given voice, and the first and second remain deeply disturbing. But as far as can be, they are reconciled, at least to the point where the poet can live with them. That *is* the decisive experience, the complex occasion, deeply felt but sovereignly shaped.

No wonder that right to the end Goethe went on saying "poetic substance is the substance of one's own life."[53] But that could have unwelcome consequences:

> I now have another particular torment that good, sensible, benevolently inclined people want to interpret my poems and think that for the fullest insight it is indispensable to know the very special circumstances [*Spezialissima*] in which and from which the poems arose, whereas they ought to be content that somebody has raised the special circumstances [*das Speziale*] to such a general level that without more ado they can take them over into their own special being [*ihre eigene Spezialität*].[54]

What began as a complaint against the public has turned into a concise poetics of occasions. From the originating circumstances to a finished poem should be a one-way street. It is fine to see not just *the fact that*, but *the way in which* an occasion has generated a poem. To follow the creative process back to its origins may help prevent the poem being taken for granted, as if it were just a block of print timelessly and undynamically present on the page. Print is inert until enlivened by the reader's imagination as the poem unfolds—one more instance of emotion recollected in tranquility, this time on the reader's part. What is not legitimate is to reverse the direction and turn the form itself back into the "very special circumstances" from which it arose.

Undoing poems with the facts that lay behind them is what nineteenth-century Goethe scholarship is commonly blamed for, and it did sometimes cross the line from interpretation into biographical reduction. But the baby has since been thrown out with the bath-water. For fear of slipping into crude biographism, over-cautious practice often seeks to deny poetry its personal origin and import. Students are told, don't for heaven's sake use the poet's name, but say rather "the speaker," in German "das lyrische Ich" (the lyrical persona). These are all squeamish abstractions, or allegedly conscious constructs by the poet himself, even when the utterance of a real individual's emotion is part of an unbreakable declared nexus, as in that dedicatory poem of Goethe's to *Faust*, or in the "Marienbad Elegy," a cry of unmistakably personal pain that cannot be ascribed to a "generalized poetic voice."[55] "Raising special circumstances to a general level" so that readers can "take them over into their own being" is not an *im*personal but a *trans*personal process, a bridging of the gap between individual and collective, an invitation to empathy from the firm ground of identity. An epigram of 1785 hits off the paradox of uniqueness and community: "Alle gleichen wir uns, denn wir sind eines Geschlechtes; / Allen gleichen wir nicht, sagt einem jeden das Herz." (All of us are alike, members all of one species. / We are not all the same, everyone says in his heart.)[56]

Outside the seminar room, more relaxed Common Readers don't think of a poem as a cool construct. Except where it is an evident role-play, as in a poem like Goethe's "Prometheus" or "Ganymed," they assume they are hearing the voice of a real person with something to communicate, an assumption that Goethe was prominent in creating—the genesis of modern poetry-reading is largely his doing. The poet's voice then becomes increasingly distinctive as the scope of our reading widens, since except in classroom exercises we commonly read not just single poems but a substantial part of a poet's work. Characteristic themes and motifs recur across the texts, impressions accumulate, readings cross-fertilize. The result is not a factual biography, but it is a coherent poetic personality. This is what ultimately underlies Goethe's famous statement that his works were all fragments of a great confession[57]—usually read foregrounding the idea of confession, the emphasis needs to be as much on "fragments," and the single great corpus they go to make up. It was precisely the purpose of his autobiography to provide the matrix that would give them coherence. The foreword to that work quotes a friend's letter requesting such an account. Together with Goethe's commentary, it is the largest-scale program and fullest justification for genetic explanation.[58]

The old idea of the writer's development may be too simple and systematic, but it can be broken down into the successive explorations of that one person's experience, experiments conducted on self, substance, and style, with no necessary teleology beyond the outcome of unplanned trial and error.[59] In Goethe's case the resulting variety is so great as to defy at first the quest for cohesion. Looking back, he said of his beginnings: "I really had no style. With every work I had to grope my way tentatively forward, depending how the subject was constituted."[60] Variety followed necessarily from the dependence on occasions. But there is a balancing constancy over sixty years of uninterrupted lyrical writing and several inner and outer renewals. They all have an unmistakable voice. As Nietzsche said, "Every mind has its sound."[61]

Yet the sound of Goethe's mind proved in a remarkable and moving way to be shareable by another poetic voice. At the heart of his late Persian collection the *West-Östlicher Divan*, in the Book of Suleika, four poems spoken by the fictive beloved were written by the real-life love of Goethe's sixties, Marianne von Willemer. She thus joined in a real dialogue secretly woven into the lyrical fiction. For decades she (and Goethe) had kept her part in its genesis a secret, until it came out through a chance of conversation with the writer Wilhelm Grimm. At first not believed by some, and then vastly exaggerated by others into the notion that Marianne von Willemer perhaps wrote even more of the collection, the case for her authorship of the four poems she claimed as hers, and for no more, is firm.[62]

Genesis of a Classicism

For all his immense poetic power, Goethe was no literary theorist on the grand scale, though he knew in retrospect what his practice of occasions meant and had achieved. Yet behind it lay a potential theory of creativity waiting to be formulated. Luckily someone was at hand whose private problems and analytical power inspired him to turn this potential into a grand account of poetic typology and cultural history. Schiller told Goethe, "I lacked the object, the body, for some speculative ideas, and you put me on the track of them."[63] Goethe had himself become an occasion.

Schiller, ten years the younger man, had admired Goethe's writing since his youth. For the last decade of his short life, he was to have the privilege and pleasure of observing and collaborating in the genesis of further major works. He too had begun his career with a sensational success, the drama *The Brigands*, but it brought him a ban from his ruler, the Duke of Württemberg, on all further writing. The only option was to escape and gamble on making a literary living in some other state; but on top of the problems of surviving in exile, he found his creative impulse flagging, inhibited by his critical consciousness:

> The boldness, the living fire that I had before I knew a single rule is something I've been lacking now for several years. I *see* myself creating and shaping, I observe the play of enthusiasm, and my imagination acts the less freely for knowing that it is no longer without witnesses.[64]

The cure seemed to be yet further critical consciousness, in the hope that it might homeopathically restore spontaneous creation as a second nature. From that crisis, and the deeper delving into philosophy, Schiller's monumental essays in aesthetics stemmed.

Beside this tortuous process, Goethe's creativity seemed enviably straightforward, its results unproblematic. At first the spectacle of such ease generated an acute love-hatred in the ambitious Schiller. That became unreserved love (Schiller's term) when their distant acquaintance turned into a working partnership and cordial friendship, and he could feel himself recognized by the one contemporary who mattered to him. But he still needed to fathom what made them so different, not just as individuals but as types, and types representative of the whole course of Western cultural history. An immense birthday letter he wrote Goethe in August 1794 distinguished an intuitive, spontaneous creativity (Goethe's) from a speculative, analytical kind (Schiller's own). "I seem to be writing a treatise," Schiller ended his letter. It did indeed become, in yet another genesis, a full-blown treatise, *Über naïve und sentimentalische Dichtung* (*On Primal and Reflective Poetry*).[65] Schiller's term "naïve" meant unselfconscious writing, immediately rendering a directly experienced nature, while "sentimentalisch" meant writing that is hyperconscious both in the act of creation and in the attitude to a world from which the writer has been cut off by the complexity of modern culture. The contrasting characters and creative modes of these two eighteenth-century writers fitted into (or, seen genetically, provided the inspiration for) a dual vision of literature, going back to the Greeks, who were harmoniously integrated in their world, and coming down to the Moderns, who were only ever able to yearn elegiacally for a lost world, or to conjure it up as a wistful idyll, or to satirize present reality in the light of the ideal. The contrast is caught in Schiller's epigrammatic formulation, "The Greeks had natural feeling. We have a feeling for the Natural."[66]

Goethe and Schiller, in common with all their contemporaries, were located at a historical watershed. The quarrel of the Ancients and the Moderns was a long familiar issue. Now Schiller was explaining the weaknesses of the Moderns by their location in cultural time, but he did allow them, a touch grudgingly, the compensation of modern spiritual complexity. The Ancients rendered the world itself, a perfect poetic match though necessarily limited through its very objectivity; the Moderns' response to the world was an imperfect match, but limitless in its forms of subjectivity. The modern preponderance of spirit over matter could be a ground for criticism—Christian writing, Klopstock for example, comes in for some straight talking as unsensuous, not plastic, not visual enough.[67] But at least there can be some credit for both sides, as there had to be at the individual level if the reflective Schiller was to hold his head high in the relationship with his primal friend.

Even so, some are more equal than others. Goethe, nowhere named in the treatise but recognizable in the examples Schiller singles out for praise, himself represents the ideal. As one of a few rare spirits—Shakespeare, Cervantes, Molière are others—he is either a throw-back to the primal quality of the Ancients, or its miraculous reconstitution in and despite modern times.

Schiller's ultimate ideal would have been a reconciliation of primal and reflective in a reflective idyll—a logical impossibility, given the mutually exclusive terms in which he had defined the two phenomena. What could, however, be achieved in practice was a balance of subject and object, spirit and flesh, mind and world. While waiting for the far-off poetic millennium, there could at least be mutual aid: the analytical Schiller could help the intuitive Goethe to organise the materials for projects (*Faust*, *Wilhelm Meister's Apprenticeship*) that had grown almost too large for the grasp. In return Goethe's very concrete example could be the model for Schiller to earth his poetic high-mindedness in the grim world of the Thirty Years War and produce the greatest of

German historical dramas, the *Wallenstein* trilogy. Such integration was worthy of being called a classicism. Their friendship and cooperation, amazingly harmonious for two such antithetical creative personalities, was the genesis of the last Classicism in European literature, named for its small-town location: Weimar.

7: Live and Learn: *Werther* and *Wilhelm Meister*

Matters of Life and Death

JUST HOW FAR Goethe's poetic substance grew out of the substance of his own life was shown and confessed in his sensational first novel. In 1772 a colleague at the Imperial Court at Wetzlar, Karl Wilhelm Jerusalem, was driven to suicide by social and career frustrations and unhappy love for a married woman. In the same place and time Goethe was smitten with the likewise unavailable fiancée of another colleague, Johann Christian Kestner. The following year he wrote *The Sufferings of Young Werther*, inspired, after that period of gestation, by the shock of Jerusalem's death, down to minute detail: the culminating scenes are an extensive montage of Kestner's letters recording the circumstances of the suicide and the burial.[1] Some of the most moving passages in all of German prose are Kestner's formulations that Goethe borrowed verbatim: creativity lay in seeing the potential of sober report to make a somber ending after so much high emotion. Less was more.

Goethe's infatuation with Kestner's Charlotte gave him empathy with the dead man's situation: "I have added my feelings to his story, and so it makes a marvelous whole"[2]—to be precise, it makes a lyrical prose narrative of a man overwhelmed at the novel's happy beginning by the beauty of the natural world, then as the mood darkens, overwhelmed by its implacable destructiveness; first ecstatic at the deep affinity he feels with Lotte, then in despair as she dutifully represses the love for him that he is rightly sure she feels. All this is conveyed wholly by Werther's letters to a never-heard correspondent: a one-way epistolary novel. At the end, an "Editor's Report" maintains the fiction of real documents assiduously brought together by this anonymous author since Werther's death.

The closeness to the lives of four real people became widely known, generating a public interest in proportion to the novel's sensational success. That was potentially embarrassing for the Kestners, though in the end they took it well. "If you could feel the thousandth part of what 'Werther' is for a thousand hearts," Goethe cajoled them, "you wouldn't count the cost of what you've contributed." For Lotte "to know her name is being pronounced with reverence by a thousand sacred lips is surely compensation for any concerns."[3]

The sensation generated legends. First, that there was a wave of suicides by young men dressed in Werther costume (as Goethe himself and his companions were on their Swiss journey—that much obviously was a fashion). But no suicide *à la Werther*, let alone a wave of them, has ever been documented.[4] A letter from Friedrich Nicolai to Isaak Iselin of January 17, 1775, does record that "a hysterical young person" poisoned him- (or her-?) self after reading *Werther*: so, unnamed and not Werther's method. Likewise in 1778 Christel von Lassberg drowned herself from unhappy love in the Ilm at Weimar, allegedly with a copy of the novel in her pocket:[5] so, wrong sex, a time-lag, and again a different method. Goethe himself speaks in his autobiography, long after the event, about how friends believed the novel *might* be imitated to the point of suicide, but with no sign that anyone did.[6] Werther's legendary emulators remain elusive.

For Goethe's own part, the English graveyard poetry of Young and others had long led him to reflect on suicide; he had even kept a dagger at his bedside, experimentally pressing it "a few inches" [*sic!*] into his chest. Failing to manage it, he "threw off all this grotesque hypochondria and resolved to live"[7]—this at a time before *Werther* was even conceived. It looks as if Goethe was safe from suicide well before the emotional crisis over Lotte.

Yet in later years he was responsible for the personal leg of the legend, writing about the "efforts and decisions it cost [him], to escape from the waves of death."[8] But this was in a letter of condolence to his old friend Zelter, whose son had just killed himself, and Goethe was drawn into a mood of dark solidarity. Earlier, in the midst of revising the novel, he remarked sardonically that "the author was wrong not to shoot himself when he'd finished writing it."[9] But at that point he is going through a bad phase with his not-quite-lover Charlotte von Stein, and is plainly self-dramatizing and fishing for sympathy. Earlier, nearer to the writing of *Werther*, his references to "hang-ish and hangworthy thoughts," and to "not wanting to shoot [him]self just yet," sound decidedly ironic—the second phrase could almost be Heine.[10]

The unreality of the suicide threat is only half the issue. The other half is the claim that writing the story was a sufficient therapy to cure the impulse—hardly a negligible question for our survey of literary genesis. Yet if by fathoming the experiences he shared with Jerusalem, and by formulating them through Werther with such clarity and power, Goethe did indeed work them out of his system and save himself, why did these literary processes do nothing for Werther, distancing, clarifying, and calming? For the letters are fictionally his, his words, expressing his thoughts, insights, visions. As Goethe's creation, they are a recognized classic of

German prose. Can they be merely Goethe's means to portray Werther, with no therapeutic gain for Werther himself, engaged as he is in an identical creativity?

No gain for Werther must indeed have been Goethe's attitude, conscious or not, since the few other writings that the suicide leaves behind are dismissed by the editor as mere short essays and disjointed thoughts.[11] Inconsistently, Werther is thus left without the beneficial effect Goethe later claimed had been decisive for himself. As the young Thomas Mann reflected when he was creating his own unhappy outsiders, "To portray a human being unfit for life and fated to die, a writer only needs to give himself—leaving out the creativity."[12] But Werther patently possesses it. Scholarship now commonly writes him off as a creative failure, though earlier critics took the equivalence in substance of author and character seriously: "Werther is a great lyrical writer [. . .] but beside and behind this lyricism we hear Goethe's own," or "Goethe gives Werther his own language and visual power."[13]

At one point Goethe does allow Werther the full clear-sightedness about his fate that the letter sequence embodies, but it is a passage only added in the revised version of 1787. Perhaps it was Goethe's own clear-sightedness on reworking his early text that made him want Werther to share it. But as Werther's letters are all in Wilhelm's hands, hence not accessible to be read over by Werther, Goethe has to introduce as a means something never mentioned in the first version:

> My diary, which I've been neglecting for some time, fell into my hands again today, and I am astounded at how wittingly, step by step, I went into all that! How I always saw my condition so clearly and yet acted like a child; how I now still see just as clearly, and there is still no sign of improvement.[14]

It's true that Werther has earlier had moments of self-awareness. For example, one letter records how he has told himself he won't go to see Lotte again, then, in a later continuation of the same letter, that he couldn't resist, and went after all. But after the diary has provided a moment of full clarity, it is never mentioned again. It seems Werther only remembers it this once, when it "fell into [his] hands." He evidently hadn't been keeping it for some time before, or since; and it can't have survived among the packets he sealed up before dying, or it would have been an invaluable help to the editor in reconstructing Werther's final hours. Its destruction was provided for in advance before Goethe even thought of adding it, for the first version of the text mentions that Werther disposed of a lot of papers before his death.[15]

Perhaps Goethe himself soon forgot he had introduced the diary, since it's never mentioned again. A good thing too, because it created more problems than it solved. To begin with, to have made more of it would have seriously damaged Werther's image as the writer of spontaneous impassioned letters. He would have had to be imagined practicing some kind of double-entry bookkeeping, either first drafting his letters in the diary or afterwards copying them into it. Moreover, the repeated act of writing would necessarily have redoubled the therapeutic effect, helping to rescue Werther in the way Goethe alleged that it rescued himself. It couldn't be allowed to do that since, placed at that central point, it would have aborted the tragic fiction halfway. Instead, however clear-sighted Werther is about his past course, he only foresees more of the same inescapably happening. If anything, *his* writing, unlike Goethe's, must be understood to have taken him deeper into his obsession rather than out of it, constantly twisting the knife in the wound.

So the whole notion of writing as Goethe's self-therapy is best abandoned as a legend. But what Jerusalem's suicide and its fictional derivate did do was to cast a shadow over the exuberant embracing of life that fills Goethe's early poetry. Light now meets darkness. That much was a sobering lesson learnt. Werther's suicide remained a point of reference for darker moods, down to the extreme of that bitter suggestion in the old man's poem "To Werther," that in abandoning life the young suicide hadn't missed much.

Once again, as with some early poems of Goethe's, revision had been of dubious value. Ironically, he had recognized the risks entailed by revision in the very text of the first version that he still went on to revise. Werther loves to tell the children a story; they protest when he changes anything second time round, and he has "learned from that how an author must necessarily damage his book through a . . . second, altered edition of his story, however much it may have been poetically improved."[16]

Yet revise it he did. Eight years later, the novel that had apparently first gone down on paper with scarcely a correction[17] was substantially extended, not just by the diary motif. Goethe was once again aware that revision was "delicate and dangerous," indeed flatly against nature, as he emphasizes by a grotesque corporeal metaphor: "I've been through my 'Werther' and am having it written out as a manuscript; he is going back into his mother's body; you shall see him after his rebirth."[18]

Commitment

At the same time Goethe was having another manuscript written out: the first three books of *Wilhelm Meister's Theatrical Mission*,[19] a novel for which he was again drawing on his personal substance, this time as a theatrical author. His early reputation rested, alongside *Werther*, on the historical drama *Götz von Berlichingen*. So Goethe was already in good measure a man of the theater and could write about it from the inside.

The high-sounding title—"mission"—suggests more than just the writing and putting on of plays. It echoes a contemporary movement aimed at affecting the real world, of which a young writer among writers might well feel part. From the 1760s on there was much talk of a "national theater" that would be a more settled and substantial institution than the offerings of travelling players on makeshift stages, and would be more widely accessible than the court theaters that put on largely French plays for the nobility.

There were shaky attempts at self-styled national theaters—in Vienna, Mannheim, Hamburg. When the Hamburg project failed, Lessing reflected ruefully what a naïve idea it had been to give Germans a national theater when they weren't yet a nation. The political patchwork of three hundred pieces, large states like Prussia, Austria, and Bavaria and polities too small to deserve the name, meant there was no coherent audience and—assuming a nation would want to see itself represented on stage—no congenial subject matter either. This non-nation seemed to Lessing to have no character at all, other than that of slavishly copying the French.[20] He had long argued, against the Francophile reformer Johann Christoph Gottsched, that Germany's true affinity was with English culture, with Shakespeare rather than with Corneille. In order to see that, you only had to look at some scenes he quotes from an "authentic old" German Faust play (he had in fact written them himself).[21]

Lessing was talking about moral character, expressly not about the political order. Other writers, Schiller for one, less despairing of a national character, thought the normal causality could be reversed—that a national theater didn't have to wait on the existence of a nation, but might actually help to create one, cart before horse.

> If in all dramas *one* main characteristic dominated, if our poets would agree among themselves and set up a firm alliance for this purpose—if strict selection guided their work, if their brush were devoted only to popular subjects—in a word, if we had the experience of a national stage, then we would also become a nation.[22]

That was what the ancient Greek dramatists had done—and, incidentally, what Goethe declined to do after his success with *Götz*, when he sensed a demand for more national-historical material but was reluctant to produce mere popular sequels.

Schiller's exhortation comes from the lecture "What effect can a good standing theater really have?" given to a literary society in Mannheim, where for the last few months he had been house-dramatist in the Rhineland Palatinate's national theater. He was not a great success, not popular with the actors, late in delivering plays, which then turned out to be too uncomfortably subversive for the management, and by his mere presence a diplomatic embarrassment vis-à-vis the Duke of Württemberg, from whose service he had absconded to become a free writer.

Schiller is on his way out and knows it, so he has nothing to lose in putting forward radical answers to what, as the word "really" in his title shows, was a currently much discussed issue. Theater, he continues, could be the communal channel through which "clearer ideas and principles will flow down through all the arteries of the people"; "the fog of barbarity and superstition will vanish, night yield place to light."[23] This is classic Enlightenment thinking, but to link theater and nationhood is also radical in an explicitly political way. The very notion of a unified German nation was a threat to the independence of all those absolutist ministates. Through the nineteenth century, such broader German patriotism would be felt to be as much a danger to the status quo as a French-style revolution.

Goethe's new central figure is the son of a business family who feels commerce is pitch on the wings of his spirit. His emotions and imagination badly need a way out from the constriction of small-town bourgeois life. He becomes fixated on the theater as a path to higher fulfillment. (He was not unique in his problem or its hoped-for solution. Anton Reiser, in the novel of that name, has identical problems and aspirations.)[24] Wilhelm's impulse goes back to the puppet-theater and amateur dramatics of his childhood. An affair with an actress draws him further in. Then, sent to collect money owed to the family firm, he falls in with a troupe of actors, helps them out, and at the end joins an established theater. Chance propels him into acting as a stand-in, with some success. He has written plays and believes he has it in him to make a literary career. There is talk of the great influence the theater could have on the shaping of a nation and the world,[25] of the actor as close kin to the preacher, bringing not the word of God but the voice of nature to human hearts (1,15:34). He comes to see himself as the creator of a future national theater, for which he had heard so many people sigh (1,16:49). Hence the title "Wilhelm Meister's Theatrical Mission." The odd choice of surname for his character promises at least a future mastery.

Overall, the novel gives a rich and sympathetic picture of "the whole theater business,"[26] starting with the actor-troupes who were the raw material for a more stable stage culture, but whose lively naïve beginnings risked being over-reformed on French classical lines. The fictional Madame de Retti is a portrait of the influential manageress Caroline Neuber, who was involved in Gottsched's theater reforms but came to regret that so much native vitality had been lost in the process. The novel registers the radical shift of theatrical model from French to English when, for Wilhelm as for Goethe, Shakespeare comes as a revelation, his art nothing short of reality itself.[27] Throughout, high cultural aspirations mingle with theatrical low life, like a material woven of silk and crude hemp,[28] but it is a mixture that Wilhelm in the end realistically accepts.[29] It is, though, the end of only half a book.

There are obvious reasons why this version of the novel stayed unfinished. For a fictional Wilhelm to have fulfilled his dream of creating a national theater would have been contrary to the facts: the theatrical mission hadn't been achieved in Germany, by Goethe or anyone else, so it couldn't be achieved by his "beloved dramatic image."[30] By the 1780s all he had to show was his own establishment at a minor court, more as administrator than poet, yet obliged to write entertainments for the court that interrupted his serious projects, and at best able to put on plays in a theater that was local, not national. Altogether it was a far cry from the grand ambitions his hero begins with, which Goethe had at some stage shared.[31] Perhaps after all the cart couldn't be put before the horse, theater could not create a nation but needed a prior national reality in which to take root and grow.

So was the novel's grandiose title from the first ironical? Elegiac rather, in proportion as the dream, private and public, had already faded when Goethe began writing. The text has too many signs of sympathy and whole-hearted commitment to be read as ironic. In particular, Wilhelm's positive decision in favor of the theater at the close of the provisionally final book 6 is emphatic. Goethe's irony is reserved for the people who failed to support the native culture, specifically the nobility, who are observed in a castle giving hospitality of sorts to the actors but never serious about their art, always distracted by trivial pursuits. (Goethe had by now had plenty of mixed experience of the upper classes, including a visit by Prince Heinrich of Prussia, Frederick the Great's brother, which yielded "observations shot on the wing.")[32]

The fact remains that sympathy and commitment to the theater had reached a dead end, and with them the novel seemingly had too. When Goethe slipped out of Carlsbad at 3 a.m. on September 3, 1786, heading for Italy—a positively dramatic escape from the court and his Weimar responsibilities—it was one of the works he took with him, at least mentally. He had recently received a not altogether funny birthday-card purporting to be from his unfinished works, asking him to get a move on and complete them. Of four dramas, *Iphigenie auf Tauris*, *Egmont*, *Torquato Tasso*, and *Faust*, the first two would indeed be completed in Italy. He also mentions having new thoughts enough on Wilhelm, but there is no sign that anything came of them down south. Yet so massive an undertaking—six books written, six more planned—was not to be lightly abandoned. Once Goethe was back from Italy in the autumn of 1788, he had to face up to making something of it.

Retractation

Still it was more than two years before pen touched paper, and no wonder. At such a distance from the original inspiration, Goethe felt more like the work's editor than its author,[33] out of touch with the childhood memories and the feel for the young hero's organic growth that had made the writing so palpably alive. Its program had been to "work artfully towards naturalness."[34] Such effects were no longer a priority for a writer matured and reoriented by two years spent among Classical remains and Renaissance art. To write now about the aspirations of an earlier self seemed to him at most a "pseudo-confession."[35] So what new angle could make the old material fruitful? Nothing short of a fundamental change of attitude that goes beyond elegy, even beyond sympathy. It is announced in the new title: *Wilhelm Meister's Apprenticeship*.

The new conception[36] treats the old ambition as an aberration; the story of a young man's bohemian adventure becomes a novel of his education, of trial and error, overwhelmingly error. This consists in being weaned off theater, rejecting and regretting his once deeply felt involvement and his proven talent. His generous impulses are disclaimed and discredited. "Master" no more, he is now humorously labelled "Wilhelm Scholar";[37] in the title concept he is of course a mere apprentice. It is true he does establish himself for a while as an actor with a reputable company, even as a director (HA 7:345); but he soon drifts frictionlessly away (7:490), leaving the novel's final books to show emphatically that he is now directed by others, in particular by a masonic-style Society of the Tower, which, unaccountably but benevolently, has had him in view all along. He is left to acquiesce and conform, even to wish he had earlier been better guided rather than left to his own devices. In retrospect he is to "drink his error in full draughts"—an assurance that he is not to regret any of his past foolishnesses rings hollow (7:495). Henceforth venture becomes caution, active development declines into passive socialization. "I leave myself entirely in the hands of my friends," Wilhelm finally says, "it is in vain to strive after one's own will in this world" (7:537). Scarcely any room is left for natural growth, which is elsewhere Goethe's deepest and most fruitful idea.

Correspondingly little survives in the *Apprenticeship* of the old impulses and their language of commitment, only enough to show what it was that Wilhelm has been cured of. His entire past is judged to have been a false turning based on an illusion about himself. In a retrospect of some decades later, Goethe is emphatic not just that this is the reworked novel's message, but that it was always there, from the very first conception. He recalls the time when he took up the project again, and links it back to its roots in the (not named) *Theatrical Mission*:

The beginnings of "Wilhelm Meister" had been long quiescent. They arose from an obscure presentiment of the great truth: that a person may often want to try something for which nature has denied them the talent [. . .] an inner feeling warns them to desist, but they cannot see things clearly and are driven along a false path to a false purpose, without realizing what's happening. [This is] what has been called dilettantism.[38]

Goethe's statement totally misrepresents the book's origins. When he wrote these *Annals* c. 1819/20, he was relying on distant memory, and the later reworking of the novel will have long since overlaid its true beginnings in his mind, without any conscious falsification. The fact remains that nowhere in the *Theatrical Mission* is any such "great truth" hinted at, not even obscurely.

Readers of the *Apprenticeship*, at the time of publication and for more than a century after, had no way of knowing how the first version had read, how wholeheartedly Wilhelm's impulses and achievements had there been presented—in fact they had no way of knowing that there ever *was* a first version at all, much less that a direct linear narrative had been turned into a recursive, self-cancelling one. For the *Theatrical Mission* had entirely vanished, its manuscript probably destroyed by Goethe after he completed the reworking. But by fortunate chance, Barbara Schulthess of Zurich and her daughter, friends since Goethe's Swiss journey of 1775, transcribed the whole text he had sent them—he regularly did send various friends his work-in-progress. The transcript then went underground until it turned up in the family's papers in 1910.[39]

Throughout the genesis of the *Apprenticeship*, Goethe notably never quotes the original title or anything else from the content of the *Mission*, not even in his letters to Schiller, his close collaborator on the revised novel. The most he ever says, after following Schiller's advice and "using the scissors on some theoretical-practical twaddle" that had found its way into the new text, is that "one never quite gets rid of remnants of the earlier treatment."[40] He never says anything about the exact nature of that treatment—at least not in writing. The two had many long meetings, with intensive talk on the novel's narrative strategy and detail, so who knows? But the absence of any mention of the *Theatrical Mission* from their correspondence remains telling. As it happens, Schiller's own early experience— "I am better acquainted [with the theater business] than I have cause to wish"[41]—might have qualified him to sympathize with the original Wilhelm, and to judge how far he was actually more than a dilettante.

Disposing of an old manuscript after reworking it was Goethe's common practice. But why did he have so radical a change of mind and intention in the *Apprenticeship*? There was more to the shift in his attitude than mere elapse of time, or personal maturing and a new aesthetic. Larger things had shifted. The French Revolution had transformed the European political scene. At the highpoint of its horrors, in 1793, Goethe was just back from accompanying Duke Carl August on the disastrous Austro-German invasion of France, which had set out to restore the monarchy, and from witnessing the subsequent siege of Mainz by French forces.[42] He needed a sheet-anchor in troubled times: "I'm wondering what to start on in the New Year, one must attach oneself with main force to something. I think it will be my old novel."[43] Old indeed—a whole eight years since book 6 was completed in November 1785. That made it the more open to reshaping. Goethe later admitted to the "limitless effort to deal poetically with this most terrible of events [the Revolution] in its causes and consequences."[44] Politics, consciously or not, would be a significant pressure on the new version.

For there had been, in calmer times, political implications and potential consequences to the national theater movement. Culture was to help unify a nation. No such outcome had been brought about. At most, by the mid seventeen-nineties Goethe's and Schiller's creative and combative efforts were beginning to give German literature an influential center in Weimar. That was achievement enough to make Goethe resent a published criticism that Germany lacked prose works of classic quality—this in 1795, when he was in the midst of completing and publishing the *Apprenticeship*, his own major prose work. His irate response points out that the necessary conditions for "classic" writers and works were not present in Germany: no single center of cultural life, no history of great events, no common spirit, no tradition for writers to learn from—all this and much else was lacking.[45] An outstanding national author could only be expected from a nation—which Germany was not. Yet it couldn't be blamed for being politically a set of fragments. Nor (this is the political recantation towards which everything moves) nor were the radical upheavals (*Umwälzungen*) desirable that could prepare classic works—that is, by bringing about the unified structure out of which they might grow. Goethe is looking across at the extreme upheavals in France. Political chaos, regicide, and a Reign of Terror would be too high a price to pay for the creation of a single nation and the possibility of a national literature.

His argument thus confronts, consciously or not, those earlier ambitions for the theater's role. It becomes clear why they had to be rejected through Wilhelm's person. It would have been embarrassing at this critical moment in history to appear sympathetic, even in a nostalgic fiction, to the initiatives of the 1770s. It wasn't enough that they should fail; they had to be expressly deplored. *Wilhelm Meister's Apprenticeship* becomes part of a conservative withdrawal.

Crucially, at the personal level, by losing his self-confidence and giving up his freedom to act according to his own lights, Wilhelm is renouncing the central human right that the Enlightenment had fought to secure: to think for oneself and not be controlled by "guardians" (*Vormünder*). These are not the governmental guardians of Plato's *Republic*, but, as in Kant's classic essay of 1784, "What is Enlightenment?," the metaphorical equivalents of a child's guardians, parental or other, in whose eyes the People are mere children.[46] The role of a guardian is explicitly celebrated by one of Wilhelm's personal guides:

> It is incredible what an educated man can do for himself and others when, without wanting to dominate, he has sensibility [*Gemüt*] enough to be the guardian of many, leads them to do at the right time what they would all really like to do and guides them to their purposes, which they mostly have very well in view, and are only not finding the right way. (608)

Behind the gentle liberal tone can be heard the authoritarian certainty of knowing better than themselves what the many "really" want. In a world made insecure by revolution, authority needed to be reasserted. Even the temperamentally less conservative Schiller, faced with the horrors of 1793, briefly gave house-room to the notion of guardianly power (*vormundschaftliche Gewalt*), which the human race had demonstrably not grown out of needing.[47]

It is sometimes said, to explain Goethe's turn against the theater, that he had simply lost his belief in its effectiveness. On the contrary, in the 1790s he tried to use it repeatedly (though not very successfully) in dramas and dramatic fragments that treated political and revolutionary themes critically. It was all part of what he ruefully labelled his "limitless effort to deal poetically" with the revolution.

In these and in other genres, Goethe is on a new mission; he strives for balance, satirizing extremes of subversion, reaction, or injustice;[48] he shows some sympathy for an idealist who dies in revolutionary Paris, but declares a resolve to defend a placid German burgher way of life against unwanted turbulence.[49] At root, he is opposed to political trial-and-error—and what was the revolution but (in the scientist and aphorist Lichtenberg's phrase) "experimental politics"?[50] The spread of liberal ideas was already dangerous. Change should come from above, but even that couldn't be trusted: "A certain sense of freedom, a striving for democracy, had spread to the upper classes. People didn't seem to realize what all must first be lost so as to reach any sort of ambiguous gain."[51] The upshot of this attempt at balance was a pragmatic—clearly not altogether disinterested—conservatism, a preference for the frying-pan of moderate absolutism over the fire of radical change.

Goethe duly tried to persuade the Weimar community—again notably trusting to the effect theater could have on the people—that this was where their interests lay. Epilogues to some of the plays he put on in the court theater carried exhortations to contentment with the status quo, Biedermeier *avant la lettre*. They speak of "the joy that domesticity, love, friendship, trustingness may grant," these are "goods that are common to us all, in whatever station, high or low, fortune has placed us." (Reconciling people to their lowly "station" is a hallmark of the conservative.) These social goods are allegedly independent of politics and power: "No tyrant can rob us of them, the best of princes cannot give them." Goldoni's play *War* is to remind the audience of the present wars and "make [them] feel the happiness of the tranquility that [they] here enjoy far from all misery."[52] These pieces went almost unnoticed until the newest, chronologically ordered, complete works put the spotlight on them.

But one text, a celebrated epigram, also appears in a new light against this historical and political background:

> Zur Nation euch zu bilden, ihr hoffet es, Deutsche, vergebens;
> Bildet, ihr könnt es, dafür freier zu Menschen euch aus![53]

[Germans, you hope in vain to make yourselves into a nation,
Make yourselves rather—you can!—free human beings instead.]

Usually read simply as a piece of humane high-mindedness, it is in fact specifically discouraging notions of national unity and preaching a non-political kind of freedom. It clearly belongs to Goethe's cautious conservatism.

Genesis (and Failed Genesis) of a Genre

Goethe doesn't just show an education: he makes Wilhelm conscious of the process even as it is happening. So much so that he projects it into his past as something he always intended. Against the narrow views of his commercially minded cousin Werner, who now runs the family business, he claims that from his youth it was always "obscurely my wish and my intention to educate myself, just as I am." The active verb ("mich auszubilden"), and the phrase "just as I am" ("ganz wie ich da bin") suggest a spontaneous process[54] that would make the most of his true nature rather than a training by others such as he is about to undergo—to that extent a remaining link between the novel's two versions. But education as such, and particularly reeducation after a mistaken development, played no part at all in the *Theatrical Mission*. It has now become dominant.

The interactions of self and society in *Wilhelm Meister's Apprenticeship* set a pattern for later German writing.[55] The novel of education, the *Bildungsroman*, became the alternative to the social novel of the English, French, and Russian traditions. It is always the story of the central figure's formation—experiences, errors, socialization—which necessarily has to happen somewhere, so not in a vacuum, yet it doesn't focus on the fabric and ethos of a broader society. It can be argued, as Lessing, Schiller, and Goethe all argued, that Germany lacked the structures to support literature, and this must apply even more to the novel than to the drama. As if by magic the first recognizably European-style social novel arose in Germany promptly after the first unification under Prussia in 1871. Theodor Fontane's novels are dense with the realities of a new order, and are clear-sighted about its faults.

In the meantime, Goethe's example inspired Adalbert Stifter's *Indian Summer* (*Der Nachsommer*, 1857) and Gottfried Keller's *Green Henry* (*Der grüne Heinrich*, 1854/5), similarly massive histories of a young man's trials and errors, where guidance leads to harmony with the surrounding world. In every case, the character's line of development has points of contact with his author's own past—the Bildungsroman is the closest of all narrative genres to autobiography. That central statement of Wilhelm's in the *Apprenticeship* about his deep-rooted commitment to personal fulfillment exactly echoes a confession of Goethe's, dating indeed from the time the *Mission* was first being worked on:

> This desire to raise the pyramid of my existence, whose firmly founded base is made clear to me, to the highest possible pinnacle, outweighs everything else and hardly allows me to forget it for a moment.[56]

The sheer bulk typical of the *Bildungsroman* allows for—or is the result of—a long and tortuous development. The tradition outdoes itself in the twists and turns that shaped its later most prominent exemplar, Thomas Mann's *Magic Mountain* (1924). Consciously a parody of *Wilhelm Meisters Apprenticeship* but ultimately serious, it too features a young man hemmed in by rival educators and only gradually emerging from naïve passivity. It again discreetly shadows a personal development of its author. The line is not decisively broken until Günter Grass's *Tin Drum* (1959) with the ineducably anarchic Oskar Matzerath.

A new genesis undoes the old. Turning the *Theatrical Mission* into the *Apprenticeship* meant that a young man's adventure was aborted and his valuable impulses disclaimed. But it also meant that an alternative form of the novel was crowded out. The *Theatrical Mission* is more concrete, more colorful, livelier, richer in social reality, closer in its almost picaresque informality to the mode of (say) Fielding's *Joseph Andrews*, as against the more cerebral intricacy of the *Apprenticeship*. A Fielding style was perhaps too down-to-earth for a Goethe intent now on high literature, which included rescuing the novelist from his still unprestigious status as only, in Schiller's phrase, the half-brother of the poet.[57] Critical opinion mostly goes along with the orthodoxy that says Goethe's reworked text is a masterpiece beyond all comparison superior to its first form. But it is worth recalling how the *Mission*'s first presenter, seeing with fresh eyes this rediscovered and highly characteristic early work of Goethe's, appreciated its richness and vividness and lamented their loss with a cry of "how could Goethe undo this?"

> If it is permissible for a great writer to be ruthless towards himself, all too ruthless for [the interests of] humanity when he feels the strength to create something new and not yet known, if it is permissible for him to reject what he gave birth to in his creative hours, then in this case Goethe made ample use of that right. He discarded the most delicate breath of these souls; he tore to pieces with violent hand what had once so firmly arisen to make a splendid structure . . .[58]

It is ultimately a lament for the path historically not taken, the non-genesis of a social novel in Germany.

Part IV

Nineteenth- and Twentieth-Century German

8: Writing on the Run: Georg Büchner's Revolutions

Agitator

THE YEAR IS 1834: he sits at his manuscript, fearing arrest at any moment. The Darmstadt police were his Muses, he would later say, a sardonic angle on the urgency of this genesis. He needs money. He is still at home, but there's a ladder against the back garden wall for a quick getaway. Some of his fellow-conspirators are already safely over the border, in nearby Strasbourg or in Switzerland. The less lucky ones are or soon will be in jail, betrayed by informers and *agents provocateurs*, facing years of confinement, interrogation, sometimes torture. His closest collaborator, the pastor Friedrich Ludwig Weidig, defiant in adversity but finally despairing after three years of solitary confinement, will slash his veins; the authorities soon find him, but they leave him to bleed to death, a judicial murder.

Büchner has been involved in plans to free some of the prisoners, which is one reason why he has stayed on in Darmstadt, but the plan has collapsed: the bribed guard has been withdrawn from service. The imprisoned colleagues will haunt Büchner's conscience and his imagination—he knows that such pressures would have slowly broken him. Once safe in exile he will write to the family of his relief that the constant threat of arrest has been lifted, though Darmstadt has requested extradition in a "wanted" notice now in circulation. Phantasies of imprisonment will visit the typhus delirium of the young man's last days, which will be very soon.

The present manuscript apart, he is hardly yet a writer. He has coauthored with Weidig an inflammatory pamphlet, which is mainly what has got him into this trouble. Otherwise he is just a medical student in his early twenties, with two years at the University of Strasbourg behind him and a third more locally, at Giessen, Justus Liebig's university. Now he is working at home for his examinations and doing some private teaching for would-be medical students; there are anatomical diagrams all over his desk. These also served, his brother Ludwig would recall, to hide the manuscript from his father, a respected senior medic whose social standing helped keep the police at bay. He doesn't know about his promising son's political doings, so had better not know about the text that is meant to be a lifeline to a new start elsewhere. True, Georg's letters to the family from Strasbourg had already made no secret of his views—that only violence would serve against the violence of an oppressive system which the family apparently regarded as the "*legal state of affairs*" (*Zustand*); that he was committed to fighting against it "with *mouth* and *hand*"; but also, reassuringly, that he had taken no part in recent action, if only because he regarded the present chances of success to be nil.[1]

In 1834 Büchner founded branches in Giessen and Darmstadt of a clandestine Society for the Rights of Man and the Citizen, on a model he knew from Strasbourg. That spring or summer he wrote his pamphlet, *The Hessian Messenger*,[2] designed to rouse up the down-trodden subjects of Hesse-Darmstadt against their rulers. There were already stirrings in the air, wafting across from the latest French revolution of July 1830. Since the 1815 post-Napoleonic Restoration, Metternich's Europe had been living in fear of just such a renewal, uncertain which of Europe's peoples would embody the spirit of revolution and make it a reality again, in Heine's neat coining a "Volkwerdung" (a play on "Fleischwerdung," the Christian term for incarnation). It came as no surprise that in the event it was the French. They had the power of precedent, and the restored Bourbon monarchy had been a comic disaster. Would upheaval spread across the border? Even if it did, a fragmented Germany—still thirty-odd separate states, though reduced under Napoleon's sway by a factor of ten—lacked the cohesion to be transformed by central action such as was possible through Paris.

An age of anxiety for the German authorities was nevertheless a time of hope for liberals and radicals. Büchner belonged emphatically to the second group, and was located at its revolutionary extreme. He rejected liberal efforts at constitutional reform as a bourgeois compromise with power that would leave the lower classes no better off than before. What did freedom of the press and an extended suffrage mean to starving people? Or a constitution such as the thirty-odd German princes had promised their peoples when it was crucial that they join in the overthrow of Napoleon? Promises on which they had in any case long since reneged, in solidarity with the reactionary pan-European ancien régime that the 1815 Congress of Vienna had restored under the control of Metternich.

Büchner's pamphlet drew on a recent statistical survey of the dukedom of Hessen,[3] which set the cold figures of exploitation—the heavy tax burden on the mainly peasant population, monies that went into financing the extravagances of court and administration—in a matrix of heated part-biblical rhetoric. Its motto had a French source, Chamfort's battle-cry "War on the Palaces! Peace to the Cottages!"[4]

A Dramatist from Nowhere

Büchner's secret manuscript was not, however, another piece of agit-prop but a full-blown drama centered on the conflict between the leading figures of the first French Revolution, Danton and Robespierre; its title was *Danton's Death*. Büchner's self-discovery as a writer is the most remarkable thing about this genesis. What had made him suddenly turn to drama, turning him instantly into a mature dramatist? What gave him the confidence to send his hastily put-together manuscript to a Frankfurt liberal publisher, Johann David Friedländer, asking with a beginner's naïvety for a reply "as soon as possible," further asking Friedländer to forward it to the writer Karl Gutzkow, and in turn requesting Gutzkow to recommend the drama "as soon as possible" to Friedländer for publication—if, that is, "your *conscience as a critic should permit it*" (italics Büchner's). This is a young man in a hurry. He has written the play "in at most five weeks," and once more he asks for a "swift answer"—"if favorable, a few lines by next Wednesday (!) can rescue a miserable man from a sad situation."[5]

It was a long shot. Neither recipient of Büchner's letters can have known this would-be author from Adam. He realizes he's bursting in on Gutzkow with demands as peremptory as a highwayman's. But it works. Gutzkow is deeply impressed by the play; he does all he can to further Büchner's interests, and he becomes his friend and adviser: Don't press for a big fee—dramatic works don't sell well; don't go as far away as America, stay in close contact; from France you can earn money by writing for Friedländer's journal, *Phoenix*. (Gutzkow is the editor of its weekly literary supplement.) It is all to Gutzkow's credit as a critic and a man—not every established figure[6] is so generous to an unknown. But he realizes this young man is a hidden genius, a real prospect for German literature. *Danton's Death* shows "deep reserves, with a great deal flowing in and flowing out."[7] Friedländer duly pays ten Friedrichs d'or (c. $600) for the work, which, as a further kindness, Gutzkow offers to bring over to Darmstadt, though the publisher thinks this is risky—Gutzkow is himself a marked man and is soon going to be arrested for an "immoral" novel. In any case, Büchner has by this time already fled the country.[8] It remained for Gutzkow—better him than some less sympathetic hand—to take on the job of removing the sexual allusions and other potentially offensive material[9] so as to make Büchner's text acceptable to Friedländer; the publisher was a respectable family man with a reputation to consider. In his commitment to making the revolutionaries appear as the sexually crude beings he was sure they were, and perhaps with a young firebrand's desire to shock the public, Büchner had decidedly called a spade a spade.

The Dramatist as Historian

That was just part of the radical truth it was his declared literary duty to represent. To his own respectable family, who had perhaps heard about his "immoral" play or soon would, he writes that the dramatic poet is nothing but a historian, superior only in making the past come tangibly alive, neither more nor less "moral" than things were in reality. Debauched atheists could only be shown as debauched and atheistical. Otherwise you might as well forbid the study of history itself, or blame God for the way he made the world. Idealistic poets created pompous puppets, not flesh-and-blood people—so it was yes to Goethe and Shakespeare, and no to Schiller.[10]

This was plainly making broader claims than any political propaganda. So what was the point of *Danton's Death*? Financing Büchner's escape was not an intrinsic purpose ("Money? I'll write a play"), merely an urgent need that it could incidentally serve. At most his crisis may have precipitated what was already in gestation. His interest in the French Revolution can't itself have been new—a modern would-be revolutionary could hope to learn lessons from the past—but for some time he had been reading it up with an intensity beyond present tactical needs. He was borrowing a succession of books from the Darmstadt court library—volumes of Thiers and Mignet, the most recent French authorities, and a variety of documentary collections, each loan never for more than five days together, which suggests precise knowledge of which material he needed. Fruitful too was a popular compilation, *Our Age: An Overview of the Most Notable Events from 1789 to 1830*,[11] which had been read aloud in the family since his schooldays.

Büchner's absorption in his project was such that it kept him from writing to his fiancée, Minna Jaeglé in Strasbourg. There were weighty reasons why:

> For days now I've kept picking up the pen, but it was impossible to write a word. I was studying the history of the Revolution. I felt as if annihilated under the hideous fatalism of history. I find in human nature a dreadful sameness, in human relations an inescapable violence, given to everybody and nobody. The individual just foam on the wave, greatness mere chance, the dominance of genius a puppet-play, a laughable struggle with an iron law, the most that can be achieved is to understand it, controlling it is impossible. It no longer occurs to me to bow down to the showy prancers and pompous statues of history. I accustomed my eye to blood. But I'm not a guillotine. The "Must" is one of the curses Man was christened with. The saying, "It must need be that offences come; but woe to the man by whom the offence cometh," is horrible. What is it in us that lies, murders, steals? I'd rather not think it through.[12]

The argument is indeed not altogether thought through. The fatalism is Büchner's, not history's, an attitude of mind, not an objective strand running through events. His horror at the necessity of violence sits oddly beside his own commitment to violence, as does the melancholy reduction of individual greatness to chance beside the energetic activism of the *Hessian Messenger* later that year. The contradiction has remained a hard nut for critics to crack, calling forth ingenious solutions.[13] The conclusion surely has to be that an unaltered resolve to act for the best in the worst of all possible worlds was just about able to coexist with an acceptance that his own actions would fall under the biblical curse, and that the end result would be as bloody as 1793, and maybe still not even better the lot of the people. The guillotine provides heads, not bread. For what the play unambiguously shows is the tragic failure of all violent politics. The new-born dramatist was balancing the revolutionary activist, forcing him to contemplate the realities of revolution, both its murderous effects and its dark psychic origins.

Büchner's fatalism was in tune with the critical reaction of nineteenth-century historians to the hopeful historiography of the Enlightenment, which the Revolution had helped to discredit. It was in his sources: Thiers and Mignet were recognized fatalists. Before long, Tolstoy's epilogue to *War and Peace* would spell out the denial of all human agency in great events. But the events themselves as Büchner shows them, despite the suprapersonal generalizations of the fatalism letter, are without historic grandeur. They are shaped, in the individual and the moment, by the impulses of whoring, lying, and murdering.

It isn't possible to follow step by step how this dark vision shaped the play over those five weeks. Gallingly, there is an unexplained six-month gap in Büchner's correspondence between August 23, 1834, and February 21, 1835, just the time when he was under acute threat of arrest and finally composing the text. It seems barely conceivable that over that span he would not have told at least Minna what he was doing, and there are reports that he was indeed writing to close friends. Not that he ever went into detail about what he was working on in the letters we do have. The fact remains that no word of his survives that touches the very core of the drama's genesis.[14]

Undaunted, scholars have tried to distinguish compositional phases—first and second sketches, later elaborations, using as coordinates the precise dates of Büchner's library loans[15] and minutely observed features of the text, the sequence of passages of montage from his sources, which shows Büchner's structural dependence on Thiers, their perceived degree of integration in his text, and some minute breaks in textual logic—all this within the narrowest of time frames, and on no material basis other than the final manuscript, which is the only thing Büchner left.[16] There are no preserved drafts or notes from his reading of the sources.

The one truly important distinction is between source-dependent sections of the drama and Büchner's own imagined passages, the ones where the authenticity of history is filled out by empathy to create flesh-and-blood characters. What Gutzkow, without any knowledge of Büchner's sources, read and was impressed by as a uniform dramatic realism is a deft combination of the two disparate elements. Crucial speeches are a word-for-word montage of documents from Büchner's reading[17]—Robespierre's lengthy harangues at the Jacobin Club in act I, scene 3 and in the National Convention in act 2, scene 7, or Danton's defense before the Revolutionary Tribunal in act 3, scene 4, and act 3, scene 9. But St Just's speeches in act 2, scene 7, which sound just as convincing—chillingly so, indeed—are not montage; they, and the character in which they are grounded, are Büchner's conception, albeit true to what is known of the real man's ruthlessness. When, however, a weary Danton broods on the absurdity and tedium of existence, his nihilism lies wholly outside anything the sources say. So does his probing into the deep motives for action, as he uses words from Büchner's "fatalism" letter on the curse of historical necessity (the "Muss"). So does Thomas Payne [sic] preaching atheism[18] to the prisoners awaiting execution in act 3, scene 1.

These passages are no mere superficial gestures towards profundity by a bitter young man. Büchner's reading of philosophy was as serious as his study of medicine and his engagement in politics—a further aspect of his extraordinary range and intellectual energy. He was already planning a course on German philosophy in the wake of Descartes and Spinoza for a hoped-for university position, in parallel with projected lectures on the anatomy that was his main qualification. Long dismissed as mere excerpts derived from a secondary source,[19] his preparatory work on Descartes and Spinoza was remarkably thorough, including his own translation of texts till then only available in Latin.[20]

Adding an imagined existentialist angle to Danton's source-based speeches makes him a more complex character, to the point of a wholly credible contradiction, between the inertia of a tired revolutionary, which is part of Büchner's conception, and the energy of the historical Danton. Stung by unjust charges and a gerrymandered jury, the real Danton defended himself in a day-long speech that had "stupendous effect."[21]

The way the jury's membership has been fixed and the tribunal's procedures skewed against Danton and his fellow accused makes this a world not of grand historical gestures but of vicious in-fighting and personal score-settling. It barely rises to the level of ideology in the conflict between Robespierre, whose "virtue ruling through terror" means liquidating successive groups, and Danton, who with his easy-living moderates wants to call a halt to the endless executions.[22] Danton himself was once as extreme as anyone, responsible in September 1792 for the massacre of hundreds of imprisoned priests and other suspects who, it was feared, might get free and stab the Revolution in the back as the Austrian armies advanced on Paris. That was necessary to save the Republic—it was the curse of the "Must." Now Danton hears the ghostly accusation "September" echoing through the streets.[23] His obsession with his own personal guilt is another Büchner invention.

The corrupt justice by which Danton is framed and killed fits two of the terms of Büchner's question, "What is it in us that lies [. . .] and murders?" The words are put in Danton's mouth, with the added verb, "whores." That wasn't a word Büchner could well use in the letter to his fiancée, but it now becomes a subtle motif. First in the crude form, in Danton's libertine life-style, the opposite of Robespierre's virtue ("he wants to halt the horses of the revolution at the brothel door"). But then more subtly in Danton's question: isn't all this virtue of Robespierre's— ostentatiously not getting drunk, not profiteering, not sleeping around— itself a lie, a perverse reverse form of self-indulgence, a not-whoring for the pleasure of feeling superior? Vice and virtue are reduced to the same basic impulse. We are all epicureans indulging in our different pleasures. Thus Danton in their verbal battle at act 1, scene 6. It is enough to shake Robespierre's self-righteous convictions, to the point where he asks himself: "What is it in me that is lying to the other half? [. . .] Sin is in the thought. Whether the thought becomes deed, whether the body acts it out, is mere chance." But St Just is there on cue to stiffen Robespierre's resolve. It is another fine piece of historical imagining. And in the end, Robespierre's virtue pays off: image against image, he wins out over Danton in the competition for popular support.

Scientist

By the time *Danton's Death* appeared,[24] Büchner was safe in Strasbourg, free to reside there so long as he wasn't politically active, the usual condition imposed on refugees by a host country. Now he threw himself into his science and completed a thesis in French on the nervous system of the barbel, a fish plentiful in the river at Strasbourg. Based on Büchner's skilled preparation of specimens,[25] it was highly regarded by his French teachers. Delivered in a set of three lectures (Büchner was an effective speaker) then published in a learned journal, it continued to be taken seriously by later anatomical researchers. There was nevertheless no chance of employment in France. There were, however, possibilities at the University of Zurich, a liberal institution just founded in 1833, which still had gaps in its lecture program. Its rector was the distinguished anatomist (likewise an exile from Germany for political reasons) Lorenz Oken. Büchner put out feelers, and in September 1836 Zurich awarded him a doctorate with prospects of a teaching function. He moved there in mid-October and gave the sample lecture required to secure the status of *Privatdozent*.[26] A career beckoned.

Now that the planned courses were about to become a reality, his references are sardonic—he is going to Zurich "as a superfluous member of society to lecture to my fellow-men on something highly superfluous, namely German philosophical systems since Descartes and Spinoza."[27] He has always been skeptical about the terms with which philosophy works: "I'm throwing myself with all my force into philosophy, the technical language is dreadful, I think that for human matters one must find human expression."[28] He strikes an equally negative tone about his science, writing to Gutzkow, currently in prison, that he too is imprisoned, in tedious scientific work: "Day and night at the repellent business [no doubt the messy dissections], I don't understand where I got the patience."[29] Gutzkow gently and perceptively reprimands him: "Don't be unjust to your studies; for it seems to me it's to them you owe your main strength, I mean your rare quality of clear-sightedness, [*Unbefangenheit*] I would almost say your autopsy, which speaks out of everything you write."[30]

The scientific work continues, perforce a practical priority now that anatomy rather than philosophy is to be the subject of his first course; but even more than the professional science, literature is becoming Büchner's deepest commitment: "The best of it is, my imagination is active, and the mechanical occupation of specimen-preparation leaves room for it."[31] He has "the pleasure of creating [his] poetic productions." For some reason he imagines that Shakespeare had a demanding day job and could only write at night—"and I, who am not fit to loose his shoe-string, am much better placed."[32] It was his last but one letter before typhus ended his life.

Autopsy

Just what Büchner was writing or had written by 1836/37 is something of a mystery. A comedy, *Leonce and Lena*, was put together hastily for a competition that promised prize money but was submitted too late for the deadline. Beyond that, letters speak of "*my two dramas.*" They must be well advanced, since he declares himself not satisfied with them.[33] Soon afterwards, he speaks of *Leonce and Lena* "*with two more dramas,*" which he will be bringing out (*erscheinen lassen*), so not just finishing, but publishing, "at latest within a week."[34] Of these so emphatically announced plays there is no trace. It is most unlikely Büchner was referring to his translation of two plays by Victor Hugo, hack-work put his way by Karl Gutzkow who was editing a collected edition of Hugo's works. Büchner had no high regard for Hugo, and spoke only of "my translation." Rumors were later put about of a play on the Renaissance author Pietro Aretino, and of its loss or suppression by Minna as, once more, "immoral." But again there is no trace, of it or of any other text anywhere near complete.[35]

There is however a fragment[36] that was paradoxically to become Büchner's most significant and influential work. *Woyzeck* is of all geneses the most clearly still in flux, a bundle of manuscripts in four distinct but partly overlapping sequences where the main characters have different names—Louis and Margreth or Franz and Marie—and the incomplete action has divergent endings, themselves only implied, Woyzeck's suicide or his trial for murdering his mistress. That was the real Woyzeck's crime—Büchner was once again working from documents, the records of a long-running controversy in which the traditional conception of criminal guilt was called in question by a liberal defense of diminished responsibility.[37] Büchner is likely to have known about several similar cases that were running—and publicized—at the same time. (All this was well before the English judiciary formulated the MacNaughton rules on the criteria for diminished responsibility.) Lengthy examination of the real Woyzeck's psychological state and accounts of his past behavior still resulted in a death sentence, and a public beheading in an elaborate public show in Leipzig in 1824.

Woyzeck links Büchner's science with his social sympathies in a terse down-to-earth style far removed from the grand rhetoric of the politicians in *Danton's Death*. He is following an artistic principle he has recently put in the mouth of the eighteenth-century dramatist Lenz in an extraordinary short story, a revolutionary realism that fills two eloquent pages, beginning "One should try for once going deep into the life of the most insignificant being and rendering it in all its twitches and hints, the whole minute, scarcely noticed play of the features. [. . .] You must love humanity so as to penetrate the particular being of each one, none must be too lowly, none too ugly, only then can you understand them."[38]

There is a lot to make Woyzeck twitch. He is the victim of everything in and around him, of his own psychic and physical constitution and of a social Grand Mechanism every bit as ruthless as the one that is seen operating in the high politics of Shakespeare's histories. A squaddie at the bottom of the army hierarchy, he is also a poor physical specimen, further depleted by a grotesque diet of nothing but peas, which he is kept on in the service of a doctor's crazy experiments; he has visions and voices and an obsession with being pursued by the Freemasons; he loses the affections of his highly sexed common-law wife Marie to a strapping drum major, who also beats him up in a tavern brawl—one thing after another. The portrayal of Woyzeck appeals, on behalf of a lower class that had never before been foregrounded in literature, to the eighteenth century's ethos of human sympathy through drama—"Sympathetic people are the best people."[39] Yet the play is no mere tear-jerker but the outwardly detached diagnosis of a grim case: in Gutzkow's term, an autopsy.

Deciding which aspect of Woyzeck's misery dominates is left, given the inchoate state of the text, in the hands of editors and stage producers. This leaves even more openings than usual for "Regietheater," the German theatrical practice of playing fast and loose with classic texts. Physiology, psychology, pathology, social protest, powerful sexuality, and plain jealousy are themes to choose between and variously combine. Not to mention bleak symbolic interludes—a fairground show of a horse parodying human behavior, Woyzeck's baby son playing with an idiot, an old grandmother telling the tale of a child lost in a cold universe. Or the recurring dark existential motif, Man, be natural, you're created of dust, sand, muck. Do you want to be more than dust, sand, muck?[40]

So it matters what element you begin with in arranging the text from the raw manuscript materials. In the first edition, put together by the Austrian writer Karl Emil Franzos in 1879, Woyzeck is first seen shaving his superior officer, who sets verbal traps for his underling's simple mind, reproves him for his lack of bourgeois morals, and crudely hints at Marie's infidelity (if he hurries he might find a hair on a pair of lips. . . "Captain sir, I'm a poor devil with nothing else in the world, captain sir, if you're joking. . . ." When the mocked man struggles to articulate his own view from the depths of his poverty and simple-mindedness, he is only mocked the more for it: "There he goes, philosophizing again Woyzeck."[41] (Addressing someone as "he" is itself degrading, with roots in German feudal usage.)

In contrast, Fritz Bergemann's edition, canonical from the 1920s on, opens with Woyzeck's delusions about the Freemasons, as he and his comrade Andres cut sticks out in the fields. And would the play end with Woyzeck's death, in the pond where he tries to dispose of the murder weapon, or with his arrest and trial? Both are suggested at points in the manuscripts: both remain undeveloped.

As with the attempt at a genetic sequencing of *Danton's Death*, editors follow the orthodox principle of trying to make out Büchner's latest intention among the scattered scenes and divergent lines of action. But there *was* no clear latest intention, just a set of options all in play, everything in flux.[42] The first manuscript starts with the fairground scene and ends with the police. The second starts with the stick-cutting and ends with Marie still alive and trying to pray. The third starts with the stick-cutting and ends with Woyzeck giving his possessions away to Andres. The fourth is just two scenes, at a professor's house and the child with the idiot. The first manuscript sequence is the only one that has anything like an ending, a policeman rubbing his hands over this really good murder. All this within a genetic time frame not much greater than the five weeks it took to write *Danton's Death*. For Büchner just may have begun writing *Woyzeck* in Strasbourg, but the pressure of his scientific preparation work clearly left little time for his precious literary work, and it seems likely the sketches date from the very end of Büchner's life.

The conscientious editor trying, as editors all finally must, to construct a viable reading text, is torn between the demand for a unified action and fidelity to the manuscripts, with the pull of otherwise successful scenes that don't fit a unifying line.[43] There is a distant echo here of Goethe's problem putting *Faust I* together from disparate and sometimes incompatible pieces, with the difference that in this case no solutions were reached before Büchner's death. As with *Faust*, here too, if on a smaller scale, the only way to read these dynamic fragments is synoptically, excluding no trees from the wood in order to make up for ourselves Büchner's shifting image of the pressures to which a poor man—poor in every possible sense—was subject. That at least does justice to the disparate impulses that Büchner didn't live to sort out and realize.

It is remarkable that the text itself survived at all. When the family belatedly brought out Büchner's collected writings in 1850, they rejected the *Woyzeck* manuscript as a batch of illegible and probably undesirable scribblings. When Karl Emil Franzos rescued it for his edition, he used chemicals to make it more legible, but the long-term effect of this treatment made it even less legible for later editors. Franzos misread the name as Wozzeck, a title which was then perpetuated in Alban Berg's opera of 1920. (Büchner's manuscripts themselves have no title.) Never staged until 1913, the play's realistic precision and social impulse, its revolutionary form dating from decades before Naturalism and Expressionism, quickly made it and its author modern classics for a liberal audience.

Büchner's premature death interrupted the genesis not just of a single work but of what would surely have been an extraordinary career, scientific, literary, or political, or perhaps all three. His political commitment is clear, though it would have been at best the politics of exile, for which Zurich was something of a center—Lenin too would later stay in Zurich, in the very same Spiegelgasse where Büchner lodged—but with the frustrating limitations on political activity that the Swiss authorities imposed. Büchner might have moved to Paris, where like Heinrich Heine and Ludwig Börne he could have written freely on politics, probably even more fiercely polemical than either of them. As for science, here Büchner's career was well launched, although a published *Woyzeck* might have queered his pitch with the medical profession through its slashing satire on an ambitious doctor who conducts grotesque experiments on a helpless human subject.

But of the three career strands, Büchner's enormous poetic potential leaves no doubt. He is mature from his first work, a writer almost without juvenilia, his full powers already realized by the age of twenty-four. His literary afterlife[44] is a tantalizing compensation for a loss that can only be guessed at.

9: "The Best-Laid Schemes...": Thomas Mann Unplanned

Out of Himself

IN A SUBLIME PUT-DOWN, Bertolt Brecht once said of Thomas Mann, author of some of the most monumental and highly regarded novels of the twentieth century, "I always found his short stories really quite good."[1] In his beginnings Mann did indeed think of himself as no more than a short-story writer with no higher formal ambitions. A favorite author and model was Maupassant. Mann's first major work had to be drawn out of him by circumstances to which his talent responded with amazing sophistication (he was still in his early twenties). The pattern repeated itself. Throughout his career ever larger undertakings grew out of initial small-scale plans. In contrast, a phase of career-conscious grand designs through which he hoped to confirm his early success proved arid—the desired masterpieces couldn't be written to order. Fortunately, these grand projects became superfluous when an unforeseen impulse took over.

In 1897 the young Thomas Mann succeeded in placing a piece with Samuel Fischer's *Neue Rundschau*. Fischer, then *the* publisher of the avant-garde, was impressed enough to reprint it as the title story for a volume with five other already published stories of Mann's. *Little Herr Friedemann* appeared in the "Collection Fischer," gratifyingly alongside some then-esteemed names—Herman Bang, Hermann Bahr, Peter Altenberg. It was well received, was even compared with Chekhov's beginnings. It was no best-seller—by 1900 there were still 1597 copies left from a print-run of 2000. Still, Fischer kept faith with his beginner. He had already invited him to write a novel, "even if it's not so long." That was intended not so much to set a limit as to encourage Mann to go beyond his present range. A longer work could incidentally pay higher royalties.[2]

It was an offer a beginner couldn't refuse, but it posed problems besides just length. Mann's early stories were grotesque and pathological cases of human oddity, of suffering and social exclusion, all narrated with a cool detachment that suggested (was surely meant to suggest) a maturity beyond the young author's experience. It had sources in the ironists who had shaped Mann's outlook—Heine and, especially, Nietzsche.

Early readers were impressed by the stylistic virtuosity, though sometimes uneasy with an irony that implied no positive values.

This mode would hardly fill the larger narrative form, the materials too slight and the manner too corrosive to sustain interest over two hundred and fifty pages, which was the target Mann now set himself on the pattern of novels by two Scandinavian writers popular at that time, Lie and Kielland. What could serve his turn? Where was material on the right scale to be found? What—the question is simple but vital, and it would tax Thomas Mann throughout his career—what did he *know* enough to write about? He noted Baudelaire's advice, "A writer must be very industrious, he must read a lot in the lexicon."[3] A novel lives by reflecting a complex world and its social structures. What was the young Thomas Mann's range? He was a young hopeful free-floating on the fringes of Munich society, of modest independent means since the death of his father and the winding up of the family firm had given him and his elder brother Heinrich the freedom to chance their arms as writers.

Even that much substance and connection to society, as the younger generation of a somewhat passé Lübeck merchant family, had been further weakened by doctrines current in the day. The brothers' literary talents and ambitions marked them out, and they duly saw themselves, as decadent, unhealthy ("neurasthenic" was a buzz-word of the day), offshoots of a grand old tree, clear signs and consequences of its decline.[4] But might not precisely that make a substantial subject for a novel, the family's decline, with the counterpoint of a new type arising from within it, the Artist—like themselves?

Mann had already been planning one more story about a suffering outsider, this time a boy with outstanding musical gifts. The situation, as in his other early stories, would have been set wholly in a narrative present, would have opened *in ultimas res*, with no spelling out of a prehistory; the decline from healthy antecedents would have been taken for granted. On Mann's latecomer scale of values, earlier stages would have merited no more attention in this than in his other tragic tales. Only the exceptional counted. How much, after all, was there to be said about self-confident burghers, masters of commerce, and their no doubt boringly normal families? Since, according to Tolstoy, all happy families are alike, there would not be much interest there.

And yet... There was distinctive substance in the generations before degeneration, and it lay ready to hand in Mann's own youthful experience of the world he had grown up in, together with the insights and reminiscences ready to hand from elderly relatives who were rooted in that stable past. And perhaps not so totally stable, or happy, either. There must surely have been telltale early signs, cracks in the solid façade, parts of a steady process of decline: no abrupt abyss, but a long downward slope, still unambiguous enough to suggest the title Mann first planned for his novel, "Abwärts" (The way down).[5] Symptoms of decadence could be introduced in discreet doses from one generation to the next.

Mann now had his material and a clear angle. Ultimately he would be pleading his own cause, reconstructing the history that had led down to an artist like himself. He soon sketched the preceding generations. The first few pages of a notebook of 1897 and early 1898 trace the line back from the death of little Hanno, the "sensitive late-comer" of the original short-story conception, to Old Johann, his grandfather; also to Hanno's uncle Christian, an eccentric and finally unbalanced character, a link back to the short-story writer's stock-in-trade of grotesque figures. But the real family history provided more substantial, less typecast characters, for whom a new narrative manner and even a measure of sympathy could develop. In the novel's early sections, an aunt's disastrous marriage inspires a tragicomic episode that for long stretches absorbs the attention of author and reader. The fictional Tony Buddenbrook's first marriage is forced on her for the firm's commercial advantage (it turns out to have the opposite effect) and a second, equally disastrous marriage by the family's need to expunge the blemish of the first divorce. Together the two episodes set a powerful moral theme going: the damage done to private lives by the idolized idea of family and firm. That extends to other family members. Tony's brother Thomas has a socially unacceptable early love-affair with a shopgirl, and a subsequent cold marriage. For all their affluence and solid façade, the Buddenbrooks are scarcely ever a happy family.

On Tolstoy's principle, all the better. Their substance lures Mann well beyond the original plan. More and more is found in the subject, and that draws more and more out of the author. The story acquires factual foundations through targeted enquiries, including a detailed questionnaire to which an obliging Uncle Wilhelm Marty provides answers that make almost three closely printed pages in Mann's published notebooks.[6] The writing still didn't go easily—in retrospect he will call it "three years of torture." Yet as the work grew under his hands, so did his respect for it, "so that I demanded an ever higher style from myself."[7] The project feeds on itself. Higher style doesn't mean grandiose or pretentious, simply a manner that took a serious subject seriously, a fundamental change of attitude from the sardonic early stories.

Structurally Mann drew strength from several great predecessors. The Goncourt brothers had first shown him how to link short episodes into a longer line. Later, Tolstoy was the vital example for coping with material quantity and social range. Dickens was the model for a mellow humor. A new maturity is clear from any piecemeal comparison with the early style. In place of sharp effects there is a leisurely pace and a more tolerant, rounded treatment of character. Ingenious fresh chapter-openings vary what could have become a monotonous record of hatchings, matchings, and dispatchings in the family, and of ups and downs in the firm's fortunes. Most strikingly original is the way Hanno's death is conveyed through a bald rehearsal of the course of typhus, lifted direct (true to Baudelaire's maxim) from a lexicon: a classic piece of montage. Verbal irony is now kept in check, but there are fine ironic structures, as when Tony's first husband—virtually imposed on her by her father as a good match—is revealed as a swindler, or when the firm's jubilee celebrations fall on the same day as a massive loss that has been brought about by Thomas departing from their time-honored practices, just so as to prove his modern toughness.

The change of title from "Abwarts" to *Buddenbrooks* is a decisive shift. The family's name as the novel's title, without even a definite article, suggests a familiar local reality, to be treated with respect even in its less happy days. Their loss is demoted to the sub-title: "Decline of a Family." Paradoxically, the family's rich substance resists concentration on the decline theme.

All this affected the novel's length. The planned two hundred and fifty pages were now running to a thousand. Fischer had suggested a longer work, but not this long! He decreed that the manuscript would need to be cut by half, though he realized this was an immense imposition on the young author. Whereupon Mann wrote what he later called the best letter of his life (sadly it isn't preserved) making the case for the book's full length as essential to its conception. Fischer and his chief reader Moritz Heimann conscientiously reread the manuscript—a fine testimony to the literary conscience of a not just commercially motivated publisher—and relented. "Well, you won't always write four-volume novels."[8] (As if!) *Buddenbrooks* appeared in 1901, uncut, in two volumes, to critical acclaim. A popular one-volume edition two years later made it a best-seller, which it has remained ever since, what Germans call a "house-book," found on the shelves of otherwise not necessarily literary families. The successive plans of author and publisher for a short story, a medium-length novel, and an abridged version, had all ganged agley—to everyone's gain.

Falling Short

Mann was clear that his first novel had been "a masterpiece," but he feared that "[his] powers could not reach that level again . . . under the immense pressure of public expectation."[9] *Buddenbrooks* had extended his technical range but exhausted his one material source. What next? He was left to himself, brooding on the situation of a writer lacking substance—in the psychological sense too, of standing outside normal life, looking on and alternately scorning and yearning for the fulfillments that less complex beings enjoyed. Making this his theme in wistful or satirical novellas (*Tonio Kröger*, *Tristan*—both minor successes) only intensified and publicized the problem. His position on the outside of society became an obsession, blocking the path to anything else. At best, but this proved no solution, he drew on real-life types as allegories for the writer's unreality. In *Royal Highness* (1909) a Ruritanian prince leads a purely symbolic existence to meet his people's need for ceremony. In *Confessions of the Confidence Man Felix Krull* the conman cheats a credulous public. When Mann revealed that the narrative of a princely life wasn't social analysis but all about himself, its already unfavorable reception (found too lightweight from the author of *Buddenbrooks*) collapsed further: "pretentiously self-centered" was the drift. Carefully planned allegory is, with rare exceptions, the coldest of literary forms.

Felix Krull would at least have been self-critical, perilously so indeed for the writer's serious reputation, but its writing didn't flow, and in 1911 it was abandoned. (A "Childhood" section was published in 1922, but not until 1954 was a text completed, as a declared first part that left this final novel technically a fragment.) Meanwhile Mann's one drama, *Fiorenza*, had been "a fiasco"[10]—wordy and heavy with read-up Renaissance, another allegory that made Savonarola's hatred of Florence's "vanities" stand for Mann's resentment of the art-obsessed, unliterary city he lived in, Munich.

He went on planning—what else could a highly self-conscious writer do? As *Buddenbrooks* receded ever further into the past, career anxiety set in: "I'm now thirty. It's time to think of a masterpiece."[11] The plans were correspondingly ambitious, but none was being realized: "The 'Frederick,' 'Maja,' the novellas that I'd like to write could become masterpieces, but one consumes oneself in plans and despairs of getting started."[12] Together they would have made an impressive portfolio: a novel on Frederick the Great as contribution to national pride and the author's cultural status; "Maja" a social tapestry with a Munich setting to equal the Lübeck of *Buddenbrooks*; an essay "Mind and Art" (Geist und Kunst) attacking current German anti-intellectualism, a worthy successor to Schiller's classic eighteenth-century treatise "Über naïve und sentimentalische Dichtung."[13] They did in the end all get written. Just not by Thomas Mann...

Force mineure

... but as the imagined and named works[14] of the mature Gustav von Aschenbach in *Death in Venice*. By age fifty-three (Mann was still only thirty-five) Aschenbach is a recognized master and pillar of the national culture. In a chapter of pastiche literary history, interposed in the narrative while Aschenbach is preparing to leave for Venice to ease his writer's block, Mann heaps on this alter ego the reputation he had hoped to achieve himself. In the novella he could happily pass on those frustrating plans, because he had suddenly been carried beyond the need for planning.

For experiences of his own in Venice had provided compelling material and a matching emotion. The figures and incidents that line Aschenbach's route to death—the ominous figure at the Munich North Cemetery, the sordid steamship, the disgusting old drunken gay, the unlicensed gondolier, Aschenbach's abortive attempt to leave the city, the outbreak of cholera, the honest clerk in the travel bureau, the sinister ballad-singer, and above all the beautiful Polish boy—all were given, they had an "innate symbolism" that only needed placing.[15] The boy was the inspiration, and Mann brought home from Venice "a very bizarre thing, serious and pure in tone, a case of pederasty in an aging artist. 'Hm, hm,' I hear you say, but it is very proper."[16]

Soon however the tone became less jaunty. "I'm tormented by a work that is turning out more and more to be an impossible conception." Doubts continued for a year, but he had taken too much trouble to give it up now: it must be finished somehow.[17] Yet with publication arrangements already under way, he still can't find the ending.[18] Why it was an impossible conception is clear enough. Since the German royal court scandals of the 1900s and Oscar Wilde's sensational self-destruction, homosexuality was a taboo theme. Even a "very proper" treatment risked identifying the author with his protagonist. By now a family man, a prominent writer and a public figure, Thomas Mann had a lot to lose.

He was, as his wife well knew, homosexual—which Aschenbach (a point rarely made) is initially not. Besides their respective ages, it is the one significant difference between them, commonly overlooked because so much else is directly modelled on Mann's time in Venice. If Aschenbach had been homosexual from the outset, it would have been the familiar situation of an experienced gay observer always on the lookout and responding fully at once, a routine, even potentially boring narrative line. The subtlety of the novella is to show a sudden infatuation surprising a man long widowed and never before homosexually inclined—what he slowly discovers in himself is explicitly the renewal of "past feelings, early delicious sufferings of the heart which had died away in the strict discipline of his life and were now returning *so strangely transformed*."[19] That gradual transformation is what gives the novella its dramatic nerve and perfect pacing.

The encounter with the Polish boy was an inspiration, if anything in Mann's writing life ever was. It demanded a response, if only out of loyalty to his orientation. Years later Mann recalled the episode and what it meant for his self-perception at the time:

> Weißt du noch? Höherer Rausch, ein außerordentlich Fühlen
> Kam auch wohl über dich einmal und warf dich danieder,
> Dass du lagst, die Stirn in den Händen. Hymnisch erhob sich
> Da deine Seele, es drängte der ringende Geist zum Gesange
> Unter Tränen sich hin. (GW 8:495)

[Remember? Intoxication, an extraordinary feeling
Came over you too on one occasion, and threw you
Down, your head in your hands. To hymnic impulse your spirit
Rose, amid tears your struggling mind pressed urgently upwards
Into song.]

The lines are part of his answer to the question with which the opuscule opens: Am I a poet? More importantly for a German, Am I a "Dichter"? The word distinguishes not verse from prose but traditional high quality from the writings of a mere modern "Literat." That made it a handy weapon for conservative critics, and Thomas Mann—ironist, intellectual, and child of a foreign mother—had often been their victim. He liked to claim equal entitlement for his own coolly deliberate writing—"anch' io sono poeta." But this time writing had an altogether different feel, "hymnic impulse" gave rise to "song"! There may even have been a first draft in verse—hexameters and fragments of hexameter rhythm are present in the final text, most strikingly ". . . Ruhte die Blüte des Hauptes in unvergleichlicher Anmut" (. . . the bloom of the head reposed in unsurpassable beauty; 2.1:534).

Certainly he had been taken poetically out of himself. Unfortunately it didn't last, for

leider blieb alles beim Alten.
Denn ein versachlichend Mühen begann da, ein kältend Bemeistern,—
Siehe, es ward dir das trunkene Lied zur sittlichen Fabel.

[Alas it all stayed as it had been:
There began a process of sobering, mastering, cooling.
Lo! The drunken song turned into an ethical fable.]

The narrative sees Aschenbach's growing passion with increasingly critical detachment; it is labelled not just an infatuation, but an aberration.

What if the hymnic impulse had been sustained? What positive view of pederasty would have been possible in literature? Other cultures, other values. Mann turned eagerly to the Greeks: Plato's *Symposium* and *Phaidros* and the *Erotikos* of Plutarch,[20] dialogues that treat the potential of homosexuality to inspire courage in battle, resistance to tyranny, and the creation of poetry and philosophy. The texts are amply excerpted in Mann's work-notes, and numerous phrases and motifs are taken over into the novella's final text.[21]

All this was in tune with the first exalted mood. It offered a rationale for homosexuality and a defense of Mann's own orientation against the prejudices of contemporary German society. In a crucial scene, Aschenbach fulfils one of the Platonic conditions by writing on the beach with

Tadzio in full view and the music of the boy's Polish voice in his ears. He had travelled to refresh his weary creativity, and that now seems to have happened. He writes a short prose piece that will be posthumously much admired.[22] So perhaps it needn't have been *death* in Venice at all, or at worst an elegiac end after a triumphant return to creativity. Yet the fulfillment doesn't go unquestioned, for immediately after writing, Aschenbach feels "exhausted, shattered even," as if "his conscience was accusing him of a wild excess." A good thing, the narrator comments, "that the world knows only the beautiful work, not the circumstances of its genesis" (2.1:556).

In a long letter of self-interpretation, one of his fullest ever, Mann quotes those verses about his emotional crisis and explains the move from drunken song to ethical fable by "the difference between the dionysian spirit of irresponsibly individualistic outflowing lyric" and "the apolline spirit of objectively bound moral and social epic."[23] Implicitly it was no contest. Further, there were the necessities of his own nature, a tendency to Naturalist objectivity, a very un-Greek Protestant bourgeois puritanism, a profoundly pessimistic mistrust of passion as such. . . All of which doesn't do much more than restate in elevated terms the problems of writing about a taboo subject. Ultimately, in this letter one homosexual was making excuses to another for his retreat to conventional morality, half-affirming and half-masking his own orientation. Alongside the verses that evoked his Venice emotion, Mann inconsistently claims to have deliberately added the homosexual aspect so as to make an existing project, on the aged Goethe's famous infatuation with a seventeen-year-old girl, more extreme. (There is no other sign that such a project ever existed.)

After this complex genesis, the final text oscillates between positive and negative—surely the reason why Mann couldn't till the last minute find an ending for the story. Was it to be a condemnation of Aschenbach or a celebration of his restored poetic power? On a first reading, condemnation is decisive, both verbally and concretely in the record of the way he pursues Tadzio and the family through an infected Venice, fails to warn them of the epidemic for fear he will lose the boy forever, and positively welcomes this aberration in the outside world that so thrillingly matches his own.

Yet heavy moral emphasis is so unlike Thomas Mann's usual mode that it already calls itself in question. Ironically, it sounds like the assertive moralizing of another of Aschenbach's works, the novella "A Miserable Wretch" (Ein Elender), a moral position now undermined by his own actions and inaction. Mann does indeed say in the letter to Carl Maria Weber that the position of the moralist can only be adopted ironically. And the text's heavy-handed judgments are offset in the final balance by the positive elements that remain the story's "hymnic core,"[24] namely the descriptions of Tadzio, which are rapturous to the point of visionary: "In mounting delight he believed he was seeing the Beautiful itself, form as the divine idea," one of Plato's eternal ideas. But—oscillation again—where the work-note reads unambiguously "he contemplates the eternal forms, the Beautiful itself,'" the text only says it is what he *believes* he is seeing; and it is followed by the sober comment "That was intoxication, and greedily the aging artist welcomed it" (2.1:553). Is a work-note simply by nature shorthand, or is the reservation (only "he believes") a sign of that cooling process?

"Intoxication," at all events, points forward to Aschenbach's dream of a cultic orgy that carries him beyond the aesthetic-cum-erotic pleasure of watching Tadzio into the very different Greek realm of a violent "visitation" by the Alien God Dionysos, the bringer of natural renewal but also the releaser of deep and destructive urges.[25] Since Dionysos reputedly came from India, which was also the known source of cholera, a set of connections begins ("Beziehungen"—a favorite concept of Thomas Mann's) between medical and mythical, literal meaning and subterranean significance.

But before Aschenbach's final loss of control, the narrative's moral balance has been subtly embodied in a single sentence at the decisive highpoint of feeling. At the very end of chapter 4, he has been confronted and outraged by Tadzio's open and provocative smile:

> And leaning back, with arms hanging loose, overwhelmed and with repeated shivers running over him, he whispered the standing formula of yearning,—impossible here, absurd, depraved, ludicrous and sacred still, venerable even here too: "I love you."[26]

After the four negative adjectives, we expect an adversative, "*but* sacred still." Instead, more subtly, "*and* sacred still" reads as a simple continuation of the list. Rejection is ambushed by acceptance. It is an appeal for the reconciliation of values.

The outcome nevertheless remains death in Venice—Aschenbach dies of cholera. The epidemic, hushed up by the Italian authorities, was after all a major part of the reality Mann was reworking (what Aschenbach learns from the honest clerk in the travel bureau about cholera's origins and movements across the globe is another extensive montage of lexicon material)[27] and death is in any case the high-minded artistic option: "Dignity is rescued alone by death ('tragedy', the 'sea'—the solution, 'way out' and refuge of all higher love.)"[28] In the context of Mann's career, the tragedy was to help restore his serious reputation after his "descent to the flatlands of optimism"—thus the (resented) comment of his friend Kurt Martens on *Royal Highness*, where a happy ending with a royal marriage encoded Mann's own marriage to Katia Pringsheim.

A subtle balance is maintained right to the end, which without celebrating Aschenbach does restore some of his lost status. When he collapses on the beach, he has yet again been contemplating Tadzio, who stands statuesque against the background of the open sea, a "pale and lovely psychagogue." So the boy now doubles as Hermes, mythical conductor of souls to death. And as the series of strange figures Aschenbach has encountered merge into one dark Dionysian identity, they constitute a second layer of meaning discreetly present beneath the Naturalistic surface, nothing short of a Fate. The coherence of levels and the enriched meaning of motifs that came together is surely what gave Mann the feeling, as he recorded in an autobiographical sketch, of being at moments "serenely borne along as never before" (GW, 11:124).

The coda-like closing page visualizes the passage in Plato's *Symposium* where Diotima evokes the initiate who has been "brought at last to the shore of the sea of beauty" and now looks beyond the distraction of any single physical exemplar to "the knowledge of Beauty itself."[29] The novella thus ends on an elevated positive note.

To Mann's relief, the impossible conception was for the most part read respectfully and even admired. His writerly reputation was repaired. At worst his old enemy Alfred Kerr gibed that he had made pederasty acceptable to the middle classes—not so wide of the mark neither, especially when later seconded by the high-end culture of Luchino Visconti's film adaptation and Benjamin Britten's opera. So the ethical fable had successfully offset the drunken song, or at least shielded it for purposes of public viewing. Yet if those confessional verses of Mann's are to be believed, he felt the success was a deeper failure ("der tiefere Fehlschlag") that left a bitter taste in the mouth.[30]

Germs of an Epic

Encounters with a rather milder malady proved strangely congruent with the Venice affair, and creatively fruitful. In 1912 Katia Mann suffered a lung infection that necessitated more than one sanatorium stay. Thomas, already primed by her letters, "went to visit for three weeks," as the eventual story of Hans Castorp will read. He saw for himself a new set of bizarre characters, felt the physical and psychological effects of high altitude, and, when he caught a cold and consulted the head specialist, was invited "with a profitable smile" to stay for the full treatment. It all suggested a comic sequel, and by July 1913 he was working on "a humorous, grotesque counterpart to Death in Venice,"[31] something akin, as he later suggested, to the satyr-play that follows and parodies a Greek tragedy.[32] Once more a life of settled order would be overturned by physical and emotional forces in an outlandish location.

Who was to be the victim? Not another writer this time, but a normal young man of impeccable upbringing who is about to embark on a very practical career as a marine engineer, altogether a typical product of a Hansa city, Hamburg this time instead of Lübeck. Hans Castorp, blonde and fully at home in his environment, is very much in the mold of those ideal well-adjusted people towards whom Mann's autobiographical early stories, *Tonio Kröger* especially, expressed a mixture of yearning and scorning, of "oh to be like them" and "what do they know?" There would be *Schadenfreude* in seeing the stolid Hanseatic ethos exposed to a sanatorium's decadent sick community.

It would be a matching novella with many motifs echoing its predecessor. Like Aschenbach, Hans plans a short stay, intends to return home refreshed but unchanged, briefly tries to escape from the deeply unsettling milieu, is soon in thrall to the charms of a Slavonic coresident, admits he is in love, resists being sobered up, revels in his changed physical and emotional state, stays on as a patient (has love generated disease, or disease love?) and eventually. . .? Something would turn up.

It did, with a vengeance, in 1914. The outbreak of war generated in Thomas Mann a militant enthusiasm unlooked for in such a clear-eyed outsider, a severe shock to the liberal intellectuals, who had thought he was one of them. But precisely the historical moment was calculated to draw the outsider into the warmth, the fever heat even, of the national collective. Against *entente* propaganda attacking the barbarism of a land that had invaded France via neutral Belgium, shelled cathedrals, and shot civilians, Mann wrote polemical essays asserting Germany's more profound culture, all clichés of the day. Materials for his abandoned Frederick novel went into the most substantial of them, "Frederick and the Great Coalition," which identified Germany's actions with the mission of the Realpolitiker king, setting him against a superficial Enlightenment Voltaire.[33] That set Thomas Mann against his brother, an outspoken critic of Germany's actions, who in response to Thomas's effusions went public with his own historical hero. Heinrich's essay on Émile Zola and the military establishment that victimized Dreyfus was a thinly veiled "J'accuse" directed at the Kaiser and his generals. The Manns' brotherly relations had always been delicate, competitive. Now the two were at daggers drawn.

This was no time for the planned comic novella. But work-in-progress can sometimes be wrenched round to meet a transformed reality. The original plan started growing into "a story with basically pedagogical-political intentions,"[34] and eventually into a full-length novel. The intention of the novella had been to denormalize a normal young man through contact with disease and "the most seductive power, death." That involved the author avowing his own sympathy with death as an existential position. But by March 1917 it is Hans Castorp's own "unvirtuous sympathy with death" that is keeping him high up in the sanatorium.[35] The mountain itself becomes a positive symbol in Mann's wartime ideology. Its greater elevation plus the organic secrets of tuberculosis and its treatment can be made to stand allegorically for the superiority of German culture in its battle with the superficiality of Western civilization. (In a weird self-positioning of the day, Germany saw itself as neither Western nor a mere civilization.) The plot soon acquires champions for both sets of values, a Protestant pastor Bunge (later replaced by the sinister Jesuit Naphta) and the secular intellectual Lodovico Settembrini, conscious educators both, who struggle—in abstract terms, since the narrative setting is still pre-war—for Hans Castorp's soul.[36] It has become a Bildungsroman.

Yet in another bizarre concept, politics is itself part of the nexus that Mann rejects, along with democracy, rationality, and the literature of activist intellectuals, foremost among them his brother. Settembrini is the fall-guy in whom Heinrich is satirized. Politics is what the others do, the West, Britain, France especially (Heinrich was a known Francophile). In the oldest of conservative tricks—"*You* are rocking the boat. *We* are just a stable boat"—Thomas's politics claims to be innocent of politics. The massive polemical work he went on to labor over throughout the second half of the war, when writing fiction was no longer feasible, he duly titled "Considerations of an Unpolitical Man" (*Betrachtungen eines Unpolitischen*). Heinrich is nowhere named but everywhere present in it as the emblematic "Zivilisationsliterat," a term of contempt that can be rendered by something like "civilization-monger."

The novella plan had been long lost to sight behind historical events and their fallout. These now threatened to overwhelm the novel it had become. So a further reason for a separate work thrashing out all the issues that war and fraternal conflict had raised was to reduce in some measure the hypertrophying debate between two opposed champions, to unburden the novel as far as possible, looking towards a time when events would allow Mann to get back to composing fiction.

Bulk was not the only problem (that incidentally remained unsolved—*The Magic Mountain* ended up as another two-volume thousand-page opus). The other problem was yet further change, in the outside world and in the author's attitudes to it. Thomas Mann ended the war as a prominent conservative and nationalist. Defeat, the Kaiser's abdication, a revolution and the declaration of the Weimar Republic— the kind of things he loathed but had gloomily foreseen—made him yesterday's man, and he knew it. He took refuge briefly in the niche of idyll, writing the poem on his daughter's christening and a prose account of walks with his dog.

Meantime, he was looking round for vestiges or new beginnings of conservatism. He was clear that this had to be intellectually respectable. Unfortunately, the conservatism he saw in the chaos of postwar politics was reactionary, backward-looking to the point of barbarism and violence, culminating in the death of Walter Rathenau, not the first but the most prominent politician to be assassinated by right-wing extremists. Violence from both extreme Right and extreme Left was directed against the republic, whose very existence neither accepted.

How and where else on the political spectrum could a decent national life be made possible? There was no bringing back the monarchy, or the old authoritarian structures, or the assertive pride of a rising power, which had been broken by defeat. Harking back to these things was a rotten Romanticism; they were historically dead, a death that could no longer even fascinate as something decadent and intriguing. The national life had to go on in a pragmatically accepted present. The republic might not be an object of love, but it could and should be accepted as the best political option available. Mann became through his support for the Weimar Republic a "Vernunftrepublikaner," a rational republican, a term of the day that half-apologized for both elements. He went public with it, and was much reviled by the Right, who had counted on him as one of theirs.

So the sympathy with death that had been celebrated in the still unfinished novel now became a negative motif, and on that the novel's conception pivoted. Hans Castorp still gains depth through the contact with death, but in the central chapter "Snow" he realizes crucially—the sentence is even printed in italics—that "for the sake of goodness and love Man must not allow death to have dominion over his thinking" (GW 3:686). Its phrasing seems abstract, but the value-conflict of the day gives it very concrete reference. "Death" is that blind and eventually violent attachment to the past—the rotten Romanticism. Other emphases change to match. Mann has reversed his vocabulary, in both fiction and public statements, to meet an increasingly desperate political situation. Where he had still, in the early twenties, rejected "Western" rationality, by 1930 he is appearing on a Berlin platform to deliver "An Appeal to Reason" (GW, 11:870—90). The once satirized Settembrini becomes a more positive figure who would gladly have subscribed to what his author is now bravely saying in public. Meanwhile the once passive Hans Castorp cheekily gets his own word in edgewise in the endless debates he only half understands between the Italian and the Jesuit—a welcome comic touch. He is duly slapped down for his forwardness, yet he is making a claim for the ordinary person's democratic right, and need, to take a view on big questions. Whose "Bildung" is this anyway? In fact, not just his, but his author's too. It is part of the Bildungsroman tradition that protagonist and author have learned something together as the work proceeds.

And the final *Magic Mountain* that at last appeared in 1924? The change from sardonic novella to novel of wartime politics, from unreal conservatism to republican flexibility, from reveling in ideas of death to an enlightened humanism—that whole tortuous unplanned development has been driven by events over twelve years of German and European catastrophe. The ideologies of the day—of war and postwar—are miraculously contained and kept in focus from a new angle under the one original metaphor. It was a magic mountain indeed, a masterly response to a complex situation that had doomed other writers' grand projects—Hugo von Hofmannsthal's *Andreas*, Robert Musil's *Man without Qualities*—to stay uncompleted.

Spelling It Out

"This natural narrative"—the biblical Joseph story—"is extremely charming, only it appears too short, and one feels called to spell it out in detail."[37] Thus Goethe. What he omitted to do was amply made good by Thomas Mann in *Joseph and His Brethren*. After *Buddenbrooks* and *The Magic Mountain*, he can hardly have been surprised to find that something he had planned small—it was to be one of a triptych of novellas on religious subjects—yet again grew, this time further than ever before: four volumes and two thousand pages. Its genesis is a story of massive material acquisition in new fields of history, archeology, Old Testament studies, myth, and theological speculation, all fully documented. Interwoven with it is the story of Mann's exile from 1934. The long haul to completion in America (the first two volumes had been completed, and volume 1 already published, in Germany) helped psychologically to hold him together in the stress of exile. Yet for all the vast scope of the materials, the compositional process was undeviating and unproblematic—paradoxically, given its length, it was the simplest case in a lifetime of complex geneses. The most monumental of his works arose almost without a hitch from yet another modest original plan.

The Devil in Detail

More straightforward still by Mann's account was the genesis of *Doktor Faustus*,[38] his postwar reckoning with German cultural history and its part in the political catastrophe. For once in his life, he planned something on a large scale from the outset, and was able straightaway to deploy all its strands and motifs. Not only that, but for once he began composing swiftly, as if under the pressure of inspiration.

Yet the conception already had a long previous history. Simply, subsequent events had now filled it with a terrible content never foreseen. The roots of the work reach as far back as a note of 1904/5:

> Novella or for "Maja": The syphilitic artist: as Dr. Faustus, has sold himself to the Devil. The effect of the poison is intoxication, stimulus, inspiration; in raptures of enthusiasm he is allowed to create

wonderful works of genius, the Devil guides his hand. But finally *the Devil carries him off*: paralysis.[39]

The idea was born of post-*Buddenbrooks* frustration and fear of creative impotence, but itself failed to be written. The artist's devilish solution was too extreme to make a plausible narrative for the modernity of 1900, even if there had been the kind of double-layer explanations, medicine and myth, that was soon to give *Death in Venice* its dual structure. The Faust plan was left on one side, never further sketched out. It surfaces three decades later at a moment in the thirties early in Mann's exile, when he is thinking how to respond to Nazism. The "Faust novella" would be "a free symbol for the condition and fate of Europe," and a literary work might have more effect than a direct political statement.[40] Nothing comes of either alternative, and the idea goes underground again; but it has started to acquire solid modern reference as new realities have made the sinister Faust myth plausible. A decade later, disease is likewise not too strong a metaphor for Nazism, which has infected and almost destroyed European civilization beyond what could be even imagined in 1934.

Once again, direct statement is not enough, and the strands of German intellectual and political history have to be captured in an allegory. It centers on the fictional composer Adrian Leverkühn and is fleshed out with real social subplots and cultural flashbacks. A hyperintellectual artist's creative dead-end and the way out that he devises in a rigid new musical order[41] are presented as a parallel to Germany's temptation and self-abandonment to an irrational—not fruitfully Dionysian but "dis-Dionysian"—new political order. Leverkühn "is" Faust "is" Germany "is" also Nietzsche, whose biography (complete with syphilitic infection) Mann borrows. Nietzsche is relevant because some of his ideas were a source of the irrationalism on which Nazism fed. And in some measure Leverkühn "is" also Thomas Mann, who could confess his own irrational temptations of long ago and, to the horror of his American patroness, the influential publisher's wife Agnes Meyer, could see in them a connection with the rise of Fascism. They were

> tendencies of the time, in the air long before the word "fascism" existed, and scarcely recognizable in the phenomenon that bears that name. Yet in spirit they are in some measure connected with it, morally they served to prepare the way for it. I had these tendencies in me as much as anyone.[42]

All the terms of Mann's equations are persuasive when taken singly, though in combination they become dizzyingly tortuous.[43] But they are a heroic attempt to grasp the greatest political disaster of modern times in an immense literary structure. And its basis was that far-off original sketch that had remained latent, waiting to be force-fed by the brutality of history.

Falling in Love Again

The Faust novel was Mann's last great work, though still not his last work. He wrote a short (for him) novel reworking the medieval legend of Pope Gregory, and a novella (this time it stays just that) that probes more sardonically than *The Magic Mountain* the causal relation of love and disease.[44]

Casting around then for a way to fill in time before dying, he at last took up *The Confessions of Felix Krull* again. Conceived way back in 1911, with fragments published in the twenties and thirties,[45] and most recently edged out as too frivolous by the Faust theme, it now seemed an unproblematic choice. It hardly even needed a plan—Mann just had to pick up the thread of the story and recapture the comic light touch. Career's end, moreover, was a safe time for his own personal confessions, and in any case the idea of the artist as con-man duping a gullible public was no longer a live issue, amply outdated by Mann's four decades of humanistic and political commitment. Krull's further adventures could be conceived, and were in due course enjoyed by a grateful public (the book became a best seller) without depending on the original allegorical equation of the writer with a confidence trickster.

So what, in the subject, was still—or again—live? If Krull was no longer an embodiment and confession of his author, what was Krull to him? And what did Mann mean when he called it "the homosexual novel"?[46] This late in life, he is strangely preoccupied with his sexuality. In his diary he looks back over a lifetime of non-fulfillment, remembers all the young men he has loved and on whom he has bestowed, unnamed (so he now names them) "a kind of immortality." They are "a gallery no 'literary history' will record."[47] (He would have been surprised!) Even more to the point, he is now "enormously alert and full of painful desire for all beauty of that kind." His potency is restored through feelings he has not known for twenty-five years. They are intensified by his approaching end,[48] though at times death seems positively inviting because he "can no longer stand the longing for the 'divine boy.'"[49] True, he sometimes sees his ideal incarnated, in a young sportsman or an attentive waiter in a St. Moritz hotel,[50] giving rise to

> a general mourning for my life and its love, this deepest felt, crazy, and yet passionately affirmed enthusiasm for the charm, *incomparable and not surpassed by anything in the world*, of the young male, which was always my happiness and my misery.[51]

His homoerotic feelings were always "the deepest thing in me, the basis of my art." "In your breath my word is given shape," he quotes from a poem by Michelangelo, in whose writing he sees "the Platonic arousal which always interprets thralldom to beauty as a love of god and the spirit."[52] We are back on the beach with Aschenbach, writing with Tadzio in sight, back with Potiphar's wife Mut-em-enet, whose passion for Joseph finds expression in words that Mann had written in the days when he loved Paul Ehrenberg. As with Proust, the montage makes persuasive fiction: love is love is love.

So the late continuation of the Krull project now rests on a reversal. Where in 1911 the young Felix stood allegorically for the young writer-*subject* Thomas Mann, now the still timelessly young Krull becomes the *object* of the old Thomas Mann's loving admiration. The newly written sections celebrate Krull's attractiveness—to homosexuals cruising the streets of Frankfurt, and later to the lonely Lord Kilmarnock, who invites him to give up work as a waiter and become his resident butler in Scotland (GW 7:479). It is Kilmarnock, who, at seventy-five, Mann's own present age, now stands for the author. In him Mann has fallen in love with his own creation.

Even more actively, the romantic novelist Diane Houpflé delights in having Krull as her lover, the youthful opposite of the hairy-chested male type she detests. The chapter-long celebration of her special taste in men culminates in a near-verbatim montage of the diary entry quoted above. Mann only had to turn his confession of a passion for young *men* into her passion for *young* men:

> I live in my so-called perversion, in the love of my life, which is the basis of everything I am, in the happiness and misery of this enthusiasm, with its precious vow that nothing, nothing in the whole range of experience can equal the charm of youthful early manhood.[53]

If this is a touch too serious for a comic novel, Mann's own confession is too well masked in the adapted diary entry to be an open confession at all. Its vehemence is the measure of his feelings, encoding it is the measure of his reserve. But once again, the materials of a fiction from decades ago have been turned to a very different purpose from the original.

For all Mann's emphasis on a life of mourning and misery, and though he talked down the pleasures of international fame, there were times when he could see his life as "a *happy and blessed* life, its foundation cheerful, so to speak sunny, and by this everything after all is determined."[54] Above all he could accept that he had to be as he was to produce what he did: "For a productive individual, the question remains always: What comes of it all—whatever the nature of 'it all' may be."[55]

10: Description of a Struggle: Kafka's Half-Escape

In memoriam Malcolm Pasley

The Wound Breaks Open

As THESE STUDIES GO, Kafka is a case in the diagnostic sense. Perhaps not just all unhappy families, as Tolstoy wrote, but all unhappy individuals are unhappy in their own way. Kafka's misery was complex, each strand having its own pathology and paradoxes: a deep feeling of physical and psychological inferiority and of exclusion from common human contact; dissatisfaction with his body and appearance, although he was tall, good-looking, and always elegantly dressed; uneasy family relations, especially with his dominating father, a powerful self-made businessman; a feeling that he lived among but not in his family, stranger than a stranger, lonelier than Robinson Crusoe on his island, yet also not wholly belonging to the traditional Jewish world, or Zionism; a sense of intellectual failure from the time of his schooling onwards; the frustration of an unloved office job, and the responsibility for a rashly launched further family enterprise, both of which consumed time and energies that might have been used for writing.

Writing was a yearned-for compensation, but also a further source of misery when, as so often, it failed to flow. Even so, it dominated his life, in childhood as a premonition, later as a hope, later still as despair.[1] Was he a writer? He was sure he was nothing else. Reflections on that status and attempts to achieve it fill his diaries. Rather than everyday events, they record his creative starts (overwhelmingly unsuccessful) and the ebb and flow of his self-confidence. The above chapter title, borrowed from an early collection of his sketches, exactly fits Kafka's life-long struggle to prove himself.

Not that the creative fulfillment Kafka hoped for would have made for a happy life. As a writer, he would still be left with loneliness and exclusion. An early piece, the delicate prose-poem "An unhappy bachelor," movingly foresees the realities of a solitary life.[2] Marriage and family were in his eyes an ideal fulfillment, just not for him. He came as near as being engaged—twice—to Felice Bauer, and over six years wrote her 400 eloquent love-letters (they make 750 closely printed pages) but twice broke off the engagement. His writing routine, deep into the small hours, would have made him an unsociable husband.[3] Conversely, which was what mattered to him more, keeping more normal hours would have put paid to his writing. His diary during the first engagement weighs the pros and cons of marrying, and the balance is negative.[4]

Occasional bursts of inspiration kept his hopes alive, most powerfully a breakthrough in September 1912 when, as he wrote to Milena Jesenská in 1920, "the wound first broke open in a long night."[5] Written immediately after it happened, it is the most graphic of all accounts of literary genesis:

> I wrote this story, "The Judgment," in the night of the 22nd to 23rd from ten in the evening to six in the morning, in one go. I could hardly pull my stiff legs out from under the desk. The fearful effort and joy as the story developed before me as I moved forward in a surge of water. Several times in this night I carried my weight on my back. How everything can be dared, how for all, for the strangest ideas a great fire is prepared in which they pass away and are resurrected. How it turned blue outside the window. A car drove by. Two men went over the bridge. At two o'clock I looked at the clock for the last time. As the maid first went through the room outside I wrote the final sentence. Switching the lamp off and daylight. The slight pains round my heart. The tiredness that went away in the middle of the night. Went trembling into my sister's room. Reading it to her. Before that, I stretched and said to the maid: "I've been writing till now." The sight of the untouched bed, as if it had just been carried in. The conviction confirmed that with my novel I've been in the shameful shallows of writing. This is the only way to write, only in such coherence, with such complete opening of body and soul. Spent morning in bed. My eyes all the time clear. Many feelings while I was writing: for example, the pleasure at having something beautiful for Max's Arcadia, thoughts of Freud naturally, [. . .] and of my "Urban world."[6]

This is inspiration, if anything ever was. The story's effect bears it out. When Kafka two days later read it to his friend Oscar Baum's family and circle, it brought tears to his eyes, an emotion that previously only performing the works of other writers had done. "The story's undoubted quality was confirmed."[7]

Kafka had meant to write a story about a war, starting with an observer looking down from a high window at a crowd crossing a bridge.[8] Under his hands—or rather, taken out of his hands—the impulse became involuntarily something quite different, a conversation between a son and a widowed father that suddenly turns into mortal conflict. It starts from a question about Georg Bendemann's coming marriage—should he announce it to a friend in Russia whose business is not going well? (The fiancée has mysteriously said, "With friends like that, you shouldn't have got engaged.") Father queries whether the friend even exists, though he has earlier met and not liked him ("Do you really have this friend in St Petersburg?"). Yet it now turns out that father and friend are actually in league ("He would be a son after my own heart") against Georg, whose efforts to supplant him at home and in the family firm his father has seen through. And now the son is asserting himself by marrying, just because the "repulsive goose lifted her skirts." Seemingly a weak old man, the father is still a giant in his dressing-gown. Lovingly put to bed, he repeatedly asks "Am I well tucked in?" only to rise up, "strong enough for you, too strong for you," and condemn Georg to death by drowning. Exit Georg: he crosses the road, seizes the rails of the bridge "like a hungry man his nourishment," and with a cry "Dear parents, I always loved you," throws himself over.

Reading the proofs the following February, a puzzled Kafka writes down such connections as have become clear to him. "I have to do this, because the story came out of me"—here the motif of opening body and soul becomes fully visceral—"like a real birth, covered in filth and slime and only I have the hand that can penetrate through to the body and the desire to do it."[9] It is the most drastic instance of the recurrent birth metaphor. The birth had all too clearly come from the quick of life: a tyrannical father like the one central to Kafka's existence; he himself present in thin disguise, for the number of letters in the son's name, Georg, matches Franz, the surname Bende- (ignoring the neutral suffix "-mann"), matches Kafka, with the vowels in the same places; the fiancée's name, Frieda Brandenfeld, shares initials with Kafka's new acquaintance and soon-to-be fiancée, Felice Bauer, while the "-feld" (field) part of the name connects with Felice's surname "Bauer" (peasant).[10] To cap all, Kafka's sister Ottla recognized the setting as the family flat.

A connection Kafka doesn't make is between the repulsive goose's lifted skirts and the crude attitudes to sex and sex education of his father (who also habitually went about the flat in his dressing-gown). Other connections Kafka thought he could make out may seem as puzzling as the story itself: that the friend is "the greatest common element" between father and son; that his fiancée "lives" only through the friend; that only because Georg "has nothing" does the judgment take such devastating effect. Kafka lists the connections in a letter to Felice, asking whether she can find any straightforward, coherent sense in the story. He himself can't—he can't explain anything. It's as obscure as any poem.[11] Even more mysteriously, he notes in his diary that Georg's fiancée is the cause of his downfall. Also that indirectly he has Felice to thank for the story. He duly dedicated the published text to her.[12]

"The Judgment" is a bizarre triumph. What mattered more for the moment than any piecemeal or overall interpretation was the sense that his inner life—those strangest ideas he speaks of—had been swept up in a "great fire" and "resurrected," that is, brought to new literary life. The experience had at last given him the confidence he needed, for a while at least. From early on, writing had been his ambition, his addiction, and his frustration. "I am made of literature, I am nothing else and can be nothing else."[13] The realization was there early: "When it became clear to my organism that writing was the most productive direction of my being, everything pressed that way and left all capacities standing empty that were to do with the pleasures of sex, eating, drinking, philosophical reflection, music especially. I lost weight"—a typical bodily metaphor—"in all those directions. I had to, because my powers were so slight in total that only when combined could they halfway serve the purpose of writing." So he mustn't lament that he can't bear to have a lover, knows as little of love as of music, celebrates New Year's Eve with a frugal vegetarian meal. . . Now he only needs to escape from his insurance-office job—that other oppressive part of his existence—to begin his real life, "when, in step with my works, my face will at last naturally grow old."[14]

What keeps him going is the hope for, and occasional experience of, writing in a state of elevation or intense emotion ("Erhebung," "Ergriffenheit"), something that—paradox again—"I fear more than I yearn for, however much I do yearn for it."[15] He has been writing short pieces since 1904, and since 1910 the diary has been a vital channel to keep his pen active—it upset him whenever for a few days he didn't write. He had headaches and sleeplessness to contend with, and often a state of anomie that left him staring at his fingers. "There were years," he confesses late on to his father, "when I spent more time lazing on the sofa, in the best of health, than you in your whole life, illnesses included."[16]

The diaries are a quarry but also a graveyard of geneses, fragments abandoned after a sentence, a paragraph, or several pages. Sometimes an opening is immediately written out afresh, even several times over, as if Kafka needs the energy of a new run-up that may carry him a bit further this time; but it still doesn't. Sometimes a narrative develops and begins to read well, but is abandoned for no obvious flaw.[17] "The Judgment" is a rare instance of a sustained and completed creation, for Kafka a first fully convincing genesis.

Most concretely, the experience of writing it gave him the impetus to launch into a new novel, *The Man Who Disappeared* (*Der Verschollene*).[18] Its first chapter follows in the diary immediately after the genesis of "The Judgment." So far from the "shameful shallows" of the earlier (unidentified) novel, he was now, so Max Brod recorded, "in unbelievable ecstasy," once more writing through night after night.[19] True, subjective inspiration didn't guarantee lasting satisfaction, and he was later to reject 550 pages of it as wasted work,[20] cherishing only the first chapter, "The

Stoker," as in some not entirely clear way a rounded success, and keen to publish it as a declared fragment.

Yet in another twist of his hypersensitivity, Kafka shied away from publishing as much as he aspired to it. Publication was a desired and logical consummation—why else write?—yet also a painful revelation of his private world and all his weaknesses. It was paradoxically damaging to be pleased with himself when he put together old journal pieces for a first volume, *Betrachtung* (Reflection).[21] "Don't overrate what I write," he warned himself, "that way I make what I have to write unattainable."[22] Pressure to publish came in any case largely from Max Brod, including an introduction to his own publisher, the Rowohlt Verlag. In an extraordinary symbiosis, alongside his own literary career Brod became Kafka's impresario, for the rest of his life doing everything to further the visibility and reputation of his shy friend. At the extreme of self-effacement, Kafka wrote to his later publisher Kurt Wolff that he would always rather have his manuscripts sent back to him than published.[23] (Wolff, the promoter of so much talent from the Expressionist generation, was the most encouraging publisher imaginable, reassuring Kafka that he strongly believed in his work even while reporting minimal annual sales.)

It can be difficult to follow Kafka's judgments on his own production, positive or (far more often) severely negative. Either way, stories became for him intensely real physical presences. An unsuccessful text has "gaps you could push a hand through, one sentence rubs against another like the tongue on a hollow tooth."[24] Or he will "jump into my novella even if it cuts my face to pieces."[25] Or he is "repulsed by all three stories."[26]

What, concretely, had "The Judgment" achieved? Privately, psychologically, its happenings and compulsive images had brought to the surface deep traumas and anxieties. Yet beyond identifiable personal pain, Kafka felt an obligation to bring into the open "the monstrous world that I have in my head. But how to liberate myself, and liberate it, without tearing myself apart? And a thousand times sooner tear myself apart than keep it back or bury it within me. That is what I'm here for, that is quite clear to me."[27] It sounds very much like another birth. The mixture of expressive impulse and painful constriction is characteristic. It is there again in a letter to Felice where he says the things he wants to say to her are like a press of people struggling to get through a narrow door,[28] impulse and frustration equally clear.

Beyond Realism

Alongside trauma, there is the compelling illogic of dreams. They too are part of what Kafka felt obliged to make public. "From the viewpoint of literature, my destiny is very simple. My feeling for the representation of my dream-like inner life makes everything else secondary and in a terrible way stunted, and the stunting process is continuing."[29] The dreams that emerge are more like nightmares. Georg Bendemann is forced to commit suicide, Gregor Samsa is transformed into a beetle, the Penal Colony centers on an elaborate punishment machine, Josef K. in *The Trial* is inexplicably condemned and executed. Arbitrary judgment is accepted as legitimate; guilt remains obscure but unquestioned.

Hardly any text of Kafka's lacks the feeling of unease and foreboding; narrative is almost always in a minor key. Alongside the extreme examples in his fiction, the diaries contain as many again, and worse. Punishment and torture were ingrained in Kafka's feelings, going deep into the self-harmingly masochistic. "Today once again for the first time the pleasure of imagining a knife turned in my heart"; "Constantly the imagination of a bright butcher's knife that thrusts into me in great haste and with mechanical regularity, and cuts off thin slices that through the speed of the work fly away almost in rolls"; "To be pulled in through the ground-floor window of a house by a rope round my neck and ruthlessly, as by someone who doesn't take much note, torn bloody and in shreds through all the ceilings, furniture, walls, and attics until on the roof the empty noose appears which in breaking through the roof tiles has lost my remains."[30] He imagines a "bizarre court procedure" whereby a man sentenced to death is stabbed in his own room by the executioner. The victim thinks it can't possibly happen: they're going through the motions, after which he will just be imprisoned. To which the executioner replies, unwrapping his daggers: "You're thinking of fairy tales where a servant is ordered to expose a child but doesn't. That is a fairy tale, this isn't a fairy tale."[31] All these instances are close to the ending of *The Trial*, where Josef K is executed. On the other end of procedures, Kafka sees himself as the operator of a torture instrument that is punishing an innocent Felice for the injustice he himself has committed[32]—their difficult relationship already generates this grim metaphorical scenario. The larger fictions are only a part, seemingly a truthful part, of a disturbed and disturbing mind-set. It was indeed a "monstrous world"[33] he had in his head.

Once he is reading his own work, Kafka doesn't revel in the dark visions but looks at them with cool objectivity. He calls "Metamorphosis" an "exceptionally revolting story."[34] Put together in one volume, "The Judgment" and "In the Penal Colony" would be a "dreadful combination."[35] Yet precisely this mixture is a possibility he discussed with his publisher Kurt Wolff: a proposed volume "Punishments" was to contain "The Judgment," "Metamorphosis," and "In the Penal Colony," while an alternative suggestion was a volume entitled "Sons," which would have contained "The Judgment," "Metamorphosis," and "The Stoker." The overlap between the two schemes is telling. Being a son and having to be punished are very close.[36]

These are self-evidently not realistic worlds—but then, the advanced fiction of the day had long bidden farewell to straightforward realism. That tradition was not even a baseline to work from, but something to be completely escaped from. Kafka never produced an explicit poetics—he seems always to have been driven rather than consciously driving—but there are a few statements, ambitious and more than a little puzzling, of what he thought he was doing and what, on fortunate occasions, happened when the writing went well:

> Remarkable, mysterious, perhaps dangerous, perhaps liberating consolation of writing: leaping out of the deadly routine [of] act—observation, act—observation, by creating a higher kind of observation, higher, not sharper, and the higher it is, the less accessible from the "routine," the more independent it becomes, the more it follows its own laws of movement, the more incalculable, joyful, its ascending way.[37]

It is easier to see this as a farewell to banal realism than to say quite what is being celebrated in its place. Likewise when he says he can feel satisfied for a time by work like "A Country Doctor," "but I feel happy only if I can raise the world into the Pure, the True, the Immutable."[38] In both passages, the image of ascent to a new level makes emphatic claims, but just what constitutes purity, truth, and immutability, and what higher kind of observation his fictions seek to attain, is not made clear.

They do certainly become independent, with their own laws of movement, and the overall line of development in the sequence of Kafka's works rises clearly from a base in ordinary observation. The two trauma-inspired stories, "The Judgment" and "Metamorphosis," still have one foot in domestic realities—a recognizable family flat, a father-son chat about family matters, the pressure of a new working day—before they descend into nightmare. "What do you say to the terrible things that play out in our house?" Kafka reportedly asked an acquaintance.[39] They are reactions to a very specific emotional pressure, as Kafka recognized even as he was writing "The Judgment," with his "thoughts of Freud, naturally." It is the nightmare elements that have made him famous, above all "the bug story," as his publisher Kurt Wolff offhandedly called "Metamorphosis."[40] It is a striking, even crude, metaphor for a son's alienation within the family. But as yet these stories lack the density and coherence of a wholly dream world.

That is compellingly achieved in "A Country Doctor." No longer limited to embodying specific personal pain as in "The Judgment," nor dominated by one aggressive metaphor as in "Metamorphosis," the narrative is released into a freestanding and free-moving fiction. Any précis is problematic, since the compulsiveness of dream depends on any and every inconsequential yet vivid detail: The doctor-narrator's carriage stands ready to respond to an urgent call ten miles away through a snowstorm, but his horse is dead; an unknown farmhand provides two splendid replacements from the pigsty, but then assaults the maid Rosa, who is left to his mercies as the doctor is driven off—and instantly arrives. The patient, a sick boy, asks to be allowed to die, but is entirely well. The doctor still worries about the maid being raped, but suddenly the boy is dying after all of an immense wound crawling with thick worms. The family are demanding the impossible, old beliefs have died, they are misusing the doctor for sacred purposes, threatening to sacrifice him, they undress him and put him into bed with the boy, who is now said to have been born with the wound, which however would be cured with two strokes of an axe. The doctor hastily gathers up his fur and starts the journey back. His practice is ruined, a successor has stolen it, at home Rosa must by now be the farmhand's victim. Suddenly the perspective widens: "Nackt, dem Froste dieses unglückseligsten Zeitalters ausgesetzt mit irdischem Wagen, unirdischen Pferden, treibe ich mich alter Mann umher." (Naked, exposed to the frost of this most unhappy age, with an earthly coach and unearthly horses I wander around, an old man.) His fur drags behind the carriage, irretrievable. "Einmal dem Fehlläuten der Nachtglocke gefolgt—es ist niemals gutzumachen." (Once the false ringing of the night-bell is followed, it can never be made good.)[41]

Everything is suggestive and disturbing. Unease is physical, sexual, metaphysical. The "icy age"—the story was written in the third winter of the First World War—is a reference to the wider world, rare in Kafka. It echoes an earlier image for his own existence as "a useless post covered in snow and hoarfrost, driven askew into a churned-up field on the edge of a great plain on a dark winter's night."[42] But the doctor's narrative has gone beyond private trauma; there is no father-figure, no father-son conflict, no unhappy family. If writing was Kafka's way to escape from his father, writing itself needed to escape from that obsessive domestic theme. Otherwise it was only a half-escape, as when "a worm's rear half is trodden on and the front half tears itself away."[43] But "A Country Doctor" is fully free, concerned now with that wider theme of a mission, a calling, real or illusory—it was originally meant to go into a volume with the title "Responsibility" (Verantwortung). Well might Kafka feel satisfied for a time by this remarkable story. But he still dedicated the volume to his father.

The story's dense coherence suggests it was written in one of the heightened moods Kafka longed for. The problem was how to sustain that condition long enough to create something even of novella length. The idea for "Metamorphosis" spontaneously "came to me in my misery this morning in bed."[44] After several nights spent working on it, he noted that "this kind of story ought to be written with at most one interruption, in twice 10 hours" so as to have "its natural pull and storm, which it had in my head last Sunday."[45] So here was already a compromise between inspiration and application. He had "damaged" the story with his intermittent working method, and on top of that he now had to break off for a business trip. The story had an "unreadable ending" and was "imperfect to its very roots." Meanwhile he still had a novel at the back of his mind, but a novel needed a different order of discipline, a whole other way of working. The desired heightened states were too transitory and unpredictable to be relied on for the longer haul.

Novelist?

This most influential of twentieth-century novelists never completed a novel. He repeatedly spoke of the need to succeed in a longer work that would motivate his writing, but without the motivation how could he achieve the longer work? It was a vicious circle. It was not for want of trying. In October 1914 he took two weeks off from the office to work on *The Trial*, got nowhere with that, but instead dashed off "In the Penal Colony" and "The Nature Theater of Oklahoma," a final chapter for *The Man who Disappeared*—which he had already abandoned a year earlier. He was clearly taking refuge from the larger task in two lesser ones. He felt "unable to write further." His diary entry reads: "I am at the final limit, before which perhaps I am to sit again for years, in order then to begin another story that remains unfinished."[46] (There are echoes here, or anticipations, of the parable "Before the Law.") Kurt Wolff, unaware equally of Kafka's intention and inability to write a novel, encouraged him to do just that. Kafka surprisingly saw his American novel conception as a "straight imitation" of *David Copperfield*, but also as an improvement on Dickens's "unthinking powerful flow" and his "chunks of crude characterization."[47] But what constructive means were available to him? Those larger conceptions, *The Trial* and *The Castle*, lack the temporal scaffolding and material accumulation on which the great nineteenth-century novels, from Balzac and Tolstoy down to Thomas Mann's *Buddenbrooks*, were built up. Kafka doesn't seem to have planned the structure of his—chapter titles were added after the chapters were written—and the only thing that was foreseen from the start in *The Trial* was that it would end with Josef K's execution. Rather, Kafka seems to start writing out of a present imagined situation, simply following his pen, beginning as if from nothing. "One has to write as if in a dark tunnel, not knowing how the characters will develop," he told Max Brod. It is exceptional that *The Trial* had that clear intended ending,[48] though it was still left to Brod to order the preserved drafts and give the story a clear sequence after Kafka's death.[49]

The sensational impact of Kafka's novels, for all their inchoate final state, is not in doubt. Yet his strictly artistic successes are the perfectly formed medium-length pieces to which he increasingly gravitated.

Escaping from work on *The Trial* into those two alternative shorter texts wasn't a weakness; rather it showed his true direction. The more concise stories grow out of a single situation or metaphor—as indeed do *The Trial* and *The Castle*—but unlike the novel fragments, they round this to a controlled unity and conclusion. Down to the dense concise pieces of Kafka's last years, they demonstrate his true talent.

Artists

Kafka was at least by now more his own man, free of his extreme obsessions and violent visions (he abandoned *The Trial* in late January 1915 as an "artistic failure"[50]) and able to reflect with humorous detachment on the nature of art and the artist's position. Which is not to say that his conclusions are straightforward. The artist theme, ubiquitous in modern writing from Mann and Hesse to Joyce and Camus, is nowhere rendered so bizarrely and teasingly as in Kafka's fables: of a singing mouse and her status in the mouse community; of an animal tirelessly extending and repairing its burrow, threatened on all sides by enemies; of a circus acrobat who refuses to descend from his trapeze; of a now neglected starvation artist whose one-time success with the public had rested on the misprision that fasting was difficult for him, hence an achievement.[51]

Almost everything in the mouse fable is no sooner stated than contradicted by what reads like the work of a murine ethnologist. Apparently the mice are carried away by Josefine's singing, though as a people they are unmusical. She is unique in loving, communicating, and preserving music, but in private they admit it's nothing special. Is it even music at all? It's surely just whistling, and all mice can whistle. Yet nor is it just whistling when you see her close up; it's sufficient that this mouse is publicly doing an everyday thing—just as cracking nuts in public wouldn't simply be nut-cracking but an art previously not remarked on because universal, yet paradoxically more of an art if performed less well than most mice can. Processions go to hear her, especially in times of crisis, but sometimes a crowd has to be organized and directed. And does she really have that much effect? How elevated is her art? Because of her status she demands to be spared having to work for a living, but the mouse people aren't having that. She struggles for recognition against her enemies, though in fact she has none. The mice wonder whether they treasure her singing as anything more than a distant memory of a lost tradition. In her decline she will gradually be forgotten, freed from the earthly ills she believes all Chosen Ones have to suffer.[52]

Is all this serious, or simply humor? Humorous Kafka certainly could be, and he often only needs to be read with that pre-setting to come across with less gloomy effect. But he was too serious for mere whimsy. Yet it is hard to see how the story's twists and turns can be consistently mapped on to specific concerns of any one artist or artist type. The title, which gives the Mouse People equal status with the protagonist, has tempted some to see its subject as art and the Jews, and Kafka was Jewish; but it wasn't otherwise his central problem. Here too the details don't all fit, any more than they fit any other monothematic reading. Kafka was in any case—that much is clear from the working methods and problems sketched above—not an allegorist, not that is systematically encoding abstractions in fictions. The mouse story is rather a play of glancing insights into the relation between an artist and her talent, her ambitions, and her public—"play" in the full sense. For once the situation is conceived, it can be explored, imaginatively lived in, and enjoyed, by both author and reader, in the unsettled and unsettling way an Escher picture can be enjoyed, but with only one certain outcome: that the relation of art and artist to the world isn't easy.

The same is true of the creature in his great burrow, his devoted labors constantly disturbed by threatening noises from somewhere around him, his expeditions and returns perilous. In contrast, the trapeze artist, with his literally elevated art, is positively indulged by the Circus Impresario; when he requests a second trapeze, it's ordered at once for the next performance. Yet the "First Sorrow" he felt over this idiosyncratic need is a harbinger of others. As they travel to the new venue (with the trapeze artist of course accommodated up in the luggage-rack) the first worry-wrinkles already appear on his forehead.

Most radical but in the end most positive is the case of the starvation artist. At first sight the parallel with display-fasting seems to discredit art absolutely as a perversion of normal life. The protagonist's fasts were once a fashionable feature of the fairground; spectators marveled at the scoreboard as he approached the forty-day mark. But interest has since waned, he lies forgotten in his neglected cage, to be finally replaced by a frighteningly vigorous panther, who is at once a hit with the crowds: in his brute normality, "there was nothing wrong with *him*." Instinct and vitality trump asceticism (in a textual variant, the contrast figure was a cannibal). As the hunger artist lies dying, he confesses to the supervisor who sweeps him out of his cage that his fasting was never difficult, it was all he ever wanted to do, so he should never have been admired for it. His showmanship was a deceit, his art no achievement, its object to that extent unreal, valueless.

But isn't rather the reverse true? He still fasts on "because I have to, I can do no other." Why not? "Because I couldn't find the food I liked. If I had found it, I would have made no fuss and eaten my fill, like you and everyone." So there did exist a positive object of desire and a valid appetite for it. The artist's world, the world of the spirit, was not a perversion of normality, but had—has—its own distinct reality, elusive, unusual, yet still compelling.[53]

The compulsion, surely not by chance, echoes Luther's historic words: "Here I stand and can do no other." But Kafka's age was in thrall to a vitalism derived from Nietzsche, according to which art, philosophy, and even morality were essentially abnormal, decadent. Restoring vital instinct was allegedly the way to a renewed culture. That left artists with a guilty conscience that went to the roots of their existence and their calling. Kafka, for all his feelings of guilt and deficiency, stands out against this mode of anti-intellectualism to which others yielded.[54] He was not responding passively to a pervasive influence, in the way then current, but critically to his own well-documented reading of Nietzsche. This provided the images—panther, tiger, or lion (the notorious "blond beast" of the *Genealogie der Moral*)—in which Nietzsche had represented the primal human instincts with careless relish. He made a sick animal in a cage stand for the ancient Germans whom Christianity had tamed. Kafka was, so to speak, playing Nietzsche on the philosopher's home ground of the emblematic imagination, in order to arrive at diametrically opposed conclusions.

Kafka's own flair for striking images made him sensitive to other people's, and there is more than one occasion when he borrows from the two thinkers who, against the alleged German tendency to dry abstraction, owe their widespread influence precisely to the power of their imagery. The other is Nietzsche's master, Schopenhauer, whom Kafka held in high esteem precisely as "an artist in language. That is where his thinking comes from."[55] In just that way, Schopenhauer the great pessimist characterized the world as "a punishment institution, a penal colony."[56] Even more suggestively he compared our vain attempts to understand reality from the outside, which yields only images and names, to a man "who goes round a castle, vainly seeking a way in and meantime sketching the façades."[57]

Sometimes Kafka's artistic self-concern goes so far as to take works of his own as secret referents for a story, setting harmless puzzles and sometimes providing a clue. The descriptive piece "Eleven sons," so he told Max Brod, referred to eleven of his own stories. Similarly, though left without this kind of key, the story "A Father's Worries," with its mysterious figure Odradek, on whom a lot of scholarly ink has been expended, really (if that concept can apply to anything in Kafka) refers to a story, "The Hunter Gracchus," that was causing him problems.[58] Again, even as he was writing about legal procedures in *The Trial*, Kafka slipped into writing about his own writing and *its* problems. When Josef K. has dismissed his lawyer and now has to compose the required documents himself, he reflects: "What was at stake wasn't just the legal submission, for which perhaps a spell of leave would have been enough, [. . .] it was a matter of a whole trial [Prozess] whose duration couldn't be known." But what Kafka first inadvertently wrote was: "What is at stake is a whole process [Prozess] whose length can't be known in advance."[59] The present tenses, and "length," not "duration," show that a preoccupation with the author's own problems has edged out those of the fictional figure. Writing *The Trial* was indeed a trial of Kafka himself, to see whether, after his first failed attempt at writing a novel, he could at last complete one.

"The Secret King"

Throughout, Kafka's style is already remarkable enough through its constantly even tone and objective lucidity, its unruffled calm. But it stands out the more through the paradoxical contrast with the extraordinary content (as does, behind it, the orderly, clear handwriting of his manuscripts). Kafka's language is sometimes thought of as Prague German, but even within that known idiolect his voice is unique. For Hermann Hesse it made Kafka, sensational substance apart, "the secret king of the German language."[60]

One of the marked features of Kafka's style is its rhythm, which is embodied in a punctuation that diverges from standard practice. In the original drafts, for example of *The Castle*, Kafka's prose is urgent, nervous, linking successive events and perceptions closely with no more than commas between. When Max Brod edited the posthumous works, he "corrected" Kafka's usage, as if an author's original punctuation were not part of his narrative style, but merely (as has been mistakenly argued) one of the "accidentals," spelling is another, that are distinct from the significant, "substantive" elements of the text.[61] Yet the pattern of punctuation is what sets up the rhythm that most nearly conveys an author's voice.[62]

There is a striking difference in effect between short, end-stopped sentences, and a linked sequence that turns them into a "flowing parataxis,"[63] Kafka's original form, which Pasley restored in the Frankfurt critical edition. Such syntactically unorthodox structures are, needless to say, a much-used option in modern prose narrative.[64]

True, Kafka himself sometimes adjusted his texts to the standard conventions for publication, but when writing he kept up his deviant practice to the end, as witness the late unfinished story "A Dog's Researches," where it is a prominent feature of a lengthy text.

Genesis of a Reputation

From being scarcely known in his lifetime, excluded (if he was ever even noticed) by the Nazis as a Jew and later rejected by Marxist literary critics as a decadent modernist, Kafka became a central figure in postwar culture across the Western world. Briefly in the Prague Spring and permanently after the fall of communism, he was accepted and celebrated in the country of his birth. At the basis of it all was Max Brod's tireless editing and promoting of Kafka's work—the unfinished novels had at least been published before the Second World War. Brod subsequently rescued all Kafka's manuscripts from a succession of twentieth-century wars and invasions in an odyssey that took them from Prague to a Tel Aviv archive, thence to a New York publishing house, on to a Zurich bank-vault, and finally to Oxford's Bodleian Library.[65] That Brod didn't follow Kafka's instructions to burn all his unpublished work after his death[66] has caused raised eyebrows. It has been plausibly argued that Kafka must have known that Brod, of all people, wouldn't do what he was requesting. At all events, Brod's was the right decision. Too much has been lost to literature through the intervention of descendants and other short-sighted survivors. Kafka's case, in a double irony, reverses this relation: the author asks a survivor to destroy his work, and by the same action prevents it. Brod, generously, always looked forward to a full critical edition of the works he had so faithfully promoted. (The *Times Literary Supplement* nicely titled its review of the first volume of the new edition "Not by Brod alone.")

Kafka certainly came to have an extraordinary status, in and beyond literature. "Anti-classical times, it seems, can't do without classics," wrote the bibliographer Paul Raabe[67] at a time when Germany's established classics—Goethe, Schiller, Thomas Mann—were being treated with skepticism and suspicion by a politically radical generation. It was virtually a qualification of the new idols to have been outsiders, leading unhappy, even tragic lives: Hölderlin, Kleist, Büchner. Kafka plainly fitted.

W. H. Auden went further, singling Kafka out as "nearest to our times, as Dante, Shakespeare, Goethe were to theirs . . . he is so important for us because his problems are the problems of present-day people."[68] That was a massive claim to make compared with the scope, complexity, and quality of the other three writers named. But is the imputation to "us" of problems shared with Kafka even plausible? "Kafkaesque" is established in common parlance (and in the OED) for situations that are irrational, unjust, oppressive, or just frustrating to the helpless human being. The usage derives most obviously—though users may never have read these texts—from the legal structure of *The Trial* and the administrative hierarchy of *The Castle*. These in turn are assumed to have their roots in Kafka's position in the industrial insurance office that assessed workers' claims (and mostly rejected them, contrary to Kafka's own sympathies). But the frustration of Kafka's sad figures have a metaphysical suggestiveness that goes beyond (or stops short of) labor relations and the other harsh experiences of the modern world. The moods of *The Trial* and *The Castle* hardly dominate contemporary existence. The social and political realities that do press down on humanity everywhere are more convincingly Orwellian than Kafkaesque. Kafka was not, in any serious sense of the word, predicting tyranny; Orwell was. Overall Kafka doesn't offer the range of human experience or emotion for which we value the great novelists; while Kafkaesque is too blunt an analytical tool even for a widely shared psychological state, if such existed. Rather it encourages feelings of anxiety and vicarious victimhood that are inauthentic and defeatist. We are not all Ks.

The ever-pugnacious Edmund Wilson, going to the opposite extreme, asked "how one could possibly take Kafka for either a great artist or a moral guide." He compared Kafka to the Brocken specter, "a human shadow thrown on the mist in such a way that it seems monstrous and remote when it may really be quite close at hand."[69] And indeed, as we get closer to Kafka, away from the two main novels and to the other works, especially the diaries, the cliché reference gets weaker, Kafka appears less vaguely "Kafkaesque," the picture of his misery looms larger, more distinctive and peculiar to him. "I don't believe there are people whose inner state is like mine, well, I can just about imagine such people, but that the secret raven flies constantly round their heads as it does round mine, that I can't even imagine."[70] As ever, Kafka is straightaway thinking in images, but their sense—the uniqueness of his own inner state—is plain. True, since at latest the eighteenth century, literature has been the route by which unique private experience is laid open to public awareness and sympathy. Yet sympathy for, and even empathy with, a special case must be able to stop short of an identification through which a whole culture embraces a disabling pessimism. There are many other options, not least the comparators Auden named, who are decidedly not a thing of the past.

Kafka himself rarely generalized and didn't see his own work as generalizing. Least of all would this most modest of writers have seen himself or the fictional figures with whom he shares initials or name-patterns—Josef K. in *The Trial*, K. in *The Castle*[71]—as Everyman. He did recall in his diary an early wish to "achieve a view of life and persuade others of it in writing,"[72] but the force of the wish is at once attenuated by the usual self-subversions, and the passage was deleted. Just twice he looks outside his private misery to evoke a grim present world, once in the passage quoted above from "Ein Landarzt," and then in a letter to Kurt Wolff, where he agrees that "In der Strafkolonie" is painful, but adds that "our general and my particular time was and is very painful," so that he is "at least outwardly an undoubted contemporary."[73] This too is a formulation from the midst of an unprecedentedly terrible war.

Only late on, when he knows he is dying, does Kafka engage in general philosophical, even mystical, reflections, as ever, subtle, paradoxical, teasing. "The true way goes over a wire, which is not stretched up high but barely above the ground. It seems meant more to trip up than to be walked across" (1).[74] "In the struggle between you and the world, take the world's side" (52). "A. is a virtuoso and heaven is his witness" (49).

"Only our concept of time makes us speak of the Last Judgment, really it is a permanent summary court" (40). "You are the set task, no pupil far and wide" (22). There is often a play with religious motifs, Paradise, the Fall, Evil, Free Will: "The German word 'sein' means both 'to be' and 'to belong to him'" (46). Repeatedly there is too the sense of a reliable existential core: "Human beings cannot live without a permanent trust in something indestructible in itself" (50). "The Indestructible is One; every individual human being is it and at the same time it is common to them all, hence their unparalleled inseparable connection" (70/71).[75] Though the aphorism sequence is not systematic enough to make a coherent doctrine, it has a recurrent positive note that is not at all Kafkaesque. Perhaps the Indestructible (das Unzerstörbare) that Kafka sensed was the ultimate source of the Immutable (das Unveränderliche) that he aspired to capture in his writing.

Back to the Beginning

At the same late stage, in very different mode Kafka penned a 100-page letter to his father, an explicit statement of the obsession at the root of his work: "My writing was about you." The letter's length and unfulfilled purpose—it was never sent—lift it out of the category of mere correspondence into Kafka's oeuvre proper, which it crowns with total lucidity in a manuscript clearly written in full flow, with barely a correction. It completes the circle that began with the "The Judgment," filling in the real-life character and actions of the giant figure in his dressing-gown and stating the case against Hermann Kafka for making his son into the unhappy man he became. Despite the achieved diversity of Kafka's fiction, that originating trauma has never gone away. It smolders on here.

The letter is virtually a handbook on how not to raise a child. Never treated with physical cruelty, Kafka was early made miserable by the want of fatherly love, remembering especially an incident when he was left out on the balcony as a punishment for pestering his father in the night for a drink of water. He always felt he was nothing to his father, was never vouchsafed a kind look, was never taken gently by the hand. Later on, everything was calculated to undermine his self-confidence. There was only irony and contempt for his enthusiasms, for his friends, for anyone he admired. As a hard-nosed commercial operator who thought of his employees as "paid enemies," Hermann Kafka seemed to his son to rule the world from his armchair. Indeed, it was as if his physical presence was spread out over a map of the globe, and any area he covered was off limits for Franz, above all marriage. There was no recognition for his son's publications, the center of his existence, just saying "Put it on the bedside table" while he went on with his card game. It all left Kafka with a "limitless feeling of guilt." "Remembering this, I once wrote of someone

'He fears the shame will still survive him'"—a near-quotation of Josef K's dying thought on the last page of *The Trial*.

Kafka was well aware he was writing "an advocate's letter," with all the tricks of that trade, hinting that there was much more that could be brought in evidence. Yet typically, the dialectic of doubt and self-questioning present in virtually everything Kafka wrote sets in powerfully at the end and he imagines his father's exhaustive reply. In dizzying twists and turns, the ventriloquized paternal voice uncovers the ways the accusing son has managed to prove him guilty but then purports magnanimously to forgive him, yet still finally leave his guilt clear between the lines. Franz is unfitted for life, but has conveniently made his father responsible for that, including the failure to marry, which was never actually prevented. He has let himself be towed through life, parasitic on his father right down to this construct of a letter. Kafka in a further twist replies to the reply, admits that things can't in reality fit together as completely as in his version; but at least he and his imagined father between them have now jointly come close enough to the truth to make their real living and dying easier.

The letter was never sent, and for Franz not much living was left.

Appendix: From Manuscripts to Editions

The final phase in the history of the manuscripts dates from a chance contact between Malcolm Pasley and a great-nephew of Kafka's, Michael Steiner, then a student in Oxford, and through him with his mother, one of Kafka's four nieces, who were the family's only survivors of the Holocaust. They, it emerged, were the manuscripts' legal owners. Till then it had been commonly assumed the *de facto* owner was their devoted preserver, Max Brod. Brod indeed continued to claim that the manuscript specifically of *The Trial* had been a personal gift to him from Kafka—one more contradiction of Kafka's stated wish that Brod should destroy all his unpublished writings. This one manuscript was auctioned off by Brod's partner after his death.

Through Pasley's diplomacy the nieces agreed to place the remaining manuscripts in the Bodleian on permanent revocable loan. Legendary among British Germanists is Pasley's winter journey across Europe in his small car (a Fiat, not a Beetle) to take receipt of the papers and bring them back to Oxford. The nieces' loan was later converted into an outright gift that made the Bodleian joint owner with the family—an act of enormous generosity on their part, given that in 1988 the manuscript of *The Trial* had cost the Marbach literary archive £1 million at auction.

The Bodleian became the center of Kafka scholarship, specifically of the critical edition published by the S. Fischer Verlag, with Pasley *primus inter pares* in the editorial team, himself editing *The Trial* and *The*

Castle and coediting the diaries. There was then a further grand project, of a complete facsimile edition of the manuscript materials launched by the Stroemfeld Verlag of K. D. Wolff. It began with a rash announcement of its all-embracing scope before the copyright holders had even been informed, let alone their permission requested, and as a consequence there were unnecessary frictions over access and rights between the would-be publisher, the Bodleian, and Mrs. Steiner, advised by Pasley. These were with time fortunately resolved.

But equally rash were the initial claims for the value of the facsimile edition. They make clear by contraries the proper relation of manuscript to printed text. The editors' introduction spoiled sound sense through a narrow obsession:

> Anyone who likes Kafka is interested in the characters and the pattern of his handwriting. And anyone who works on Kafka wants to know "what is written." For that, he doesn't need a so-called "reading text" but alongside the facsimile a minute transcription of the manuscript along with detailed descriptions of the movement of manuscripts within the Kafka Nachlass and their provenance (indications of locations and owners).[76]

Facsimiles can indeed serve the curiosity of a lay readership, and the professional needs of scholars, who don't then need to travel to see the original in its fixed location. But it goes too far to say that people interested in Kafka, at either level, "don't need"—not just don't *only* need—a "so-called (!) reading text." Literature exists for all of us primarily as "reading texts," which it is the responsibility of editors and publishers to produce as scrupulously as possible. Nor is the view tenable that "problems aren't there to be solved, but to be shown up and understood as such."[77] The dichotomy is again false: problems are there to be *both* "shown up and understood as such," *and*, as far as humanly possible, solved. Only then can a reading text—an easily readable text—be established. Editors who do this are not selling their readers short, but serving their interests.

11: Atomic Beginnings: Brecht, Galileo, and After

Orbiting Ourselves

SCIENCE IS THE CENTER of educated modern awareness, the source of the most reliable knowledge about what and where mankind is. When Karl Marx declared religion was the opium of the people, he followed it up with a scientific metaphor urging people to concentrate instead on purely human concerns. Disillusioned by the critique of religion, Man was to "move around himself and thereby around his real sun. Religion is only the illusory sun, which moves around Man all the time he does not move around himself."[1]

The metaphor is decidedly hit-and-miss. Orbiting ourselves is hard to visualize—we have to be simultaneously the sun at the center and the earth going round it. And it never was an illusory sun, only ever the real sun, of which there were illusory perceptions. But the metaphor remains striking, and its reference is clear, to Copernicus and Galileo who set the sun at the center of the universe in place of the earth. That revolution became (to stay with astronomical metaphors) a fixed star in the history of science, enlightenment, and human progress, emerging in the seventeenth century, but in principle timeless. Science was a bridgehead in the campaign to replace religious and philosophical dogma with a tenable, testable worldview, often at great personal risk to the innovator. Scientific discovery was damned as religious heresy. Accordingly, the monument to the Polish astronomer Copernicus in the church of St Anne in Kraków is dedicated to "the man who dared (auso)," which picks up the motto "dare to know" (sapere aude) from Kant's great essay of 1784, *What is Enlightenment?* Aptly so, since not just science but specifically astronomy was consciously a model for Enlightenment thinkers because of its diametrical reversal of a set way of thinking.[2]

The two astronomers naturally figured in the pantheon of Marxism. Their example was once again timely when science and freedom of thought came under attack in Nazi Germany, driving intellectuals, writers, and scientists (among them fourteen Nobel laureates and twenty-six professors of theoretical physics) into exile. The life of Galileo was an obvious dramatic subject.

But not for that a simple one to handle. Galileo's conflict with the authorities was a clear-cut issue of innovation versus orthodoxy, but there had to be enough scientific substance to bring the issue dramatically alive. The dialogue in the brief scene "Physicists" of Brecht's *Fear and Misery of the Third Reich* from the same year as *Galileo*, 1938, uses a montage of scientific terminology that the audience needn't understand in order to see the point: the "German" physics Nazism demanded was still using Jewish advances, Einstein's work especially, but dared not admit it.[3]

The basic facts of the shift from geocentric to heliocentric are general knowledge, but to make a stage play they needed spelling out as human experience and social impact. Conversely, human drama had to be always transparent for the intellectual principle. It was the old problem of the didactic work, the *pièce à thèse*. In the last few years Brecht had been writing didactic plays, "Lehrstücke," sometimes targeting specifically working-class audiences in a tradition that went back to the nineteenth century. Beyond their political purpose, they are unappealing texts, never meant to "entertain," hard in tone, their necessarily dogmatic message only occasionally offset by looking at the same situation from opposite angles—for instance, whether an individual should willingly sacrifice himself for the Cause.[4]

Exile

But Brecht now no longer had this audience, or indeed any audience at all. Exile is virtually a German literary tradition, counting among its number Heine, Börne, Büchner, Nietzsche, Marx, and in the Nazi period virtually the whole Weimar literary, intellectual, and musical culture that mattered, starting with Thomas and Heinrich Mann. On February 28, 1933, the day after the Reichstag fire, Brecht joined the exodus himself, leaving Berlin for Prague and the further wanderings of exile—Sanary-sur-mer (for a time the gathering-place of exiled German writers), Svendborg, Moscow, Stockholm, Helsinki, and eventually California, near Hollywood (a longer-term gathering point of the German diaspora, where writers hoped to find work in film).

Exiles lack not only a home country to give them a feeling of rootedness, but also the concrete institutions that make literary communication possible—publishers, theaters, journals. These were to be years in which Brecht could only write for the drawer, constantly frustrated in his attempts to find somewhere to publish, broadcast, or stage what paradoxically became his finest works. Host countries were again (see above on Georg Büchner) chary of anything political that might cause diplomatic trouble with the regime the exiles had escaped from. Typically, Brecht had to put a notice in a Stockholm newspaper saying that his *Galileo* contained nothing hostile to contemporary Germany or Italy.

That remained the situation until after the war, when he was able to return to Germany and establish what became a celebrated theater of his own in East Berlin. For the present, the creative and political impulse was nevertheless sustained, perhaps all the more urgently now that a divided society had become a monolithic tyranny. Yet the new works, which put an end to the series of agitprop fables, somewhat relaxed the ideological tautness of the writing. Text flowed more freely, substantial, demotic, witty, yet rising at times to a rhetoric that Brecht himself only half-jokingly called Schillerian.[5] Ultimately it was the richness of history and the complexity of real characters and dilemmas that took his writing to a new level, though he wasn't too happy with what he saw as a backsliding from his theory and practice of "epic theater." (The scope and force of *Galileo* and *Mother Courage* would seem to be precisely what the term suggests, but that wasn't what he meant by it.)[6]

Brecht wrote the first draft of his *Leben des Galilei* in three weeks in 1938 in Denmark, where he could draw on help with the science from Christian Møller, an assistant of the atomic physicist Niels Bohr. The opening scene combines Galileo's grand vision of a new age opened up by science with the minutiae of the Ptolemaic and Copernican systems. The astronomical reversal is deftly brought into focus by having the scientist explain it to his landlady's thirteen-year-old son. He carries Andrea around on a chair to simulate the earth's real movement in relation to a washstand sun. What is education for the boy is a refresher course in basic astronomy for the audience. A humorous pedagogy solves the presentational problem, also not forgetting the economics of scientific research—an underpaid Galileo has to waste his time teaching dim aristocrats in order to boost his income and be able to afford books and food for his double appetite.

Physics-Physicality

For Galileo's scientific curiosity and his gourmet tastes have a common earthy source. The opening scene is duly dominated not just by his intellect but by his physical presence as he washes and dries his ample form (think of Charles Laughton, creator of the role in the play's first two productions in America in 1947). Galileo's physicality is later crucial when he is threatened by the instruments of the Inquisition, but to begin with it is the vital source of his motivation—research is another fundamental appetite, "scarcely less pleasurable and peremptory than the reproductive urge."[7] Not for nothing is the science called Physics.

Its other source is the practical good sense Galileo has observed guiding craftsmen and artificers to new answers in the Venice Arsenal and shipyards,[8] humble practitioners of what the learnèd called "techne," a thing of no status beside their higher rational knowledge, "episteme," yet the real key to understanding how the world works. But orthodoxy stuck obstinately to its a priori rationality, scorning the basics as base. So the scholars of the Florence court refuse even to look through Galileo's telescope at the newly discovered moons of Jupiter, whose orbits disproved the existence of the crystal spheres to which the stars were allegedly fixed. The evidence of their eyes was as nothing against the authority of Aristotle and Scripture—what must not be, could not possibly be. For them the clearly visible moons must somehow be inside the telescope. . .

This much is a kind of desperate comedy before matters turn grim. When they do, the story is anything but heroic. Galileo's recantation under the threat of torture is a blow for his circle. In a fine scene of suspense, they wait to hear whether he has recanted, briefly rejoicing that there has been no public signal of his submission, until the fateful bell tells them otherwise. Andrea, by now a grown-up member of the scientist's circle, greets the returned Galileo with the cutting comment "Unhappy the land that has no heroes"; to which Galileo replies with the more profoundly critical "Unhappy the land that needs heroes."

Andrea's logic is realistic but demanding. Galileo's logic, if traced back from cause to preceding cause, implies a kind of Utopia: there would be no need for heroes if there were no Inquisition; no Inquisition would mean no dogma; no dogma would mean there was no single dominant church; without such a church there would be an open society of varied and tolerated beliefs. It is the logic of ordinary people who want a life that can be led in safety and freedom from oppression, without the need for heroics. Brecht's Mother Courage is even more dismissive of the need for special effort: "Anywhere there's great virtues, something's rotten[. . .] Because if a general or a king's plumb stupid, and he leads his men up shit alley, they have to be desperate brave, that's a virtue, too. If he's mean and doesn't recruit enough soldiers, every one of them has to be a Hercules. And if he's a slacker and doesn't care about anything, they have to be as cunning as serpents or they're done for. It takes special loyalty, if he expects them to do too much. All virtues a proper country and a good general don't need. In a good country you don't need virtues, everybody can be just ordinary, middling bright, and for all I care, cowards."[9] It is a tradition that goes back to Falstaff on the empty value of honor, and to Shaw's Blüntschli with chocolate in his pistol-holster.

How much of a surprise Galileo's recantation was is hard to say—it took a brave man to resist the Inquisition's techniques. But would the virtue of heroism, to the point of death, have even been a victory? Giordano Bruno, unrepentant and burned at the stake for his beliefs, may have been an example more discouraging than inspiring to free enquiry. But Brecht takes the consequences seriously, as damaging not just for science. His deepest concern is the social impact of Galileo's retractation. Astronomy had become for a time the gossip of the marketplace, and

Galileo's teachings were "a foretaste of the future"; a satirical balladeer sings of a world turned upside-down (or right way up) actually echoing Marx's phrase about people "orbiting themselves" where once they had to go round their betters. Every relationship is being transformed on the model of the earth-sun reversal. The bricklayer will build a house to live in himself, princes will have to black their own boots, cardinals will pay no regard to the Pope, and a wife will look around for another "fixed star" (Fixstern/ Fickstern) able to do as well as her husband. In sum, "Who wouldn't fancy being his own lord and master?" The multitude "learned about doubt. They snatched the telescopes out of our hands and had them trained on their tormentors, prince, official, public moralist."[10] But all that, so the plot runs, has been thrown into reverse by Galileo's betrayal of his scientific discoveries.

One wonders about these effects, positive and negative—the sturdy seeds of revolt arising from a scientific revolution or the tightened screws of oppression that follow on its withdrawal. Historical drama commonly plays fast and loose with the facts, and such intangible influences on people's outlook and action are ill-defined "facts," their causal workings an open question of cultural history. Brecht treats them as instant and unambiguous.

But then he had a message, or rather, more than one message at different times in the play's genesis, making the play itself in the end ambiguous. The shifts are dictated by the situations and events of the thirties and forties, from the Danish version of 1937/38, via the California version of 1947, to the Berlin version of 1955/56.

Politics of Freedom

In February 1933 the Nazis assumed power. With all democratic freedoms abolished, justice became the servant of the one-party state, prominently in the trial of the Bulgarian communist Georgy Dimitroff, who was accused of causing the Reichstag fire. Brecht had already thought of building up a theater of celebrated court cases, and Galileo's trial was now all the more relevant. Incidentally, 1933 was the four-hundredth anniversary of his recantation. Brecht was later to insist that the issue could not, in present circumstances, be science versus religion so much as freedom of thought versus authority—the Church just happened to be its embodiment in the Galileo case. Nor was Nazism the only present parallel. This was also the period (1936–38) of the Soviet show trials, which the communist Brecht had difficulty coming to terms with, as Moscow had with him.[11]

But what positive message could be brought out of Galileo's seemingly total failure? An early title for the play is his famous reassertion that "the earth does move" (eppur si muove) but he never speaks these words in any of the play's three versions.[12] These all follow the astronomer's life story—the play's final title is *Life of Galileo*—to the bitter end in his years of house arrest under the close supervision of the Church, which seemingly confirmed his defeat (Goethe called it his "sad semi-martyrdom."[13]) The crucial last-but-one scene, the intellectual climax of all three versions, has Andrea visiting the nearly blind old man. Commissioned by other scientists to ascertain the state of Galileo's health, he remains bitter to the point of hostility over Galileo's betrayal of science: ultimately Galileo had betrayed intellectual freedom, the freedom to teach what one knew, and the belief in the power of facts and reasons, which is the basis of all non-superstitious thinking.

In the 1938/39 Danish version, the best that is allowed to be said for Galileo is that some of his earlier friends believed he had recanted so as, by surviving, to continue his scientific work; but this he denies—it was simply the fear of death.[14] And the best he himself can claim is that physics and astronomy will be able to leave his case behind and go on with their research. Yet meantime, and it may be a long meantime, his hard-won authority has been handed back to the Church. His final judgment on himself is that science cannot use and "cannot tolerate in its ranks someone like me who failed to stand up for reason,"[15] phrasing that sounds more than a little like the formulas of twentieth-century communist self-criticism.

In an earlier scene unique to this first version, Galileo has at least begun to make practical amends. A workman in the house ostensibly to repair the chimney has been trying to help smuggle out Galileo's new scientific writings, so far with no success.[16] So the conversation has to get round to suggesting Andrea shall attempt it. After much pseudo-contrition and ironic acceptance of the Church's control over him, Galileo wrenches the dialogue round to a quite different confession: that he has indeed been writing another book. The directness—"I must alas confess that I have suffered relapses"—is dramatically a touch crude, as is Andrea's instant realization that this must be the *Discorsi*, the "Discussions on Two New Sciences."[17] Galileo has been docilely handing over every page to the authorities, who tolerate his habit of writing; but he has secretly copied everything and hidden it away, aptly inside a globe. With plain double meaning, he says he "lives in constant fear, in constant fear" [*sic*, repeated] that these writings may somehow get into the wrong hands and be read abroad "where people don't know the extraordinarily weighty arguments of the Inquisition as I do." And he follows up almost immediately by "wondering" whether "somebody" might risk taking them out to a waiting Europe?[18] Exit Andrea with the manuscript and Galileo's topical warning ringing in his ears: "Great parts of this world lie in darkness. There it has grown even deeper. Take care when you travel through Germany with the truth under your coat."[19] But the rescue of the manuscript creates an upbeat, quietly triumphal ending.

In the 1947 California version[20] the early view of "some friends" that Galileo's recantation was a subtle strategy for continuing his work is picked up positively and elaborated by Andrea. He takes back his bitter criticism—it is true that Galileo returned from the Inquisition with stained hands, but "better stained than empty." Contrary to what Galileo taught him when he was a boy, in the opening scene, "the shortest line between two points may be a crooked one."

And the new book is now finished, a product of the same old urge, what the Pope-scientist Barberini called "the itch." A satisfying consistency balances the two reactions of Galileo's physical being, the past fear of pain with the renewed appetite for science. For a moment he is half-persuaded by Andrea's praise for his supposed tactics. "Sounds realistic. Sounds like me. New science ... new ethics." But only half. His final judgment on himself remains damning, that science cannot tolerate a man like him in its ranks.[21] ("In case anyone is interested, this is also the judgment of the play-writer," wrote Brecht.[22]) Here too Andrea is drawn into the role of smuggler, but now more subtly. The scheme is improvised on the spot, only made possible through the chance of Andrea's visit. There has been no earlier effort to get the manuscript out: the conspiracy with a workman has been cut.

Sins?

But most significantly, the fallen physicist's self-indictment has acquired an element new to this version:

> "You may in time discover all there is to be discovered, but if you yield to coercion your progress must be a progress away from the bulk of humanity. The gulf between you and humanity might even grow so wide that the sound of your cheering at some new achievement could be echoed by a universal howl of horror."[23]

The reference is clear. Work on this text with Charles Laughton was in progress precisely at the moment the first atomic bombs were dropped in February 1945:

> Overnight the biography of the founder of modern physics read differently. The infernal effect of the Big Bomb cast a new, sharper light on Galileo's conflict with the authorities of his day. We had very few changes to make, not a single one to the structure.[24]

Historical drama is commonly as much about the present as the past. Brecht's response to events is admirably prompt, and Galileo's ominous prediction is an overture to decades of debate and protest in the shadow of the nuclear threat. But the insertion does violence to Brecht's original conception more than he realizes.

True, the outward structure hasn't been affected, just a few words have been added to that final speech. But they suffice to change a properly Galileo play into something fundamentally different. The new atomic preoccupation has no link to Galileo's own guilt, which Brecht calls "the original sin of the modern sciences."[25] Up to now, the problem was that Galileo had missed a "unique opportunity" to stand up for science and free thought. Science itself was a positive force, simply not applied when the chance offered. If that was a sin on Galileo's part, it was a sin of *omission*. What twentieth-century scientists had done in devising the bomb and making it available to politicians and the military was a sin of *commission*, for which there was no parallel in Galileo's career. When he sells the Venetians a plagiarized telescope it is only a comic prologue to its serious use in revolutionizing astronomy; it contained no threat to the human race. Nor was the bomb, in any plausible line of scientific descent, "the ultimate fruit of Galileo's laws of motion."[26] Rather, Brecht's new message was an indictment of a quite different science, far beyond the age of Galileo and unconnected with his work. It belonged by rights in a different drama, an Einstein drama—which Brecht would later conceive but not live to write.

Yet the final 1955–56 Berlin version, which expands and confirms but doesn't essentially change the California text,[27] still ends with the triumphal moment when the *Discorsi* are rescued from permanent suppression by the Church. The emphasis is once more (or, genetically speaking, is still) on the positive potential of science. Galileo's new work is going to revitalize research across Europe, and will again implicitly serve social advance. Andrea's final words are optimistic: "We are really just at the beginning." Clearly what is meant cannot be the beginning of the grim development predicted in Galileo's self-accusation, which is spelled out in Brecht's assertion outside the text that "the great discoveries and inventions have become only an ever more terrible threat to humanity."[28] Keeping the hopeful ending unchanged completed the final version's inner inconsistency. It hadn't been possible to make a consistent drama out of both claims: that Galileo betrayed science and society by recanting and that he betrayed mankind by initiating fundamental work in physics. What Brecht's genetically divided structure does however do is unwittingly to express the two-edged nature of modern science.

Responsibility

For Brecht to indict the whole of science was to tip the baby out with the bathwater; but such was the immediate atomic trauma. Yet even within nuclear science, it was not quite that simple. Science was not without a conscience of its own. After Hiroshima, physicists fled government service. It had become a disgrace to discover anything. Their intensive commitment to building the bomb was followed by efforts to dissuade the United States government from using it; a Committee on Social and Political Implications was supported by dozens of signatures. It could already be foreseen that postwar politics would generate an arms race. The development of the hydrogen bomb (ten thousand times as powerful as an ordinary atomic bomb) was resisted most dramatically by America's leading nuclear scientist, head of Los Alamos and "father of the atom bomb," J. Robert Oppenheimer. This resistance, and his efforts to bring about international agreement on nuclear limitation, led to proceedings against him as a threat to national security resulting in the withdrawal of his security clearance. What the investigating committee represented as communist-inspired disloyalty to his country he defended as loyalty to the human race—not far short of practicing the Hippocratic oath as proposed by Galileo. If there had indeed been an "intellectual betrayal," it was the betrayal of the spirit of science when it handed over its results to the military; instead of free and open investigation, it became a top-secret activity, its laboratories under military control. This was once more the stuff of drama, which was duly realized in Heinar Kipphardt's scenic adaptation of the committee transcripts.[29] Its relevance to Brecht's *Galileo* was obvious to his successors at the Berliner Ensemble, who combined the two conceptions in productions of the 1960s.[30]

The prospect of an arms race wasn't yet part of Galileo/Brecht's wholesale rejection of science. It could only have strengthened his position. But he had set up a large theme that was pushed further in dramatic variations. In Friedrich Dürrenmatt's black comedy *Physicists*, Möbius, the "greatest scientist of all time," has taken refuge for himself and his dangerous theories in an asylum, play-acting the delusion that he is King Solomon. The scientific agents of rival powers pursue him, also in the disguise of patients suffering delusions, a "Newton" and an "Einstein." Each is compelled to kill a nurse who was about to blow their cover. Neither of the unnamed powers they serve wins out. The asylum's mad Directress had long since copied Möbius's manuscripts before he destroyed them (the reversal of a *Galileo* motif) and has used them to build an empire. The three scientists are left to stew in what is now their asylum prison.

An arms race between rival powers had been a reality well before the Cold War. What if German scientists in the nineteen-forties had made the bomb first? Why didn't they? Were they just not smart enough? Or did they miscalculate the nature and quantity of material needed for fission and chain reaction? Or was it, ironically, because anti-Semitism had gifted émigré Jewish science to the Allies, so that the chickens came home to roost on the other side? Or had some decisive player put the brakes on the German program? Who was in a position to make it succeed or to ensure that it didn't? The answer to both questions could only be Germany's outstanding physicist, Werner Heisenberg.

In Michael Frayn's *Copenhagen* the ghosts of three crucial figures go over these questions again and again, reliving Heisenberg's visit to Nils Bohr and his wife in Copenhagen in 1941. Why did Heisenberg come? Was it to make clear how likely German research was to succeed or how far it was from succeeding? Or did he want to find out what Bohr knew about the progress of the Allies' program (which Bohr would soon escape to join)? Or was it to moot an agreement by both sides to prevent the bomb being developed? Or was it to warn the half-Jewish Bohr of Nazi plans to send all Denmark's Jews to their death? (An internal tip-off and remarkable collusion by the German embassy meant they nearly all escaped in the nick of time.) Or was it to get from Bohr, Heisenberg's one-time supervisor and a father figure for a whole generation of physicists, a blessing for his work on the bomb, in recognition that a German scientist had to do his best for his country, however deeply it was in the wrong, when the alternative was the possible atomic destruction by the enemy of everything dear to him?

The answers remain tantalizingly unclear, and no decisive clarity is added by the extensive debate among historians, nor even by the transcripts from the Farm Hall center where a number of captured German atomic scientists were held after the war for six months in comfortable detention and their conversations recorded. Frayn notes "discrepancies in every aspect of the evidence relating to this [Copenhagen] meeting."[31] His play is effectively a sequel to *Galileo* but shifts the question of scientists' responsibility that Brecht posed in general terms on to the personal plane, of a single scientist's motivation and actions.

Which is where Brecht in the last year of his life goes back to it, with the greatest figure in twentieth-century science at the center. His title *Life of Einstein* echoes his *Life of Galileo*, but the project never got beyond first sketches—just two pages survive. Some lines of argument however are clear. When the Nazis burn Einstein's writings, he is confident his work will survive—he himself may be at risk, but "the great formula [$E = mc^2$] cannot be taken back." That same certainty turns sour when his theories have had their fearful effect: "In the end he knows that his triumph has been transformed into his defeat, as he cannot take back the great formula after its deadliness has been shown."

If abstract science has been transformed, so too have the victors in the Second World War: "E. hands the deadly weapon to the enemy of fascism [. . .] And the enemy of fascism becomes a fascist."[32] Brecht wasn't alone in this view of America in the McCarthy era. It was emphatically shared by the leading anti-fascist émigré, Thomas Mann, an observer otherwise as far removed from Brecht's positions as it was possible to be. Disillusion with the political direction his adopted country was taking drove Mann to return to Europe.

Like Dürrenmatt after him, Brecht places the scientist between two competing powers. "X gives one side his formula because it is protecting him. From the first X [. . .] fails to see the similarity in their faces." That is the standard Marxist equation of fascism and Western capitalism—a plague on both their houses. There is, however, one positive alternative: "Unclear and undefinable for him there exists a third power, outside and within the two (communism)." Implicitly, communism alone is politically blameless, though by the time Brecht's drafts were written it was already one of the two major parties in the new Cold War confrontation.

According to the critic Ernst Schumacher's reminiscences, Brecht still meant to stage a formal trial of "the consequences of 'pure science' and its isolation from the progressive forces in society."[33] There is indeed a brief note, "Progress in knowledge about nature. Alongside standstill in knowledge about society. Turns deadly." But knowledge about society no longer means the broad enlightening effect Galileo hoped for. "Progressive forces" in Brecht's postwar vocabulary is a partisan political conception.

Power against Power

With *Galileo* Brecht had put his finger on a new kind of tragic situation, and this whole clutch of dramas has a new angle on the old dramatic theme of power. No longer personal power (Creon over Antigone, Elizabeth over Mary Queen of Scots) or power struggles (Shakespeare's English kings and his Roman patricians) or revolutions against despotic rule (Don Carlos and Posa against King Philip). For the first time, a pure intellectual power that might, in an old philosophers' dream, have transformed the real world is appropriated by its *realpolitisch* opposite. At issue is a power that inheres in natural forces, whether it will be used, and whether it can be controlled. On the evil side, it is not power oppressing a people or a rival party, but the power to destroy a swathe, or the whole, of humanity. It is the genesis of a new genre of drama for an irreversibly atomic age.

12: Knowing and Partly Knowing: Paul Celan's Mission

As It Happened

ONE OF THE CLEAREST of genetic accounts concerns a now celebrated poem from Paul Celan's last and posthumous collection, *Schneepart*:

DU LIEGST im großen Gelausche,
umbuscht, umflockt.
Geh du zur Spree, geh zur Havel,
geh zu den Fleischerhaken
zu den roten Äppelstaken
aus Schweden—
Es kommt der Tisch mit den Gaben,
er biegt um ein Eden—
Der Mann ward zum Sieb, die Frau
mußte schwimmen, die Sau,
für sich, für keinen, für jeden—
Der Landwehrkanal wird nicht rauschen
Nichts
    stockt.

[YOU LIE in the great listening,
Embuscht, enflaked.
Just you go to the Spree, go to the Havel,
go to the meat-hooks,
to the red Äppelstaken
From Sweden—
Now the table is coming with the gifts,
it bends round an Eden—
The man became a sieve, the woman
had to swim, the sow,
for herself, for no one, for all—
The Landwehr Canal will not murmur.
Nothing
    stops.]

The poem is a work of extreme concision and allusiveness, a spare sonnet (rhymed abcd dece ffea [-] b) ending with a bleak historical reflection. It isn't one of the most obscure poems of a difficult poet—at least it has some obvious real-life references, to Berlin with the rivers Spree and Havel and the Landwehr canal, to winter and Christmas, to something Swedish, to some kind of Eden, to the implied deaths of two people. But what joins these things to make an overall sense isn't immediately clear. Light is however thrown by a report of the experiences that lie behind the poem, as provided in some detail by the critic Peter Szondi, who was one of Celan's companions on his only ever extensive visit to Berlin.

Celan was there in December 1967 to give readings, in the Akademie der Künste and the Comparative Literature Department of the Free University. He was put up in the Academy's accommodation in the Hansa Quarter, in a room whose large windows looked out on the bushes of the Tiergarten. During the day, he met friends, was shown round, and took in the Advent atmosphere. The market had traditional Swedish wreaths decorated with candles and apples on sticks. One of Celan's friends accompanied him to the Plötzensee execution chamber, where the resistance conspirators of July 20, 1944 were hanged from meat hooks, their death writhings filmed for Hitler's delectation. Then on an evening when Celan had nothing to read, Szondi lent him a recently published book about the deaths in January 1919 of the communist politicians and leaders of the Spartacist rising, Rosa Luxemburg and Karl Liebknecht. They were murdered by members of the Garde-Kavallerie-Schützen-Division in its HQ, the Hotel Eden. Szondi pointed out the building to Celan when they went past. It had by then been turned into an apartment block, still bearing the name "Eden." The Landwehr Canal, into which Rosa Luxemburg's body was thrown, was not far away.[1] The murder was not a random act but part of a lawless violence that increasingly destabilized the Weimar Republic and dominated the Nazi regime which followed.

The random materials of Celan's stay in Berlin interlock perfectly—which is not to say that the act of imagination needed to bring them together was simple. It can to some extent be followed in Celan's work notes and drafts in the Bonn or Tübingen critical editions. The change from "I lay" to the opening "you lie" intensifies the immediate personal pressure, leading into the injunction to himself "just you go to the Spree," which replaces "who will greet the Spree," itself echoing words of Hölderlin's about another river.[2] "Round the Eden hotel" is changed to expose plain "Eden" as a rhyme for what precedes and what follows. "What stops?" and "you stop" are replaced by the firm general statement "Nothing / Stops."

Knowledge and After

Knowing why these materials are there, in that form, allows a coherent reading, in contrast to the bemusement of complete ignorance, or the puzzlement of partial knowledge (it must be Berlin, but what are butcher's hooks doing in a poem, and who are the man and woman, and what horror has happened to them?). A historically informed reader just might make the connections unaided—I recall an older German colleague who had lived through these times doing just that.[3] But the information is a welcome help for the rest of us: without it, the poem can't be understood, let alone its force felt. We hardly need relevance theory to tell us that ignorance cannot be bliss.

Yet Szondi, after providing the necessary background, grows anxious lest knowledge be taken to be itself an adequate interpretation and damage the poem's autonomous status—as if knowledge remained inert and did nothing for the receptive imagination. Yet what status can a poem have when its real referents remain obscure? What is the abstract principle of "autonomy" and what is its value?

The concept has roots in the eighteenth century, when literature first had to liberate itself from religious and social control by claiming the rights of a distinct aesthetic realm in which anything can be freely said. It was not meant to become a self-sufficient abstraction, much less to limit the scope of reference to realities—rather the reverse.

Szondi further argued that to see as mere coincidences the link between Christmas and Plötzensee, or between a paradisal Eden and a locus of murder and modern forgetfulness, would be to miss seeing Celan's fundamental belief "that the good is simultaneously evil, and evil in whatever way has something good about it."[4] Not only is this assertion bizarre—Celan knew very well the absolute reality of evil: his people and his family had suffered fatally from it in the Holocaust; there was nothing good in that—it is also itself a claim to knowledge, of a generality that takes us right away from the realities the poem treats: an allegedly deeper knowledge based, if on anything, on personal acquaintance with the poet. (Szondi isn't the only critic to make use of that privilege.) And it is precisely those ironic coincidences that make the poem so eloquent. That is surely part of the power of poetry: to shape random experience into a significant pattern, whether of harmony or dissonance.

Yes, there is still plenty of interpreting to be done—to establish that the opening is indeed the speaker addressing himself, and that the line of sense is the clash between his present ease and the horrors of the past. Also to appreciate the poem's form, its skeletal sonnet structure, broken rhythms, yet cohesive use of rhyme. Celan rarely used rhyme in his later work, but here, as so often in poetry generally, coincidental echoes create meaningful connections, this time stark contrasts: the hideous meat hooks rhyme with the festive wreaths, which themselves have points impaling apples ("-haken," "-staken"), the national origin of these decorations happens to rhyme with the building's name, and the same rhyme is carried further by a simple pronoun to give the idea of a communist dying in the cause of everyone ("Schweden," "Eden," "jeden"). There is a powerful jolt in the paradisal name of the murder location, which also now marks the forgetting of history. This "Eden" becomes an ironic obstacle to the coming of the traditional Christmas table full of presents. (An early draft reads, more drastically still, a "table full of corpses.")[5] Festive celebration becomes a thin veneer laid over the past.

The rhyme of woman and sow ("Frau/Sau") is authentic quotation from the killers' anti-Semitic usage. The whole sonnet is embraced by the near-rhymes "-lausche / rauschen" which mark two silences. At the poem's opening it is the audible quiet in the grounds outside a guest bedroom, soon to be disallowed, as if to say "all very well for you," by the harsh reminders of history.[6] The very different silence at the close marks the failure of historical memory. The canal makes no sound, is a flow of forgetfulness, Lethe, leaving the world all around to go about its business without a glance back: "Nichts / stockt." It's as if the line-break marks a moment of waiting, for a response that doesn't come. The word echoes Lucile's lament at the end of Georg Büchner's *Danton's Death*, when she is waiting for her Camille to be guillotined: "The stream of life ought to stop [stocken] when even just one drop [of blood] is spilt. . . . No, I will sit here and scream, so that everything stands still in shock, everything stops and nothing moves any more."[7]

Commemorating

Tragic commemoration is a time-honored poetic practice, made more necessary than ever by modern history. Anna Akhmatova, in a small house in the Petersburg grounds of the Sheremetev clan, transmutes their family motto, "God preserves all" (bog sokhranyaet vsyo), into the principle that poetry preserves all, recording the horrors of Stalinist Russia. In the foreword to the poem cycle *Requiem* she recalls being asked by another of the women queueing outside Kresty prison to hand in parcels for loved ones, "Can you describe this?" and answering "I can." Robert Lowell's "For the Union Dead" ends, like Celan's poem, with a reproach to historical forgetfulness. The Boston monument to soldiers of a negro regiment who died in the American Civil War "sticks like a fishbone / in the city's throat. [. . .] Everywhere, / giant finned cars nose forward like fish; / a savage servility / slides by on grease." Not least by its black subjects, Lowell's poem is a striking counterpart to Allen Tate's "Ode to the Confederate Dead." In the late twentieth century again, Yevgeny

Yevtushenko's *Baby Yar*, which Celan translated, commemorates the slaughter of thousands of Jews by the SS.

We must be all the more grateful when light is shed on a difficult poem such as "Du liegst," allowing it to communicate its call to remember. We are hard put to it to grasp the sense of much of Celan's poetry, with which the Common Reader reaches the limits of literary understanding, an extreme case even within a modern cultural scene where difficulty to the point of obscurity has practically become a convention, as if it were the only guarantee of poetic integrity. Celan provides a major occupation for professional scholars, and even they are often taxed as nowhere else to find a point of access for interpretation to begin. Their tone has from the first been correspondingly modest, tentative, explicit about the depth of difficulty. They confess to "attempting a decipherment, as of written characters that have become almost illegible."[8] They recognize that "the traditional means of reading do not work," that even to begin applying them "to texts that one calls obscure falsifies the reading."[9] Even Celan's admiring biographer-translator calls the late poems "so cryptic as to seem like signals from another planet."[10] It follows that the most straightforward but highly labor-intensive approach is to delve—it is indeed a kind of archaeology—in search of hard evidence of meaning, of the kind Szondi was able to provide for this one poem.[11]

Private Languages

Knowledge is thus both crucial and controversial, and the withholding of knowledge a largely modern problem. In poems of an earlier lyrical tradition, the knowledge necessary to understanding a poem was presented in the poem as part of the creative act, a communicative courtesy on the part of a writer reaching out to readers. A text might be difficult, but there was in principle no obscuring of sense. Since the twentieth century, the writer-reader relationship has been increasingly reversed, for complex reasons, including an instinctive post-Romantic reluctance to wear one's heart on one's sleeve, so that it is now the reader's responsibility to go to meet the poet, searching for sense across each new unmarked terrain.

Yet the roots of the matter once again run back into the eighteenth century, the point where poetry began to focus ever more on individual experience. The more unique this experience was, the greater the potential barrier to understanding. Writers' letters and diaries and any biographical documents became needed sources of enlightenment. Goethe's joke "See the poet's private archive under L." as background to an early love poem[12] was recognizing a serious issue, for each poet's usage and range of reference was truly a distinctive archive. A writer who could be captured by a standard lexicon would not be much good.[13] These are the seeds of the critical editions of modern writers.

If the barrier to understanding poems has become more impenetrable in our time, does that mean poetry has totally changed its nature? Around the nineteen-fifties it was fashionable to put a brave face on it and celebrate an allegedly new kind of lyrical utterance, beside which the idea of a poetry rooted in experience and having something graspable to say about it was naïve. The new mode was termed "absolute" lyric, "whose sounds seem to proceed from no human mouth and no longer need to penetrate to any human ear."[14] Its representatives (typically, Mallarmé, Valéry, Eliot) embodied "a hard love that wishes to remain unused and speaks into confusion or vacuity rather than to us."[15] The pursuit of meaning was allegedly otiose, since poetry only signified itself.[16] The selection obviously begged the question by wholly leaving out the alternative line of modern poets like Brecht, Neruda, or Mayakovsky. Gottfried Benn spoke of art's "attempt, in the general decline of meaningful content, to experience itself as content and to make a new style out of this experience."[17] But that made poetry purely self-referential. What then was poetry's value? Why would anyone want to read it?

Critics have continued to play the game without questioning the new rules, insisting that poetry necessarily has a special exactitude even while they note its obscurity,[18] and ultimately accepting, in Bernard Böschenstein's term, its "necessary insolubility."[19] To be sure, it is possible to mount a sophisticated argument in defense of difficult poetry, and to forestall criticism with a high-handed epigraph from Mozart's *Così fan tutte*, "Cara semplicità, quanto mi piaci",[20] but the broad cultural loss, for a not necessarily simple-minded poetry readership, remains.

It is tempting at first sight to place Celan in the trend Hugo Friedrich described. Yet Celan felt himself to be, in a wholly traditional way, "an individuality speaking from the particular angle of his existence.[21] And it is clear from an informed reading of "Du liegst" that a poem can have roots in reality just as much as poems ever did, merely not reveal them to a first approach—a veiled "Erlebnislyrik." Celan was unhappy to see his poetry called hermetic; sometimes he simply denied it, famously telling his biographer Israel Chalfen to "just keep on reading. The understanding will come by itself."[22] When reviewers in 1968 called his poems "verschlüsselt" (encoded), he replied that every word had a real referent (*Wirklichkeitsbezug*), which they were failing to see.[23] The two things are of course not a contradiction, since it is precisely the nature of a code that it does have real referents which are designed to be decoded. Then in his Büchner prize speech, Celan was openly provocative, quoting from Pascal: "Do not reproach us with a lack of clarity, since that is what we profess."[24] Yet he also there maintained that his poems were "holding a course towards something [. . .] perhaps an approachable other person"[25] Or perhaps, in a more random drift, a poem was a message in a bottle,[26] lonely but in motion, seeking a conversation, even if a despairing one.

More pessimistically, "the poem today unmistakably shows a strong tendency to fall silent" (verstummen). It is left unclear whether that is by deliberate choice or under some unstated external pressure.

Celan's poetics thus oscillates between recognizing and denying the difficulty of his own poems. Late in life he planned a lecture on poetic obscurity, but the surviving sketches do little to resolve the contradiction.[27]

Mission

The question is the more pressing given the task Celan set himself, which was nothing less than to commemorate the fate of the Jews murdered in the Holocaust, his parents included. He felt himself to be an exposed representative, "perhaps one of the last who must live out to the end the destiny of the Jewish spirit in Europe."[28] In one of his clearest utterances he exhorts himself to have his say. "Speak you too, / speak as the final one, / speak your word," a word that must cast a necessary shadow. ("Sprich auch du"). And there is certainly nothing obscure about his first and most famous commemorative act, "Todesfuge" (Death Fugue).[29]

"Todesfuge" is a poem of incantatory power, a part metaphorical, part literal evocation of the death camps, spoken in claustrophobically repetitive phrasing by an imagined chorus of prisoners: "Schwarze Milch der Frühe wir trinken sie abends / wir trinken sie mittags und morgens wir trinken sie nachts / wir trinken und trinken" (Black milk from early, we drink it evenings / we drink it midday and mornings we drink it at nights / we drink it and drink it). Milk is a symbol for their day-in, day-out suffering. The reality is a commandant who sets his dogs on them, forces them to dig graves, though some corpses will finally be incinerated and rise as smoke—"wir schaufeln ein Grab in den Lüften, da liegt man nicht eng" (we're shoveling graves in the air, there's plenty of room there), makes them play violins for a dance of death, may at any moment shoot them out of hand—his eye is blue, his aim is true[30] and at dusk he writes to his Margarete in Germany. Her blonde hair is set alongside the "ashen" hair ("ashen" whether by natural color or through incineration) of an imagined Jewish victim Sulamith, her name that of the beloved in the Song of Songs.

Among the motifs that the poem weaves together in compelling dactylic rhythms, one stands out as precisely capturing the horror and arrogance of Nazism: "Der Tod ist ein Meister aus Deutschland"—"Death is a master from Germany." If "Todesfuge" is the best-known poem in twentieth-century German writing, then this is the obsessively recalled phrase, its creator "the poet whose word we carry in us."[31] "It hit Germans at their most sensitive point, Meisterschaft, mastery: work ethic, quality product, proficiency."[32] The poem has been recited in the

Bundestag at Holocaust commemoration, and representations of Margarete and Sulamith figure in the giant canvases with which Anselm Kiefer takes issue with the German past. The poem has achieved Celan's aim by itself and remains surely the center, if not the sole sufficient cause, of the public recognition he enjoys.

But there were negative responses, too, to that dramatic beginning, which surely helped determine the mode and problems of Celan's later writing. Apart from the accusations of plagiarism (among the many sources "Todesfuge" had drawn on, from the Old Testament on, there were modern poems that Celan must have known)[33] the poem was also widely accused of beautifying its grim subject, turning atrocity into aesthetic pleasure. It led to Theodor Adorno's foolish pronouncement that to write poems at all after Auschwitz was barbaric,[34] a clear category mistake, since it would only be barbaric to indulge in aesthetic pleasure while forgetting the historical realities—and forgetting was what Celan's poem, to put it mildly, made impossible. Artistic creation remains a natural and necessary response to any occurrence, including the most hideous. To have shaped a response effectively did not mean betraying the victims. These critics failed to say what a proper poetic response to the Holocaust would look like. It is admittedly a much-debated problem, but they were measuring Celan's poem against an unstated criterion.

The poet was himself deeply dissatisfied, first on finding that, in a truly perverse reading, people were taking his poem as a gesture of reconciliation between Jews and Germans. That made it an unintended aid to the postwar process of "coming to terms with the past" in a Germany that seemed to Celan far from de-nazified. Anti-Semitism was still very much alive (some of the criticisms of the poem struck him as having that dark motivation), old right-wing attitudes were being unashamedly reestablished, and a nationalism was resurgent as if Nazi crimes had never been. In Celan's telling Shakespearean pun, there was "something rotten in the state of D-Mark."[35] Less depressing but still unwelcome was the poem's very popularity as an anthology-piece—familiarity might well breed indifference, and he risked being a one-poem poet. He finally began refusing permission to reprint it.

Implicit, Explicit

And it looks as if Celan after all took to heart in some measure the criticism of beautifying atrocity. In 1958 he noted, with obvious self-reference, that contemporary poetry was becoming more sober, "grayer," its musicality eschewing the harmonious sound (*Wohlklang*) that "still went on blithely sounding out, with and alongside the most terrible things."[36] This was implicitly a program of his own where the gray sobriety went along with a more cryptic mode, which also had the effect of obscuring the message. At the opposite extreme from the explicitness of "Death Fugue," the commemorative intention had to be taken as read, on the universal assumption that the death of Celan's mother, and the Holocaust generally, were "the unimaginable loss that grounds *all* his writing"[37] But this is then another appeal to a general prior knowledge which, like that assumption of Szondi's about Celan's real beliefs, stands outside the poems and has to be read into rather than read out of them.[38] It guarantees a not-to-be-questioned benevolence towards the poems, almost a post-Holocaust Jewish bonus. As such it is a too-facile solution to the difficulties any single poem presents. Interpretations may work in good faith from that allegedly all-grounding knowledge, but the result may be hard to map on to the actual words of the text.

To be sure, overt allusions to the Holocaust are scattered through the corpus.[39] Any occurrence of ash or air or digging ("Es war Erde in ihnen") is bound to recall "Death Fugue." The phrase "clutching at each other" (ineinander verkrallt) in the poem "Tenebrae" unavoidably reads as the convulsive last movements of Jews in the gas chambers. "Wolfsbohne" speaks directly of his parents' deaths. These are flashes of light, or darkness, within texts that otherwise veer away from even this much explicitness. Elsewhere allusion may be specific but obscured by indirection: "They feed you with a plant-protective" ("Sie füttern") is a reference to the fact that Zyklon B was originally a horticultural chemical before it was used as a killer gas, a link that the rest of the brief text does nothing to make clear.[40] The phrase "Jewish locks, you won't turn grey" ("Mandorla") seems explicit enough, echoing an early poem "My mother's hair never grew white" ("Espenbaum"); but the refrain broadens the reference, from Jewish to human locks—as indeed the poem from which this chapter started out is more generously concerned with a wider historical forgetfulness and necessary commemoration. Not Rosa Luxemburg's Jewishness but her and Karl Liebknecht's socialism in the service of humanity is that poem's narrative and emotive center.

More powerfully explicit are what may be called anti-prayers of a disillusioned theology familiar in post-Holocaust Jewish thinking, reproaches addressed as if by Jewish victims to God for abandoning His people. In the poem "Tenebrae," "Nah sind wir, Herr, / nahe und greifbar" (Near are we, Lord, / near and graspable) echoes and undoes the still half-hopeful relation to a deity in Hölderlin's poem "Patmos": "Nah ist / Und schwer zu fassen der Gott" (Near is / and hard to grasp the god." In the age of the Holocaust, human beings might themselves have been grasped and rescued by God, but never were. Only an empty transcendence remains. "Niemand knetet uns wieder aus Erde und Lehm / niemand bespricht unsern Staub. / Niemand. // Gelobt seist du, Niemand" ("Psalm; No one kneads us again from earth and clay, / no one speaks over our dust. / No one. // Praised be thou, no one). "Hosianna" becomes "Ho, ho- /

sianna" ("Engführung"). (Where for Christian worship "hosanna" is a word of affirmation and praise, in Hebrew it is in any case an anguished appeal for help.) These examples of Celan's independent-mindedness, his practice of "Widerruf"[41] (revoking, negation) already lead over into the queston of his Judaic culture, which is amply present, though more immediately accessible to readers with a Jewish background.[42] But both categories taken together still make up only a small part of Celan's oeuvre.

In the face of such a corpus, a great deal of speculation has gone into the work of critics committed to Celan, some of whom even deny, as he did himself, that his work is hermetic. Some of the claims to be deeply moved by Celan's poems ring pretentious and inauthentic in the absence of any demonstration that their meaning has been understood. Those of lesser faith and more sober expectations can be glad of any reading of a difficult poem that draws persuasively on relevant knowledge of whatever kind to aid insight, aware that understanding Celan must be a long haul over eight increasingly demanding collections. Where words stand, as so often in his poems, in proximity on the page but in no evident coherent reference to each other, we are left observing not much more than what Gottfried Benn declared to be "the primal quality of a poet, the capacity to place words in a fascinating way."[43] But words alone do not a poem make. How they came to stand in such untransparent connection is ultimately the mystery of a poetic process that the evidence of the poem's genesis seems to have the best chance of illuminating.

For the Common Reader

Standing back from the intense activity of critics, the common reader is left with the paradox of an asserted vital message that has been made unduly difficult of access by the messenger. There is no point in saying the poet should have done better, should have done differently; one can only regret the failed communication. It decidedly doesn't help to be told by Adorno that "Celan wants to speak of the most extreme horror through silence."[44] That is a human, but not a poet's reaction to horror.

True, there was the problem of the language Celan had to use—the mother tongue that was also the mother murderers' tongue. The German language, Celan wrote,

> was, despite everything, not lost. But it now had to go through its repeated lack of answers [*Antwortlosigkeiten*], through a terrible falling silent [*Verstummen*], through the thousand darknesses of death-bearing speech. It passed through and provided no words for what happened; but it went through this happening, passed through and was able to emerge again, "enriched" by all that.[45]

The ironic quotation marks signal the burden weighing on a guilty language that had to be rescued for innocent purposes.

If that involved an actual "struggle with language,"[46] which would help account for the poems' obscurity, any implication that Celan lacked the linguistic and stylistic skill and the formal craftsmanship needed to put complex thought and feeling into whatever poetry he had wanted to create is ruled out by the quality and perceptiveness of his translations from French, Russian, and English—including sonnets of Shakespeare. The conclusion might be that, whatever his intention, much of Celan's poetry served self-expression rather than communication; that in essence he was using a private language of meditation within the matrix of a public language that had been besmirched by history.

13: Christa Wolf: A Fall from Grace

GENESIS IS ONLY COMPLETE when a work is published. Up to that point, it doesn't exist beyond the author's desk; at that point it becomes a literary reality. The date of publication is usually not important, or matters at most to a particular slice of the public, fans impatient for an expected new work. The date isn't likely to be critical, certainly not a main focus of criticism, and even less likely to transform the author's whole reputation and public standing. But that is what happened to Christa Wolf over a late, slight novella. The affair broadened into an attack on East German writers generally, a major contribution to the bitterness of that unsettled time after the fall of communism, the "Wende," then further into an attempted reckoning with all postwar German literature, West German writers included, on the grounds that they had given politics priority over art. Her small book was thus a significant catalyst to a broader, fierce East/West debate, and constitutes a substantial case with which to end this volume.

With the collapse of communism across Europe and the fall of the Berlin Wall in 1989, Christa Wolf at last decided to publish *Was bleibt*, an account written in 1979 of a writer's experience of surveillance by the East German secret police, or Stasi.[1] Its record of the pressures used to intimidate citizens could not have been published in the East while "real existing socialism" still existed. On the other hand, to have published it across the border in the West would have been an absolute break with the East German state and would almost certainly have meant Wolf having to emigrate to West Germany, as many writers had chosen or been forced to do. So the story stayed in her desk. Writing for the desk drawer in oppressive circumstances has been in modern times practically a literary genre in itself.

All Wolf's previous work had come out in both Germanies. She was reluctant to publish anything that could not appear on both sides of the divide. Her writings were an important cultural bridge, especially her most substantial novel *Kindheitsmuster* (Patterns of Childhood, 1976), which recalls experiences widely shared on both sides of the border—of having grown up in the normality of Nazi indoctrination and practice, which includes seeing a synagogue burn down and having a relative murdered in the euthanasia program for "worthless life"; the trek west in 1944 as the Russians advanced; a father returning from Russian captivity; a family visit to the old hometown, now Polish, and throughout the book an attempt to reconstruct the child she was and to understand how she came to be the person she is.

Nothing Christa Wolf wrote was on the surface politically subversive. She remained throughout her career a member of the SED (the East German Communist Party) and her unaggressive dissent stayed within the bounds of an idealistic commitment to socialism. Admittedly she had to strive to fend off the growing disillusion with a reality that failed to match the state's official ideals. Still, she went on hoping to ease change in a liberal direction, much as eighteenth-century writers had aspired to bring enlightenment to their princes. In successive phases, as the SED's cultural policy blew hot, blew cold—Erich Honecker, First Secretary of the party from 1971 to the end, once even declared that no topic was taboo, though with the proviso that writers still had to stay loyal to the socialist order—such moderate dissidents were tolerated. Christa Wolf especially, since her growing international reputation made her a prestige possession for a GDR culture none too richly endowed and slowly melting as ever more writers left. True, a certain tension remained, even some resentment of her success. "If she weren't so well known, she would have been put through the mill," was the rueful comment of Otto Gotsche, then secretary to Honecker's predecessor, Walter Ulbricht.

For she was after all purveying an alternative to the state's orthodoxies, which enforced a false optimism in denial of an often-bleak national life. Her works, written on a principle of "subjective authenticity" and rooted in the truthfulness of humane feeling and community, were a source of comfort to her home readership, as shown by the popularity of everything she published. Western critics largely saw her work as an enclave of civilized values under a dictatorship.

Westerners were indeed welcoming to East German writing generally—that was a recognized "GDR bonus." In more dramatic confrontations where radical dissidents were victimized by the authorities, most strikingly the expulsion of the satirical balladeer Wolf Biermann, the Western media at large were quick to offer support and make Cold War cultural propaganda. Such support would certainly have been afforded to Christa Wolf if the story had come out in 1979 and made her belatedly into a radical too.

But not now. By the time *Was bleibt* was published, the political world had changed. It must have seemed to Wolf, in all innocence, the moment to present the long-withheld text and share one more experience with her readers. It was received in the West very differently. Where once she had been a bright spot in a dark picture of social oppression and cultural censorship, she was now seen as a beneficiary of the communist system, the most prominent "state writer," who had enjoyed a life of privilege and ease and had shown too little civil courage on occasions when real resistance was called for. Even when she had made a bold stand, co-signing the letter of protest at Biermann's expulsion in 1972, it was asserted, and went on being maintained in the teeth of documented facts, that she had later withdrawn her signature. Now she was plainly trying to make herself out to be a victim and curry favor with the victorious West. And surely she had rewritten the text for that purpose? Demonstrably not, it appears: the only adjustments Wolf made to the text in 1989 were of small stylistic corrections that didn't affect its content.[2] But even without any calculating revision, the timing was decisive. On the pivoting-point of this untimely publication, her whole work and career were re-evaluated.[3]

What exactly does the text say? It narrates in barely veiled autobiographical terms a writer's domestic routine, dominated by the awareness that there are observers in a car regularly parked across the way, the lowest-level "security" operation, deliberately un-secret to create insecurity in the victim. There is some satire of the way three "young men fit for work" are wasting time gathering information about her every movement. Her mail is opened, and she imagines the wagonloads of letters delivered every day and sorted by significance up through a large building to ever-higher levels of security checking—a grotesque picture, but not far from the truth. The GDR did indeed pile up a mountain of trivia about its citizens, lights on and lights off, working hours and bedtime. It is best illustrated by Reiner Kunze's eloquently uncommented selection from his Stasi file, *Deckname "Lyrik."* Christa Wolf speculates about who, higher in the hierarchy, holds *her* file, relishing the power to know everything about her, perhaps a failed philosopher she once knew who has sold out to the Stasi, like one of her friends who is reported to be reporting on her. Such betrayal was common knowledge in the GDR; only the depth of its penetration into intimate circles, even families, was a shock revelation after the *Wende*.

There is self-observation and self-criticism as she compares herself with a more resolute young woman visitor, who writes well and truthfully and has suffered imprisonment as a dissident. For the young are prepared to "run on to the knives," as the narrator herself has not been. In the final episode she gives a public reading, where questions from the audience get near the quick of political protest, they again braver than she is, and needing protection by her harmless answers. People innocuously gathered outside, unable to get into the reading, are roughed up by a police intervention that was clearly a prearranged job. The whole text is a lament, not just about her own problems, but about a society where such things are the daily norm. The essential fire of her Berlin has gone out. What remained, what would remain at the personal and social level, was a more gloomy question than any Christa Wolf's writings had previously posed.

It is of course standard after the fall of dictatorships that people claim to have been victims or resisters. But it was difficult, in my reading of *Was bleibt* in 1990, and remains so in retrospect, to see the novella as a self-serving claim to victimhood. It is more a confession of the narrator's/Wolf's own inadequate resolve, and a sketch of life under GDR socialism as lived experience. Hardly surprising, then, that of the two big reviews in the liberal weekly *Die Zeit*, Volker Hage's was an appreciation of the story's artistic quality, in much the same positive vein her work normally met with.[4] But Ulrich Greiner's review in the same issue struck the new hostile note: here was the East German "State Writer" (*Staatsdichterin*) tactlessly making a song and dance about what in the GDR was an everyday happening, her writing characteristically slack (so: not just in this latest work), her stock-in-trade sentimental, the "Christa-Wolf-Sound" again allegedly out of touch with reality.[5]

This was facile dismissal, with pejorative phrasing in place of argument, and visibly fueled by aggression. Greiner admitted it wasn't literary criticism by the rules: he was forgetting the first-year lesson that fiction isn't factual report and has to be treated differently—among other things (though this he omits to say) with at least a provisional sympathy for what is offered as open confession. Later he was also to admit that he'd never been able to get on with Wolf's work, so had no business reviewing her.[6] Greiner was not alone in avowedly sweeping principles aside so as to let feeling hold sway. Reinhard Baumgart summarized the way German critics had rejected objectivity. "Carefully considered and substantial analyses" written "in distant non-German cities" appeared "weak and indecisive, compared with the strictly unobjective and shrill German controversy. [. . .] They lacked the passion for issues of principle, the relation of society and literature, morality and aesthetics."[7] It was alarming that "issues of principle" should be treated with "unobjective and shrill" assertions. But Greiner observed an unashamed need to "push through a reading. That is no academic matter. If you determine the past, you determine the future."[8] "Push through," "determine" (durchsetzen, bestimmen): this had been not literary criticism but decisionist *Realpolitik*.

Meantime Christa Wolf and fellow writers had appealed to GDR citizens at a large public meeting in Berlin to stay and make a new political start in a homeland that would continue independent, where there were indeed new shoots of democratic activity. That added to her unpopularity in the West. Surely it was ungrateful not to accept the historic opportunity to reunify Germany in its Western form? Weren't freedom and affluence preferable to the hard grind of a new start? Choosing the harder option of life in the East had been Christa Wolf's theme back to her first literary success, the novel *Der geteilte Himmel* (Divided Heaven, 1963). There was little awareness in the West that its society was not necessarily seen as an ideal in the East, where the Federal Republic seemed as much a dependency of the United States as the German Democratic Republic was of the Soviet Union. The clichés of the SED's anti-capitalist propaganda (the employment of unreconstructed Nazis in the judicial and higher-education spheres of Adenauer's Bonn "Restoration"—"Better dirty water than no water at all," Adenauer is reported to have said—and the premature release of war criminals) were of a piece with continuing geopolitics. Thus the record of the journey to Poland in *Kindheitsmuster* registers at intervals the latest bombings of North Vietnam. For pessimists there was a virtual balance of undesirables. As the traveler delayed by a flat tire says in Brecht's poem, "Ich bin nicht gern, wo ich herkomme, / Ich bin nicht gern, wo ich hinfahre. / Warum sehe ich den Radwechsel / Mit Ungeduld?" (I don't like it where I come from, / I don't like it where I'm going. / Why am I impatient / For the wheel to be changed?)[9]

Christa Wolf's appeal to her fellow citizens was the starting point for Frank Schirrmacher's editorial article in the *Frankfurter Allgemeine Zeitung*, the most serious and substantial analysis, in psychological and historical depth, of her commitment to the East German state (though it too begins with offhand dismissals: she is an overrated writer; some of her works are already forgotten). Her loyalty had all along been a reaction—as the state itself expressly was—to the experience of Nazism. The older generation of left-wing politicians who returned from concentration camps and exile to take over the GDR became father-figures, willing subjection to whom was natural in a communist "family." That only repeated the submissiveness first conditioned under the Nazis. The argument is persuasive, but it is largely pushing an open door. Schirrmacher quotes Wolf's own self-criticisms and only needs to comment "it couldn't be put more exactly."[10] That is the difficulty her critics were in: she had said it before them. But what had been literary confession, offered in all honesty, evidence for the prosecution, was exploited with judicial severity. That was made explicit by Karl Heinz Bohrer: "The arguments are now as hard as in the Civil Code."[11] But it isn't clear that this was justice.

The attack then widened, first to East German writers generally, who were accused, as Christa Wolf had been, of supporting the state by their writing, and ultimately by the mere fact of staying on in their home country instead of moving to the West like their exiled colleagues. The wider attack was visibly part of the wholesale takeover to which GDR institutions were subjected—universities, the legal system, all forms of administration.[12] Reunification was not going to mean the historical joining of two postwar literatures into a single process, but the one denying houseroom to the other.

Of course there was counterargument and defense, prominently by West German liberal intellectuals. But the response to that was to make them the targets of an even more sweeping critique. The whole of postwar German literature and intellectual life was to be seen in retrospect as dominated by "Gesinnung," a very *political* correctness that had excluded the "aesthetic" element essential to art.[13] The term was adapted by Greiner and Bohrer from Max Weber's distinction between an ethics determined by pure principle, come what may ("Gesinnungsethik") and an ethics that took responsible account of practical consequences ("Verantwortungs-ethik").[14] It was a crude fit, not clearly applicable to any individual literary work, and none were named. In denying an aesthetic element, the thesis overlooked the imaginative power that Heinrich Böll, Günter Grass, Alfred Andersch, Siegfried Lenz, Jurek Becker, and others had brought to the critical reconstruction of the Nazi past. Their work was by no means high-minded moral abstraction lacking realization in artistic form. And its motivation was precisely—to invoke Weber's other concept, "Verantwortung"—an ethics of responsibility, for historic acts and for their present remembrance. The body of writing this generated deservedly gained international recognition for its quality. (The Nobel prizes for Böll and Grass were not primarily political gestures.)

The criticism of an "unaesthetic" literature was in any case vacuous. It begged the question what "aesthetic" can even mean in isolation from the substance of real situations and their treatment. The imaginative confrontation with the twentieth-century German past has incidentally still not been completed, and perhaps it never can be. It has gone on finding impressive form in works like Bernhard Schlink's *Der Vorleser* and Ferdinand von Schirach's *Der Fall Collini*.

Only a slender thread now connected the debate back to its point of origin in Christa Wolf's novella. It was pure chance that this small cause provoked a controversy for which energies had been stored up over years, and to which new resentments were being added by the hour through the frictions of German reunification. (As the saying ran, nothing divided like unification.) How else would those energies have been let loose? The woman at the center of it all—and perhaps a woman was an easier target, especially of gutter-press attacks for which it wasn't necessary to have read her book—paid a high price. The attacks intensified when it was found that in her youth she had briefly cooperated with the Stasi, albeit only submitting positive reports on individuals so that they rejected her as unsuitable material as a collaborator, even herself suspicious. As a poem she wrote in 1999 put it, "Angenagelt / ans Kreuz Vergangenheit Jede Bewegung / treibt die Nägel / ins Fleisch"[15] (Nailed / to the cross of the Past—Every movement / drives the nails / into the flesh). The poem's title, "Prinzip Hoffnung" (The Hope Principle) is taken from the philosopher Ernst Bloch's best-known work, to evoke the emotion Christa Wolf had always struggled to sustain against the odds. But by this time, at latest, she must have applied to herself Mikhail Gorbachev's legendary words, "If you come too late, life will punish you."[16]

There are historical ironies to this story. For one thing, the years of Christa Wolf's allegedly inadequate opposition to "real existing socialism," when she accommodated herself to the state and the party in the hope of liberalizing their practice, were the same years in which the

Federal Republic's policy toward the GDR began to follow exactly the same lines. In place of the original Cold War rejection of the GDR, it was accorded the recognition it craved; East German dissidents (and those of the Eastern bloc generally, including Polish Solidarność) were no longer publicly encouraged, for fear of rocking the diplomatic boat; the rival state was "stabilized," not least by the granting of massive credits to save its tottering economy from total collapse. The "Cold Warriors of yesterday," Günter Grass commented sardonically, were suddenly "effusive peace-apostles." This new *Ostpolitik* was aimed at bringing about "change through rapprochement" (Wandel durch Annäherung) and a liberalization of the GDR for the benefit of its citizens.[17] Christa Wolf's critics don't seem to have noticed the exact match. To have done so might have blunted their vehemence.

The final irony, at the expense of both the Federal Republic and Wolf herself, is that neither of them achieved the desired liberalization by their soft tactics. When in 1989 real change came, it was through the kind of radical action they had both set themselves against, action not by prominent dissidents but by a wave of popular dissatisfaction in response to the usual falsified election figures. The result was a revolution on the streets and squares of East German cities. The citizens of the GDR did it themselves, admittedly helped by Gorbachev's Soviet Union, whose refusal to back a violent crackdown prevented bloodshed—the recent Tiananmen Square massacre threatened as a model. The Federal Republic thus enjoyed a triumph that simply fell in its lap.[18] But as a consequence it could give up sweet-talking the GDR and go back to demonizing it as the harsh dictatorship it had been. True enough, but the reverse turnabout smacked strongly of hypocrisy.[19]

The Christa Wolf affair was thus a symbol of the larger forces shaping the new Germany. At all events, the door was now open for the uneasy course of reunification. West dominated East in a political, institutional, and economic takeover, an often-brutal process, only less so than the earlier oppressive attempts to impose unity on the German people.

Afterword

Anyone who has read this far will perhaps agree that the study of literary genesis is not a pedantic unpicking of literary masterpieces but an approach that enhances the understanding and enjoyment of a text as it stands. These responses remain intact, and are simply enriched by a sense of origin and process, as thought and feeling are seen taking their eventual shape.

So Goethe was exaggerating when he gave the genetic view an absolute priority, declaring—no doubt from the feel of his own writing—that "you don't get to know works of nature and art when they're completed, you have to catch them as they come into being in order in some measure to grasp them."[1]

There have been exaggerations in the other direction too. Rousseau: "To say whether a book is good or bad, what does it matter how it was made?"[2] And Nietzsche: "Insight into a work's origin is only a matter for the physiologists and vivisectors of the mind, never ever for aesthetic people, for artists."[3]

An anthology could be put together of writers' utterances pro et contra. But why set the two perspectives against each other when they can be married? Genetic understanding, like everything else in literature, is not an obligation but an offer—a freely available extra. If the taste is acquired, there will be materials to hand for any work or author, from critical editions and any number of essays.

But isn't there a problem about how far it can be taken? The possible objects of study are endless, so that not even scholars, let alone the Common Reader, can follow through the genesis of every admired work. Yet that is no more than a truism of a familiar kind. There are too many mountains for the mountaineer to climb, too many countries for the traveler to visit, too many languages for the linguist to learn. A few symbolic instances have to suffice for most people's lifetimes. But even if we can only get to know a few works in genetic detail, we can see in these the embodiment of a constant principle that alters our feeling for whatever we read. Every text will come to life in a fresh way.

The principle of process and growth is common to nature and art—on that, Goethe was right. The link is not just rhetorical but substantive: art is essentially one more product of nature, emerging from the latest and most refined stage of human evolution. So it is fitting to end this book with the response of that great poet and scientist to a grandiose natural phenomenon in the midst of which he found himself. It is 1779 and Goethe is standing at night among the Swiss mountains, refusing to be fashionably intimidated by the Sublime, feeling on the contrary securely and typically at home:

> You can sense in the darkness the genesis and the life of these strange shapes. However and whenever it happened, these masses composed themselves by the weight and affinity of their parts, in grandeur and simplicity. Whatever revolutions later shifted them, divided them, split them, they were only single disturbances, and even the thought of such immense movement gives an exciting sense of eternal steadfastness. [...] You feel it deeply, here nothing is arbitrary, everything slowly moving eternal law.[4]

Notes

Preface

[1] Goethe, *Maximen und Reflexionen* nr. 488. Goethe, *Werke*, Hamburger Ausgabe (henceforth HA), 12:432.

[2] Goethe, *Maximen und Reflexionen* nr. 461, HA 12:429.

[3] Dr. Johnson "rejoiced to concur" with the judgment of the "common reader" on Gray's "Elegy in a Country Churchyard," "for by the commonsense of readers uncorrupted with literary prejudices, after all the refinements of subtlety and the dogmatism of learning, must be finally decided all claims to poetical honours." Samuel Johnson, *Lives of the Poets*, 2:463. The passage was made widely known by Virginia Woolf in her essay collections, *The Common Reader*, series one and two, 1915 and 1932.

[4] Beauvoir, *The Second Sex*, 113.

Introduction

[1] Milton, *Areopagitica* (1644), in *Selected Prose of John Milton*, 280.

[2] For some samples from twentieth-century writing, see Siegfried Unseld, *Von aufgegebenen Werken*. The introduction, 15–16, sketches the publisher's angle. The volume's motto is Jesus' instruction after the miracle of the loaves and fishes, "Gather up the fragments that remain, that nothing be lost" (John 6:12).

[3] Goethe to Bartholt Georg Niebuhr, November 23, 1812, *Briefe*, Hamburg edition (henceforth HAB), 3:207.

[4] Longinus, *On Sublimity*, 33.2.

[5] John Ruskin, *The Stones of Venice*, 137–38. Italics original.

[6] ". . . quandoque bonus dormitat Homerus." Horace, *Epistula ad Pisones* (*Ars poetica*), lines 358–59.

[7] Roth, *American Pastoral*, 45.

[8] Letter to Vita Sackville-West, *Congenial Spirits*, 204.

[9] Schiller to Christian Gottfried Körner, May 25, 1792, *Brw Sch/Kör* 1:452; and to Goethe, March 18, 1796, *Brw Sch/G*, 198.

[10] Eich, "Der Schriftsteller vor der Realität," quoted in Schrott and Jacobs, *Gedicht und Gehirn*, 8.

[11] "Du suchst das wort, von dem du nicht mehr weißt, / als dass es fehlt." Reiner Kunze, *die stunde mit dir selbst*, 31.

[12] Goethe, *Sämtliche Werke*, Frankfurter Ausgabe (FA), 1:4.

[13] Kleist, "Über die allmähliche Verfertigung der Gedanken beim Reden," in *Sämtliche Werke*, 2:319–23.

[14] Dieter Henrich, *Werke im Werden*, 69.

[15] Goethe, *Dichtung und Wahrheit*, Bk 16, HA 10:80.

[16] Montaigne, "On Some Verses of Vergil," in *Essais*, 3:91. For Goethe's similar horseback problem, see the opening of the chapter "Occasions: Goethe's Lyric Poetry."

[17] Balzac was dedicating the ms and proofs of "La femme supérieure" to David d'Angers, in 1843. *Oeuvres complètes*, vii: 1545.

[18] Conrad, quoted in the *Times Literary Supplement*, January 19, 2018, 4. The general point is richly supported by Ulrich von Bülow's anthology of documents from the Marbach Literary Archive, *Papierarbeiter: Autoren und ihre Archive*.

[19] Satie, *Trois morceaux en forme de poire*, 1903.

[20] Quoted in Gottfried Benn, "Probleme der Lyrik," in Benn, *Gesammelte Werke*, 1:496.

[21] A. E. Housman, "The Name and Nature of Poetry," in Housman, *Selected Prose*, 194. Further work may include testing the gift itself for "pathological passages." Benn, "Probleme der Lyrik," 507.

[22] Virginia Woolf, *A Writer's Diary*, 286.

[23] Alles geschieht im höchsten Grade unfreiwillig, aber wie in einem Sturme von Freiheits-Gefühl, von Unbedingtsein, von Macht, von Göttlichkeit . . . Die Unfreiwilligkeit des Bildes, des Gleichnisses ist das Merkwürdigste [. . .] Alles bietet sich als der nächste, der richtigste, der einfachste Ausdruck. Es scheint wirklich, um an ein Wort Zaeathustras zu erinnnern, als ob die Dinge selber herankämen und sich zum Gleichnis anböten. Nietzsche, *Ecce homo*, §3 of the chapter that deals with *Zarathustra*, in *Sämtliche Werke*, Kritische Studienausgabe (henceforth KStA) 6:339.

[24] According to the memoirs of Marie von Thurn und Taxis, Rilke spoke of the roaring of a storm in which a divine voice spoke to him, inspiring the first of the *Duino Elegies*. Nietzsche on inspiration is directly quoted by the Devil when he offers Adrian Leverkühn a new creativity in chapter 25 of Thomas Mann's *Doctor Faustus*.

[25] Nietzsche, *Menschliches, Allzumenschliches*, §§155 and 156, KStA 2:146.

[26] Joseph Haydn, program note to a Wigmore Hall performance of Symphony 52 by the English Concert, September 14, 2017.

[27] The parallel in music would be, again, Beethoven's working notebooks as against the legend of Mozart's genius for composing a work complete in his head that needed no alteration. (The twenty-fourth piano concerto would be an exception.)

[28] Woolf, *A Room of One's Own* and *Three Guineas*, 40.

²⁹ Our more familiar kind of angels are said to spend their time listening to Mozart, God himself of course to Bach. (Beethoven might disturb the higher serenity.)

³⁰ Schiller, the first of the *Briefe über Don Carlos*, in *Sämtliche Werke*, 2:227.

³¹ Hugo von Hofmannsthal, "Ungeschriebenes Nachwort zum *Rosenkavalier*," in Hofmannsthal, *Prosa* III: 43; and letter to Strauss of December 22, 1912, *Briefwechsel*, 178. The Hofmannsthal–Strauss and Goethe–Schiller interactions are richly documented in their respective correspondences.

³² Jacques Derrida, *Writing and Difference*.

³³ Roland Barthes, "The Death of the Author," repr. in David Lodge, *Modern Criticism and Theory*, 171.

³⁴ Derrida, *Writing and Difference*, 158.

³⁵ "Verständigung wohnt als Telos der menschlichen Sprache inne." Jürgen Habermas, quoted in Martin Seel, "Im Maschinenraum des Denkens," *Die Zeit*, celebratory number for Habermas's ninetieth birthday, June 12, 2019.

³⁶ Goethe, *Maxims and Reflections* 916, HA 12:495.

³⁷ Derrida, *Writing and Difference*, 287.

³⁸ Frederic Jameson, *The Prison-House of Language*. Nietzsche's subtler formulation does not use the metaphor of a prison-house at all, but refers to the constraint of language (sprachlicher Zwang) under which we necessarily operate, unsure whether it constitutes a boundary. Nietzsche, *Nachlass 1886–87*, KStA 12:193.

³⁹ Michel Foucault, "What Is an Author?" repr. Lodge, *Modern Criticism and Theory*, 198.

⁴⁰ "*Liebe als Kunstgriff.*—Wer etwas Neues wirklich *kennen* lernen will (sei es ein Mensch, ein Ereigniss, ein Buch), der thut gut, dieses Neue mit aller möglichen Liebe aufzunehmen [. . .] so dass man zum Beispiel dem Autor eines Buches den grössten Vorsprung giebt und geradezu, wie bei einem Wettrennen, mit klopfendem Herzen danach begehrt, dass er sein Ziel erreiche. Mit diesem Verfahren dringt man nämlich der neuen Sache bis an ihr Herz, bis an ihren bewegenden Punct: und dieses heisst eben sie kennen lernen. Ist man soweit, so macht der Verstand hinterdrein seine Restrictionen." Friedrich Nietzsche, *Menschliches, Allzumenschliches*, 1, §621. KStA 2:350.

⁴¹ "Das Bizarre fesselt den Blick, [. . .] das Übertriebene drängt sich auf." Hugo von Hofmannsthal, "Goethes West-Östlicher Divan," *Prosa*, III: 159.

⁴² Paul de Man, *The Resistance to Theory*, pages 12, 4, and 24 respectively.

⁴³ George Steiner, *Real Presences: Is There Anything in What We Say?*, 85.

⁴⁴ Initially in their book *Relevance: Communication and Cognition* (1986).

⁴⁵ See also Schrott and Jacobs, *Gedicht und Gehirn*, 24–28.

⁴⁶ An excellent survey is Almuth Grésillon's *Éléments de critique génétique*.

⁴⁷ "Brauch ich Zeugnisse, dass ich binn? Zeugnisse, dass ich fühle?—Nur so schätz, lieb, bet ich die Zeugnisse an, die mir darlegen, wie tausende oder einer vor mir eben das gefühlt haben, was mich kräftiget und stärket. Und so ist das Wort der Menschen mir Wort Gottes es mögens Pfaffen oder Huren gesammelt

und zum Kanon gerollt oder als Fragmente hingestreut haben. Und mit inniger Seele fall ich dem Bruder um den Hals Moses! Prophet! Evangelist! Apostel, Spinoza oder Machiavell! Darf aber auch zu iedem sagen, lieber Freund geht dir s doch wie mir!" Goethe to Johann Caspar Lavater and Johann Conrad Pfenninger, April 26, 1774, HAB 1:159.

[48] Goethe to Carl Friedrich Zelter, June 18, 1831, HAB 4:430.

[49] Schiller to Goethe, February 27, 1798. *Brw Sch/G*, 589.

[50] Rita Felski, *The Limits of Critique*.

[51] Toril Moi, *The Revolution of the Ordinary*, 217–20. For an earlier survey of the benefits and drawbacks of "Theory," and a word in favor of a return to sympathetic "tactful" reading, see Valentine Cunningham, *Reading after Theory*.

[52] "Nous ne sommes hommes et ne tenons les uns aux autres que par la parole." Montaigne "Des menteurs" (Of Liars), *Essais* 1, ix; 73.

Chapter One

[1] Bowra, *Homer*, 1.

[2] In the version by Robert Fagles, Homer, *The Iliad*.

[3] Robert Graves, *The Anger of Achilles*.

[4] W. B. Yeats, "Leda and the Swan," one of the great poems on historical causality, with its riddling question whether the mortal woman could have shared the god's foreknowledge of fate.

[5] Marlowe, *Doctor Faustus*, 5, i.

[6] Plato, *Ion*, 533d.

[7] Michael Avi-Yonah, *Ancient Scrolls*, 16.

[8] The first references to a literary work published in that form are in poems by Martial in 84 CE. Even then, the new invention took a long time to catch on. Eventually it became a distinguishing mark of Christian as against other documents.

[9] M. L. West, *The Making of the Iliad*, 51–62.

[10] Eduard Schwartz, *Zur Entstehung der Ilias*. Quoted in West, *Making of the Iliad*, 56.

[11] Longinus, *On Sublimity* (1st century CE), 33.2. Russell and Winterbottom, *Ancient Literary Criticism*, 492. Or proverbially "even Homer nods," after Horace, quoted above in the introduction.

[12] E.g., "The passage contains some fine phrases, but by the standards of Homer it may truly be said to exemplify a tired and second-hand style." Kirk, *Songs of Homer*, 168.

[13] Friedrich August Wolf, *Prolegomena to Homer*, 70.

[14] As first suggested in 1897 by Samuel Butler, *The Authoress of the Odyssey*, perhaps building on Richard Bentley's suggestion that the *Iliad* was meant for men and the *Odyssey* for women. Robert Graves turned the notion into the delightful

novel *Homer's Daughter*. For "how it really was" on Ithaca during Odysseus' absence, see Margaret Atwood, *The Penelopiad*. Pat Barker's *The Silence of the Girls* retells the action of the *Iliad* as experienced by Briseis, the captive over whom Achilles fell out with Agamemnon.

15 Bernard Knox, introduction to Fagles, *Iliad*, 9.

16 Walter Leaf, *The Iliad of Homer*, 117.

17 Knox, introduction to Fagles, *Iliad*, 3.

18 Joachim Latacz, "The Structure of the Iliad," in *Prolegomena to the Basel "Iliad" Commentary*, 161.

19 Rieu, trans. and intro., *The Iliad*, xii.

20 Jasper Griffin, *Homer*, 13.

21 Kirk, *Songs of Homer*, 253.

22 Bowra, *Homer*, 8.

23 In his novel *The File on H.*, Ismail Kadare transfers this scholarly pursuit to his native Albania, where the narrative tradition is dying out. Ironically, when the American researchers' equipment is attacked and their recordings destroyed, this becomes itself a subject for renewed local epic song.

24 Wolf, *Prolegomena*, 109. Cf. Ruth Finnegan, *Oral Poetry*, passim.

25 *Casablanca*, dir. Michael Curtiz, with Humphrey Bogart as Rick Blaine and Ingrid Bergman as Ilsa Lund (1942).

26 J. B. Hainsworth, in *Traditions of Homeric and Epic Poetry*, 1:39.

27 Their titles are listed by the ancient commentator Aelian. They cover most of the later *Iliad*, including "The Story of Alcinous" (presumably Odysseus telling his adventures to the Phaeacians), "The Interrupted Battle," and especially "The Catalogue of Ships." See Wolf, *Prolegomena*, 113. These too fail to include the fall of the city.

28 Gotthold Ephraim Lessing, *Laokoon* (1766) §18, in *Werke*, VI:119–21. Lessing argues that static description simply is not the job of poetry. So again, Homer offers no description of Helen's beauty ("in which modern writers would have luxuriated!"), but shows its effect on Troy's old men at the sight of her—a woman like that was worth a war! *Laokoon* §21, Lessing, *Werke*, VI:138.

29 Instances of repeats taken at random from Aeschylus's *Oresteia*: *Choephoroi*, lines 806–11 and 814–17; 827–30 and 834–37.

30 Sappho, papyrus fragment 16; Campbell, *Greek Lyric*, 1:66–67.

31 "A declaration of war should be a popular festival. A spectacle like a bullfight, where ministers and generals in their bathing trunks fight it out with clubs. The victor's country wins. Whereas here the wrong people are fighting each other." Erich Maria Remarque, *All Quiet on the Western Front*, 1929, chapter 3. Just occasionally, single combat is suggested by high-ups themselves. In Shakespeare's *Henry IV*, Part 1 Hal challenges Hotspur, but it is not seriously considered, and was perhaps a chivalric gesture not expected to be.

32 "Homer lived four hundred years before logic of any kind was expounded." Whitman, *Homer and the Heroic Tradition*, 12.

[33] It is only briefly glanced back at in the *Odyssey* (Od. 8:552), and not given the classic treatment until Virgil's *Aeneid*. The omission is so surprising as to be sometimes overlooked. "The *Iliad* has a climax, the fall of Troy" says John Burrow in *A History of Histories*, 475. Knox mildly cheats by evoking the fall of the city in his own graphic detail (see Fagles's translation of The Iliad, 37).

[34] The original Greek "heros" in any case only means "warrior," with no further implication of status or achievement.

[35] Robert Graves, *The Anger of Achilles*, xiv. There is one positively comic moment when Menelaus has been wounded and Agamemnon becomes the complete Job's comforter, luridly imagining his brother moldering in his grave. So good for morale! (4:196–209) Beyond the scope of the *Iliad*, Agamemnon caps his disasters by reassigning to Odysseus the armour that the late Achilles intended for Ajax. In a rage of disappointment Ajax kills himself.

[36] Graves, *Anger of Achilles*, xxii.

[37] Shakespeare strikingly follows tradition and makes him the spokesman of "degree" and "order" in *Troilus and Cressida*, 1, iii.

[38] Schiller, "Über epische und dramatische Dichtung," in Schiller, *Sämtliche Werke*, 5:790.

[39] As finely analyzed in chapter 1 of Erich Auerbach's *Mimesis: Represented Reality in Western Literature*.

[40] Arthur Hatto, introduction to the *Nibelungenlied*, 313.

[41] See Jonathan Shay, *Achilles in Vietnam: Traumatic Stress and the Undoing of Character* and *Odysseus in America; Combat Trauma and the Trials of Homecoming*.

Chapter Two

[1] Greek neuter plural "biblia," from the diminutive of "biblos," "biblion," scroll, out of which modern languages have made a (where relevant feminine) singular.

[2] Joel Rosenberg, "Ezekiel," in Alter and Kermode, *Literary Guide to the Bible*, 194.

[3] See Wolf, *Prolegomena*, 29 and 229–31.

[4] Harold Fisch, *Poetry with a Purpose*, 2.

[5] *Chronicles of Kings of Judea and Israel*, *Book of Yashar*, and *Book of Battles of Yahweh*. Alter, *Art of Biblical Narrative*, 35.

[6] The Authorised Version (AV) at 2 Samuel 21:19 reads "Elhanan slew *the brother of* Goliath," italics in the text. Italics in the AV normally indicate added words not present in the original, usually just colorless verbs, adjectives, or adverbs, such as "is," "their," "then," whose equivalent is not found in the Hebrew syntax. In this instance, they are admitting a deliberate adjustment of facts, since without the inserted words the text would contradict the account of David's heroic victory at 1 Samuel 17. Luther's text has no such insertion. On legend as politically adjusted history in ancient as in modern times, see the East German novelist Stefan Heym's satire *Der König David Bericht*, 1973.

[7] For a concise account of the canon, see Frank Kermode's chapter in Alter and Kermode's *Literary Guide to the Bible*, and Lee Macdonald, "Canon," in *Oxford Handbook of Biblical Studies*, 779.

[8] Immanuel Kant, *Die Religion innerhalb der Grenzen der bloßen Vernunft*, in *Werke* VI: 252.

[9] See Erich Auerbach, "Figura," in *Scenes from the Drama of European Literature*, 11–76.

[10] For the arguments around Moses' authorship, see Alexander Rofé, *Introduction to the Composition of the Pentateuch*. Spinoza was also among the earliest to argue that the Hebrew Bible was the work of many human authors.

[11] So named for the seventy (actually there were seventy-two) commissioned translators who all came up with identical versions of their text, transparently a myth for anyone who has ever conducted a translation class.

[12] As in the nineteenth-century standard account by L. Gaussen, *Theopneustia: The Plenary Inspiration of the Holy Scriptures*. Gaussen ducks the central question, declining (349) to "start any hypotheses as to the manner in which God dictated [the scriptures]."

[13] "The signs of a highly biased rendering of the history of the monarchy are visible to even the casual reader." George Savran, "I and 2 Kings," in Alter and Kermode, *Literary Guide to the Bible*, 146.

[14] Heinrich Heine, *Die Harzreise*, in *Sämtliche Werke*, 4:39.

[15] Donne, *Sermons* V:44 and VI:55. Quoted in David Norton, *History of the English Bible as Literature*, 105 and 150. The following pages draw gratefully on this invaluable survey of the Bible's reception.

[16] See the not notably pious Goethe: "I'm a very earthly person, for me the parables of the Prodigal Son, the Sower, the Pearl of great price and the like are more divine, if divine there has to be, than the Seven Bishops, Horns, Seals and Stars" (the grander imagery of Revelation about which his friend Lavater had been writing). Johann Wolfgang Goethe to Johann Caspar Lavater, October 28, 1779, HAB 1:279.

[17] These phases are usefully tabulated in Christopher de Hamel, *The Book: A History of the Bible*, 22–24.

[18] Their complexity is nicely captured in the story of a boy learning from a priest "how complex and mysterious were certain institutions of the Church [. . .]. I was not surprised when he told me that the fathers of the Church had written books as thick as the *Post Office Directory* and as closely printed as the law notices in the newspaper, elucidating all these difficult questions." James Joyce, "The Sisters," in Joyce, *Dubliners*, 10.

[19] Luther gave the old answer: his own (new) authority, which meant he could decry those who dissented from his readings as blasphemers, even Satan. Cf. Lyndal Roper, *Martin Luther, Renegade and Prophet*, 315–17 and passim.

[20] Recounted in Norton, *History of the English Bible*, 10–11.

[21] Luther's Bible in his final revision is reproduced, with ample documentation, in the fine two-volume edition by Hans Volz, *D. Martin Luther: Die gantze Heilige Schrifft Deudsch*. Wittenberg 1545.

[22] Volz, *Heilige Schrifft*, 1:4–7. The pirate printers remained undaunted—twelve pirated editions of the New Testament came out in 1523 alone.

[23] The Authorised Version (AV) is only the last stage in a complex history of versions and the theological issues behind them that would go far beyond present purposes. For a concise but richly illustrated account, see David Edgar, "Whose Bible Is It Anyway?," in the February 19, 2011 number of *The Guardian* marking the 400th anniversary of the AV's publication.

[24] "The King James Bible and Its Cultural Politics," in Helen Moore and Julian Reid, *Manifold Greatness*, 132.

[25] Norton, *History of the English Bible as Literature*, passim.

[26] An American apologist in 1930, quoted by Norton, *History*, 399. Italics apparently in the original. The once authoritative critic George Saintsbury couldn't imagine that any modern translation, "even Luther's German, can vie with ours" (405). How closely did Saintsbury check, and for what qualities exactly?

[27] *The New Testament*, trans. Tyndale.

[28] The AV translators, "so often praised for unlikely corporate inspiration, took over Tyndale's work. Nine-tenths of the Authorised Version's New Testament is Tyndale's." David Danniell, *William Tyndale: A Biography*, 1.

[29] Donne, *Sermons* VI:55–57. Quoted in Norton, *History*, 151.

[30] Donne, *An Introduction to the Holy Scriptures* (1669), 8–9. Quoted in Norton, *History*, 153.

[31] Robert Lowth, *Lectures on the Sacred Poetry of the Hebrews*, 1787, Lecture 33, 2:404–7. Lecture 19 has a straightforward reference to Vergil's Fourth Eclogue in a discussion of the prophets.

[32] Milton, *Paradise Regained*, 4:343–47.

[33] Sir Richard Blackmore (?1658–1729). Norton, *History*, 196.

[34] Norton, *History*, 174.

[35] The charge goes back at least to Tyndale, who decried popular stories of Robin Hood, Hercules and Hector, and "fables of love and wantonness [. . .] as filthy as heart can think, to corrupt the minds of youth withal." Danniell, *William Tyndale*, 2.

[36] Recorded in Gilbert Burnet's not unsympathetic account of Rochester's sinful life and death-bed turn. Norton, *History*, 173.

[37] For example, Thomas Babington Lord Macaulay: "If everything else in our language should perish, [the Bible] would alone suffice to show the whole extent of its beauty and power." Norton, *History*, 401.

[38] John Hays Gardiner (1906), quoted in Norton, *History*, 402.

[39] David Damrosch, "Leviticus," in Alter and Kermode, *Literary Guide to the Bible*, 66.

[40] David M. Gunn, "Joshua and Judges," in Alter and Kermode, *Literary Guide to the Bible*, 116.

[41] R. G. Kratz, "The Prophetic Literature," in Barton, *The Hebrew Bible*, 137.

[42] Auerbach, "The Scar of Odysseus" in *Mimesis*, ch. 1.

[43] Auerbach, *Mimesis*, 19–21.

[44] A rare exception is the building and equipping of the Temple described in Exodus, ch. 30, which goes into even fuller detail than Homer's description of the making of Achilles's shield. Filling in detail is, however, a feature of Jewish midrash, for example in versions of the Aramaic translation of the Pentateuch, where material is added.

[45] Goethe, *Dichtung und Wahrheit*, Bk 4, HA 9:141.

[46] Marlow, "The Human Condition," in Barton, *Hebrew Bible*, 298.

[47] Alter and Kermode in their introduction to *Literary Guide to the Bible*, 30. This is surely a "lucus a non lucendo."

[48] J. P. Fokkelman, "Exodus," "Genesis," in Alter and Kermode, *Literary Guide to the Bible*, 60, 42.

[49] Robert Alter, *Art of Biblical Narrative*, passim. Parallelism is already familiar from Lowth, lecture 19.

[50] Robert Alter, *The Art of Biblical Poetry*.

[51] See the corresponding article in John Elwolde, *Dictionary of Classical Hebrew*, 2:596. Where the AV does vary its conjunctions and the accompanying verbal forms, it can seem to lose the logical thread. See 1 Kings 2:9, in David's instructions to Solomon to kill Shimei, the meandering sequence "therefore," "for," "oughtest," "but." Contrast Luther, who renders the consistent line of thought: "but," "for," "shallst," "so that."

[52] Gerald Hammond, "English Translations of the Bible," in Alter and Kermode, *Literary Guide to the Bible*, 660.

[53] Duly noted by Goethe, who likewise has the Lord draw Mephistopheles's attention to Faust as an object to practice on.

[54] Jennie Grillo, "The Wisdom Literature," in *Hebrew Bible*, ed. Barton, 190. The apter parallel is Robert Lowth's, of Sophocles's Oedipus tragedies, discussed above.

[55] J. P. Fokkelman, "Genesis," in Alter and Kermode, *Literary Guide to the Bible*, 50.

[56] Or, with a psychologist's eye, reading the god's command as a father's pathological delusion, the intervening angel and the ram in the thicket as symbolizing the moment when Abraham suddenly realizes the horror of what he is about to do.

[57] Wilfred Owen, "The Parable of the Old Man and the Young," sensitively discussed by Alison Gray, "Reception of the Old Testament," in *Hebrew Bible*, ed. Barton, 423–29.

[58] John Barton, *A History of the Bible*, 433.

[59] C. S. Lewis, *Reflections on the Psalms*, 2.

[60] Barton, *History of the Bible*, 416.

[61] Eliot, "Religion and Literature," in *Selected Essays*, 390.

[62] "... a narrative constructed to persuade." David Jasper, "Literary Approaches," in *Hebrew Bible*, ed. Barton, 462.

[63] R. W. I. Moberly, "Theological Approaches," in *Hebrew Bible*, ed. Barton, 486.

[64] Jasper, "Literary Approaches," in *Hebrew Bible*, ed. Barton, 455.

[65] John Barton, "Reading the Bible," *London Review of Books*, May 5, 1988.

[66] Alter and Kermode, General Introduction, *Literary Guide to the Bible*, 1–2. Italics added.

[67] Cf. Reed, *"Nobody's Master."*

Chapter Three

[1] I quote Montaigne in my translation, but for the reader curious to savor his Early Modern French, I give volume and page of Alexandre Micha's paperback edition of the *Essais* (Paris: Garnier, 1969–79). Its three volumes correspond to the three books of the essays, so the numerals 1, 2, 3 in my references do double duty. Each individual essay then has its Roman numeral. Thus the reference "1, viii; 70" is to book 1, the eighth essay, and simultaneously to volume 1, p. 70 of the Micha edition. Essays quoted or referred to in the text are listed in numerical order with their full titles in the appendix at this chapter's end.

[2] Terence Cave, *How to Read Montaigne*, 4.

[3] At his father's request, Montaigne had translated from Latin a theological treatise by the Spaniard Raimond Sebond. The long "disquisition" referred to above (*Essais* 1, xii) is "An Apology for Raimond Sebond."

[4] Philippe Desan, *Montaigne*, 17.

[5] For a minute account of its organization and curriculum, see Desan, *Montaigne*, 29–37.

[6] Montaigne gives a full account of La Boétie's death in a letter of 1563 to his father. See *Essays and Letters* 1:li–lxvii (the edition, incidentally, that Virginia Woolf was reviewing in her piece on Montaigne that went into *The Common Reader*).

[7] On the successive editions and their significance, see below, the section "Layers."

[8] Thus a further inscription formerly on one of the beams, since lost. See *Essais*, Pléiade, 1316–17.

[9] See the full account immediately below, in the section "Layers."

[10] *Essais*, Pléiade, 2007, 741.

[11] This remarkable man, blind from the age of four, also transcribed the whole text of the Essays into Braille. He further wrote extensively about and for blind people, a virtual double career. There is surely no more heroic feat in European scholarship. Villey was tragically killed at fifty-four in a train crash.

[12] Alexandre Micha's edition uses oblique strokes— / ; // , /// .

[13] Quotations from here on will carry the Villey lettering, to make clear at what point each stands in the genetic chronology.

[14] See the sample page from the Exemplaire de Bordeaux that Montaigne worked on, reproduced in Donald Frame's biography, 245. Several more samples are given in Paola Iemma, *Les repentirs de l'Exemplaire de Bordeaux* (Paris: Garnier, 2004). Her term "repentir" aligns Montaigne's practice with the "pentimenti" (afterthoughts) of Renaissance painters, which can be revealed by Raman spectroscopy. His elaborations were the start of a French tradition of making voluminous additions late in printing, taken further by Balzac and Proust.

[15] For such objections as there are to the evolution thesis, see the 2007 Pléiade edition, xxxi.

[16] We shall see Goethe coping with the problem later. The Provençal troubadour Guillaume de Peiteis made light of it in his "Song of Nothing": "I thought this up once, on my horse, / While slumbering." Kehew, *Lark in the Morning*, 24.

[17] Villey located the composition of the essays of book 3 between 1585 and the spring of 1588. That means the writing process was more concentrated than with books 1 and 2. The essays in book 3 are fewer and longer.

[18] Since the base text of the entire book 3 is the 1588 (b) edition, I expressly identify only the 1595 (c) insertions.

[19] Philippe Desan paints a very different picture of a man intent at every stage of his life on a political, specifically an ambassadorial, career. This involves intricate historical references but a good deal of conjecture.

[20] A full account of the journey is given in a substantial travel journal, the first half written by a secretary, the rest by Montaigne himself, partly in (not very sound) Italian.

[21] For a graphic account of period attempts to operate on the stone, possibly fatal, see the 1601 entry in John Massingham's diary, quoted in Charles Nicholl, *The Lodger*, 60.

[22] Thus the magistrate and historian Jacques-Auguste de Thou, quoted in Frame, *Biography*, 229.

[23] The essay "On Cruelty" in book 2 has an impassioned account of the atrocities now common in France (2, xi: 101). They put the brutalities of primitive New World tribes in the shade ("On Cannibals" 1:xxxi, 258). The theme is everywhere in the *Essays*. The re-narration ("On Coaches") of the misdeeds of the Spanish conquistadors in Mexico and Peru (3, vi: 124–27) still makes uncomfortable reading.

[24] The hope was in some measure fulfilled by his late relationship (from February 1588) with Marie de Gournay, the young woman who edited the 1595 text. She at least fulfilled his hope for a friend who would come forward in response to his writings (3, ix; 194). The essay "On Presumption" ends with a passage on his love and high regard for Marie (2, xvii; 324). Grounds for suspecting she may have written and inserted it herself while working on the edition—unlike most (c) insertions in the Bordeaux copy, there is no marginal draft in Montaigne's hand—are cited by Frame, *Biography*, 277. Against that hypothesis, see Pléiade 2007, 1654.

[25] See part 2 of the *Philosophical Investigations*, the alternative readings of a trick drawing from the humorous *Fliegende Blätter*. Also reproduced in Ernst Gombrich, *Art and Illusion*, 4.

[26] "Homo sum. Humani a me nihil alienum puto." Pléiade 2007, 1313.

[27] Typically, Andreas Gryphius's sonnet "Menschliches Elend," with its many metaphors for transience, ends "Wir vergehn, wie Rauch von starken Winden."

[28] The otherwise rarely seen document is reprinted in M. A. Screech's translation of the *Essays*, lvii.

[29] Cave, *How to Read Montaigne*, 42; Kirsti Sellevold, *'J'ayme ces mots...'* passim.

[30] Quoted by Sarah Bakewell, *How to Live*, 323.

[31] André Gide, "Montaigne," 677.

[32] Nietzsche, *Unzeitgemäße Betrachtungen* 3, "Schopenhauer als Erzieher," KStA 2:348.

[33] Quoted in Gide, "Montaigne," 676.

[34] Horace, *Odes* I, xxxi, stanza 17. My translation.

[35] This is now known as the Bordeaux copy. Other jottings are preserved that did not go into Marie de Gournay's 1595 edition.

Chapter Four

I quote the Histories throughout from the Arden series of Shakespeare's works (London: Bloomsbury), using the latest edition of each of the Histories available at the time of writing.

[1] It became international headlines as a formulation from the greatest of literary voices in response to a new refugee crisis in 2016.

[2] The name is sometimes given, and even occasionally rhymed in the period, as Heminges, and it is given as Hemings in the list of actors a couple of pages later in that same First Folio. But the form without an "s" is how he co-signed that edition's prefatory matter.

[3] First Folio, F1, A 2.

[4] The unpublished works were *Macbeth, Julius Caesar, Antony and Cleopatra, Coriolanus, Cymbeline, Measure for Measure, Two Gentlemen of Verona, Henry VI, King John, Henry VIII, As You Like It, The Taming of the Shrew, The Comedy of Errors, All's Well that Ends Well, Twelfth Night, The Winter's Tale, The Tempest,* and *Othello.* This last was also published separately in 1623 while F 1 was in preparation.

[5] Emma Smith, *The Making of Shakespeare's First Folio*, 17.

[6] Francis Beaumont, "To Mr B. J," circa 1615. Quoted from manuscript in E. K. Chambers, *Shakespeare Facts and Problems*, 2:224.

[7] Stratford's vicar in his diary c. 1660, quoted in Jonathan Bate, *Soul of the Age*, 357.

[8] Smith, *Making of Shakespeare's First Folio*, 90.

[9] Thus the punning title of a chapter in Jonathan Bate's *The Genius of Shakespeare*, which traces the conceptual shift from Classical to Romantic aesthetics.

[10] *The Early Comedies* (London: Folio, 1997), 395 and 409.

[11] First Folio 1, A 2.

[12] First Folio 1, A 3.

[13] Johnson, quoted in *3 Henry VI*, 159.

[14] Quoted in Charles Nicholl, *The Lodger*, 213.

[15] On these individuals, Emma Smith, *First Folio*, 121 and passim. Her book gives a full account of the practical teamwork that went into the historic volume.

[16] *Hamlet*, 18.

[17] See Brian Vickers, *Shakespeare*, Co-author; and for a concise summary, James Shapiro, *Contested Will*, 289–92.

[18] J. K. Walton, *The Quarto Copy* 69, referring to *Hamlet*, 2, ii; 287.

[19] For an analysis of their cultural and psychological roots, see James Shapiro, *Contested Will*.

[20] See James Shapiro, *1606*.

[21] See T. J. B. Spenser, *Elizabethan Love Stories*.

[22] "To play histories [. . .] was a common entertainment." Samuel Johnson, Preface to his Shakespeare edition. Johnson, *Prose and Poetry*, 588.

[23] Quoted in *Richard II*, xliii. Daniel was the author of a poetic epic on the Wars of the Roses, almost certainly known to Shakespeare.

[24] E. M. W. Tillyard, *Shakespeare's History Plays*, 99–100.

[25] *2 Henry VI*, 2, ii, 9–27, 211.

[26] *2 Henry VI*, 214.

[27] *3 Henry VI*, 2, i, 71, 225.

[28] S. T. Bindoff, *Tudor England*, 188.

[29] It still of course is. The portrayal of violence, in film especially, has in our times been much debated, though largely over the damage it may do to young minds. Less discussed, perhaps simply taken for granted, is the appetite for violence in mature minds—for James Bond and Quentin Tarantino's films, not to mention more obscene extremes. See above on the rich variations on slaughter in the *Iliad*, which must be assumed to have been just as popular.

[30] *A Midsummer Night's Dream*, 5, i, 145–46.

[31] Marlowe, *The Complete Works*, ed. Fredson Bowers 1:82.

[32] Marlowe, *The Complete Works*, 1:77 and 79.

[33] Alexander Pope, preface to *The Works of Shakespeare*, in *Eighteenth-Century Essays on Shakespeare*, ed. D. Nichol Smith, 46. Charmingly, Pope's edition gives especially fine passages a star, as to a child's schoolwork.

[34] Samuel Johnson, *Prose and Poetry*, 506.

[35] James Shapiro, *1599*, 17.

[36] *Romeo and Juliet*, Prologue.

[37] *2 Henry VI*, 3, i, 239.

[38] See Bate, *Soul of the Age*, chapter 5, "Stratford Grammar." Bate makes the case for a more positive/creative understanding of rhetoric. Shapiro in *1599*, 320,

picks out the very Shakespearean trope of hendiadys—conceptual doublets (e.g., "... of much pith and moment"). Much, though, can be analyzed in rhetorical terms that was not consciously constructed from rhetorical principles. These, after all, themselves first evolved from natural impulses, e.g., in triads like "blood, sweat and tears."

[39] *3 Henry VI*, 2, v, 249.

[40] *1 Henry VI*, 4, iv, 242–46.

[41] *3 Henry VI* 1, iv, 215.

[42] *3 Henry VI*, 4, iii, 311.

[43] *3 Henry VI*, 5, iv, 348–51.

[44] *3 Henry VI*, 2, v, 254.

[45] Wolfgang Clemen, quoted in *3 Henry VI*, 120.

[46] *3 Henry VI*, 1, i, 191.

[47] Gibbon, *Decline and Fall of the Roman Empire*, 1:102.

[48] *3 Henry VI*, 3, iii, 285.

[49] *2 Henry VI*, 4, x, 337.

[50] *1 Henry VI*, 1, iii, 148.

[51] *3 Henry VI*, 5, ii, 345. The fallen Cardinal Wolsey arrives at the same facile wisdom-after-the-event. *Henry VIII* 4, ii, 379.

[52] *History of the Reign of King Richard III*, quoted in Susan Brigden, *New Worlds*, 172.

[53] Citizens "welcomed Henry Tudor at his accession and came to regret it." Brigden, *New Worlds*, 12. Bindoff's Tudor classic is more positive about Henry.

[54] Quartos of both were published in the same year, 1597, *Richard II* indeed first. It is followed by *Henry IV* Parts One and Two, and *Henry V*.

[55] For this bizarre doctrine see Ernst Kantorowicz, *The King's Two Bodies*. Chapter 2 spells out the example of Shakespeare's *Richard II*.

[56] *Henry V*, 4, ii and 4, viii. Arden 1965, 106, and 134.

[57] Jan Kott, *Shakespeare Our Contemporary*, chapter 1, "The Kings."

[58] Quoted in *1 Henry IV*, 27.

[59] *1 Henry IV*, 1, iii, 157 and 174.

[60] Respectively *1 Henry IV*, 4, i; 5, ii, 286 and 316; 5, iv, 330; 5, v, 337.

[61] Quoted in Bate, *Genius*, 209.

[62] Cf. Bate, *Genius*, 209. "He has somehow won himself a knighthood . . ." Just how is not usually questioned.

[63] The poet laureate John Masefield in 1911, quoted in *2 Henry IV*, 62.

[64] Nicholl, *The Lodger*, 18, 210.

[65] The classic case of historical material forcing dramatic expansion is Schiller's masterpiece on *Wallenstein*, the Habsburg generalissimo in the Thirty Years War (1798). Conceived as a single play, it burst its bounds to become two five-act

dramas, then a trilogy with a prefixed *Wallenstein's Camp* to show the army on whose loyalty-in-rebellion Wallenstein's fate will hang.

[66] *2 Henry IV*, 1, ii, 18.

[67] *2 Henry IV*, 4, ii and 5, iii, 293 and 322; and *2 Henry IV*, 5, v, 180.

[68] Goethe, "Zum Shakespeares Tag" (On Shakespeare Day) 1771, HA 12:224. It is important not to translate this as a conventional simile ("nothing so *like* nature ..."). The syntactical hard join ("nothing so Nature") shortcuts comparison to assert identity.

[69] "Wenn alles verloren wäre, was je, dieserart geschrieben, zu uns gekommen, so könnte man Poesie und Rhetorik daraus vollkommen wiederherstellen." Goethe, *Maximen und Reflexionen*, HA 12:499.

[70] Goethe was up to reading Shakespeare in the original. By 1766, in among the fluent but hilariously erratic English of his letters and poems addressed to his sister Cornelia, there are extensive quotations from William Dodd's popular anthology *The Beauties of Shakespeare* of 1752. See James Boyd, *Goethe's Knowledge of English Literature*), ch. 1.

[71] Cf. Harry Champion's Edwardian song "I'm 'Enery the eighth I am ..." The speaker has married a seven-times widow of previous namesakes, "she wouldn't have a Willy or a Sam."

[72] *1 Henry IV*, 1, i, 147.

[73] *1 Henry IV*, 5, iv, 326.

[74] *Richard II*, 1, ii, 37.

[75] The options were comically overstated in BBC television's 400th anniversary celebrations of Shakespeare's birth by a sketch in which a whole handful of actors vehemently argued for stressing each a different word in the famous line.

[76] *Macbeth*, 2, i.

[77] I discount the trivial reading of the sense as "a green one" against "a red one."

[78] Gerard Manley Hopkins, "To Robert B[ridges]."

[79] *1 Henry IV*, 3, i, 155.

[80] See Peter Ure's cogent summary in *Richard II*, xxx. For a detailed positive account of the sources, see Dominique Goy-Blanquet, *Shakespeare's Early History Plays*.

[81] The two texts are juxtaposed in full in Bate, *Genius*, 10–12.

[82] Philip Edwards, *Shakespeare: A Writer's Progress*, 106.

[83] *Henry V*, 5, ii, 156.

[84] The whole Elizabethan complex of religion, politics and ethics—plus, for good measure, the sexual rivalry of the two queens—had to wait two centuries to be brilliantly treated in Schiller's *Maria Stuart*.

[85] Under an original long title beginning "The first part of the contention betwixt the famous houses of York and Lancaster ..." (*1 Henry VI* was not printed until the First Folio of 1623.)

[86] Exceptionally in octavo, under an original long title, ending "with the whole contention between the two houses of York and Lancaster."

Transition—Tradition

[1] Hegel, *Ästhetik*, ed. Friedrich Bassenge, 2:452.

Chapter Five

[1] The "three stages" are explained fully below.

[2] A couple were published in the journal *Iris*, edited from 1774 to 1777 by Johann Georg Jacobi.

[3] The autobiography *Dichtung und Wahrheit* (Poetry and Truth), bk. 6, HA 9:223.

[4] "Auf dem See," final version, line 2. Letters to Jacobi, August 31, 1774; to Auguste von Stolberg, February 13, 1775; to Carl August, September 2, 1786; to Herder, December 27, 1788. HAB respectively 1:169; 1:177; 2:9; 2:107.

[5] Goethe to Gottlob Friedrich Ernst Schönborn, June 1–July 4, 1774, HAB 1:163.

[6] Goethe to Lavater, October 28, 1779, HAB 1:279.

[7] Goethe to Ernst Theodor Langer, November 24, 1768, HAB 1:79.

[8] The wording of Faust's opening monologue in *Urfaust*, line 6. Quotations generally are from the completed *Faust Part One*, unless, as here, there is a variant from an earlier genetic phase.

[9] ". . . das Überlieferte war nicht weit her." February 16, 1826.

[10] It is not even clear what his exact status is and where he ranks in some diabolical hierarchy. Though regularly referred to by himself and Faust as *the* Devil (e.g., 1651, 2585), he admits he is "not one of the great ones" (16410). Though he pulls rank on the witch, he forbids her to call him Satan (2504). In never-used sketches for Walpurgis night, Urian (=Satan) is said to be at the top of the mountain that Mephisto and Faust are still climbing. Why then is Mephisto a plenipotentiary in the "Prologue in Heaven"? (Just where the evil spirit fits in, who mocks the fallen Gretchen in the Cathedral scene, is unclear.)

[11] Paralipomena, in *Faust*, ed. Albrecht Schöne, 1,175.

[12] See Ernst Beutler, "Die Kindsmörderin" in his *Essays um Goethe*.

[13] The drama *Die Kindermörderin* by Heinrich Leopold Wagner (who actually poached the subject when he heard Goethe was treating it). Schiller's poem "Die Kindsmörderin," Goethe's own poem "Vor Gericht." As harrowing as any is "Das Lied vom Herren und der Magd," one of the ballads Goethe collected in Alsace during his student time at Strasburg, FA, 1:109). The problem is also the last but one of the fifty-six topics listed for Goethe's doctoral examination in law (Max Morris, *Der junge Goethe* II: 97). How Goethe treated it is not recorded.

[14] On his bad habit ("Unart") of starting works and leaving them lying, see *Italian Journey*, September 8, 1786. For his birthday a few days earlier, members of the court had sent him a humorous greeting purporting to be from his known projects, with the plea to finish them. HA 11:21, 22.

[15] "Mein Busen drängt sich nach ihm hin" (3406; My bosom yearns toward him). Identical in *Fragment*, toned down from the more drastic *Urfaust*: "Mein Schoß, Gott! drängt sich nach ihm hin" (1098; My womb, God, yearns toward him). For this Christian girl to invoke her God in mid-passion is as striking as the anatomical explicitness that points on to the tragedy of infanticide.

[16] Martha's garden: lines 3414 and 3510–14. We hear nothing more about the drug. Has Mephisto provided it? Or Faust himself—he has certainly practiced medicine (995–1006). Was it an accidental overdose? We only hear the embarrassing exchange: "*Gretchen:* Es wird ihr hoffentlich nicht schaden. *Faust:* Würd' ich sonst, Liebchen, dir es raten?" (1207–8; I hope it won't harm her; Would I otherwise recommend it, dearest?)

[17] "Their naturalness and power in relation to the rest are unbearable. So I am currently seeking to put them into verse, where the idea shines through as through a veil, but the immediate effect of the dreadful substance is toned down." Goethe to Schiller, May 5, 1798, HAB 2:343. In the event Goethe only managed to versify the very last scene. The poetic benefit of that is questionable.

[18] The fullest documentation of the genesis of Goethe's *Faust* is the monumental hybrid edition (print form plus Internet site) produced by Anne Bohnenkamp and a team at the Freies Deutsches Hochstift–Frankfurt Goethehaus (2018).

[19] As reported by a visiting friend of Goethe's, Friedrich Leopold Count Stolberg, HA 3:422.

[20] Eudo Mason, *Goethe's Faust: Genesis and Purport*, 246. There are draft poems from these years that either anticipate the moment of completion (wishful thinking) or regret that he was never able to achieve it (final resignation). See Mason, 222.

[21] Goethe's diary for that date, HA 11:9.

[22] It is first heard in scene 17 and later retained, with the title "Dull day. In the country," but nowhere given substance.

[23] Goethe to Schiller, December 2, 1794, *Brw Sch/G*, 69.

[24] Goethe to Schiller, June 22, 1797, *Brw Sch/G*, 404.

[25] This, against the conditions of the pact, is itself a moment of human fulfillment. Goethe came close to the everyday world again in Italy, trying to melt into the crowd and finding the people endlessly interesting.

[26] That is expressed in a diary note recording the poem's composition, "Zueignung an Faust." If simply a dedication to accompany the work had been meant, the note would have read "Zueignung *zu* Faust." The preposition "an" here must be governing an accusative, so the dedicatee is the work, to which the writer is dedicating himself. See Albrecht Schöne's *Faust* edition, 2:150. Schöne spoils his acute insight by the over-sophisticated argument that the speaker is not necessarily to be equated with the real Goethe. He self-evidently is: this is an author explicitly relating to his work.

[27] "Prelude on the Stage" ends with the Director's invitation to measure out the whole Creation, moving between those locations, "Vom Himmel durch die Welt zur Hölle" (239).

[28] Mason, *Genesis and Purport*, 257.

[29] *Faust, ein Fragment*, 1890–92.

[30] Presumably the sense is that her fate may drag him down from the moment he kills her brother.

[31] Slightly reworded from *Urfaust*, 1411.

[32] Goethe to Schiller, August 17, 1795, *Brw Sch/G*, 126.

[33] Goethe to Schiller, May 5, 1798, *Brw Sch/G*, 624.

[34] This could also lead him to include in *Faust, Part One* a text of little poetic value, the satirical "Walpurgisnight Dream." The extreme case from elsewhere in the Goethe corpus is the mass of maxims brought in to fill the third volume of *Wilhelm Meister's Years of Travel* when this turned out at a late prepublication stage to be short of copy. The literary pretext was to present them as the reflections of a mystical female character, whom scholarship has sometimes taken with elaborate seriousness.

[35] The history of Goethe criticism is littered with attempts to explain away difficulties (e.g., imagining some quite different "sublime spirit" in "Woodland Cave"), or to ignore whenever convenient the concrete evidence of the *Urfaust* manuscript, or to base implausible interpretations on speculative datings and arbitrary stylistic distinctions. Nobody has done more than Eudo Mason to discredit these "esoteric critics with their inexhaustible ingenuity" (*Genesis and Purport*, 44).

[36] Schöne, *Faust*, 2:312.

[37] *Goethes Gespräche*, nr. 2264, vol. 2, 106–12. The context is the fascinating report of a conversation with Goethe by the historian Heinrich Luden, newly appointed to the University of Jena. Luden could only know the 1790 *Fragment*, but he intuitively saw through to the essential genetic problems, which Goethe—against what he obviously knew—chose to deny, begging the question by an appeal to unity as something axiomatic. The young scholar duly deferred, to social rather than intellectual pressure.

[38] In the section "Israel in the Wilderness" of the notes to the *West-Östlicher Divan*. HA 2:224.

[39] "Von Zeit zu Zeit seh ich den Alten gern"; "Gebt ihr euch einmal für Poeten, So kommandiert die Poesie"; "Zwei Seelen wohnen ach! In meiner Brust"; "Hier bin ich Mensch, hier darf ich's sein"; "Das also war des Pudels Kern"; "Blut ist ein ganz besondrer Saft"; "Ihr Mann ist tot und lässt Sie grüßen"; "Er nennt's Vernunft und braucht's allein, Um tierischer als jedes Tier zu sein."

[40] John Williams's commentary to his translation of *Faust*, 452.

[41] Schöne, *Faust*, 2:585.

[42] Arguably a Faustian trait, but Euphorion is just as much another allegory, of the figure and fate of Byron. This too cuts across the Faustian plotline.

[43] In act 5, the word "soul," or a pronoun standing for it, is at last used, but only by Mephisto (11615, 11623, 11660, 11673). Goethe elsewhere uses the Aristotelean term entelechy.

[44] Goethe to Eckermann, June 6, 1831.

[45] A bizarre but persistent notion, going back to the theosophist Rudolf Steiner, holds that Faust is now embodied in the figure of the Doctor Marianus.

[46] Lessing's Faust might have been, on Enlightenment grounds. But his version was perhaps never finished, and the sole copy of such text as there was reportedly went missing in transit.

[47] Goethe to Eckermann, June 6, 1831. This, bizarrely, in a conversation that has just dwelt on the scene where the old couple and their guest are murdered by Faust's henchmen.

[48] The quotation marks in Goethe's text round the first two lines, and the emphatic typeface make it seem a statement of heavenly policy. Goethe told Eckermann (June 6, 1831) that this was the key to Faust's salvation.

[49] Most recently and massively by Michael Jaeger in a trilogy of studies culminating in *Wanderers Verstummen: Goethes Schweigen, Fausts Tragödie*.

[50] Hegel, *Vorlesungen über die Philosophie der Weltgeschichte*, 1:107.

Chapter Six

[1] To that extent a distant cousin to the accident that set Montaigne going. See Goethe's letter of November 2, 1767 to his friend Ernst Wolfgang Behrisch, HAB 1, 54. His accident likewise generated writing, a paragraph "in which the shape of my brain is modelled, confused and incoherent"—the more strikingly expressive for that when the beginner was still producing conventional Rococo poems, all controlled wit.

[2] See Wulf Segebrecht, *Das Gelegenheitsgedicht*. Not that Goethe the courtier did not also later write in the old patronage tradition. See Albrecht Schöne, *Der Briefschreiber Goethe*, 258–62.

[3] Goethe to Eckermann, September 18, 1823.

[4] Goethe to Auguste zu Stolberg, September 14, 1775, HAB 1:191.

[5] The second "Wandrers Nachtlied," "Über allen Gipfeln . . ." In Peter Johnson's enviable pun, the "Ausgabe letzter Wand."

[6] Goethe, *Dichtung und Wahrheit*, Bk 16, HA 10:80.

[7] Goethe to Auguste zu Stolberg, July 17, 1777. HAB 1:234. The poem ("Alles gaben Götter . . .," a brief meditation on the more and less auspicious gifts that come from the gods) was then probably forgotten. It was published in 1780 by Auguste's brother.

[8] Goethe to Carl August, December 23, 1775, HAB 1:201. As the letter manuscript shows, the text went down complete and without corrections.

[9] Keats to John Taylor, February 27, 1818. *The Letters of John Keats*, 107.

[10] Goethe to Eckermann, November 15, 1823.

[11] The title "To Belinda" echoes the social world of Pope's *Rape of the Lock*.

[12] To Eckermann, March 5, 1830.

[13] As Elisabeth von Türckheim, her faith and resoluteness sustained and protected her family through business disasters and the perils of the French Revolution (she had married into French Alsace). See Ernst Beutler, "Lili—Wiederholte Spiegelungen."

[14] They may well be only the survivors of a larger harvest, in which "no pinnacle of happiness, no abyss of pain but had words devoted to it." For the full autobiographical account, see *Dichtung und Wahrheit*, Bk 17. The poems to Lili included there are the only personal lyrics Goethe built into the autobiography.

[15] I leave two minor slips of the pencil uncorrected. See below.

[16] The translation draws in part on a version by David Luke, *Goethe: Selected Poems*.

[17] "Frucht" has a distant link back to the opening natal image. "Leibesfrucht" (fruit of the body = fetus).

[18] "Schwebenden Sterne" in line 14 is ungrammatical, and line 18 has the dittography "beschattetete Bucht." Line 3 of the little Lili poem has a letter missing, "liebt" instead of "liebte." I drew attention to the first in an essay of 1984, but, like everyone else, missed the other two until a fresh look in 2006. Whether they are signs of compositional haste or errors of transcription seems equally likely. Among editions, the Festausgabe says the text was "composed" (gedichtet) on the lake, the Berliner Ausgabe says it was "entered" (eingetragen) in the notebook, without suggesting how or from where.

[19] Quite unlike, that is, the bound notebook of 350 pages that Goethe filled full on his eight-week journey to Rome in 1786. The little Swiss notebook is preserved in the Weimar Goethe-Schiller Archive and was published in facsimile by Karl Koetschau and Max Morris in 1907 as volume 22 of the Schriften der Goethe-Gesellschaft. Most later editions piously leave out anything not by Goethe's hand—i.e., all the other travelers' *bouts rimés*, which help make up the story. The one exception is the Münchener Ausgabe, which prints the full sequence, albeit without the marginal marks (MA 1/2:542–43). Karl Eibl's *Goethe: Gedichte in Handschriften* prints just the last of the *bouts rimés* followed by the poem, with the marginal markings (p. 78).

[20] Goethe, *Dichtung und Wahrheit*, Bk 16, HA 10:80.

[21] "Was ich Gutes finde in Überlegungen, Gedanken, ja Ausdruck, kommt mir meist im Gehn. Sitzend bin ich zu nichts aufgelegt." Diary, March 20, 1780, Goethe, *Tagebücher* 1:107.

[22] For example, in the many accounts of Wordsworth composing and memorizing poems on foot and on horseback, or in Nietzsche's dictum "the only thoughts of value are the ones got through walking" ("Nur die *ergangenen* Gedanken haben Wert"), *Götzendämmerung*, "Sprüche und Pfeile," §34, KStA 6:64.

[23] In volume 8 of Goethe's first collected works, *Schriften*, 1787–90. The poem's effect in this edition is weakened by the spread over two pages (144–45), which splits the final eight-line stanza into four-four.

[24] A later page of the notebook also carries the first version of a poem "Schaff, das Tagwerk meiner Hände . . .," later called "Hoffnung" (Create, work of my hands

". . ." later "Hope"). It is, uniquely, in ink, and probably of a later date than the journey.

[25] Max Kommerell, *Gedanken über Gedichte*, 95.

[26] Cf. Francis Beaumont's comment quoted above in the Shakespeare chapter: "How far sometimes a mortal man may go / By the dim light of Nature."

[27] ". . . die eigentümliche Handlungsweise des menschlichen Geistes [. . .] gar nichts Besonderes." Novalis, *Heinrich von Ofterdingen*, in *Werke*, 287.

[28] Date removed: "An Schwager Kronos"; "Seefahrt." Title altered: "Maifest" > "Mailied"; "Eis-Lebens-Lied" > "Muth"; "Dem Schicksal" > "Einschränkung." Date removed and title altered "Im Herbst 1775" > "Herbstgefühl."

[29] Karl Eibl in the commentary at FA, 1:1006, restated somewhat heavy-handedly in italics at FA 2:1347.

[30] Which is what the discoverer of the new version supposed. Why then would Goethe never have used it to supplant the 1789 text? Jules Keller, *Goethe-Jahrbuch* (2000): 278–82, with facsimile, and *Études germaniques*, 2000, 685–89.

[31] Schiller to Körner, September 12, 1788: "He is now working on revising his poems." *Brw Sch/Kör* 1:219.

[32] See "Erste Weimarer Gedichtsammlung," reprinted at FA from 1:191.

[33] Goethe to Charlotte von Stein, September 26, 1779, *Briefe an Charlotte*, 1:119. "Need*ed*," suggests Lili's now achieved position has made up for what she lost by the broken engagement in 1775. The poem-gift would have been grossly tactless if it had been made, as Keller thinks (*Goethe-Jahrbuch*, 281), "shortly *before* that final break."

[34] The other being the four-line chaser "If I, dearest Lili, did not love you . . ." Its title in the Türckheim version is "Oberried vom Berge" (Oberried from the Mountain), again a precise location that Goethe, as usual, generalized in 1789 into "From the Mountain" (Vom Berge). Later editions return to the manuscript's title, "Vom Berge in die [*sic*] See." This poem too was revised for publication, but in his autobiography Goethe went back to the original, which he now found "more expressive than the version in my collected poems." *Dichtung und Wahrheit*, Bk 18, HA 10:141.

[35] Wordsworth, "Preface to Lyrical Ballads" (1802), in *Works*, ed. Stephen Gill, 611.

[36] W. B, Yeats, "The friends that have it I do wrong / When ever I remake a song, / Should know what issue is at stake: / It is myself that I remake." Untitled, Variorum edition of the poems, 778.

[37] Christian Gottfried Körner to Schiller, May 11, 1793, *Brw Sch/Kör* 2:64.

[38] As published in 1775 in the journal *Iris*; facsimile in *Goethe-Handbuch* 1:79. It is identical with a MS in the hand of Goethe's friend Johanna Fahlmer now in Freiburg. Friederike's own collection includes a copy of just the first ten lines, with minor differences. Eibl, *Gedichte in Handschriften*, 19, prints a facsimile of what can only be the MS copy-text for 1789, which tells us no more than the printed page does.

[39] "Und fort, wild wie ein Held zur Schlacht!" became "Es war getan fast eh gedacht."

[40] "Doch tausendfacher war mein Muth" became "Doch frisch und fröhlich war mein Mut."

[41] "Mein Geist war ein verzehrend Feuer," became "In meinen Adern welches Feuer!"; Mein ganzes Herz zerfloss in Glut" became "In meinem Herzen welche Glut!"

[42] Bizarrely, the estimable Max Morris, in his great compilation *Der junge Goethe*, argues, against the printing history and the natural direction of a poet's growth, that these flat phrases were the original forms. *Der junge Goethe*, 6:162.

[43] "Der Abschied, wie bedrängt, wie trübe!" became "Doch ach schon mit der Morgensonne"; "Aus deinen Blicken sprach dein Herz" became "Verengt der Abschied mir das Herz."

[44] "Du giengst, ich stund, und sah zur Erden," became "Ich ging, du standst und sahst zur Erden"; "Und sah dir nach mit nassem Blick" became "Und sahst mir nach mit nassem Blick."

[45] Respectively, the Propyläenausgabe; Goethe, *Gedichte in zeitlicher Folge*, 1923 and reprints down to today; Heinrich August Korff's *Goethe im Bildwandel seiner Lyrik*, 1958; here 1:162.

[46] Emil Staiger quotes precisely the timorous revision of that expressively cross-syntactical line in "An Schwager Kronos" as a poetic "wonder." He also quotes other revisions rather than the originals "to avoid unnecessary confusion." That actually creates confusion. Staiger, *Goethe*, 1:72–75.

[47] Goethe to Charlotte von Stein, September 25, 1779. *Briefe an Charlotte*, 1:119.

[48] Stephen Gill, *William Wordsworth: A Life*, 405.

[49] Book 10 of *Dichtung und Wahrheit* was published in 1811; Friederike died in 1813.

[50] For more detail see my next chapter, "Live and Learn: *Werther* and *Wilhelm Meister*."

[51] Cf. Goethe, *Elegie von Marienbad, Urschrift September 1823*, and the corresponding editio maior of the same date. A facsimile of Goethe's fair copy was edited by Bernhard Suphan as the annual gift to members of the Goethegesellschaft, Weimar, in 1900. Intriguingly, in 1980 the original document turned up in a Guernsey antiquarian bookseller's catalogue, a sign of British interest in Goethe in the nineteenth century. The seller and its previous provenance could not be traced. It was acquired by the Freies Deutsches Hochstift, Frankfurt am Main.

[52] In the original, "wie ich leide."

[53] "Noch ein Wort für junge Dichter" (HA 12:361).

[54] Goethe to Karl Friedrich Zelter, March 27, 1830, HAB 4:375. Cf. the poem "Geheimstes" (Most Secret) in the *West-Östlicher Divan*, HA 2:33, which satirizes biographical snoopers.

[55] Erich Trunz's commentary in HA 1:756. At most that could mean the poem has a power that allows—compels—us to enter fully into a devastating experience, but that is not what Trunz means.

[56] FA, 1:269. The same is implicit in the singular and plural noun of Wordsworth's claim to be "a man speaking to men." *Works*, ed. Gill, 603.

[57] "Bruchstücke einer großen Konfession." *Dichtung und Wahrheit*, Bk 7, HA 9:283.

[58] HA 9:7.

[59] They are well traced for the earliest years by Klaus Weimar, *Goethes Gedichte 1769–1775: Interpretationen zu einem Anfang*.

[60] *Dichtung und Wahrheit*, Bk 15, HA 10:48.

[61] "Jeder Geist hat seinen Klang." Nietzsche, *Zur Genealogie der Moral*, III, 8, KStA 5:353.

[62] For a full account, see Reed, "Was hat Marianne wirklich geschrieben? Skeptische Stimmen aus England."

[63] Schiller to Goethe, August 23, 1794, Brw Sch/G, 33.

[64] "Die lebendige Glut, die ich hatte, eh mir noch eine Regel bekannt war, vermisse ich schon seit mehreren Jahren. Ich *sehe* mich jetzt schaffen und bilden, ich beobachte das Spiel der Begeisterung, und meine Einbildungskraft beträgt sich mit minder Freiheit, seittdem sie sich nicht ohne Zeugen weiß." Schiller to Körner, May 25, 1792, Brw Sch/Kör 1:452.

[65] The English terms convey the point and power of Schiller's distinction, as the false friends "naïve" and "sentimental" do not.

[66] *Über naïve und sentimentalische Dichtung*, in Schiller, *Sämtliche Werke*, 5:711.

[67] Ibid, 5:735.

Chapter Seven

[1] See Kestner's report to Goethe of November 1772, HA 6:521–24.

[2] Goethe to Lavater, April 26, 1774, HA 6:525.

[3] Goethe to Kestner, November 21, 1774, HA 6:528. It isn't clear how far the pair did appreciate their literary status at the time. In Thomas Mann's comic novel *Lotte in Weimar* the long-widowed Charlotte, on a visit to the old poet in 1816, is all too coquettishly conscious of her place in literary history.

[4] Jürgen Stenzel reported the negative result of his researches in a letter to the *Frankfurter Allgemeine Zeitung* of December 27, 1995.

[5] Effi Biedrzynski, *Goethes Weimar*, 267.

[6] Goethe, *Dichtung und Wahrheit*, Bk 13, HA 9:588.

[7] Goethe, HA 9:585.

[8] Goethe to Karl Friedrich Zelter, December 3, 1812, HA 6:539.

[9] Goethe to Charlotte von Stein, June 25, 1786. *Briefe an Charlotte*, HA 6:530. He is working the same motif for pathetic effect in the late poem "An Werther."

[10] Goethe to Kestner, November 11 and 28, 1772, HA 6:518, 520. Cf. Heine, *Buch der Lieder*, "Die Heimkehr," lv: "Glaub nicht, dass ich mich erschieße, / Wie schlimm auch die Sachen stehn! / Das alles, meine Süße, /Ist mir schon einmal geschehn." (Don't imagine I'll be shooting myself, / Whatever fate has in store. / All this, my sweetie, / Has happened to me before.)

[11] Goethe, *Die Leiden des jungen Werthers.* Parallel texts, 268–87.

[12] Mann's marginal note to the *Werther* chapter of Albert Bielschowsky's Goethe biography 1:199. Thomas Mann Archive, Zurich.

[13] Max Herrmann in the Jubiläumsausgabe, 16: xxxviii; Morris, *Der junge Goethe*, 6:413.

[14] "Mein Tagebuch, das ich seit einiger Zeit vernachlässiget, fiel mir heut wieder in die Hände, und ich bin erstaunt, wie ich so wissentlich in das alles, Schritt vor Schritt, hineingegangen bin! Wie ich über meinen Zustand immer so klar gesehen und doch gehandelt habe wie ein Kind, jetzt noch so klar sehe, und es noch keinen Anschein zur Besserung hat." Letter of August 8, addition: Evening. Parallel texts 89, HA 6:44.

[15] Parallel texts 268; original unchanged in the 1787 version.

[16] ". . . wie ein Autor durch eine zweite, veränderte Ausgabe seiner Geschichte, und wenn sie poetisch noch so besser geworden wäre, notwendig seinem Buche schaden muss." Werther's letter of August 15, original unchanged in 1787. Parallel texts, 104–5, HA 6:51.

[17] "Das nunmehr fertige Manuskript lag im Konzept, mit wenigen Korrekturen und Abänderungen, vor mir." *Dichtung und Wahrheit*, Bk 13, HA 9:587.

[18] Goethe to Karl Ludwig von Knebel, November 21 1782, HAB 1:415. Goethe's friend Merck sardonically commented that the thing would only be "different, not better." *Dichtung und Wahrheit*, Bk 13, HA 9:572.

[19] Goethe to Knebel, same letter. Goethe worked partly by writing but mostly by dictating, to amanuenses, at this stage unnamed, also occasionally to Charlotte von Stein. Goethe would then work on the transcripts. Readings to and by friends generated welcome encouragement.

[20] In the last of the reviews in which Lessing had covered the two years of performances and sketched a poetics of drama. Gotthold Ephraim Lessing, *Hamburgische Dramaturgie*, 101st to 104th number, April 19, 1768. *Werke*, 4:698.

[21] Lessing, *Briefe die neueste Literatur betreffend*, number 17, February 16, 1759. *Werke*, 5:72.

[22] Schiller, *Was kann eine gute stehende Schaubühne eigentlich wirken?* 1784. *Werke*, 5:828–30. Earlier title, "On the effects of theater on the people"; later title, "The theater as a moral institution."

[23] Ibid.

[24] Karl Philipp Moritz, *Anton Reiser: Ein psychologischer Roman*, 1785/94.

[25] *Wilhelm Meisters theatralische Sendung*, bk 1, ch. 16, 43.

[26] Goethe to Johann Heinrich Merck, August 5, 1778. *Werke*, Weimarer Ausgabe IV:3, 328.

27 "The first page of his that I read made me his for life, and when I had finished the first play I stood there like a blind man instantaneously given sight by a miraculous hand. [. . .] And I cry: Nature! Nature! Nothing so nature as Shakespeare's characters." "On Shakespeare Day," HA 12:224–25.

28 *Werke*, Weimarer Ausgabe IV, 3:328.

29 Wilhelm Meisters *theatralische Sendung*, bk 6, ch.14, 416.

30 Goethe to Charlotte von Stein, June 24, 1782, *Briefe an Charlotte*, 1:338.

31 Narrated as Wilhelm's experience, it is "a devastating parody of the national cultural and artistic ideal at a provincial German court." Nicholas Boyle, *Goethe: The Poet and the Age*, 1:371.

32 Goethe to Charlotte von Stein, July 9, 1784, HAB 1:446.

33 Goethe to Schiller, August 27, 1794, *Brw Sch/G*, 38.

34 "am Stile gekünstelt, dass er recht natürlich werde." Goethe to Charlotte von Stein, June 14, 1784, *Briefe an Charlotte*, 2:69.

35 Goethe to Herder, May 1794, HAB 2:176.

36 I omit discussion of the Romantic/melodramatic plot elements—the figures of Mignon and the Old Harpist, and the "beautiful Amazon"—which are present in both versions.

37 "Wilhelm Schüler," Goethe to Schiller, December 6, 1794, *Brw Sch/G*, 72.

38 Goethe, *Tag- und Jahreshefte* (annals) for the years 1780–86, HA 10:432, The dating is also wrong: work on the *Apprenticeship* was not begun until 1790–91.

39 As first reported, with excerpts, by Gustav Billeter, *Goethes Wilhelm Meisters theatralische Sendung: Mitteilungen über die erste Fassung von Wilhelm Meisters Lehrjahren*. The text was published in full in the following year by Harry Maync. Erich Schmidt, discoverer of the Urfaust in similar circumstances, had acutely suspected that an *Urmeister* might somewhere be lurking.

40 Goethe to Schiller, June 18, 1795 *Brw Sch/G*, 115.

41 Schiller to Goethe, December 6, 1794, *Brw Sch/G*, 221.

42 As described much later in *Campagne in Frankreich* (1822) and *Belagerung von Mainz* (1820).

43 Goethe to Knebel, December 7, 1793, HAB 2:174.

44 Goethe, "Bedeutende Fördernis durch ein einziges geistreiches Wort," 1823, HA 13:39.

45 Goethe, *Literarischer Sansculottismus*, HA 12:239–44.

46 The authoritarian politician's view that "a people remains always childish" is put in the mouth of the Duke of Alba in Goethe's drama *Egmont* (HA 4:429). Giuliano Baioni acutely read *Wilhelm Meister's Apprenticeship* as "the end of the culture of the Enlightenment." *Goethe Jahrbuch* (1975): 110.

47 Schiller to the Prince of Schleswig-Holstein-Augustenburg, July 13, 1793, the second letter of the original drafts for the *Letters on the Aesthetic Education of Mankind*. In the final version of this passage, in Letter 5 of the full *Aesthetic*

Education, Schiller has thought better of using this reactionary term, even in a crisis, and has dropped it.

[48] *Unterhaltungen deutscher Ausgewanderten* (Conversations of German Exiles) are stories linked in a *Decameron*-like structure told by nobles—liberal or reactionary—who are fleeing before French advances into the Rhineland.

[49] In the hexameter idyll *Hermann und Dorothea*, Canto 6 and Canto 9, HA 2:485 and 514.

[50] Georg Christoph Lichtenberg, *Sudelbücher* 1, *Schriften und Briefe*, 1:899.

[51] Goethe, *Campagne in Frankreich*, HA 10:317.

[52] *Sämtliche Werke*, MA 4/1:192–203.

[53] "German national character," a text from the 1796 satirical collection, *Xenien*. HA 1:212.

[54] HA 7:290.

[55] Goethe's novel was not the first of the kind: Christoph Martin Wieland's *Agathon* (1766/67) and Karl Philipp Moritz's *Anton Reiser* (1785/94) already had a similar pattern. But Goethe's standing made his the most influential exemplar.

[56] "Diese Begierde, die Pyramide meines Daseyns, deren Basis mir angegeben und gegründet ist, so hoch als möglich in die Luft zu spizzen, überwiegt alles andre und lässt kaum Augenblickliches Vergessen zu." Goethe to Lavater, September 20, 1780. HAB 1:324.

[57] ". . . the novelist, who is only the poet's half-brother and still in such direct contact with the earth . . ." Schiller, *Über naïve und sentimentalische Dichtung*, Werke 5:741.

[58] Billeter, *Goethes Wilhelm Meisters theatralische Sendung*, 7. Continuation dots original—there was obviously more that Billeter could have said!

Chapter Eight

[1] Letter of April 6, 1833. All italics original. Büchner, *Sämtliche Werke*, ed. Henri and Rosemarie Poschmann 2:366.

[2] The title *Der hessische Landbote* was added by Weidig, who also made a lot of alterations that Büchner disapproved of.

[3] G. W. J. Wagner, *Allgemeine Statistik des Großherzogtums Hessen*, 1833. Extensive extracts are given in Gerhard Schaub's edition of *Der Hessische Landbote*, 164–75.

[4] Nicolas Chamfort's "Guerre aux palais! Paix aux chaumières!" had been taken up by the French Revolutionary armies.

[5] Both letters are dated February 21, 1835. Büchner, *Werke*, 2:391–93.

[6] Gutzkow was only two years older than Büchner, but already well known as a member of the liberal movement Young Germany. He would be banned by name along with Heine and other members of the group for subverting the social and

religious order in the Bundestag decree of December 10, 1835, repr. in Edda Ziegler, *Literarische Zensur*, 13–15.

[7] Gutzkow to Büchner, March 3, 1835, Büchner, *Werke*, 2:395.

[8] For a detailed account of the plots, plans, meetings, publications, arrests, interrogations, and much else in the prehistory to Büchner's flight, see Thomas Michael Mayer, "Georg Büchners Situation im Elternhaus und der Anlass seiner Flucht," *Georg Büchner Jahrbuch* 9 (1995–99): 33–92.

[9] This friendly bowdlerizer also deleted or altered an extraordinary quantity and range of innocent material. Büchner restored most of this by hand in copies of the published work he gave to two friends. The modern text is based on an original manuscript with many alterations and additions, held in the Weimar Goethe-Schiller Archive. It is almost certainly the only one Büchner had time to make.

[10] Büchner to his family, July 28, 1835. Büchner, *Werke*, 2:410. The rejection of Schiller is a cliché which overlooks the hard politics of the late plays, especially the *Wallenstein* trilogy and *Maria Stuart*.

[11] *Unsere Zeit, oder geschichtliche Uebersicht der merkwürdigsten Ereignisse von 1789–1830*, edited by a former officer of the French imperial army, Johann Conrad Friederich, in 120 issues/30 volumes, with supplements (Stuttgart: Wolters, 1826–30).

[12] Schon seit einigen Tagen nehme ich jeden Augenblick die Feder in die Hand, aber es war unmöglich, nur ein Wort zu schreiben. Ich studierte die Geschichte der Revolution. Ich fühlte mich wie zernichtet unter dem gräßlichen Fatalismus der Geschichte. Ich finde in der Menschennatur eine entsetzliche Gleichheit, in den menschlichen Verhältnissen eine unabwendbare Gewalt, Allen und Keinem verliehen. Der Einzelne nur Schaum auf der Welle, die Größe ein bloßer Zufall, die Herrschaft des Genies ein Puppenspiel, ein lächerliches Ringen gegen ein eisernes Gesetz, es zu erkennen das Höchste, es zu beherrschen unmöglich. Es fällt mir nicht mehr ein, vor den Paradegäulen und Eckstehern der Geschichte mich zu bücken. Ich gewöhnte mein Auge ans Blut. Aber ich bin kein Guilletinenmesser.Das *muß* ist eins von den Verdammungsworten, womit der Mensch getauft worden. Der Ausspruch: es muß ja Ärgernis kommen, aber wehe dem, durch den es kommt,—ist schauderhaft. Was ist das, was in uns lügt, mordet, stiehlt? Ich mag dem Gedanken nicht weiter nachgehen. To Minna, mid- or end of January 1834. *Werke*, 2:377. The bible reference is to Matt. 18:7.

[13] See for example Terence J. Holmes, "Georg Büchners 'Fatalismus' als Voraussetzung seiner Revolutionsstrategie," *Georg Büchner Jahrbuch* 6 (1986–87): 59–72.

[14] *Werke* 2:1057 notes the gap, but without emphasizing its genetic importance.

[15] These were meticulously established in Anna Jaspers's doctoral thesis, *Georg Büchners Trauerspiel "Dantons Tod."*

[16] Cf. Burghard Dedner, "*Dantons Tod*: Zur Rekonstruktion der Entstehung," 106–31.

[17] They make up some twenty percent of the text. Peter Becker's edition, *Dantons Tod: Die Trauerarbeit im Schönen* shows them up typographically. The greatest debts are to Thiers's history and *Our Time*.

[18] The historical Thomas Paine was a deist.

[19] Wilhelm Gottlieb Tennemann, *Geschichte der Philosophie*, 11 vols. (Leipzig: Barth, 1789–1819), itself no superficial survey.

[20] The philosophical texts receive detailed treatment for the first time in the Poschmanns' edition, Büchner, *Werke*, 2:924–1049.

[21] Simon Schama, *Citizens*, 818.

[22] An anonymous contemporary cartoon shows Robespierre executing the executioner, his final victim in a France completely depopulated by the guillotine. Reproduced in Schama, *Citizens*, 850.

[23] For a detailed account of Danton's (shared) responsibility for the massacre, see Schama, *Citizens*, 626–39.

[24] Published in serial form in *Phoenix* from January to April 1835, and in book form (400 copies) by Friedländer in mid-July.

[25] Lithographs of the specimens are reproduced in Büchner, *Werke*, 2:142.

[26] The subject of the lecture was the nerves of the skull, no doubt a deliberate echo of Oken's own Jena inaugural lecture, "On the Bones of the Skull."

[27] Büchner to his brother Wilhelm, September 2, 1836, Büchner, *Werke*, 2:448.

[28] Büchner to August Stöber, December 9, 1833, Büchner, *Werke*, 2:376.

[29] Büchner, letter of early June 1836, Büchner, *Werke*, 2:439.

[30] Gützkow, letter of June 10, 1836, Büchner, *Werke*, 2:441.

[31] Büchner to Minna Jaeglé, January 13, 1837, Büchner, *Werke*, 2:464.

[32] Büchner to Minna, January 20, 1837, Büchner, *Werke*, 2:466.

[33] Büchner to his family, September 1836, Büchner, *Werke*, 2:454.

[34] Büchner to Minna, Zurich, 1837? 2:461. Italics original in both cases.

[35] The possibilities, none of them promising, are reviewed in Jan-Christoph Hauschild, *Büchner: Eine Biographie*, 592.

[36] It is routinely held to be Büchner's last work, though Enrico de Angelis in his edition of *Woyzeck* argues it was begun at the same time as the *Hessian Messenger*.

[37] The initial document was the report by Dr. J. C. A. Clarus, published in 1824. It begins on a note of compassion, then recognizes the blessings of a shared religion and a mild government, before declaring the necessity of a strict and sacred law. Büchner, *Werke*, 2:938.

[38] "Man versuche es einmal und senke sich in das Leben der *Geringsten* und gebe es wieder, in den Zuckungen, den Andeutungen, dem ganzen feinen, kaum bemerkten Mienenspiel [. . .] Man muß die Menschheit lieben, um in das eigentümliche Wesen jedes einzudringen, es darf einem keiner zu gering, keiner zu häßlich sein, erst dann kann man sie verstehen." *Lenz*, Büchner, *Werke*, 1:234/35.

[39] "Der mitleidigste Mensch ist der beste Mensch." Gotthold Ephraim Lessing, *Briefwechsel über das Trauerspiel*, letter to Friedrich Nicolai, November 1756. Lessing, *Werke*, IV:163.

[40] "Mensch, sey natürlich, du bist geschaffe Staub, Sand, Dreck. Willst du mehr seyn als Staub, Sand, Dreck?" Büchner, *Werke*, 1:178.

[41] Büchner, *Werke*, 1:210.

[42] There are facsimile editions by Gerhard Schmid, 1981, and Enrico de Angelis, 2001.

[43] Burghard Dedner, *Woyzeck: Studienausgabe*, 205.

[44] It includes commemoration in Germany's highest literary award, the annual Georg Büchner Prize.

Chapter Nine

[1] This was Brecht's riposte when Thomas Mann remarked, to Therese Giehse apropos Brecht's *Mother Courage*, "The monster has talent." Wolfdietrich Rasch, *Zur deutschen Literatur seit der Jahrhundertwende*, 250.

[2] Samuel Fischer to TM, May 29, 1897. Samuel Fischer and Hedwig Fischer, *Briefwechsel mit Autoren*, 1:394.

[3] Charles Baudelaire, "Conseil aux jeunes littérateurs," copied into Mann's notebook 7. *Notizbücher*, 2:103.

[4] The same tree image for the growth of art out of old stock is put positively in Rilke's *Sonette an Orpheus*, 1: xvii: "Zuunterst der Alte . . ."

[5] To Otto Grautoff, August 20, 1897. TM *Briefe an Otto Grautoff*, 101. Grautoff was a school friend with whom Mann went on corresponding for several years. The manuscript of the letter breaks off after the key word, leaving it not further explained.

[6] TM, Notebook 2. *Notizbücher*, I: 92–95. The answers stand amid page after page of minute details, the tesserae that went into the novel's rich mosaic.

[7] TM to Heinrich Mann, March 27, 1901. *Thomas Mann–Heinrich Mann: Briefwechsel*, 24–25. Cited henceforth as *TM/HM*.

[8] Samuel Fischer to TM, March 23, 1901. Fischer, *Briefwechsel mit Autoren*, 1:399.

[9] TM to Richard Schaukal, April 30, 1905, *Briefe I: 1889–1913*, 320.

[10] TM to Heinrich Mann, February 18, 1905, *TM/HM* 57.

[11] TM to Heinrich Mann, December 5, 1905, *TM/HM* 66.

[12] TM to Heinrich Mann, June 11, 1906, *TM/HM* 80.

[13] The extensive notes for this never completed essay are printed in Scherrer and Wysling, *Quellenkritische Studien*, 122–233.

[14] The text also evokes already written or part-written works of Thomas Mann's own—*Buddenbrooks, Fiorenza, Felix Krull*—but without naming them by title.

[15] Thomas Mann, "A Sketch of My Life," GW, 11:124. The Polish boy has been plausibly identified as Wladimir Moes, who was eleven years old at the time.

[16] TM to Philipp Witkop, July 18, 1911, *Briefe, 1889–1936*, 90.

[17] TM to Ernst Bertram, October 16, 1911, *Thomas Mann an Ernst Bertram*, 10.

[18] TM to Heinrich Mann, April 27, 1912, *TM/HM* 121.

[19] *Der Tod in Venedig*, GKFA, 2.1:559. Italics added.

[20] Mann used Rudolf Kassner's versions of *Symposium* (1903) and *Phaidros* (1904), and the Kaltwasser translation of the *Erotikos*, reissued opportunely in 1911.

[21] See in full the commentary to *Frühe Erzählungen*, where the Arbeitsnotizen are printed complete (463–507).

[22] Whether or not composed on the beach, Mann's own short essay of the time, "Auseinandersetzung mit Wagner,'" GW, 10:840–42, was written on notepaper headed "Grand Hotel des Bains, Lido, Venise."

[23] TM to Carl Maria Weber, July 4, 1920, *Briefe 1, 1889–1936*, 177.

[24] In the letter to Carl Maria Weber Mann speaks of the story's "hymnic origin" and "hymnic core." "Origin" implies something that may meanwhile have been superseded, but "core" is something still deeply present.

[25] In the background is one of Thomas Mann's earliest and most persistent shaping influences, Nietzsche's *Birth of Tragedy from the Spirit of Music*, with its psychological and cultural dialectic of Apollo and Dionysos.

[26] "Und zurückgelehnt, mit hängenden Armen, überwältigt und mehrfach von Schauern überlaufen, flüsterte er die stehende Formel der Sehnsucht—unmöglich hier, absurd, verworfen, lächerlich und heilig doch, ehrwürdig auch hier noch: 'Ich liebe dich!'" (2.1:562).

[27] Arbeitsnotizen, 22 to 24, six-and-a-half printed pages in their published form.

[28] Arbeitsnotiz 4.

[29] *Symposium* starting at 210d, excerpted in worknote 16.

[30] *Gesang vom Kindchen*, GW, 8:1069.

[31] TM to Ernst Bertram, July 24, 1913, *Briefe an Bertram*, 18.

[32] TM to Oskar Schmitz, April 20, 1925, *Briefe III: 1924–1932*, 23/1:147.

[33] The others—"Gedanken im Kriege" of 1914, "Gedanken zum Kriege" of 1915—can be found in *Gesammelte Werke*, 13:1084.

[34] TM to Paul Amann, August 3, 1915, *Briefe an Paul Amann*, 29.

[35] TM to Paul Amann, March 25, 1917, *Briefe an Paul Amann*, 53.

[36] In an extraordinary mix, Naphta also has communist revolutionary ideas. He is said to have been based on Mann's meeting with the Hungarian Marxist Georg Lukács.

[37] Goethe, Bk 4 of *Dichtung und Wahrheit*, HA 9:141.

[38] Described in detail in TM, *Die Entstehung des Doktor Faustus—Roman eines Romans*, 1949, GW, 9.

[39] *Notizbuch 7*, page 155. *Notizbücher*, 2:121.

[40] Diary entry, February 11, 1934. *Tagebücher 1933–1934*, 321.

[41] It was sufficiently like Schoenberg's twelve-tone system to enrage its real deviser. See Mann's ironic-apologetic postscript to later editions of the novel.

[42] TM to Agnes Meyer, May 30, 1938, *Brw TM/Meyer*, 124. Mann has in mind the anti-analytical and "regenerative" impulses he shared with Aschenbach.

⁴³ I tried to capture their complex interrelation with a diagram in my *Thomas Mann: The Uses of Tradition*, 370.

⁴⁴ In *Die Betrogene* (*A Woman Deceived*, published in English as *The Black Swan*) the elderly Rosalie falls in love with a young man, her periods seem to be miraculously restored and she blossoms again, rejoicing in a mysterious boon of Mother Nature. But her bleeding comes from a fatal cancer of the womb.

⁴⁵ *Buch der Kindheit* was published in 1922 and again in 1937 with five more chapters for a book 2, ending with the scene in which Krull's virtuoso acting gets him out of military service. In a supreme bluff with the public, *Krull* was always Mann's favorite for public readings, teasing audiences who respected his high status with a work that undermined it.

⁴⁶ TM, Diary, November 25, 1950, *Tagebücher, 1949–1950*, 295.

⁴⁷ TM, July 11 and 16, 1950, *Tagebücher, 1949*–1950, 216, and 221.

⁴⁸ TM, August 28, 1950. *Tagebücher 1949–50*, 257.

⁴⁹ TM, August 6, 1950, *Tagebücher, 1949–50*, 239.

⁵⁰ The play of attraction and response with Franz Westermeier is recorded in detail in diary entries for early July 1950, just when work on *Felix Krull* was in progress.

⁵¹ einer allgemeinen Trauer um mein Leben und seine Liebe [. . .], dieser allem zum Grunde Liegenden, wahnhaften und doch leidenschaftlich behaupteten Enthusiasmus für den *unvergleichlichen, von nichts in der Welt übertroffenen* Reiz männlicher Jugend, die von jeher mein Glück und Elend [. . .], TM, August 6, 1950, *Tagebücher, 1949–50*, 238–39. Italics original.

⁵² TM, Diary, July 20, 1950, *Tagebücher, 1949–50*, 227. Cf. the essay of 1950 "Die Erotik Michelangelo's" [*apostrophe sic*], which ends with this quotation. GW 9:793.

⁵³ "Ich lebe in meiner sogenannten Verkehrtheit, in meines Lebens Liebe, die allem zum Grunde liegt was ich bin, in dem Glück und Elend dieses Enthusiasmus mit seinem teuren Schwur, dass nichts in dem ganzen Umkreis der Phänomene dem Reiz gleichkommt jugendlicher Früh-Männlichkeit." GW, 7:446.

⁵⁴ TM to Agnes Meyer, October 7, 1941, *Briefwechsel mit Agnes Meyer*, 322. Italics original.

⁵⁵ TM to Agnes Meyer, December 16, 1939, *Briefwechsel mit Agnes Meyer*, 187–88.

Chapter Ten

¹ Franz Kafka, *Brief an den Vater*, 160.

² A piece from Kafka's first published collection, *Betrachtung*; a slightly longer version in the diary for November 1911, *Tagebücher*, 249.

³ Kafka's fixed routine was 8 to 2 or 2:30, office; 3 to 3:30, lunch; sleep till 7.30; ten minutes' exercise; an hour's walk; evening meal with the family; then from 10.30 or 11.30, writing till 1, 2, or 3 o'clock, "once even 6 a.m." (as we are about to see). Letter of November 1, 1912 to Felice, *Briefe an Felice*, 67.

[4] Kafka, *Tagebücher*, August 21, 1913, 568.

[5] Kafka, *Briefe an Milena*, 235.

[6] Diese Geschichte "das Urteil" habe ich in der Nacht vom 22 zum 23 von 10 Uhr abends bis 6 Uhr früh in einem Zug geschrieben. Die vom Sitzen steif gewordenen Beine konnte ich kaum unter dem Schreibtisch hervorziehen. Die fürchterliche Anstrengung und Freude, wie sich die Geschichte vor mir entwickelte wie ich in einem Gewässer vorwärtskam. Mehrmals in dieser Nacht trug ich mein Gewicht auf dem Rücken. Wie alles gewagt werden kann, wie für alle, für die fremdesten Einfälle ein großes Feuer bereitet ist, in dem sie vergehn und auferstehn. Ein Wagen fuhr. Zwei Männer über die Brücke giengen. Um zwei Uhr schaute ich zum letztenmal auf die Uhr. Wie das Dienstmädchen zum ersten Mal durchs Vorzimmer gieng, schrieb ich den letzten Satz nieder. Auslöschen der Lampe und Tageshelle. Die leichten Herzschmerzen. Die in der Mitte der Nacht vergehende Müdigkeit. Das zitternde Eintreten ins Zimmer der Schwestern. Vorlesung. Vorher das Sichstrecken vor dem Dienstmädchen und Sagen: "Ich habe bis jetzt geschrieben." Das Aussehn des unberührten Bettes, als sei es jetzt hereingetragen worden. Die bestätigte Überzeugung, dass ich mit meinem Romanschreiben in schändlichen Niederungen des Schreibens befinde. Nur so kann geschrieben werden, nur in einem solchen Zusammenhang, mit solcher vollständigen Öffnung des Leibes und der Seele. Vormittag im Bett. Die immer klaren Augen. Viele während des Schreibens mitgeführte Gefühle: z. B. dass ich etwas Schönes für Maxens Arcadia haben werde, Gedanken an Freud natürlich[...] natürlich an meine "Die städtische Welt." FK, Diary entry for September 23, 1912, *Tagebücher*, 460. "My novel" was probably the not-preserved project "Richard und Samuel." *Arcadia* was a literary journal edited by Kafka's friend Max Brod. "The Urban World" was an early narrative fragment. See *Tagebücher*, 151.

[7] FK, September 25, 1912, *Tagebücher*, 463.

[8] FK, Letter to Felice, June 2, 1913, *Briefe an Felice*, 394.

[9] FK, February 11, 1913, *Tagebücher*, 491.

[10] In the manuscript, "-feld" is a correction to a heavily overwritten (?) "-berg."

[11] FK, letter of June 2, 1913, *Briefe an Felice*, 394.

[12] FK, August 14, 1913, *Tagebücher*, 574.

[13] FK to Felice, August 14, 1913, *Briefe an* Felice, 444.

[14] FK January 1912, *Tagebücher*, 341.

[15] FK, November 15, 1911, *Tagebücher*, 251.

[16] FK, *Brief an den Vater*, 163.

[17] E.g, "The Urban World," *Tagebücher*, 151–60, or the adventures of Ernst Liman in Constantinople, *Tagebücher*, 493–99.

[18] He announced the title in a letter to Felice of November 11, 1912, *Briefe an Felice*, 86. Max Brod published the novel posthumously as *Amerika*.

[19] Brod, *Franz Kafka: Eine Biographie*, 156.

[20] FK to Kurt Wolff, April 4, 1913. Kurt Wolff, *Briefwechsel eines Verlegers*, 29.

[21] FK, August 11, 1912, *Tagebücher*, 428.
[22] FK, *Tagebücher*, 413.
[23] Kurt Wolff, *Autoren / Bücher / Abenteuer*, 68.
[24] FK, *Tagebücher*, 226.
[25] FK, November 15, 1910, *Tagebücher*, 126.
[26] FK, August 21, 1914, *Tagebücher* 675.
[27] FK, June 1913, *Tagebücher*, 562.
[28] FK, March 13–14, *Tagebücher*, 1913, 336.
[29] FK, August 6, 1914, *Tagebücher*, 546.
[30] FK, 220, *Tagebücher*, 560, 568. This is just a selection. Cf. further the sketch of "a husband bored through by a stake thrown from an unknown direction"; the extended episode of an outing with friends who notice he has a sword stuck in his back; or the reflections on the "most productive" place to stab, below the chin, keeping the neck muscles taut. *Tagebücher*, 559, 719, 754. See also, in the late (undated) letter to Milena Jesenská, Kafka's description and drawing of an elaborate execution machine with which he has been "preoccupied." *Briefe an Milena*, 235.
[31] FK, July 1916, *Tagebücher*, 801.
[32] FK, *Tagebücher*, 835–36.
[33] The alternative translation of "Ungeheuer" is "enormous"; but it seems unlikely Kafka was talking simply about quantity.
[34] FK to Felice, November 24, 1912, *Briefe an Felice*, 117.
[35] FK to Kurt Wolff, August 19, 1916. Wolff, *Briefwechsel*, 39.
[36] Kafka's sadomasochistic motifs, including a plausible link to Leopold von Sacher-Masoch, have been traced, most systematically by Franz Kuna in his *Literature as Corrective Punishment*.
[37] "Merkwürdiger, geheimnisvoller, vielleicht gefährlicher, vielleicht erlösender Trost des Schreibens: das Hinausspringen aus der Totschlägerreihe Tat—Beobachtung, Tat—Beobachtung, indem eine höhere Art der Betrachtung geschaffen wird, eine höhere, keine schärfere, und je höher sie ist, je unerreichbarer von der 'Reihe' aus, desto unabhängiger wird sie, desto mehr eigenen Gesetzen folgend, desto unberechenbarer, freudiger, steigender ihr Weg." FK, January 1922, *Tagebücher*, 892.
[38] FK, September 1917, 838.
[39] Johannes Urzidil, *Da geht Kafka*, 12.
[40] Wolff to Kafka, April 2, 1913. Wolff, *Briefwechsel*, 29.
[41] FK, "Ein Landarzt," in *Die Erzählungen*, 131.
[42] FK, December 5, 1914, *Tagebücher*, 704.
[43] FK, *Brief an den Vater*, 160.
[44] FK to Felice, November 17, 1912, *Briefe an Felice*, 102.
[45] FK to Felice, November 25, 1912, Briefe an Felice, 125.

[46] FK, November 30, 1914, *Tagebücher*, 702.

[47] FK, October 1917, *Tagebücher*, 841.

[48] See Malcolm Pasley, "Kafka's *Der Process*: What the Manuscript Can Tell Us," 113.

[49] Brod printed "uncompleted chapters" in an appendix. On the fate of Kafka's manuscripts generally, see the appendix to the present chapter.

[50] Letter of January 4, 1918. *Max Brod, Kafka: Eine Freundschaft*, 219. The legend of the doorkeeper was for Kafka the one successful element in the final vain laborious phase.

[51] Respectively "Josefine die Sängerin oder das Volk der Mäuse"; "Der Bau"; "Erstes Leid"; and "Ein Hungerkünstler."

[52] There is an even more flat contradiction between status and (in-)ability in a fragment of 1922 about an Olympic swimming champion who confesses at the public celebration of his triumph that he can't swim. Pasley, *Die Schrift ist unveränderlich* 171.

[53] Cf. beetle-Gregor hearing the music of his sister's violin: "It was as if he was being shown the way to the longed-for unknown food," and a diary entry of February 1922: ". . . attacked by supremely powerful enemies from right and left I can't escape from right or left, the way leads only forward, hungry animal, to eatable food, breathable air, a free life, even if beyond life." *Tagebücher*, 903.

[54] Among them Thomas Mann, Rilke, and Gottfried Benn. See Reed, "Nietzsche's Animals: Idea, Image and Influence," 159–219.

[55] Gustav Janouch, *Gespräche mit Kafka*, 49. Kafka later made Janouch a present of the Insel volume of Arthur Schopenhauer's sayings *Über Schriftstellerei und Stil*.

[56] Arthur Schopenhauer, *Nachträge [zum] Leiden der Welt*, in *Sämtliche Werke* 6:321. The last phrase is in English in the original.

[57] Schopenhauer, *Die Welt als Wille und Vorstellung*, book 2, §18, SW 2:118. The last detail matches K's claim to be a surveyor. Numerous real buildings have been proposed as the model for Kafka's *Castle*. More fully on the Schopenhauer contact, see Reed, "Kafka und Schopenhauer: Philosophisches Denken und dichterisches Bild."

[58] See Pasley, "Kafkas halbprivate Spielereien," in *Die Schrift ist unveränderlich*, 61–84.

[59] Pasley, "Kafka's *Der Process*," 116.

[60] Quoted by Kurt Wolff, *Autoren / Bücher / Abenteuer*, 74.

[61] W. W. Greg, "Rationale of Copy-Text," 21. Spelling is by no means "accidental" either, but at very least atmospheric: when Milton spells landscape "lantskip," we are reading as with seventeenth-century eyes; and when Jane Austen spells "freind," "greif" or "beleive," we are following the pen in the parlour down to the finest detail.

[62] See the comparisons of manuscript with early published text by Pasley, "Zu Kafkas Interpunktion," in Pasley, *Die Schrift ist unveränderlich*, 121–44.

⁶³ Pasley, *Die Schrift ist unveränderlich*, 125.

⁶⁴ A contrasting example of short, firmly end-stopped sentences—stop-start parataxis—would be Hemingway's style, which aims at an abrupt, hard-bitten feel.

⁶⁵ For a full account of this final phase and the critical editions that have been based on the manuscripts, see the appendix to this chapter.

⁶⁶ Once in conversation, as reported by Brod in *Die Weltbühne*, July 1924, and twice in written form, on a slip found in Kafka's desk after his death, and in a never-sent letter of November (?) 29, 1922.

⁶⁷ In a 1970 Fischer Verlag paperback edition of Kafka, *Erzählungen*, 390.

⁶⁸ Quoted by Kurt Wolff, *Autoren / Bücher / Abenteuer*, 74.

⁶⁹ Edmund Wilson, "A Dissenting Opinion on Kafka," 97, 91.

⁷⁰ FK, October 1920, *Tagebücher*, 865.

⁷¹ Intriguingly, Kafka began writing *The Castle* in the first person—"Es war spätabends, als ich ankam"—then, from page 25 recto of the manuscript, shifted to "K" as the subject, and corrected all preceding pages back to the opening, "Es war spätabends, als K. ankam." Paradoxically, as my colleague Dirk Meyer pointed out, the change actually strengthens the link between character and author: first person narratives are ten-a-penny, but there is only one K.

⁷² FK, February 15, 1920, *Tagebücher*, 855.

⁷³ October 11, 1916, Wolff, *Briefe*, 41.

⁷⁴ The bracketed numbers in this paragraph are for individual notes in the text Brod published as "Reflections on Sin, Suffering, Hope and the True Way."

⁷⁵ The concept of the Indestructible is probably derived from Schopenhauer's central thesis of an indestructible life force, the Will, as the underlying reality of which all beings are objectifications. As in his response to Nietzsche's ideas, Kafka gives the arch-pessimist's negative vision a contrary positive direction.

⁷⁶ Roland Reuss in the introductory volume of the *Historisch-kritische Ausgabe sämtlicher Handschriften, Drucke und Typoskripte Franz Kafkas*, 16. The same issues arose over the same group's earlier Hölderlin edition.

⁷⁷ Ibid.

Chapter Eleven

¹ Karl Marx, *Kritik der Hegel'schen Rechtsphilosophie*, in *Frühschriften*, 208.

² See Reed, "Umkehrungen: Astronomie als Modell für die Aufklärung."

³ Bertolt Brecht, *Werke*, 4:382 and 537.

⁴ The twin plays *Der Jasager* and its revision *Der Neinsager* (The Yea-sayer and the Nay-sayer).

⁵ Werner Hecht, ed., *Materialien zu Brechts "Leben des Galilei,"* 139.

⁶ "Epic theater" hardly conveys his intention, which was to prevent the "culinary" enjoyment of theater and make the audience stand back and coolly analyze the politics of a dramatic situation. It has nothing to do with a historical sweep of the

kind Thomas Hardy attempted in *The Dynasts*, the grand panorama of the Napoleonic Wars, which in his foreword he called "epic-drama."

[7] Hecht, *Materialien zu Galilei*, 139.

[8] This in an early fragment, *Werke*, 5:110–12.

[9] Brecht, *Mother Courage*, scene 2, in *Werke*, 6:23.

[10] Brecht, *Werke*, 5:179.

[11] See Stephen Parker, *Bertolt Brecht*, ch. 20.

[12] Brecht as author and director continually adjusted his texts, so the notion of final versions is too neat; many alternative drafts exist. See Tom Kuhn; "The Politics of the Changeable Text," 132–49; and *Brecht and the Writer's Workshop: Fatzer and Other Dramatic Projects*, ed. Tom Kuhn and Charlotte Ryland. The three versions I quote are the ones printed in the Berlin edition.

[13] Goethe in his history of color theory, HA 14:98.

[14] Brecht, *Werke*, 5:99.

[15] Brecht, *Werke*, 5:102.

[16] Brecht, *Werke*, 5:95.

[17] Brecht, *Werke*, 5:103.

[18] Brecht, *Werke* 5:104.

[19] Brecht, *Werke* 5:106.

[20] The published text credits Laughton with the adaptation. Laughton knew no German but did work closely with Brecht on building the role. (The tapes are preserved on which he sent Brecht his comments from Britain.) Other translations exist, but the partnership of the two non-linguists may explain the occasional stylistic awkwardness in this one.

[21] Brecht, *Werke*, 5:178 and 180.

[22] Hecht, *Materialien*, 37.

[23] Brecht, *Werke*, 5:180.

[24] "Ungeschminktes Bild einer neuen Zeit," introduction to the American version, in Hecht, *Materialien*, 10.

[25] "Preis oder Verdammung des Galilei?" in Hecht, *Materialien*, 12.

[26] "Notaten zu einzelnen Szenen," in Hecht, *Materialien*, 51.

[27] Probably closely related to a German version premiered in Zurich in 1943.

[28] Brecht, "Bedrohung der Menschheit durch Erfindungen" (Hecht's title) in Hecht, *Materialien*, 24. Brecht had approached this idea as early as 1939 in an essay "Über experimentelles Theater," which shows some enthusiasm for scientific advances, specifically the recent splitting of the atom by German scientists as described in a radio interview by Niels Bohr. But already there is a premonition of the things that might follow. *Werke*, 22/1:549.

[29] Heinar Kipphardt, *In der Sache J. Robert Oppenheimer*.

[30] See Manfred Wekwerth, *Schriften: Arbeit mit Brecht*, 219–21.

[31] "Post-Postcript," in *Plays*, 4:153. For an illuminating account of German physicists in the Nazi period, their traditional apolitical attitudes, responses to Nazism, ambitions, and moral failures, see Philip Ball, *Serving the Reich: The Struggle for the Soul of Physics under Hitler*.

[32] All quotations from Brecht's sketches begin at *Werke*, 10/2:985.

[33] Quoted in *Werke*, 10/2:1294–95.

Chapter Twelve

[1] Peter Szondi, *Celan-Studien*, 116–22.

[2] "Geh aber nun und grüße / Die schöne Garonne." Hölderlin, "Andenken."

[3] Herbert Göpfert, the distinguished editor of Schiller and Lessing, at an IVG Congress in Göttingen in 1985.

[4] Szondi, "Eden." *Celan-Studien*, 123. It should be noted that Szondi's essay was left unfinished at his death.

[5] Celan, *Werke: Historisch-kritische Ausgabe*, 10/2:60.

[6] The syntactically unnecessary "Du" (it is sometimes left out when the poem is quoted, e.g., by Hans Georg Gadamer in *Wer bin Ich und wer bist Du?* 127) makes the command more emphatic. Hence the insertion of "just you" before the imperative "go" in my rough version.

[7] "Stocken" is a halting or interrupted movement—the heart missing a beat, or traffic in a motorway tailback. Celan had quoted this passage from *Danton's Death* in his acceptance speech for the Büchner prize. Celan, *Der Meridian*, 42.

[8] Hans-Georg Gadamer, "Wer bin ich . . .," 7.

[9] Peter Szondi, "Eden," *Celan-Studien*, 47.

[10] John Felstiner, *Paul Celan: Poet, Survivor, Jew*, 230.

[11] See Peter Horst Neumann, "Was muss ich wissen, um zu verstehen?," on the poem "Die Schleuse," inspired by a visit of Celan's to Nelly Sachs in Stockholm.

[12] See above, chapter 6, "Occasions: Goethe's Lyric Poetry."

[13] "Wenn einem Autor ein Lexikon nachkommen kann, so taugt er nichts." Goethe, *Maximen und Reflexionen*, 916, HA 12:495.

[14] Hugo Friedrich, *Struktur der modernen Lyrik*, 83.

[15] Friedrich, *Struktur der modernen Lyrik*, 152.

[16] Hans Robert Jauss, in *Zur Lyrik-Diskussion*, Wege der Forschung (Darmstadt: Wissenschaftliche Buchgesellschaft, 1966), 365.

[17] Benn, "Probleme der Lyrik," 1:500.

[18] E.g., Peter Michelsen on Celan's poem "Fadensonnen," in *Gedichte und Interpretationen 6, Gegenwart*, 124. Any effect of imprecision is put down, typically, to "the inattention [*Flüchtigkeit*] of readers," an all too easy let-out.

[19] Bernhard Böschenstein, "Die notwendige Unauflöslichkeit: Reflexionen über die Dunkelheit in der deutschen und französischen Dichtung von Hölderlin bis Celan," 329–44.

20 "Dear simplicity, how I love you." Malcolm Bowie, *Mallarmé and the Art of Being Difficult*.

21 ". . . unter dem besonderen Neigungswinkel seines Daseins." Celan, *Der Meridian und andere Prosa*, 55.

22 Israel Chalfen, *Paul Celan: Eine Biographie seiner Jugend*, 7.

23 Quoted in Wolfgang Emmerich, *Paul Celan*, 11.

24 "Ne nous reprochez pas le manque de clarté, puisque nous en faisons profession." *Der Meridian*, 51. It is one of Pascal's *Pensées* (fragment 435 from the section "Foundations of Religion, and Answer to the Objections"). Celan had it from the Russian thinker Lev Shestov.

25 "ein ansprechbares Du vielleicht." Celan, *Der Meridian*, 38. For a programmatic self-description, see Celan's letter of November 22, 1958, to Gottfried Bermann Fischer, in Gottfried Bermann Fischer and Brigitte Bermann Fischer, *Briefwechsel mit Autoren*, 2:617.

26 Bremen acceptance speech, *Der Meridian*, 39. The metaphor was borrowed from Osip Mandelstam, whom Celan admired and translated.

27 Celan, "Vortragsprojekt "Von der Dunkelheit des Dichterischen," 131–52.

28 Celan, letter of August 2, 1948, quoted in Felstiner, *Paul Celan: Poet, Survivor, Jew*, 57.

29 Its first published form, in Romanian translation, bore the title "Death Tango," which is truer to the poem's dominant rhythms.

30 As in a notable scene in Stephen Spielberg's film *Schindler's List / Schindler's Ark*.

31 Reiner Kunze, *die stunde mit dir selbst*, 21.

32 Lorenz Jäger, *Frankfurter Allgemeine Zeitung*, June 25, 2003.

33 For a fair overview of this controversy, see Wolfgang Emmerich, "Paul Celans Weg vom 'schönen Gedicht' zur 'graueren Sprache,'" 359–84.

34 Adorno, "Prismen ohne Leitbild," *Schriften*, 10/1: 217.

35 Celan, letter of February 8, 1962, quoted in Felstiner, *Paul Celan: Poet, Survivor, Jew*, 191.

36 Reply to a survey of the Paris Librairie Flinker. In *Der Meridian und andere Prosa*, 21.

37 Felstiner, *Paul Celan: Poet, Survivor, Jew*, 191. Italics added.

38 This applies even more to the attempt to read Celan's poems as politically committed, clear though his left-wing sympathies were. Cf. Marlies Janz, *Vom Engagement absoluter Poesie*.

39 Celan nowhere uses the words "Holocaust" or "Shoah" but only ever refers to "the thing that happened" (das Geschehene). He is at his most explicit as translator (so, not author) of the text accompanying Alain Resnais's film about the death camps, *Night and Fog*, of 1956.

40 Ruven Karr, "Die Gaskammer in Paul Celans Dichtung," 42.

[41] The term, first used by Götz Wienold, is discussed by Jerry Glenn, *Paul Celan*, 25.

[42] Felstiner, for example, whose commentary-cum-translations in *Selected Poems and Prose of Paul Celan* throw much light, while inevitably often remaining more speculative than definitive.

[43] ". . . das Wort faszinierend ansetzen, das können Sie, oder das können Sie nicht." Benn, *Probleme der Lyrik*, 510.

[44] Quoted in Thomas C. Connolly, *Paul Celan's Unfinished Poetics*, 86.

[45] Celan, Bremen acceptance speech, *Der Meridian und andere Prosa*, 38.

[46] ". . . though the rhythms might later compact or rupture, his words grow strange or few, [he] kept up the struggle with language that makes him Europe's leading postwar poet." Felstiner, *Paul Celan: Poet, Survivor, Jew*, xxii.

Chapter Thirteen

[1] Wolf, *Was bleibt*, 1990.

[2] See the Nachwort to *Was bleibt*, in Christa Wolf, *Werke*, ed. Sonja Hilzinger, 10:320–22, and in more detail Carsten Gansel, "Erinnerung, Aufstörung und 'blinde Flecken,'" 27–38. Both draw on manuscripts held in the Archive of the Berlin Akademie der Künste.

[3] Documented in Thomas Anz, ed., *"Es geht nicht um Christa Wolf."* Anz reprints the most important contributions to the controversy and provides an annotated list of many others. Anz's title is apt.

[4] Volker Hage, "Kunstvolle Prosa." In Anz, *"Es geht nicht um Christa Wolf,"* 71–76.

[5] Ulrich Greiner, "Mangel an Feingefühl," in Anz, *"Es geht nicht um Christa Wolf,"* 66, 69.

[6] Greiner, in a further untitled contribution in Anz, *"Es geht nicht um Christa Wolf,"* 245.

[7] Reinhart Baumgart, "Der neudeutsche Literaturstreit," 73. It was indeed not easy to place one's own "carefully considered analyses" in the publications of a Germany that wanted to keep the matter to itself.

[8] Greiner, "Die deutsche Gesinnungsästhetik," in Anz, *"Es geht nicht um Christa Wolf,"* 208.

[9] Bertolt Brecht, "Der Radwechsel," tellingly, the first of the *Buckower Elegien*. Brecht, *Werke*, 4:1009.

[10] Frank Schirrmacher, "Dem Druck des härteren, strengeren Lebens standhalten," June 2, 1990. Anz, *"Es geht nicht um Christa Wolf,"* 77–89.

[11] Bohrer, "Kulturschutzgebiet DDR?," *Merkur* 500, November 1990.

[12] As a striking illustration, Inga Markovitz's *Die Abwicklung* describes the Western takeover of the law courts in two contrasted administrative regions, Berlin and Brandenburg. One made a clean sweep of GDR personnel and practice; the other made beneficial use of local officials and experience.

¹³ Greiner, "Die deutsche Gesinnungsästhetik," in Anz, *"Es geht nicht um Christa Wolf,"* 208–16.

¹⁴ Max Weber, "Der Beruf zur Politik," 174–75.

¹⁵ Wolf, *Werke*, 10:302.

¹⁶ "Wer zu spät kommt, den bestraft das Leben" was Gorbachev's warning to the GDR gerontocracy on the occasion of the country's fortieth anniversary celebration on October 7, 1989, just a month and two days before the wall fell.

¹⁷ For an absorbing account of the way *Ostpolitik* developed, not just as the work of West German chancellor Willy Brandt but eventually as a cross-party policy, see Timothy Garton Ash, *In Europe's Name*.

¹⁸ There had always been a ministry responsible, under a succession of titles, for German-German matters, but it had made no plans for the event of reunification.

¹⁹ On this abrupt "double-reverse," see Garton Ash, *In Europe's Name*, 214.

Afterword

¹ "Natur- und Kunstwerke lernt man nicht kennen, wenn sie fertig sind, man muss sie im Entstehen aufhaschen, um sie einigermaßen zu begreifen." Goethe to Zelter, August 4, 1803, HAB 2:454.

² Rousseau, Preface to *La nouvelle Héloise*.

³ Nietzsche, *Zur Genealogie der Moral*, III, §4, KStA 5:341. He does, however, concede that the artist is the necessary "womb and fertile soil" (Mutterschoß und Nährboden) out of which art grows.

⁴ "Man ahndet im Dunkeln die Entstehung und das Leben dieser seltsamen Gestalten. Es mag geschehen seyn wie und wann es wolle, so haben sich diese Massen nach der Schweere und Aehnlichkeit ihrer Theile gros und einfach zusammengesetzt. Was für Revolutionen sie nachhero bewegt, getrennt, gespalten haben, so sind auch diese auch nur einzelne Erschütterungen gewesen und selbst der Gedanke einer so ungeheuren Bewegung giebt ein höhes Gefühl von ewiger Festigkeit. Die Zeit hat auch gebunden an die ewige Geseze, bald mehr, bald weniger auf sie gewirkt. [. . .] Man fühlt tief, hier ist nichts willkürliches, alles langsam bewegendes ewiges Gesez [. . .]" Goethe to Charlotte von Stein, October 3, 1779, *Briefe an Charlotte*, 1:121–22.

Bibliography

Abbreviations used for Goethe editions and correspondence (full details below):

Brw Sch/G   Correspondence Schiller–Goethe
Brw Sch/Kör   Correspondence Schiller–Körner
FA   Frankfurter Ausgabe
HA   Hamburger Ausgabe
HAB   Hamburger Ausgabe Briefe (letters)
MA   Münchener Ausgabe

Adorno, Theodor W. "Prismen ohne Leitbild." In *Kulturkritik und Gesellschaft* 1, in *Gesammelte Schriften*, 10./1:, 11–30. Frankfurt am Main: Suhrkamp, 1977.
Aeschylus. *Oresteia*: *Choephoroi*.
Alter, Robert. *The Art of Biblical Narrative*. New York: Basic Books, 2011.
———. *The Art of Biblical Poetry*. New York: Basic Books, 1985.
Alter, Robert, and Frank Kermode, eds. *The Literary Guide to the Bible*. Cambridge, MA: Belknap/Harvard University Press, 1999.
Anz, Thomas, ed. *"Es geht nicht um Christa Wolf": Der Literaturstreit im vereinten Deutschland*. Munich: Spangenberg, 1991.
Atwood, Margaret. *The Penelopiad*. New York: Grove, 2005.
Auerbach, Erich. "Figura." In *Scenes from the Drama of European Literature*. Manchester: Manchester University Press, 1959.
———. *Mimesis: Dargestellte Wirklichkeit in der abendländischen Literatur*. Bern: Francke, 1946.
Avi-Yonah, Michael. *Ancient Scrolls*. London: Cassell, 1973.
Baioni, Giuliano. "Zur gesellschaftlichen Idee der deutschen Klassik." *Goethe Jahrbuch* (1975): 73–127.
Bakewell, Sarah. *How to Live: A Life of Montaigne in One Question and Twenty Answers*. London: Vintage, 2011.
Ball, Philip. *Serving the Reich: The Struggle for the Soul of Physics under Hitler*. London: Vintage, 2013.
Balzac, Honoré de. *Oeuvres complètes*. Paris: Pléiade, 1977.
Barker, Pat. *The Silence of the Girls*. London: Penguin, 2018.
Barthes, Roland. "The Death of the Author." Repr. in Lodge, *Modern Criticism and Theory*, 311–16.
Barton, John, ed. *The Hebrew Bible: A Critical Companion*. Princeton, NJ: Princeton University Press, 2016.

———. *A History of the Bible*. London: Allen Lane, 2019.
———. "Reading the Bible." *London Review of Books*, May 5, 1988.
Bate, Jonathan. *The Genius of Shakespeare*. London: Picador, 1997.
———. *Soul of the Age: The Life, Mind and World of William Shakespeare*. London: Penguin, 2008.
Baumgart, Reinhart. "Der neudeutsche Literaturstreit." In *Vom gegenwärtigen Zustand der deutschen Literatur*. Text + Kritik 113 (1992): 63–71.
Beauvoir, Simone de. *The Second Sex*. London: Everyman, 1993.
Benn, Gottfried. "Probleme der Lyrik." In *Gesammelte Werke* 1:494–532. Wiesbaden: Limes, 1965.
Beutler, Ernst. "Die Kindsmörderin." In *Essays um Goethe*, 87–101. Bremen: Schünemann, 1957.
———. "Lili—Wiederholte Spiegelungen." In *Essays um Goethe*, 191–331. Bremen: Schünemann, 1957.
Biedrzynski, Effi. *Goethes Weimar: Lexikon der Personen und Schauplätze*. Zurich: Artemis, 1992.
Bielschowsky, Albert. *Goethe: Sein Leben und seine Werke*. 2 vols. Munich: Beck, 1905.
Billeter, Gustav. *Goethes Wilhelm Meisters theatralische Sendung: Mitteilungen über die erste Fassung von Wilhelm Meisters Lehrjahren*. Zurich: Rascher, 1910.
Bindoff, S. T. *Tudor England*. London: Pelican, 1950.
Bohrer, Karl Heinz. "Kulturschutzgebiet DDR?" *Merkur* 500, November 1990.
Böschenstein, Bernhard. "Die notwendige Unauflöslichkeit: Reflexionen ueber die Dunkelheit in der deutschen und französischen Dichtung von Hölderlin bis Celan." *Zeitwende* 46 (1975): 329–44.
Bowie, Malcolm. *Mallarmé and the Art of Being Difficult*. Oxford: Legenda, 1978.
Bowra, Maurice. *Homer*. London: Duckworth, 1972.
Boyd, James. *Goethe's Knowledge of English Literature*. Oxford: Oxford University Press, 1932.
Boyle, Nicholas. *Goethe: The Poet and the Age*, vol. 1. Oxford: Oxford University Press, 1991.
Brecht, Bertolt. *Werke: Große Berliner Ausgabe*. 31 vols. Berlin: Aufbau, 1988–2000.
Brigden, Susan. *New Worlds, Lost Worlds: The Rule of the Tudors, 1485–1603*. London: Allen Lane, 2001.
Brod, Max. *Franz Kafka: eine Biographie*. Frankfurt am Main: Fischer, 1954.
Büchner, Georg. *Dantons Tod: Die Trauerarbeit im Schönen*. Edited by Peter Becker. Frankfurt am Main: Syndikat, 1980.
———. *Der hessische Landbote*. Edited by Gerhard Schaub. Munich: Hanser, 1976.
———. *Sämtliche Werke*. Edited by Henri and Rosemarie Poschmann. Frankfurt am Main: Deutscher Klassiker Verlag, 1999.

———. *Woyzeck: Faksimile-Transkription*. Edited by Gerhard Schmid. Wiesbaden: Reichert, 1981.

———. *Woyzeck: Faksimile, Transkription, Emendation und Lesetext*. Edited by Enrico de Angelis. Munich: Saur, 2001.

———. *Woyzeck: Studienausgabe*. Edited by Burghard Dedner. Stuttgart: Reclam, 1999.

Bülow, Ulrich von. *Papierarbeiter: Autoren und ihre Archive*. Göttingen: Wallstein, 2018.

Burrow, John. *A History of Histories: Epics, Chronicles, Romances and Inquiries from Herodotus and Thucydides to the Twentieth Century*. London: Penguin, 2007.

Butler, Samuel. *The Authoress of the Odyssey*. New York: Longmans, Green, 1897.

Campbell, D. A., ed. *Greek Lyric*, vol. 1. Loeb Classical Library. Cambridge, MA: Harvard University Press, 1990.

Casablanca. Dir. Michael Curtiz (1942).

Cave, Terence. *How to Read Montaigne*. London: Granta, 2007.

Celan, Paul. *Der Meridian und andere Prosa*. Frankfurt am Main: Suhrkamp, 1988.

———. "Vortragsprojekt 'Von der Dunkelheit des Dichterischen.'" In Celan, *"Mikrolithen sind's, Steinchen": Die Prosa aus dem Nachlaß*, edited by Barbara Wiedemann and Bertrand Badiou, 131–52. Frankfurt am Main: Suhrkamp, 2005.

———. *Werke: Historisch-kritische Ausgabe*. 16 vols. Frankfurt am Main: Suhrkamp, 1999.

Chalfen, Israel. *Paul Celan: Eine Biographie seiner Jugend*. Frankfurt am Main: Insel, 1979.

Chambers, E. K. *William Shakespeare: Facts and Problems*. 2 vols. Oxford: Oxford University Press, 1930.

Connolly, Thomas C. *Paul Celan's Unfinished Poetics*. Cambridge: Legenda, 2018.

Cunningham, Valentine. *Reading after Theory*. Oxford: Blackwell, 2002.

Damrosch, David. "Leviticus." In Alter and Kermode, *Literary Guide to the Bible*, 66–77.

Danniell, David. *William Tyndale: A Biography*. New Haven, CT: Yale University Press, 1994.

de Hamel, Christopher. *The Book: A History of the Bible*. London: Phaidon, 2014.

de Man, Paul. *The Resistance to Theory*. Manchester: Manchester University Press, 1986.

Dedner, Burghard. "*Dantons Tod*: Zur Rekonstruktion der Entstehung anhand der Quellenverarbeitung." *Georg Büchner Jahrbuch* 6 (1986): 106–31.

Derrida, Jacques. *Writing and Difference*. London: Routledge, 1976.

Desan, Philippe, ed. *Dictionnaire Michel de Montaigne*. Paris: Champion, 2007.

———. *Montaigne: A Life*. Princeton, NJ: Princeton University Press, 2017.
Dodd, William. *The Beauties of Shakespeare, regularly selected from each play*. London, 1752.
Edgar, David. "Whose Bible Is It Anyway?" *Guardian*, February 19, 2011.
Edwards, Philip. *Shakespeare: A Writer's Progress*. Oxford: Oxford University Press, 1986.
Eibl, Karl. *Goethe: Gedichte in Handschriften*. Frankfurt am Main: Insel, 1999.
Eliot, T. S. "Religion and Literature." In *Selected Essays*, 388–401. London: Faber, 1958.
Emmerich, Wolfgang. *Paul Celan*. Hamburg: Rowohlt, 1999.
———. "Paul Celans Weg vom 'schönen Gedicht' zur 'graueren Sprache': Die windschiefe Rezeption der 'Todesfuge' und ihre Folgen." In *Jüdische Autoren Ostmitteleuropas im 20. Jahrhundert*, edited by Hans-Henning Hahn and Jens Stüben, 359–84. New York: Lang, 2000.
Fagles, Robert, trans. Homer, *The Iliad / The Odyssey*. London: Penguin, 1998.
Felski, Rita. *The Limits of Critique*. Chicago: University of Chicago Press, 2017.
Felstiner, John. *Paul Celan: Poet, Survivor, Jew*. New Haven, CT: Yale University Press, 1995.
———, ed. *Selected Poems and Prose of Paul Celan*. New York: Norton, 2001.
Finnegan, Ruth. *Oral Poetry*. Cambridge: Cambridge University Press, 1977.
Fisch, Harold. *Poetry with a Purpose*. Bloomington: Indiana University Press, 1988.
Fischer, Gottfried Bermann, and Brigitte Bermann Fischer. *Briefwechsel mit Autoren*. 2 vols. Edited by Reiner Stach with an introduction by Bernhard Zeller. Frankfurt am Main: Fischer, 1989–1990.
Fokkelman, J. P. "Exodus." In Alter and Kermode, *Literary Guide to the Bible*, 56–65.
———. "Genesis." In Alter and Kermode, *Literary Guide to the Bible*, 36–55.
Foucault, Michel. "What Is an Author?" Repr. in Lodge, *Modern Criticism and Theory*, 281–93.
Frame, Donald. *Montaigne: A Biography*. New York: Harcourt Brace, 1965.
Frayn, Michael. *Copenhagen*. "Post-Postcript." In *Plays*, 4:140–225. London: Methuen, 2010.
Friederich, Johann Conrad, ed. *Unsere Zeit, oder geschichtliche Uebersicht der merkwürdigsten Ereignisse von 1789–1830*. Stuttgart: Wolters, 1826–30.
Friedrich, Hugo. *Struktur der modernen Lyrik*. Hamburg: Rowohlt, 1956.
Gadamer, Hans Georg. *Wer bin Ich und wer bist Du?* Frankfurt am Main: Suhrkamp, 1973.
Gansel, Carsten. "Erinnerung, Aufstörung und 'blinde Flecken' im Werk von Christa Wolf." In *Christa Wolf: Im Strom der Erinnerung*, edited by Carsten Gansel, 27–38. Göttingen: Vandenhoeck & Ruprecht, 2014.
Garton Ash, Timothy. *In Europe's Name: Germany and the Divided Continent*. London: Cape, 1993.

Gaussen, L. *Theopneustia: The Plenary Inspiration of the Holy Scriptures*. London: Passmore, 1841.

Gibbon, Edward. *The Decline and Fall of the Roman Empire*. Edited by David Womersley. London: Penguin, 1994.

Gide, André. "Montaigne." In *Essais critiques*, 664–84. Paris: Pléiade, 1999.

Gill, Stephen. *William Wordsworth: A Life*. Oxford: Oxford University Press, 1989.

Glenn, Jerry. *Paul Celan*. New York: Twayne, 1973.

Goethe, Johann Wolfgang von. *Briefe*. 4 vols. Hamburg: Wegner, 1962–67. Abbreviated as HAB.

———. *Briefwechsel zwischen Schiller und Goethe*. Edited by Emil Staiger. Frankfurt am Main: Insel, 1966. Abbreviated as *Brw Sch/G*.

———. *Elegie von Marienbad, Urschrift September 1823*. Edited by Jürgen Behrens and Christoph Michel. Frankfurt am Main: Insel, 1991.

———. *Faust*. Edited by Albrecht Schöne. Frankfurt am Main: Deutscher Klassiker Verlag 2005.

———. *Faust*. Translation and commentary by John Williams. London: Wordsworth, 2007.

———. *Faust: Historisch-kritische Edition*. Edited by Anne Bohnenkamp, Silke Henke, Gerrit Brüning, Katrin Henzel, Fotis Jannidis, and Dietmar Pravida. Frankfurt am Main: Wallstein, 2018.

———. *Gedichte in zeitlicher Folge*. Leipzig: Insel, 1923.

———. *Goethes Briefe an Charlotte von Stein*. Berlin: Deutsche Bibliothek, n.d.

———. *Goethes Briefe an Charlotte von Stein*. 2 vols. Berlin: Deutsche Bibliothek, n.d.

———. *Goethes Gespräche*. Edited by Flodoard von Biedermann. Zurich: Artemis, 1965.

———. *Die Leiden des jungen Werther(s)*. Parallel texts of the 1774 and 1787 versions. Edited by Mathias Luserke. Stuttgart: Reclam, 1999.

———. *Sämtliche Werke*. Frankfurter Ausgabe. Frankfurt: Deutscher Klassiker Verlag, 1987. Abbreviated as FA.

———. *Sämtliche Werke*, Münchener Ausgabe. Munich: Hanser, 1998. Abbreviated as MA.

———. *Sämtliche Werke*. Propyläenausgabe. Munich: Müller, 1932.

———. *Schriften*. 8 vols. Leipzig: Göschen; Vienna, Stahelin, 1787–90.

———. *Selected Poems*. Edited and translated by David Luke. London: Libris, 1999.

———. *Selected Poems*. Edited and translated by John Whaley. London: Dent, 1999.

———. *Tagebücher*. Vol. 1.i. Stuttgart: Metzler, 1998.

———. *Werke*. Hamburger Ausgabe. Edited by Erich Trunz. 14 vols. Hamburg: Wegner, 1948 and reprints. Abbreviated as HA.

———. *Werke*. Jubiläumsausgabe. Stuttgart: Cotta, 1907.

———. *Werke*. Weimarer Ausgabe. 143 vols. Weimar: Böhlau, 1887–1919.

———. *Wilhelm Meisters theatralische Sendung*. Edited by Harry Maync. Stuttgart: Cotta, 1911.
Goethe-Handbuch. 5 vols. Edited by Bernd Witte, Theo Buck, Hans-Dietrich Dahnke, Regine Otto, and Peter Schmidt. Stuttgart: Metzler, 1996–98.
Gombrich, Ernst. *Art and Illusion*. London: Phaidon, 1962.
Goy-Blanquet, Dominique. *Shakespeare's Early History Plays: From Chronicle to Stage*. Oxford: Oxford University Press, 2003.
Graves, Robert. *The Anger of Achilles*. London: Cassell, 1960.
———. *Homer's Daughter*. London: Cassell, 1955.
Gray, Alison. "Reception of the Old Testament." In Barton, *Hebrew Bible: Critical Companion*, 423–29.
Greg, W. W. "The Rationale of Copy-Text." *Studies in Bibliography* 3 (1950): 19–32.
Greiner, Ulrich. "Die deutsche Gesinnungsästhetik." In Anz, *"Es geht nicht um Christa Wolf,"* 208–16.
———. "Mangel an Feingefühl." In Anz, *Es geht nicht um Christa Wolf*, 66–70.
Grésillon, Almuth. *Éléments de critique génétique: Lire les manuscrits*. Paris: P.U.F., 1994.
Griffin, Jasper. *Homer*. Oxford: Oxford University Press, 1980.
Grillo, Jennie. "The Wisdom Literature." In Barton, *Hebrew Bible: Critical Companion*, 183–205.
Gunn, David M. "Joshua and Judges." In Alter and Kermode, *Literary Guide to the Bible*, 102–20.
Hage, Volker. "Kunstvolle Prosa." *Die Zeit*, June 1, 1990. Reprinted in Anz, *"Es geht nicht um Christa Wolf,"* 71–76.
Hainsworth, J. B. "Ancient Greek." In *Traditions of Homeric and Epic Poetry*. Oxford: Oxford University Press, 1980.
Hammond, Gerald. "English Translations of the Bible." In Alter and Kermode, *Literary Guide to the Bible*, 647–67.
Hatto, Arthur. Introduction to the *Nibelungenlied*, 299–404. Harmondsworth, UK: Penguin, 1965.
Hauschild, Jan-Christoph. *Georg Büchner: eine Biographie*. Hamburg: Rowohlt, 1993.
Hecht, Werner, ed. *Materialien zu Brechts "Leben des Galilei."* Frankfurt am Main: Suhrkamp, 1970.
Hegel, G. W. F. *Ästhetik*. Edited by Friedrich Bassenge. 2 vols. Frankfurt am Main: Europäische Verlagsanstalt, 1966.
———. *Vorlesungen über die Philosophie der Weltgeschichte*. Hamburg: Meiner, 1980.
Heine, Heinrich. *Sämtliche Werke*. Leipzig: Insel, 1910.
Henrich, Dieter. *Werke im Werden: Über die Genesis philosophischer Einsichten*. Munich: Beck, 2011.
Heym, Stefan. *Der König David Bericht*. Berlin: Reclam, 1973.
Hilzinger, Sonja. Nachwort to *Was bleibt*. In Christa Wolf, *Werke*, edited by Sonja Hilzinger, 10:32–22. Munich: Luchterhand, 2002.

Hofmannsthal, Hugo von. *Prosa III*. Frankfurt am Main: Fischer, 1964.
Hofmannsthal, Hugo von, and Richard Strauss. *Briefwechsel*. Zurich: Atlantis, 1955.
Holmes, Terence J. "Georg Büchners "Fatalismus" als Voraussetzung seiner Revolutionsstrategie." *Georg Büchner Jahrbuch* 6 (1986–87): 59–72.
Homer. *The Iliad / The Odyssey*. Translated by Robert Fagles. London: Penguin, 1998.
Horace. *Epistula ad Pisones* (*Ars poetica*). Leipzig: Insel, 1921.
Housman, A. E. *Selected Prose*. Cambridge: Cambridge University Press, 1961.
Iemma, Paola. *Les repentirs de l'Exemplaire de Bordeaux*. Paris: Garnier, 2004.
Jaeger, Michael. *Wanderers Verstummen: Goethes Schweigen, Fausts Tragödie*. Würzburg: Königshausen & Neumann, 2014.
Jameson, Frederic. *The Prison-House of Language*. Princeton, NJ: Princeton University Press, 1972.
Janouch, Gustav. *Gespräche mit Kafka*. Frankfurt am Main: Fischer, 1961.
Janz, Marlies. *Vom Engagement absoluter Poesie: Zur Lyrik und Ästhetik Paul Celans*. Frankfurt am Main: Syndikat, 1976.
Jasper, David. "Literary Approaches." In Barton, *Hebrew Bible: Critical Companion*, 455–79.
Jaspers, Anna. *Georg Büchners Trauerspiel "Dantons Tod."* Marburg, 1918.
Johnson, Samuel. *Lives of the Poets*. Oxford: Oxford University Press, 1952.
———. *Prose and Poetry*. Edited by Mona Wilson. London: Reynard, 1970.
Joyce, James. "The Sisters." In *Dubliners*, 7–16. London: Penguin, 1956.
Kadare, Ismail. *The File on H*. New York: Garland, 1997.
Kafka, Franz. *Brief an den Vater*. Facsimile and transcription. Edited by Joachim Unseld. Frankfurt am Main: Suhrkamp, 1994.
———. *Briefe an Felice*. Frankfurt am Main: Fischer, 1967.
———. *Briefe an Milena*. Frankfurt am Main: Fischer, 1986.
———. *Historisch-kritische Ausgabe sämtlicher Handschriften, Drucke und Typoskripte Franz Kafkas*. Edited by Roland Reuss and Peter Staengle. Basel: Stroemfeld, 1995.
———. *Tagebücher*. Edited by Hans-Gerd Koch, Michael Müller, and Malcolm Pasley. Frankfurt am Main: S. Fischer, 1990.
Kant, Immanuel. *Werke*. 11 vols. Berlin: Cassirer, 1912–22.
Kantorowicz, Ernst. *The King's Two Bodies*. Princeton, NJ: Princeton University Press, 1957.
Karr, Ruven. "Die Gaskammer in Paul Celans Dichtung." In *Celan und der Holocaust*, edited by Karr, 35–43. Hannover: Wehrhahn, 2015.
Keats, John. *The Letters of John Keats*. Edited by Maurice Buxton Forman. 4th ed. London: Oxford University Press, 1952.
Kehew, Robert, ed. *Lark in the Morning: The Verses of the Troubadours*. Chicago: University of Chicago Press, 2005.
Kipphardt, Heinar. *In der Sache J. Robert Oppenheimer*. Frankfurt am Main: Suhrkamp, 1964.

Kirk, G. S. *The Songs of Homer*. Cambridge: Cambridge University Press, 1962.
Kleist, Heinrich von. *Sämtliche Werke*. Edited by Helmut Sembdner. Munich: Hanser, 1961.
Knox, Bernard. Introduction to Fagles, *Iliad*.
Kommerell, Max. *Gedanken über Gedichte*. Frankfurt am Main: Klostermann, 1943.
Korff, Heinrich August. *Goethe im Bildwandel seiner Lyrik*. 2 vols. Hanau: Dausien, 1958.
Kott, Jan. *Shakespeare: Our Contemporary*. London: Penguin, 1965.
Kratz, R. G. "The Prophetic Literature." In Barton, *The Hebrew Bible: A Critical Companion*, 133–59.
Kuhn, Tom. "The Politics of the Changeable Text." *Oxford German Studies* 18, no. 1 (1989–90): 132–49.
Kuhn, Tom, and Charlotte Ryland. *Brecht and the Writer's Workshop: Fatzer and Other Dramatic Projects*. London: Methuen, 2019.
Kuna, Franz. *Literature as Corrective Punishment*. London: Elek, 1974.
Kunze, Reiner. *Deckname "Lyrik."* Frankfurt am Main: S. Fischer, 1990.
———. *die stunde mit dir selbst*. Frankfurt am Main: Fischer, 2018.
Latacz, Joachim. "The Structure of the Iliad." In *Homer's Iliad: Prolegomena to the Basel Commentary*. Berlin: De Gruyter, 2015.
Leaf, Walter. *The Iliad of Homer*. Cambridge: Cambridge University Press, 1902.
Lessing, Gotthold Ephraim. *Werke*. 8 vols. Edited by Herbert Göpfert. Munich: Hanser, 1970–79.
Lewis, C. S. *Reflections on the Psalms*. London: Fount, 1998.
Lichtenberg, Georg Christoph. *Schriften und Briefe*. Munich: Hanser, 1992.
Lodge, David, ed. *Modern Criticism and Theory*. London: Longman, 1988.
Longinus. *On Sublimity*. In *Ancient Literary Criticism*, edited by D. A. Russell and M. Winterbottom, 462–503. Oxford: Oxford University Press, 1972.
Lowth, Robert. *Lectures on the Sacred Poetry of the Hebrews*, 1787. London: Routledge, 1995.
Luther, Martin. *D. Martin Luther: Die gantze Heilige Schrifft Deudsch*. Wittenberg 1545. Edited by Hans Volz. Munich: Rogner & Bernhard, 1972.
Macdonald, Lee. "Canon." In *Oxford Handbook of Biblical Studies*. Oxford: Oxford University Press, 2008.
Mann, Thomas. "Arbeitsnotizen" to *Der Tod in Venedig*, in *Große kommentierte Frankfurter Ausgabe* (*GKFA*), 2.2.
———. *Briefe 1889–1913*. In *GKFA*, vol. 21. Frankfurt am Main: Fischer: 2009.
———. *Briefe 1889–1936*. Frankfurt am Main: Fischer, 1961.
———. *Briefe III: 1924–1932*, Frankfurt am Main: Fischer. 2013. In *GKFA*, 23.1.
———. *Briefe an Otto Grautoff*. Frankfurt am Main: Fischer, 1975.

———. *Briefe an Paul Amann*. Lübeck: Schmidt-Römhild, 1959.
———. *Briefwechsel mit Agnes Meyer 1937–1955*. Frankfurt am Main: Fischer, 1992.
———. *Frühe Erzählungen*. Edited by T. J. Reed and M. Herwig. In *Große kommentierte Frankfurter Ausgabe (GKFA)* vols. 2.1 (text) and 2.2 (commentary). Frankfurt am Main: Fischer, 2002.
———. *Gesammelte Werke*. Vols. 12 and 13. Frankfurt am Main: Fischer, 1960/1974.
———. *Notizbücher*, 2 vols. Edited by Hans Wysling and Yvonne Schmidlin. Frankfurt am Main: Fischer, 1991.
———. *Tagebücher 1933–1934*. Frankfurt am Main: Fischer, 1977.
———. *Tagebücher 1949–1950*. Frankfurt am Main: Fischer, 1991.
———. *Thomas Mann an Ernst Bertram*. Pfullingen: Neske, 1960.
Mann, Thomas, and Heinrich Mann. *Thomas Mann–Heinrich Mann: Briefwechsel*. Frankfurt am Main: Fischer, 1984. Abbreviated as *TM/HM*.
Markovitz, Inga. *Die Abwicklung*. Munich: Beck, 1993.
Marlow, Hilary. "The Human Condition." In Barton, *The Hebrew Bible: A Critical Companion*, 293–311.
Marlowe, Christopher. *The Complete Works*. Edited by Fredson Bowers. Cambridge: Cambridge University Press, 1981.
Marx, Karl. *Die Frühschriften*. Edited by Siegfried Landshut. Stuttgart: Kröner, 1962.
Mason, Eudo. *Goethe's Faust: Its Genesis and Purport*. Berkeley: University of California Press, 1967.
Mayer, Thomas Michael. "Georg Büchners Situation im Elternhaus und der Anlass seiner Flucht." *Georg Büchner Jahrbuch* 9 (1995–99): 33–92.
Michelsen, Peter. "Liedlos: Paul Celans 'Fadensonnen.'" In Gegenwart, vol. 6 of *Gedichte und Interpretationen*, edited by Walter Hinck, 123–39. Stuttgart: Reclam, 1982.
Milton, John. *Areopagitica* (1644). In *Selected Prose of John Milton*. Oxford: Oxford University Press, 1949.
Moberly, R. W. I. "Theological Approaches." In Barton, *Hebrew Bible: Critical Companion*, 481–506.
Moi, Toril. *The Revolution of the Ordinary*. Chicago: University of Chicago Press, 2018.
Montaigne, Michel de. *Essais*. Edited with introduction by Alexandre Micha. 3 vols. Paris: Garnier, 1969–79.
———. *Essais*. Edited by Jean Balsamo, Michel Magnien, and Catherine Magnien-Simonin. Paris: Pléiade, 2007.
———. *Essays and Letters*. 5 vols. London: Navarre Society, 1923.
———. *Essays of Michel de Montaigne*. Translated by M. A. Screech. London: Penguin, 1991.
Moore, Helen, and Julian Reid. *Manifold Greatness: The Making of the King James Bible*. Oxford: Bodleian Library, 2011.
Morris, Max. *Der junge Goethe*. Leipzig: Insel, 1909–12.

Neumann, Peter Horst. "Was muss ich wissen, um zu verstehen?" Paul Celans 'Die Schleuse.' Ein Gedicht für Nelly Sachs." *Celan-Jahrbuch* 4 (1991): 27–38.

New Testament, The. Translated by William Tyndale (The 1526 text). Edited by W. R. Cooper. London: British Library, 2000.

Nicholl, Charles. *The Lodger: Shakespeare on Silver Street*. London: Penguin, 2007.

Nietzsche, Friedrich. *Sämtliche Werke*, Kritische Studienausgabe (KStA). Berlin: De Gruyter, 1980.

Norton, David. *A History of the English Bible as Literature*. Cambridge: Cambridge University Press, 2000.

Novalis. *Heinrich von Ofterdingen*. In *Werke*, vol. 1. Stuttgart: Kohlhammer, 1966.

Parker, Stephen. *Bertolt Brecht: A Literary Life*. London: Bloomsbury, 2014.

Pasley, Malcolm. "Kafka's *Der Process*: What the Manuscript Can Tell Us." *Oxford German Studies* 18/19 (1989/90): 109–18.

———. "Kafkas halbprivate Spielereien." In Pasley, *Die Schrift ist unveränderlich*, 61–84.

———, ed. *Max Brod–Franz Kafka: Eine Freundschaft*. Frankfurt am Main: Fischer, 1989.

———. *"Die Schrift ist unveränderlich": Essays zu Kafka*. Frankfurt am Main: Fischer, 1995.

Plato. *Ion*.

Pope, Alexander. Preface to *The Works of Shakespeare*. In *Eighteenth-Century Essays on Shakespeare*, edited by D. Nichol Smith, 101–9. Oxford: Oxford University Press, 1963.

Rasch, Wolfdietrich. *Zur deutschen Literatur seit der Jahrhundertwende*. Stuttgart: Metzler, 1957.

Reed, T. J. "Kafka und Schopenhauer: Philosophisches Denken und dichterisches Bild." *Euphorion* 59 (1963): 160–72.

———. "Nietzsche's Animals: Idea, Image and Influence." In *Nietzsche, Imagery and Thought*, edited by Malcolm Pasley, 159–219. London: Methuen, 1978.

———. *"Nobody's Master." Goethe and the Authority of the Writer*. An inaugural lecture. Oxford: Oxford University Press, 1987.

———. *Thomas Mann: The Uses of Tradition*. Oxford: Clarendon, 1974; 2nd ed., 1996.

———. "Umkehrungen: Astronomie als Modell für die Aufklärung." *Jahrbuch des Freien Deutschen Hochstifts* (2007): 1–19.

———. "Was hat Marianne wirklich geschrieben? Skeptische Stimmen aus England." In *Liber amicorum: Katharina Mommsen zum 85. Geburtstag*, 466–81. Bonn: Bernstein, 2010.

Remarque, Erich Maria. *All Quiet on the Western Front*. Berlin: Propyläen, 1929.

Rieu, E. V., trans. and intro. *The Iliad*. London: Penguin, 1950.

Rofé, Alexander. *Introduction to the Composition of the Pentateuch.* Sheffield, UK: Sheffield Academic Press, 1999.
Roper, Lyndal. *Martin Luther, Renegade and Prophet.* London: Bodley Head, 2016.
Rosenberg, Joel. "Ezekiel." In Alter and Kermode, *Literary Guide to the Bible*, 184–206.
Roth, Philip. *American Pastoral.* London: Cape, 1997.
Ruskin, John. *The Stones of Venice.* London: Folio, 2003.
Satie, Erik. *Trois morceaux en forme de poire.* Piano duet for four hands. 1903.
Savran, George. "I and 2 Kings." In Alter and Kermode, *Literary Guide to the Bible*, 146–64.
Schama, Simon. *Citizens: A Chronicle of the French Revolution.* London: Penguin, 1989.
Scherrer, Paul, and Hans Wysling. *Quellenkritische Studien zum Werk Thomas Manns.* Bern: Francke, 1967.
Schiller, Friedrich von. *Sämtliche Werke.* Edited by Herbert Göpfert. Munich: Hanser, 1960–67.
———. *Schillers Briefwechsel mit Körner.* Leipzig: Beit, 1874. Abbreviated *Brw Sch/Kör*.
Schiller, Friedrich, and Johann Wolfgang von Goethe. *Der Briefwechsel zwischen Schiller und Goethe.* Edited by Emil Staiger. 2 vols. Frankfurt am Main: Insel, 1966. Abbreviated as *Brw Sch/G*.
Schirrmacher, Frank. "Dem Druck des härteren, strengeren Lebens standhalten." *Frankfurter Allgemeine Zeitung*, June 2, 1990. Reprinted in Anz, *"Es geht nicht um Christa Wolf,"* 77–89.
Schöne, Albrecht. *Der Briefschreiber Goethe.* Munich: Beck, 2015.
Schopenhauer, Arthur. *Sämtliche Werke.* Edited by Arthur Hübscher. Wiesbaden: Brockhaus, 1948.
Schrott, Raoul, and Arthur Jacobs. *Gedicht und Gehirn: Wie wir unsere Wirklichkeit konstruieren.* Munich: Hanser, 2011.
Schwartz, Eduard. *Zur Entstehung der Ilias.* Strasbourg, 1918.
Seel, Martin. "Im Maschinenraum des Denkens." *Die Zeit*, June 12, 2019.
Segebrecht, Wulf. *Das Gelegenheitsgedicht: Ein Beitrag zur Geschichte und Poetik der deutschen Lyrik.* Stuttgart: Metzler, 1977.
Sellevold, Kirsti. *'J'ayme ces mots . . .': expressions linguistiques de doute dans les Essais de Montaigne.* Paris: Garnier, 2004.
The Arden Shakespeare: The Histories. London: Bloomsbury, 1980–2015.
Shakespeare, William. *The Complete Plays.* London: Folio, 1997.
Shapiro, James. *1599: A Year in the Life of William Shakespeare.* London: Faber, 2005.
———. *1606: Shakespeare and the Year of Lear.* London: Faber, 2015.
———. *Contested Will: Who Wrote Shakespeare?* London: Faber, 2007.
Shay, Jonathan. *Achilles in Vietnam: Traumatic Stress and the Undoing of Character.* New York: Scribner, 1994.
———. *Odysseus in America: Combat Trauma and the Trials of Homecoming.* New York: Scribner, 2002.

Smith, Emma. *The Making of Shakespeare's First Folio*. Oxford: Oxford University Press, 2015.
Spenser, T. J. B. *Elizabethan Love Stories*. Oxford: Oxford University Press, 1968.
Sperber, Dan, and Deirdre Wilson. *Relevance: Communication and Cognition*. Oxford: Blackwell, 1986.
Staiger, Emil. *Goethe*. 3 vols. Zurich: Atlantis, 1952.
Steiner, George. *Real Presences: Is There Anything in What We Say?* London: Faber, 1969.
Szondi, Peter. *Celan-Studien*. Frankfurt am Main: Suhrkamp, 1972.
———. "Versuch über die Unverständlichkeit des modernen Gedichts." In Szondi, *Celan-Studien*, 47–111.
Tennemann, Wilhelm Gottlieb. *Geschichte der Philosophie*. 11 vols. Leipzig: Barth, 1789–1819.
Tillyard, E. M. W. *Shakespeare's History Plays*. London: Penguin, 1964.
Unseld, Siegfried, ed. *Von aufgegebenen Werken*. Frankfurt am Main: Suhrkamp, 1968.
Unsere Zeit, oder geschichtliche Uebersicht der merkwürdigsten Ereignisse von 1789–1830. Edited by Johann Conrad Friederich. 30 vols. with supplements. Stuttgart: Wolters, 1826–30.
Urzidil, Johannes. *Da geht Kafka*. Zurich: Artemis, 1965.
Vickers, Brian. *Shakespeare, Co-author: A Historical Study of the Five Collaborative Plays*. Oxford: Oxford University Press, 2004.
Wagner, G. W. J. *Allgemeine Statistik des Großherzogtums Hessen*, 1833.
Walton, J. K. *The Quarto Copy for the First Folio*. Dublin: Dublin University Press, 1971.
Weber, Max. "Der Beruf zur Politik." In Weber, *Soziologie, Weltgeschichtliche Analysen, Politik*, 167–85. Stuttgart: Kröner, 1968.
Weimar, Klaus. *Goethes Gedichte 1769–1775: Interpretationen zu einem Anfang*. Paderborn: Schöningh, 1982.
Wekwerth, Manfred. *Schriften: Arbeit mit Brecht*. Berlin: Aufbau, 1975.
West, M. L. *The Making of the Iliad*. Oxford: Oxford University Press, 2017.
Whitman, Cedric. *Homer and the Heroic Tradition*. Cambridge, MA: Harvard University Press, 1958.
Wieland, Christoph Martin. *Agathon*. 1766/67.
Wilson, Edmund. "A Dissenting Opinion on Kafka." In *Kafka: A Collection of Critical Essays*, edited by Ronald Gray, 91–97. Englewood Cliffs, NJ: Prentice Hall, 1962.
Wolf, Christa. *Was bleibt*. Frankfurt am Main: Luchterhand, 1990.
Wolf, Friedrich August. *Prolegomena to Homer*. Translated by Anthony Grafton. Princeton, NJ: Princeton University Press, 1988.
Wolff, Kurt. *Autoren / Bücher / Abenteuer*. Berlin: Wagenbach, 1965.
———. *Briefwechsel eines Verlegers 1911–1963*. Edited by Bernhard Zeller and Ellen Otten. Frankfurt am Main: Scheffler, 1966.
Woolf, Virginia. *Congenial Spirits: The Selected Letters of Virginia Woolf*. London: Hogarth, 1990.

———. *"A Room of One's Own" and "Three Guineas."* Oxford: Oxford University Press, 1992.
———. *A Writer's Diary.* London: Hogarth, 1954.
Wordsworth, William. "Preface to Lyrical Ballads" (1802). In *Works*, edited by Stephen Gill, 595–615. Oxford: Oxford University Press, 2008.
Yeats, W. B. *Poems.* Variorum edition. New York: MacMillan, 1957.
Ziegler, Edda. *Literarische Zensur in Deutschland, 1819–1848.* Munich: Hanser, 1983.

Index

Adenauer, Konrad, 235
Adorno, Theodor, 227, 229
Aeschylus, 28
Akhmatova, Anna, 223
allegory, 40, 51, 178, 188, 201, 259
Altenberg, Peter, 174
Alter, Robert, 52
Andersch, Alfred, 236
Anna Amalia, Duchess of Saxe-Weimar, 112
anthropology, 8
Apocrypha, 41
Apollo, 75, 129, 181
Aretino, Pietro, 170
Aristarchus, 20
Aristotle, 13
Athanasius, 40
Auden, W. H., 204
audience, role of, 8
Auerbach, Erich, 49, 53
Augustine, 45
Austen, Jane, 53
author, authorship, writer, 2, 8, 53, 76, 82, 191

Bahr, Hermann, 174
ballads, pre-*Iliad*, 21
Balzac, Honoré de, 5, 199
Bandello, Matteo, 84
Bang, Hermann, 174
Baroque, 72
Barthes, Roland, 10
Baudelaire, Charles, 175, 176
Bauer, Felice, 191, 193, 196
Baum, Oscar, 192
Baumgard, Reinhart, 234
Beaumont, Francis, 79
Beauvoir, Simone de, xii
Becker, Jurek, 236
Beckett, Samuel, 12

Beecher Stowe, Harriet, 47
Beethoven, Ludwig van, 6
Benn, Gottfried, 225
Berg, Alban, 173
Bergmann, Fritz, 172
Biermann, Wolf, 232, 233
"Big Guys," 30, 32
Bildungsroman, 157–58, 186
biography, biographism, 10
birth, procreation, literary parenthood, 1, 4
blank page, 5
Bloch, Ernst, 236
Bohr, Nils, 218
Bohrer, Karl Heinz, 235
Böll, Heinrich, 236
Börne, Ludwig, 173, 210
Böschenstein, Bernard, 225
boustrophedon, 22
Bowra, Maurice, 29
Brandt, Susanne Margarete, 107
Brantôme, Pierre de Bourdelles, Abbé, 70
Brecht, Bertolt, 8, 32, 81, 82, 95, 100, 174, 235; epic theater, 211
Brecht, Bertolt, works by: *Fear and Misery of the Third Reich*, 210; *Life of Galileo*, 32, ch. 11 *passim*; *Mutter Courage*, 211, 212
Brion, Friederike, 133, 138
Britten, Benjamin, 183
Brod, Max, 192, 193, 195, 199, 202, 203, 204
Brooke, Rupert, 36
Büchner, Georg, 7, 95, 100, 204, 210
Büchner, Georg, works by: *Danton's Death*, 165–69, 223; *Hessian Messenger*, 164, 167; *Lenz*, 171; *Leonce und Lena*, 170, 171; *Woyzeck*, 7, 171–73

Burbage, Richard, 82
Burke, Edmund, 31, 50, 51

Camus, Albert, 200
canon, xii, 38, 40, 41
Carl August, Duke of Saxe-Weimar, 126, 133, 155
Cathars, 40
Cato, 74
Celan, Paul, 100
celebration, 8
Cervantes, Miguel, 144
Chalfen, Israel, 226
Chamfort, Nicolas, 164
Chekhov, Anton, 174
Chomsky, Noam, 4
Chosen People, 39, 42, 47, 48
Churchill, Winston, 86
Cicero, 46
Classicism, 144
codex, 22
Coleridge, Samuel Taylor, 7, 9, 41
Coleridge, Samuel Taylor, works by: *Kubla Khan*, 7; *Lyrical Balllads*, 9
collaboration, 9
Common Reader, xii, 25, 74, 142, 224, 229, 239
communicative nexus, 1, 9, 14, 15
Communism, 213, 231, 232
Condell, Henry, 78, 80, 81, 82
Conrad, Joseph, 5, 52
Copernicus, Nicolaus, 209
Corneille, Pierre, 150
Cotta, Johann Friedrich, 114
Cowley, Abraham, 46, 47, 48
Crane, Ralph, 83
creation, conscious or spontaneous, 7
critical debate, pleasure of, 11
critique génétique, 15

da Vinci, Leonardo, 73
Daniel, Samuel, 85
Dante, xii, 204
Danton, Georges, 98, 165, 172
d'Aubignac, François Hédelin Abbé, 20
de Brach, Pierre, 74
de Gournay, Marie, 62, 76

de la Boétie, Étienne, 59, 60, 250
de Man, Paul, 13, 14
deconstruction, 11
Dekker, Thomas, 83
Demosthenes, 65
Derrida, Jacques, 10
Descartes, René, 73, 165, 170
Dickens, Charles, 176
Dimitroff, Georgy, 213
Dingelstedt, Franz von, 97
Dionysos, 182, 183, 188
Donne, John, 42, 46
Drayton, Michael, 29
Dreyfus, Alfred, 184
du Bellay, Joachim, 35
Dürrenmatt, Friedrich, 217, 219

Eckermann, Johann Peter, 105, 114
Ehrenberg, Paul, 190
Eich, Günther, 3
Eichhorn, Johann Gottfried, 38
Einstein, Albert, 216, 217, 218
Eliot, George, 8
Eliot, T. S., 52, 225
Elizabeth I, Queen, 86, 91, 92, 94, 98
Empedocles, 65
Enlightenment, 103, 151, 156, 184, 209, 259n46
Epaminondas, 74
Escher, Moritz Cornelis, 201
Eustathius, 20
evolution, 1
experience, poetry of (Erlebnisdichtung), 125, 129
Expressionism, 173, 195

Fagles, Robert, 23
Fascism, 188
fashion, intellectual, 13
Fielding, Henry, 158
Fischer, Samuel, 174, 177
Flaubert, Gustave, 79
Fletcher, John, 98
Fodor, Jerry, 4
Fontane, Theodor, 158
form, 5
Foucault, Michel, 10, 12
Frame, Donald, 65

Franzos, Karl Emil, 172, 173
Frayn, Michael, 218
Frederick the Great, 184
French Revolution, 155–57, 166–69
Freud, Sigmund, 192, 197
Friedländer, Johann David, 165
Friedrich, Hugo, 225

Galilei, Galileo, 209, 210, 212, 213, 214, 216
Galilei, Galileo, works by: *Discorsi*, 214, 216
gender, xi
genealogies, biblical, 48
geology, 1
Gibbon, Edward, 50, 90
Gilgamesh, 39
"given" stanzas, 6
Göchhausen, Louise von, 112
Goethe, Cornelia (sister), 127
Goethe, Johann Wolfgang von, xi, xii, 1, 2, 4, 5, 7, 8, 11, 13, 33, 41, 49, 66, 79, 94, 95, 100, 166, 181, 187, 204, 214, 224, 239
Goethe, Johann Wolfgang von, poems by: "Alle gleichen wir uns," 142; "An Belinden," 128; "An Schwager Kronos," 133, 139; "An Werther," 140, 148; "Auf dem See," 129–135; "Aussöhnung," 140; Dedication to "Faust," 142; "Deutscher National-Charakter," 157; Eis-Lebens-Lied," 133; "Ganymed," 104, 142; "Gehab dich wohl . . .," 126; "Holde Lili . . .," 126; "Lilis Park," 132; "Marienbader Elegie," 127, 139; "Prometheus," 104, 142; "Seefahrt," 133; "Trilogie der Leidenschaft," 140; "Über allen Gipfeln, 125; "Vermächtnis," 125; "Vom Berge . . .," 130; "Willkommen und Abschied," 135–39
Goethe, Johann Wolfgang von, works by: *Annals*, 154; *Der ewige Jude*, 126; *Egmont*, 152; *Faust*, 2, 103–24, 125, 142, 144, 152, 173; *Faust, ein Fragment*, 109–2; *Götz von Berlichingen*, 95, 100, 112, 148; *Iphigenie auf Tauris*, 113, 122, 152; *Sufferings of Young Werther*, 103, 112, 127, 139, 140, 146–49; *Torquato Tasso*, 113, 140, 152; "Urfaust," 108–17; *West-Östlicher Divan*, 13, 127; *Wilhelm Meister*, 9, 113, 144;149–58; *Wilhelm Meister's Theatrical Mission*, 149, 151–52, 153, 154, 155, 157, 158–59; *Xenien*, 9
Goldoni, Carlo, 157
Goncourt, Edmond and Jules de, 176
Gorbachev, Mikhail, 236, 237
Gotsche, Otto, 232
Gottsched, Johann Christoph, 150
Grand Mechanism, 93, 98, 171
Grass, Günter, 158, 236, 237
Grautoff, Otto, 269n5
Graves, Robert, 20, 31
Greiner, Ulrich, 234
Grimm, Wilhelm, 142
Gryphius, Andreas, 252n27
guslari, 26
Gutzkow, Karl, 165, 168, 170, 171

Habermas, Jürgen, 11
Hafiz, 15
Hage, Volker, 234
Hall (chronicler), 85, 97
Harington, Sir John, 93
Haydn, Joseph, 7
Hegel, Georg Wilhelm Friedrich, 100, 124
Heimann, Moritz, 177
Heine, Heinrich, 5, 42, 147, 164, 173, 174, 210
Heinrich, Prince of Prussia, 152
Heisenberg, Werner, 217, 218
Heminge, John, 78, 80, 81, 82
Henry VII, King, 92
Herder, Johann Gottfried, 50
Hermes, 183
Hesse, Hermann, 200, 203
Heyne, Christian Gottlob, 38
hierarchy, 30, 32
historiography, 42

Hofmannsthal, Hugo von, 9, 12, 187
Hofmannsthal, Hugo von, works by: *Andreas*, 187; *Ariadne*, 9
Hölderlin, Friedrich, 129, 204
Hollinshed, Raphael, 85, 97
Homer, 48, 49, 68
Homer, works by: *Iliad*, 2, 9, 19–36; *Odyssey*, 19, 33–36
Homosexuality, 179–90
Honecker, Erich, 232
Horace, 2, 75, 84
Horace, works by: *Art of Poetry*, 2
Hugo, Victor, 170
humanism: its ethos, 15; its pedagogic deficit, 14; its return, 16; as term of abuse, 10
Hume, David, 95

inconsistencies, 2, 19, 26
infallibility, 42
inspiration, 7, 21, 41–43, 131, 192, 199
intention, 5
intolerance, 40
Iselin, Isaak, 147

Jaegle, Minna, 166, 167, 170
Jameson. Frederic, 12
Jerome, Saint, 44
Jerusalem, Karl Wilhelm, 146, 147, 149
Jesenská, Milena, 192
Jesus, 40, 41, 43, 52, 74, 241
Johann Friedrich, Duke of Saxe-Weimar, 45
Johnson, Samuel, xi, 83, 88
Jonson, Ben, 79, 80, 82, 89
Joyce, James, 200

Kafka, Franz, 4, 61
Kafka, Franz, works by: "The Burrow," 201; *The Castle*, 199, 200, 203, 204, 205; "A Country Doctor," 197–98, 205; "A Dog's Researches," 203; "A Father's Worries," 202; "First Sorrow," 201; "A Hunger Artist," 201; "The Hunter Gracchus," 202; "In the Penal Colony," 196, 205; "Josephine, the Singer or the Mouse Folk," 200; "The Judgment," 192–96, 206; *Letter to [My] Father*, 206; *The Man Who Disappeared (America)* 194; "Metamorphosis," 196, 197; *The Trial*, 196, 199, 200, 202, 203, 204, 205, 207
Kafka, Hermann (father), 200, 206
Kafka, Ottla (sister), 193
Kant, Immanuel, 7, 40, 156, 209
Kant, Immanuel, works by: *Critique of Pure Reason*, 7; *What Is Enlightenment?* 156, 209
Karl Eugen, Duke of Württemberg, 143
Keats, John, 127
Keller, Gottfried, 158
Kermode, Frank, 52
Kerr, Alfred, 183
Kestner, Charlotte, 147
Kestner, Johann Christian, 146, 147, 263
Kiefer, Anselm, 227
Kielland, Aleander, 175
Kipphardt, Heinar, 217
Kleist, Heinrich von, 4, 132, 204
Klopstock, Friedrich Gottlieb, 129, 144
Knox, Bernard, 23, 29
Kommerell, Max, 131
Körner, Christian Gottfried, 134, 135
Kunze, Reiner, 3, 233

Language: as convention, 10; meaning indeterminate, 11; as prison-house, 12; as self-sufficient, 11
Lassberg, Christel von, 147
Laughton, Charles, 211, 215
Lavater, Johann Caspar, 104, 128, 129
Lawrence, D. H., 3
Leason, John, 83
Lenin, Vladimir Ilyich, 173
Lenz, J. M. R., 95
Lenz, Siegfried, 236
Lessing, Gotthold Ephraim, 28, 150, 158

Levetzow, Ulrike von, 139
Lewes, George Henry, 8
Lichtenberg, Georg Christoph, 156
Lie, Jonas, 175
Liebig, Justus, 163
Liebknecht, Karl, 221, 228
Linnaeus, 15
Lollards, 44
Longinus. Cassius, works by: *On the Sublime*, 2
Lord, Albert, 26
Louis XIV, 4
Lowell, Robert, 223
Lowth, Robert, 46, 47, 48
Luft, Hans, 45
Luther, Martin, 42, 44, 50, 100, 202
Luxemburg, Rosa, 221, 228

Machiavelli, Nicolò, 15, 68
Maldon, William, 44
Mallarmé, Stéphane, 12, 225
Mann, Heinrich, 175, 184, 185, 210
Mann, Thomas, 2, 5, 8, 49, 148, 158, 200, 204, 210, 218
Mann, Thomas, works by: *An Appeal to Reason*, 186; *Buddenbrooks*, 175–77, 199; *Considerations of an Unpolitical Man*, 185; *Death in Venice*, 178–83; *Doktor Faustus*, 187–88; *Felix Krull*, 178, 189–90; *Fiorenza*, 178; "Frederick," 178; *Joseph and His Brethren*, 49, 187; *Magic Mountain*, 2, 8, 11, 158, 183–87; "Maja," 178; "Mind and Art," 178; *Royal Highness*, 178, 182; *Tonio Kröger*, 177; *Tristan*, 177
Marcion, 40
Marlowe, Christopher, 20, 86, 87, 88, 103, 105, 123
Marlowe, Christopher, works by: *Doctor Faustus*, 103, 123; *Tamburlaine*, 87, 88
Martens, Kurt, 182
Marty, Wilhelm, 176
Marx, Karl, 209, 213
Marxism, 203, 209
Maupassant, Guy de, 174

Mayakovsky, Vladimir, 225
McCarthy, Joseph, 218
Metternich, Klemens von, 164
Meyer, Agnes, 188
Michelangelo, 190
Mignet, François, 166, 167
Milder-Hauptmann, Anna, 140
Milton, John, 1, 46
Mirabeau, Honoré Gabriel, comte de Riqueti, 4
Molière, Jean-Baptiste Poquelin, 144
Møller, Christian, 211
Montaigne, Michel Eyquem, Sieur de, 4, 7, 16, 46, 83, 139
More, Thomas (Sir, Saint), 44, 85, 91, 97
Moritz, Carl Phillip, works by: *Anton Reiser*, 151
Moses, 15, 41
movement, literature as, 8, 28
Mozart, Wolfgang Amadeus, 225
Muses, 32
Musil, Robert, 187

Napoleon Bonaparte, 7, 113, 114, 163, 164, 165
National Theater, 150–51
Naturalism, 173, 181, 183
Nazism, 188, 203, 209, 210, 213, 234, 235
Neruda, Pablo, 225
Neuber, Caroline, 151
Newton, Isaac, 10, 41, 217
Nicolai, Friedrich, 147
Nietzsche, Friedrich, 4, 6, 12, 66, 74, 142, 174, 202, 210, 239
Nietzsche, Friedrich, works by: *The Birth of Tragedy from the Spirit of Music*, 270n25; *The Genealogy of Morals*, 202; *Thus spake Zarathustra*, 6
Novalis, 132

Oken, Lorenz, 165
Oppenheimer, J. Robert, 217
oral performance, 27
Orwell, George, 204
Ovid, 70, 87

Owen, Wilfred, 9, 51

Paine, Thomas, 165
Parry, Milman, 25
Pascal, Blaise, works by: *Pensées*, 1, 4
Pasley, Malcolm, 191, 203, 207
Paul, Saint, 40, 42, 46
perfectionism, misplaced, 2, 36, 118, 258n35
Perrault, Charles, 20
philosophers of history, 50
Picasso, Pablo, 49
Pisistratus, 22
Plato, 10, 21, 36, 74, 71, 180, 182, 183
Plato, works by: *Cratylus*, 10; *Ion*, 21; *Phaidros*, 180; *Symposium*, 180, 183
Pliny, 68
Plutarch, 180
Pope, Alexander, 88, 95
Pringsheim, Katia, 182, 183
prophets, xii, 39, 40, 42, 43, 46, 48
Protestantism, 38, 40, 44, 181
Proust, Marcel, 190
Psalms, 39
publishers, role of, 8
punctuation, 84, 130, 203

Qumran scrolls, 38

Raabe, Paul, 204
Racine, Jean, 87, 95
Rathenau, Walther, 186
reading, as work, 11
Realism, 197
reception aesthetic, 27
register, stylistic, of Bible, 45
Remarque, Erich Maria, 30
Rembrandt, 42
revision, 1, 8, 22, 80, 117, 132, 134, 136, 138, 140, 148, 149, 233, 248, 262, 278
rhapsodes, 21, 83
rhythm, 3, 203
Rieu, E. V., 25, 33
Rilke, Rainer Maria, 8, 41

Rilke, Rainer Maria, works by: *Duino Elegies*, 8
Robespierre, Maximilien, 165
Romanticism, 186, 224
Roth, Philip, 3
Rousseau, Jean-Jacques, 11, 239
Ruskin, John, 2

Saint Exupéry, Antoine de, 53
Saint Just, Louis-Antoine de, 168, 169
Sainte-Beuve, Charles Augustin, 75
Sappho, 29, 30
Satie, Éric, works by: *Morceau en forme d'une poire*, 5
Sassoon, Siegfried, 9
Saussure, Ferdinand de, 10, 12
Schiller, Friedrich, 3, 5, 7, 9, 15, 33, 80, 113, 117, 119, 133, 135, 143, 144, 150, 151, 154, 156, 158, 166, 204, 211
Schiller, Friedrich, works by: *Don Carlos*, 9; *Maria Stuart*, 255n85, 267n10; *On Primal and Reflective Poetry*, 7, 143; *Wallenstein*, 145
Schirach, Ferdinand von, 236
Schirrmacher, Frank, 235
Schlegel, August Wilhelm, 100
Schlegel, Friedrich, 48
Schlink, Bernhard, 236
Schmidt, Erich, 112
Schöne, Albrecht, 119, 122
Schönemann-von Türckheim, Lili, 126, 127, 133, 134
Schopenhauer, Arthur, 202
Schubert, Franz, 108
Schulthess, Barbara, 154
Schumacher, Ernst, 219
Scipio, 74
scrolls, 22
Septuagint, 42
Shakespeare, 7, 15, 29, 32, 47, 48, 50, 137, 140, 144, 151, 166, 170, 204, 227, 229
Shaw, George Bernard, 32, 212
Sima Quan, 50
Socrates, 21, 74, 75
Song of Songs, 39, 40, 226
Sophocles, 46, 84

Sperber, Dan, 14
Spiess, Johann, 103, 107
Spinoza, Baruch, 15, 41, 165
Stalin, Joseph, 223
Stein, Charlotte von, 147
Steiner, George, 14
Steiner, Marianne, 207, 208
Steiner, Michael, 207
Stifter, Adalbert, 158
Strauss, Richard, 9
Strauss, Richard, works by: *Ariadne*, 9
structure, 5
style, 5
Szondi, Peter, 221, 222, 228
Szymanowska, Maria, 140

Tate, Allen, 223
teichoscopy, 23
Tennyson, Alfred Lord, 36
Terence, 72
Theatrum mundi, 72
theory, xi
"theory," 9
Thiers, Adolphe, 166, 167
Thomas, Edward, 94
Thucydides, 50
Tieck, Ludwig, 100
Tillyard, E. M. W., 85, 93
Tolstoy, Lev Nikolaevich, 7, 47, 53, 167, 176, 191, 199
translation, 33
Tudor dynasty, 92
Tyndale, William, 44, 45
typology, 7

Ulbricht. Walter, 232

Valéry, Paul, 6, 225

Villey, Pierre, 63, 64, 76, 250
Virgil, 46
Visconti, Luchino, 183
Voltaire, 50, 184
Vulgate, 44

Wolf, Friedrich August, 20, 23, 26, 38
Wolff, K. D., 208
Wolff, Kurt, 195, 196, 197, 199, 205
Weber, Carl Maria, 181
Weber, Max, 235, 236
Weidig, Friedrich Ludwig, 158
Wilde, Oscar, 179
Willemer, Marianne von, 142
Wilmot, John, 47
Wilson, Deidre, 14
Wilson, Edmund, 205
Wittgenstein, Ludwig, 73
Woolf, Virginia, xii, 3, 5, 6, 8
Wordsworth, William, 9, 134, 139, 261, 262
Wordsworth, William, works by: *Lyrical Ballads*, 9; *The Prelude*, 139
world, as object and obstacle, 7
writing, charisma of, 40
Wycliffe, John, 44

Xenophon, 74

Yeats, William Butler, 20, 134
Yevtushenko, Yevgeny, 223
Young, Edward, 147

Zelter, Karl Friedrich, 139, 147
Zenodotus, 20
Zionism, 101
Zola, Émile, 184
Zwingli, Huldrych, 45